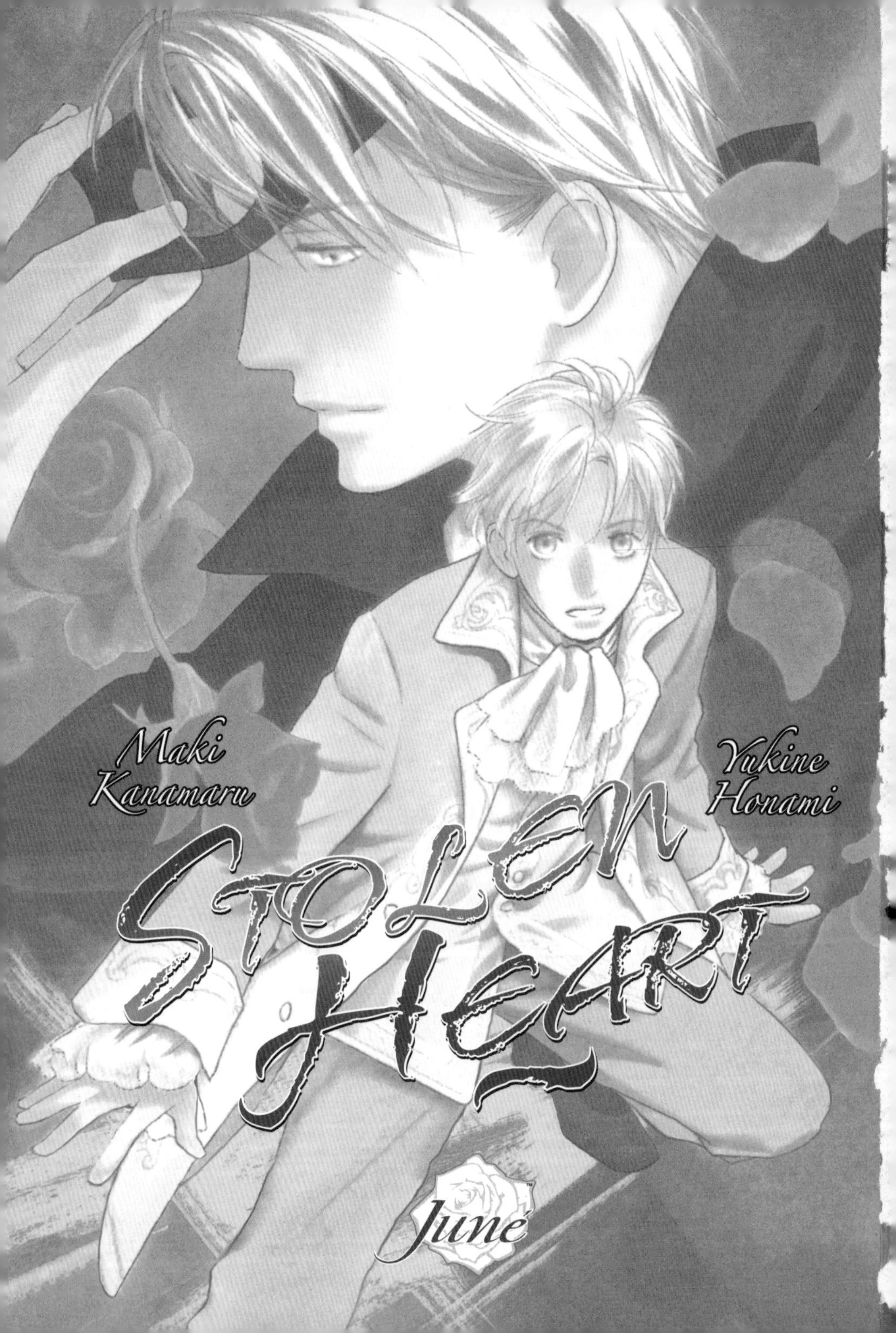
Maki
Kanamaru
Yukine
Honami
Stolen
Heart
June

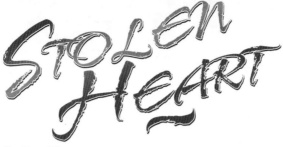

STOLEN HEART

Stolen Heart 3
Stolen Heart ~ The Beautiful Captive 35
Stolen Heart ~ The Wonderful New World 67
Be Nice 101
People Are What They Seem 115
Kiss Scandal 149
Afterword 181

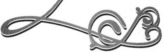

Translation .... Issei Shimizu
Lettering .... Zack Giallongo
Graphic Design .... Wendy Lee / Daryl Kuxhouse
Editing .... Daryl Kuxhouse
Editor in Chief .... Fred Lui
Publisher .... Hikaru Sasahara

English Edition Published by
DIGITAL MANGA PUBLISHING
A division of DIGITAL MANGA, Inc.
1487 W 178th Street, Suite 300
Gardena, CA 90248

www.dmpbooks.com

First Edition: September 2007
ISBN-10: 1-56970-816-9
ISBN-13: 978-1-56970-816-3

1 3 5 7 9 10 8 6 4 2

Printed in China

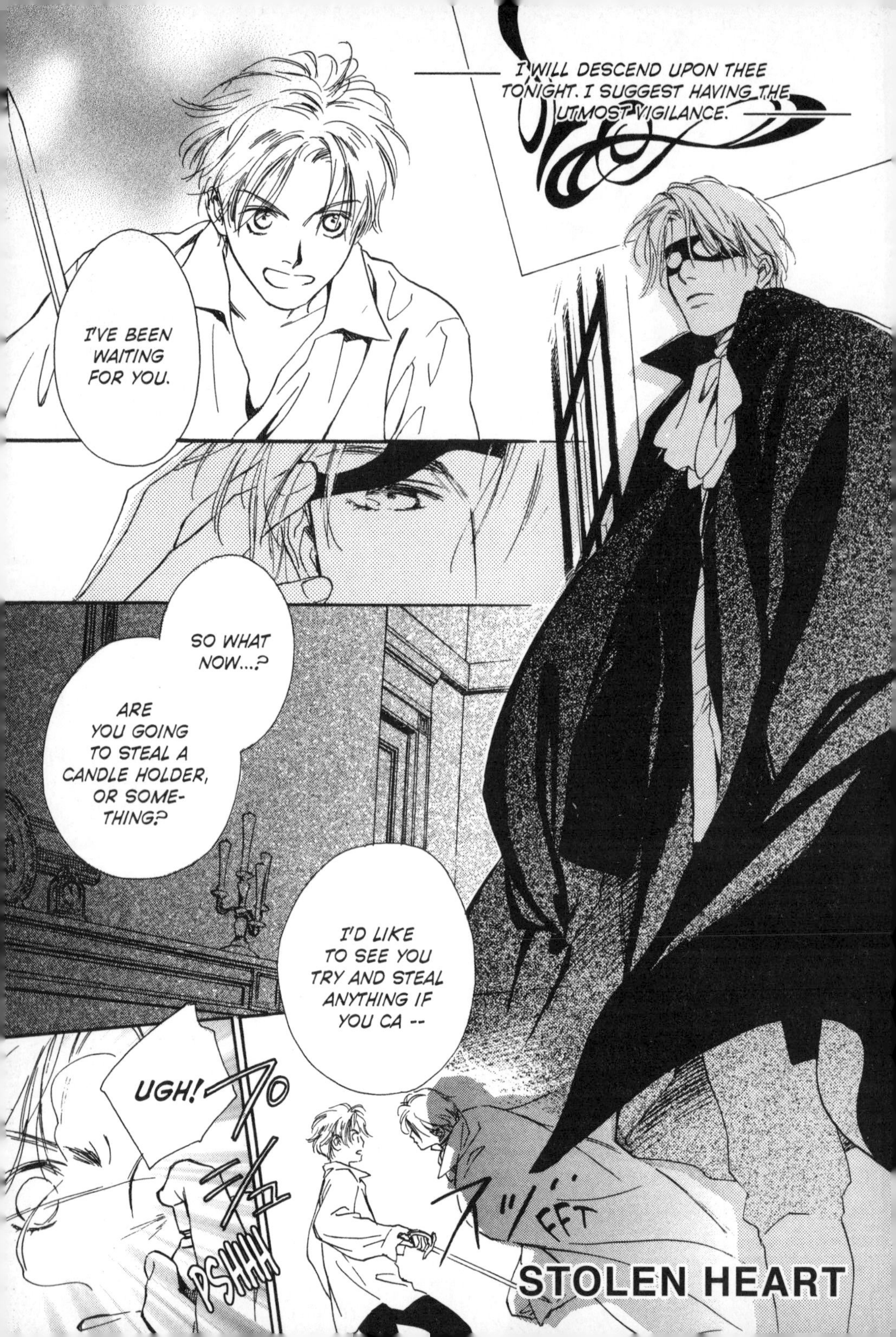
I WILL DESCEND UPON THEE TONIGHT. I SUGGEST HAVING THE UTMOST VIGILANCE.
I'VE BEEN WAITING FOR YOU.
SO WHAT NOW...?
ARE YOU GOING TO STEAL A CANDLE HOLDER, OR SOME-THING?
I'D LIKE TO SEE YOU TRY AND STEAL ANYTHING IF YOU CA --
FFT
UGH!
PSHHH
STOLEN HEART

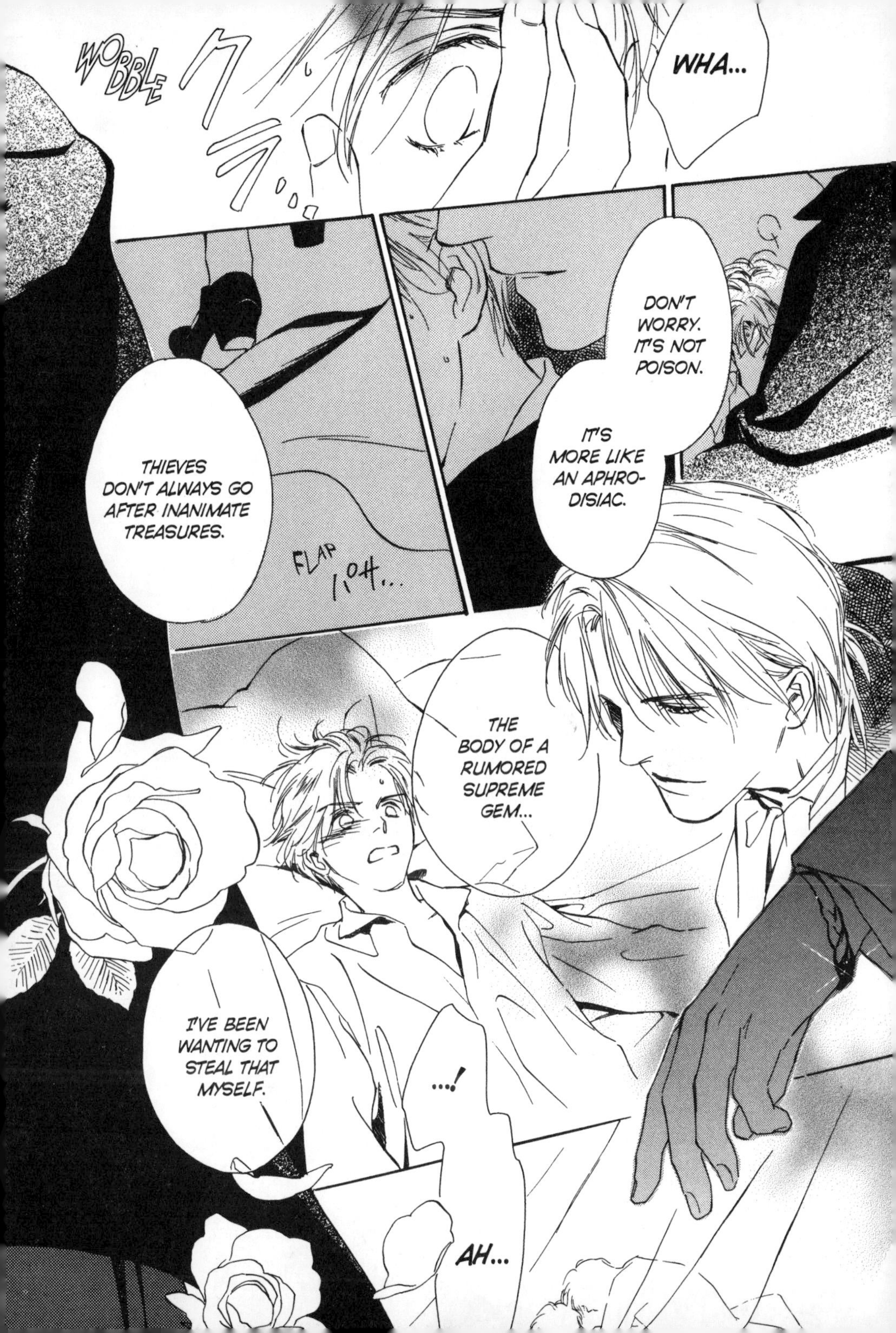
WHA...
WOBBLE
DON'T WORRY. IT'S NOT POISON.
IT'S MORE LIKE AN APHRODISIAC.
FLAP
THIEVES DON'T ALWAYS GO AFTER INANIMATE TREASURES.
THE BODY OF A RUMORED SUPREME GEM...
I'VE BEEN WANTING TO STEAL THAT MYSELF.
...!
AH...

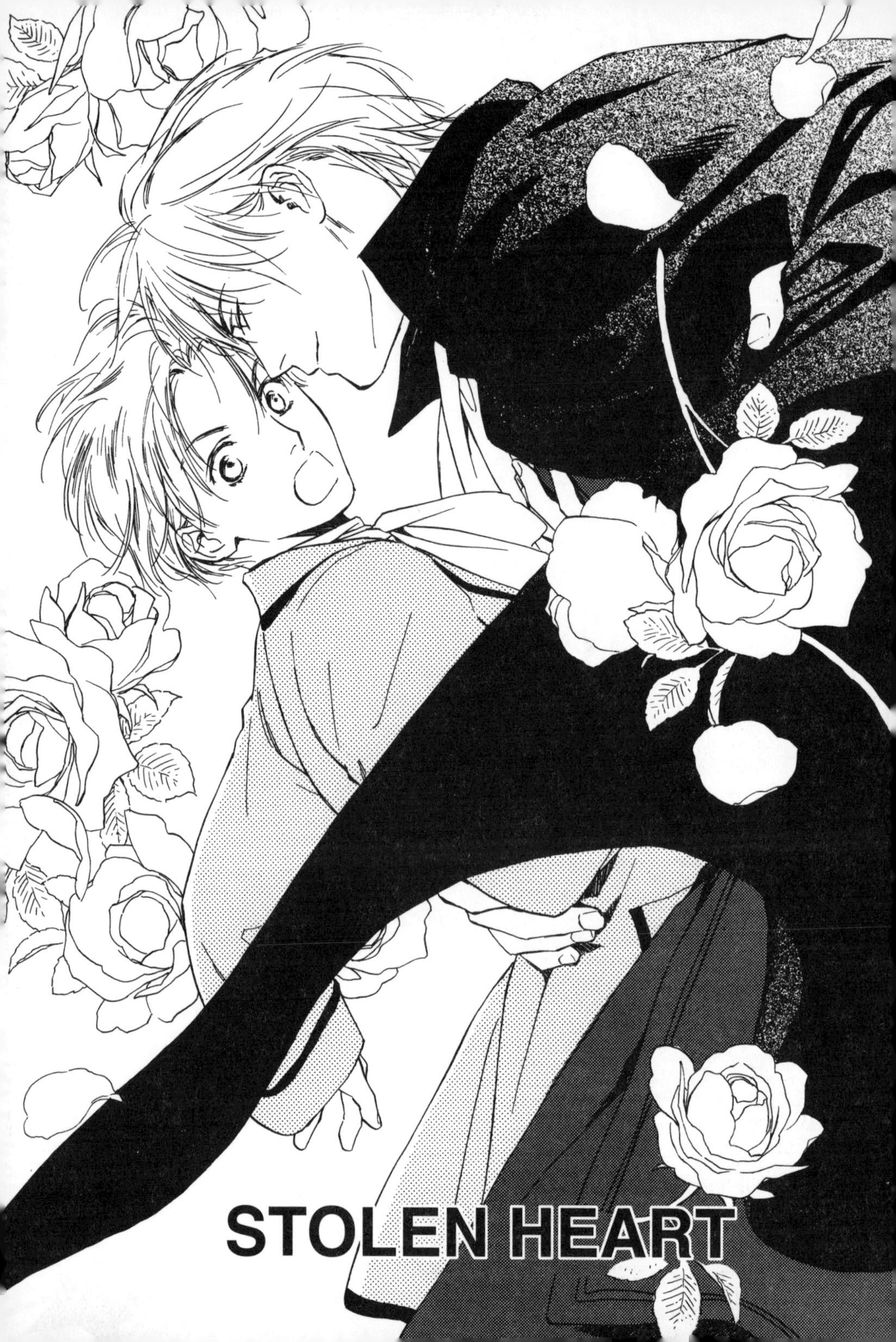
STOLEN HEART

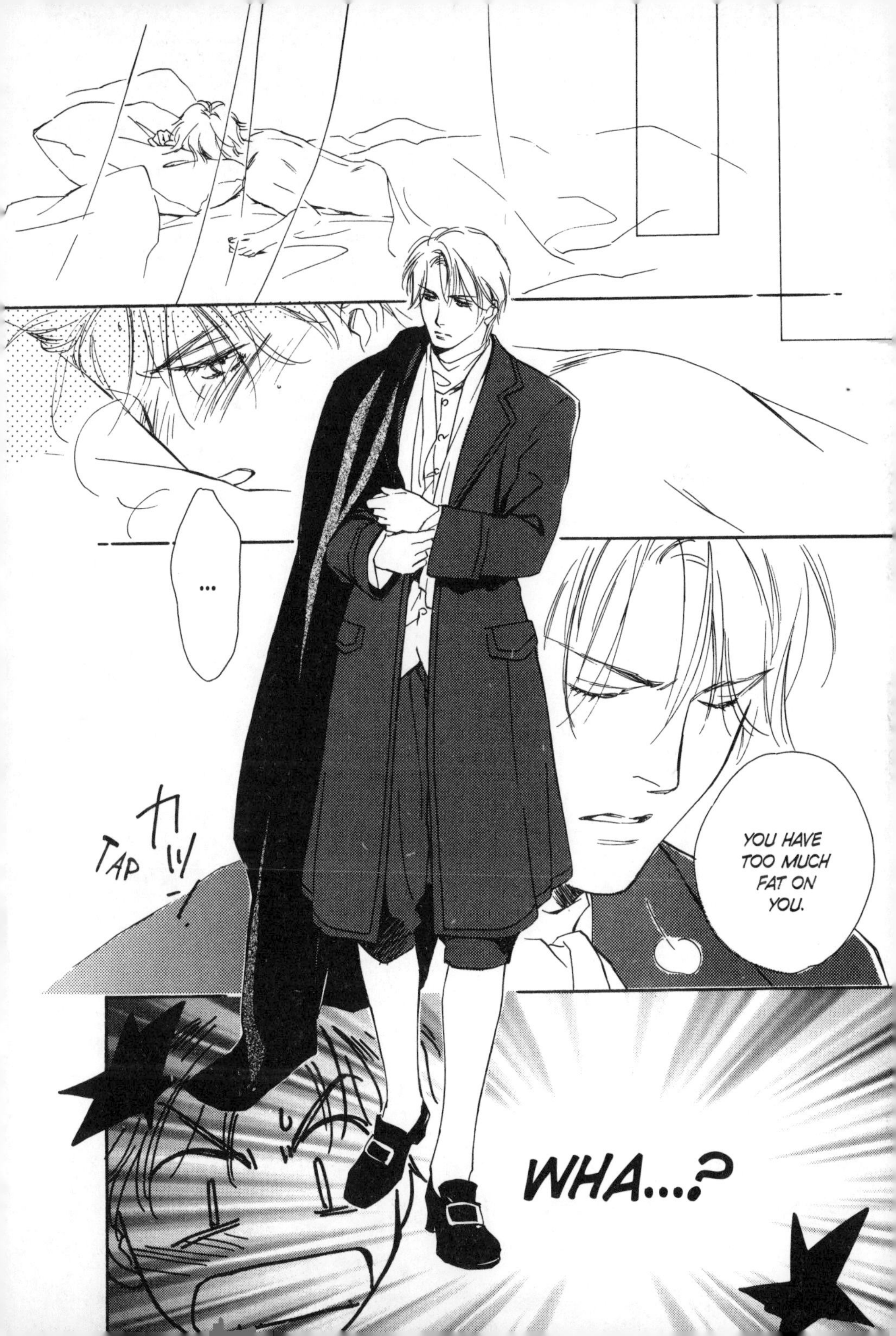
...
YOU HAVE TOO MUCH FAT ON YOU.
TAP
カッ
WHA...?

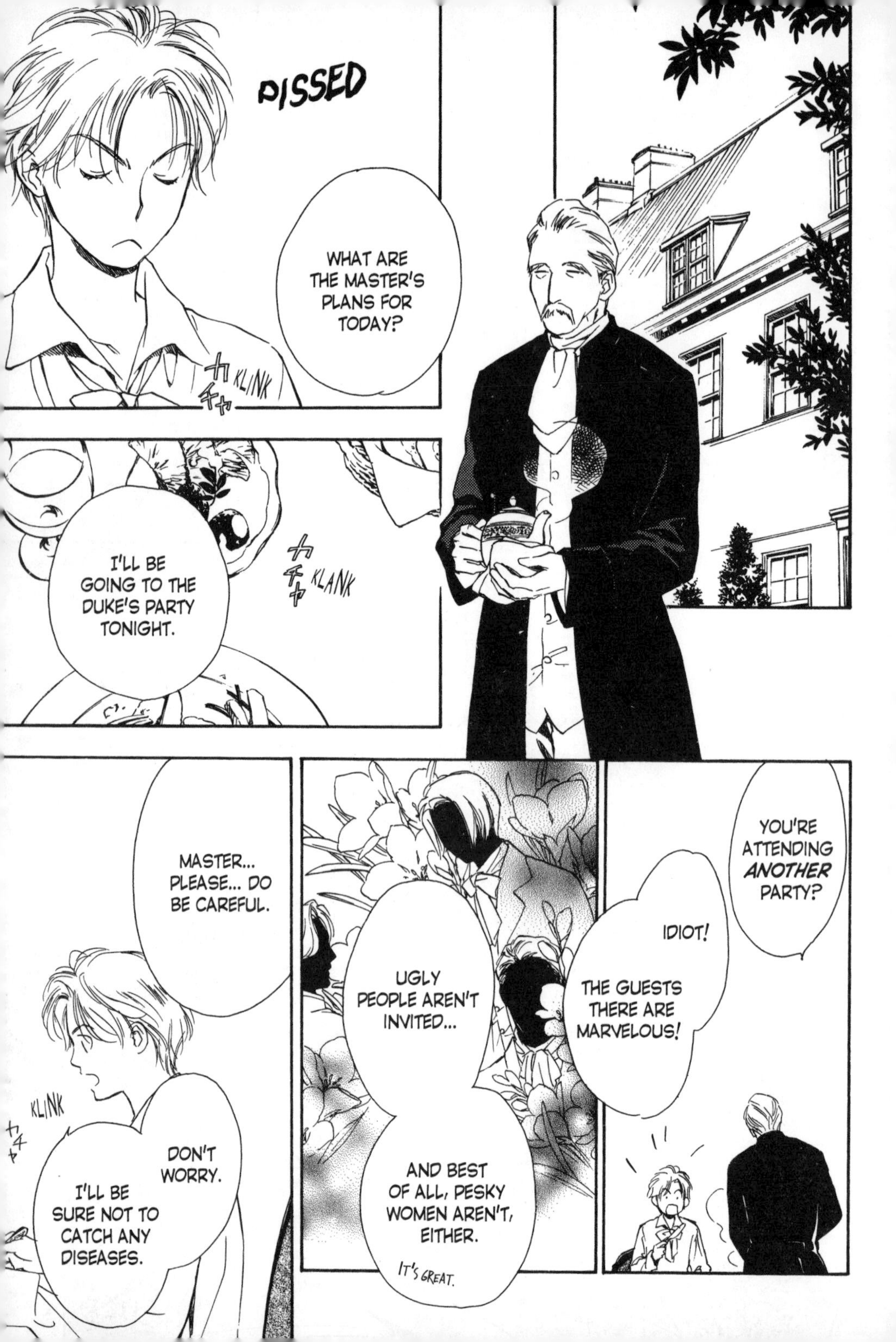
PISSED
WHAT ARE THE MASTER'S PLANS FOR TODAY?
カチャ KLINK
I'LL BE GOING TO THE DUKE'S PARTY TONIGHT.
カチャ KLANK
YOU'RE ATTENDING *ANOTHER* PARTY?
IDIOT!
THE GUESTS THERE ARE MARVELOUS!
UGLY PEOPLE AREN'T INVITED...
AND BEST OF ALL, PESKY WOMEN AREN'T, EITHER.
IT'S GREAT.
MASTER... PLEASE... DO BE CAREFUL.
カチャ KLINK
DON'T WORRY.
I'LL BE SURE NOT TO CATCH ANY DISEASES.

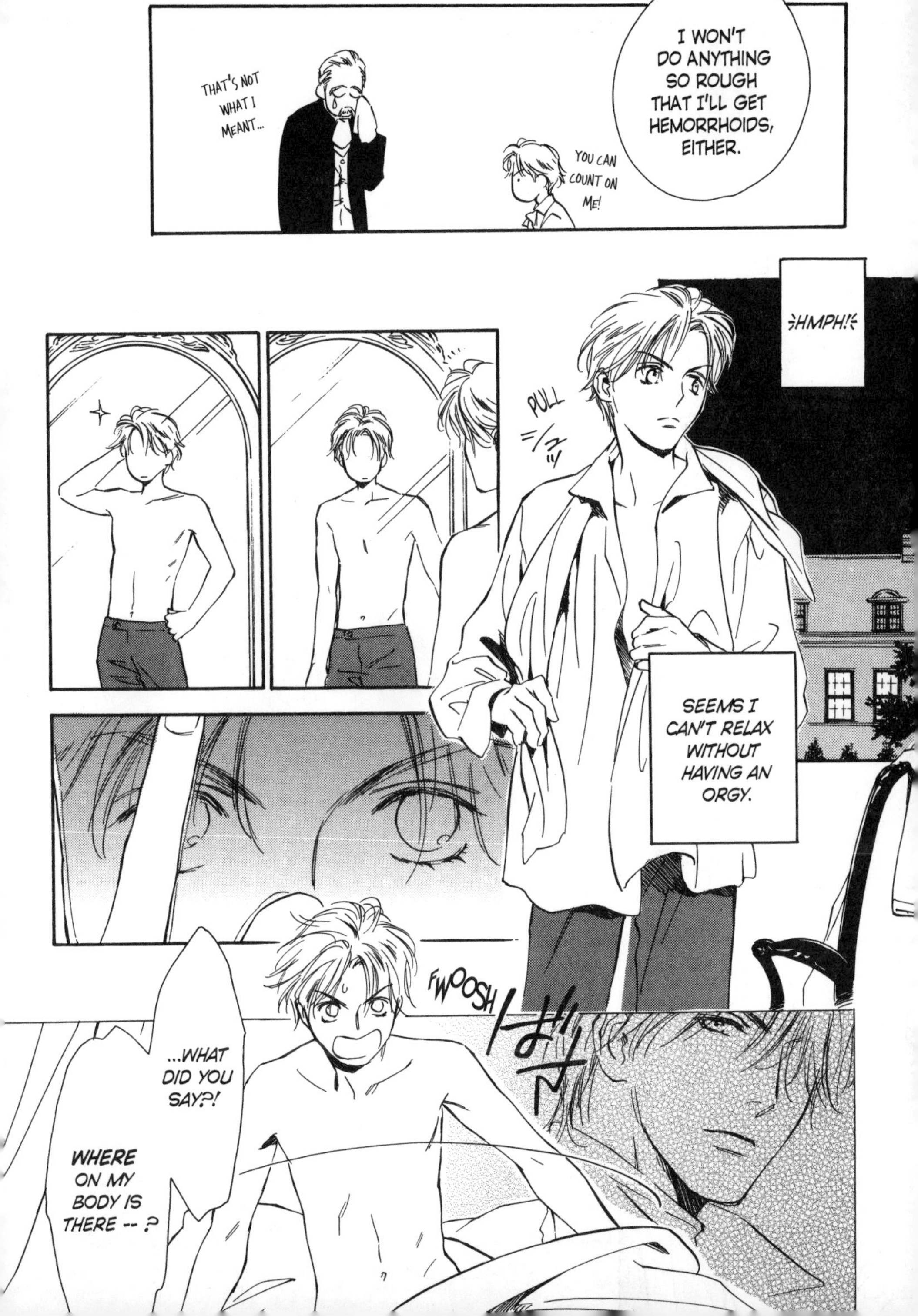
I WON'T DO ANYTHING SO ROUGH THAT I'LL GET HEMORRHOIDS, EITHER.
YOU CAN COUNT ON ME!
THAT'S NOT WHAT I MEANT...
HMPH!
PULL
SEEMS I CAN'T RELAX WITHOUT HAVING AN ORGY.
FWOOSH
...WHAT DID YOU SAY?!
WHERE ON MY BODY IS THERE -- ?

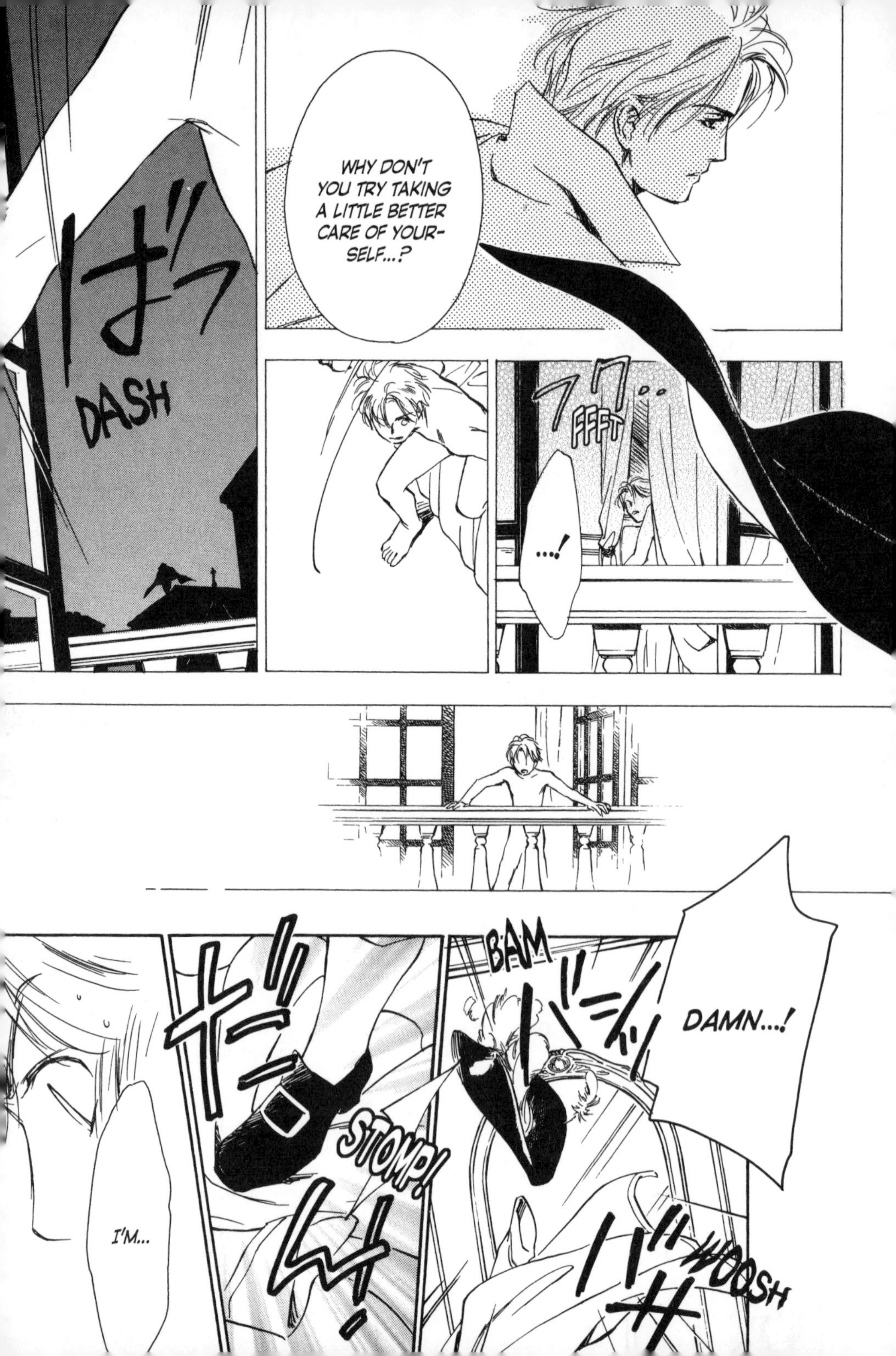

WHY DON'T YOU TRY TAKING A LITTLE BETTER CARE OF YOUR-SELF...?
FFFT
...!
DASH
BAM
DAMN...!
WOOSH
STOMP!
I'M...

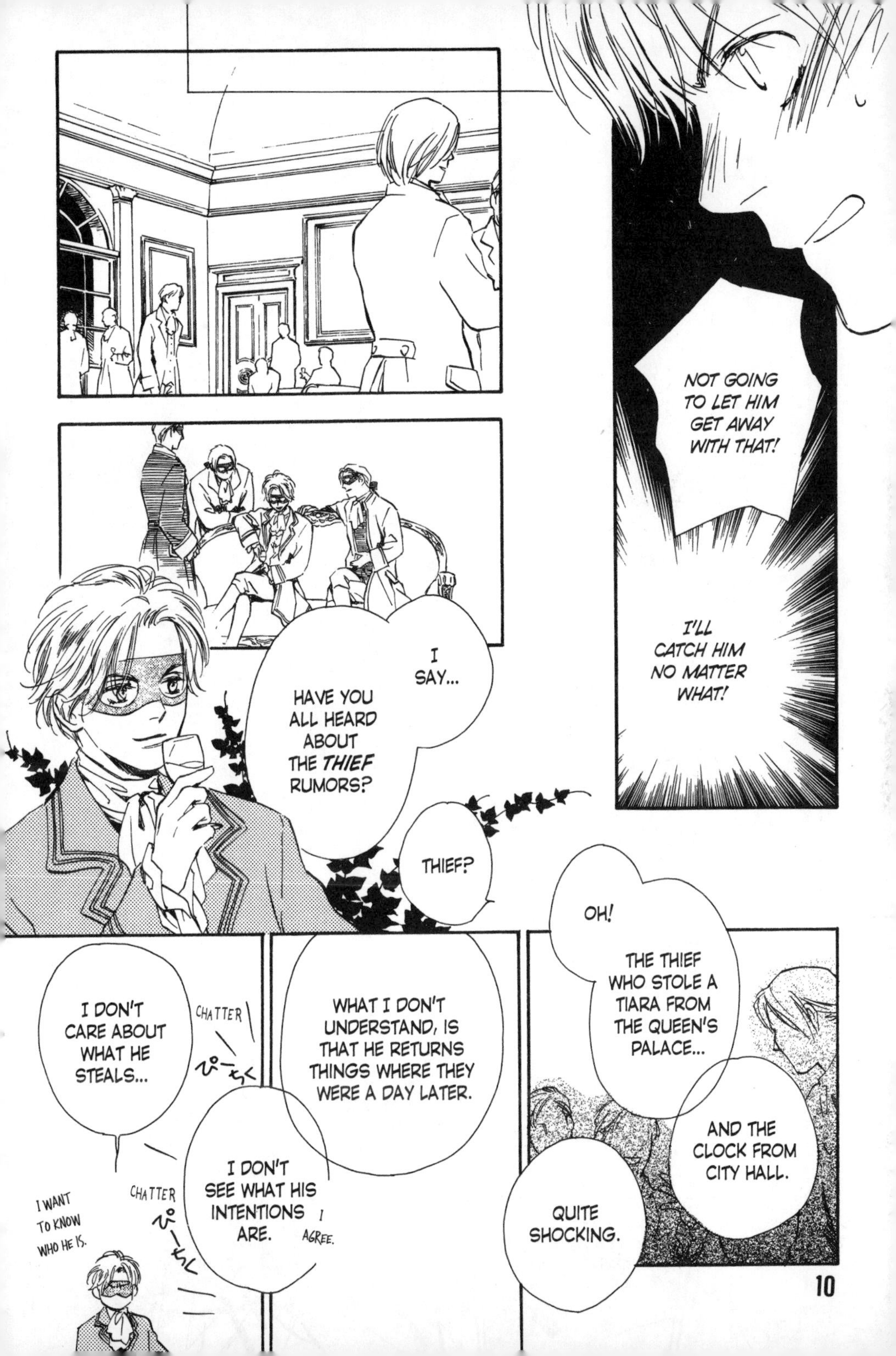
NOT GOING TO LET HIM GET AWAY WITH THAT!
I'LL CATCH HIM NO MATTER WHAT!
I SAY... HAVE YOU ALL HEARD ABOUT THE *THIEF* RUMORS?
THIEF?
OH!
THE THIEF WHO STOLE A TIARA FROM THE QUEEN'S PALACE...
AND THE CLOCK FROM CITY HALL.
QUITE SHOCKING.
WHAT I DON'T UNDERSTAND, IS THAT HE RETURNS THINGS WHERE THEY WERE A DAY LATER.
I DON'T SEE WHAT HIS INTENTIONS ARE.
I AGREE.
I DON'T CARE ABOUT WHAT HE STEALS...
CHATTER
ぴーちく
CHATTER
ぴーちく
I WANT TO KNOW WHO HE IS.

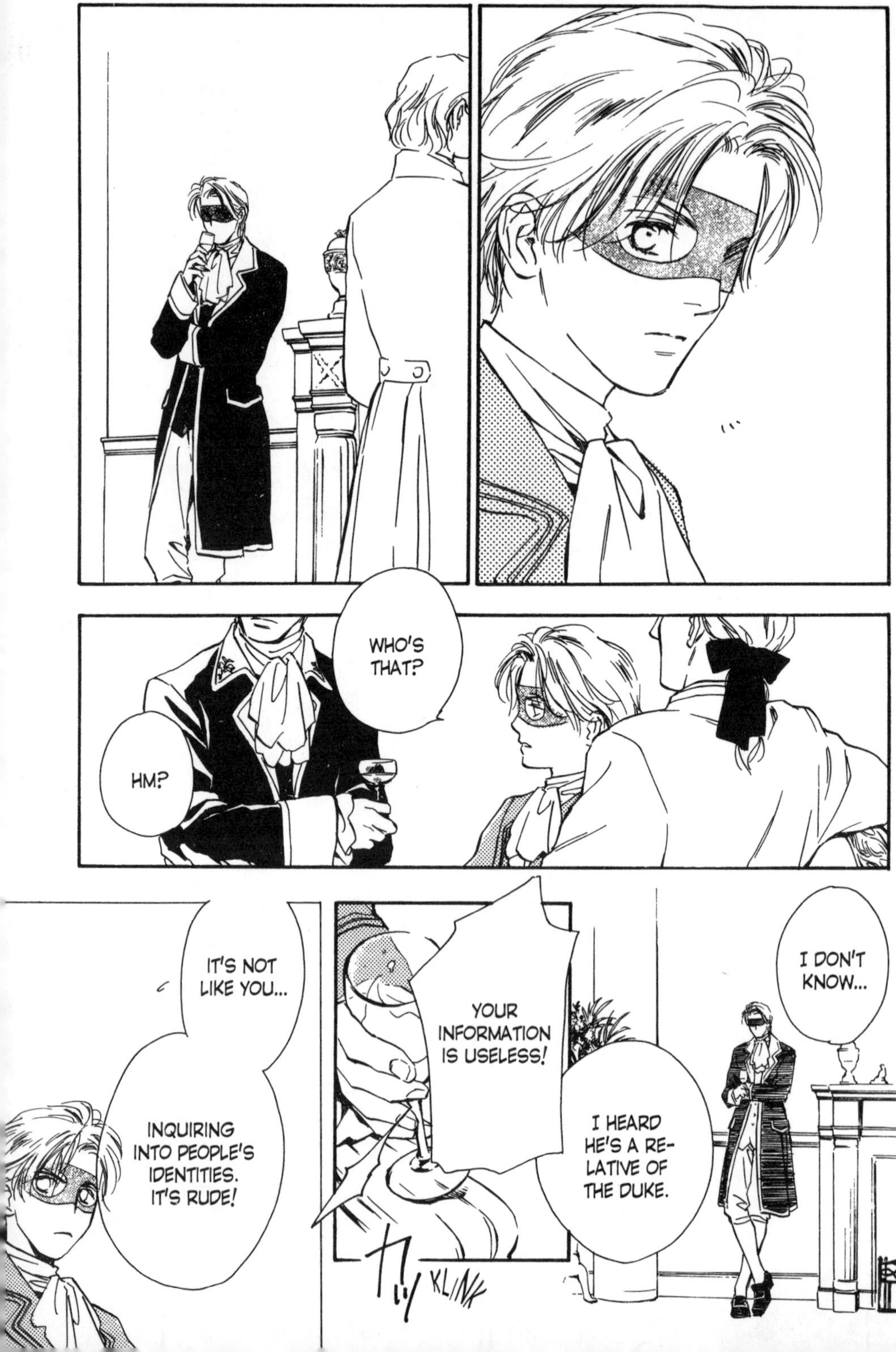
WHO'S THAT?
HM?
I DON'T KNOW...
I HEARD HE'S A RE- LATIVE OF THE DUKE.
YOUR INFORMATION IS USELESS!
KLINK
IT'S NOT LIKE YOU...
INQUIRING INTO PEOPLE'S IDENTITIES. IT'S RUDE!

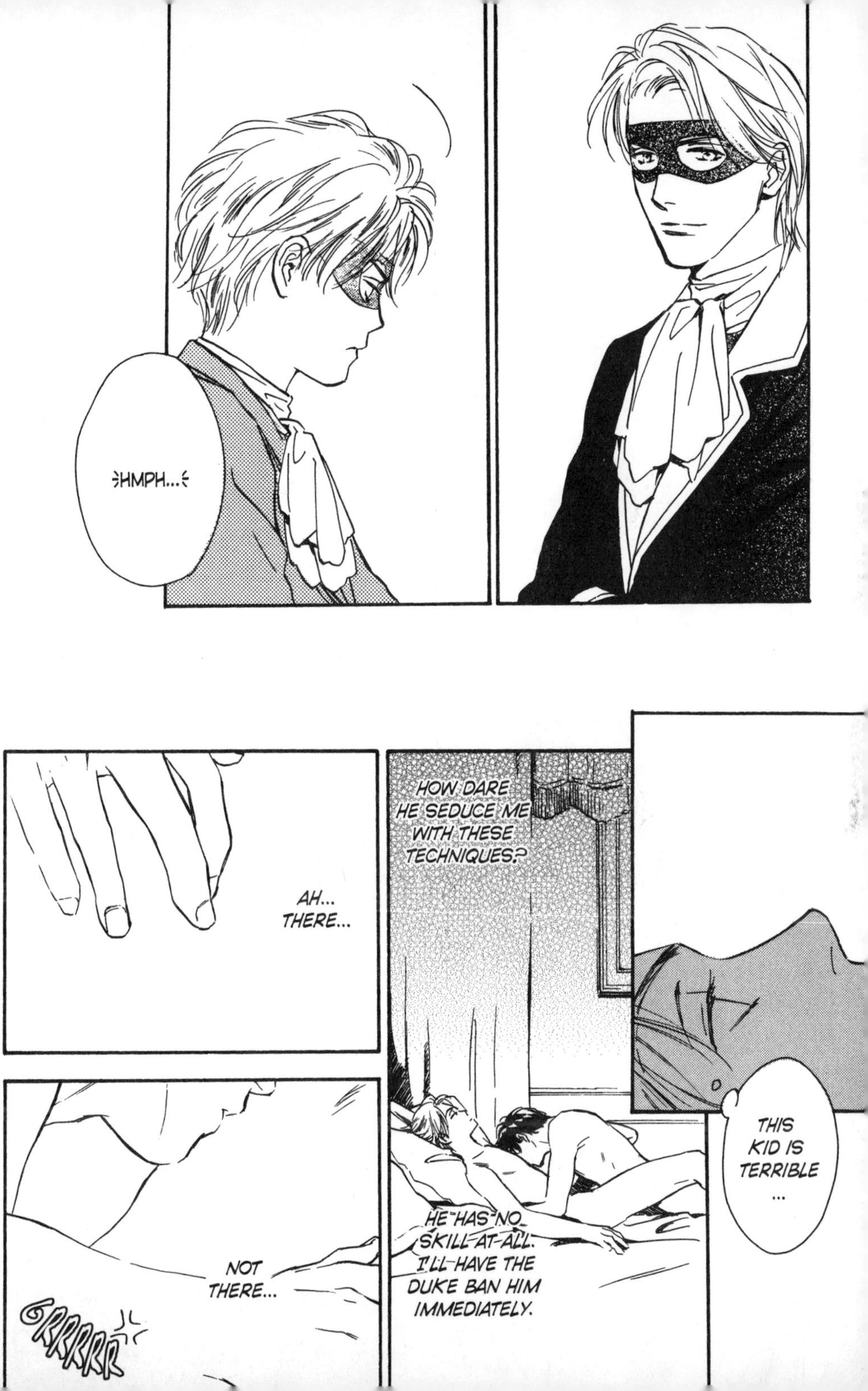
HMPH...
THIS KID IS TERRIBLE ...
HOW DARE HE SEDUCE ME WITH THESE TECHNIQUES?
HE HAS NO SKILL AT ALL. I'LL HAVE THE DUKE BAN HIM IMMEDIATELY.
AH... THERE...
NOT THERE...
GRRRRR

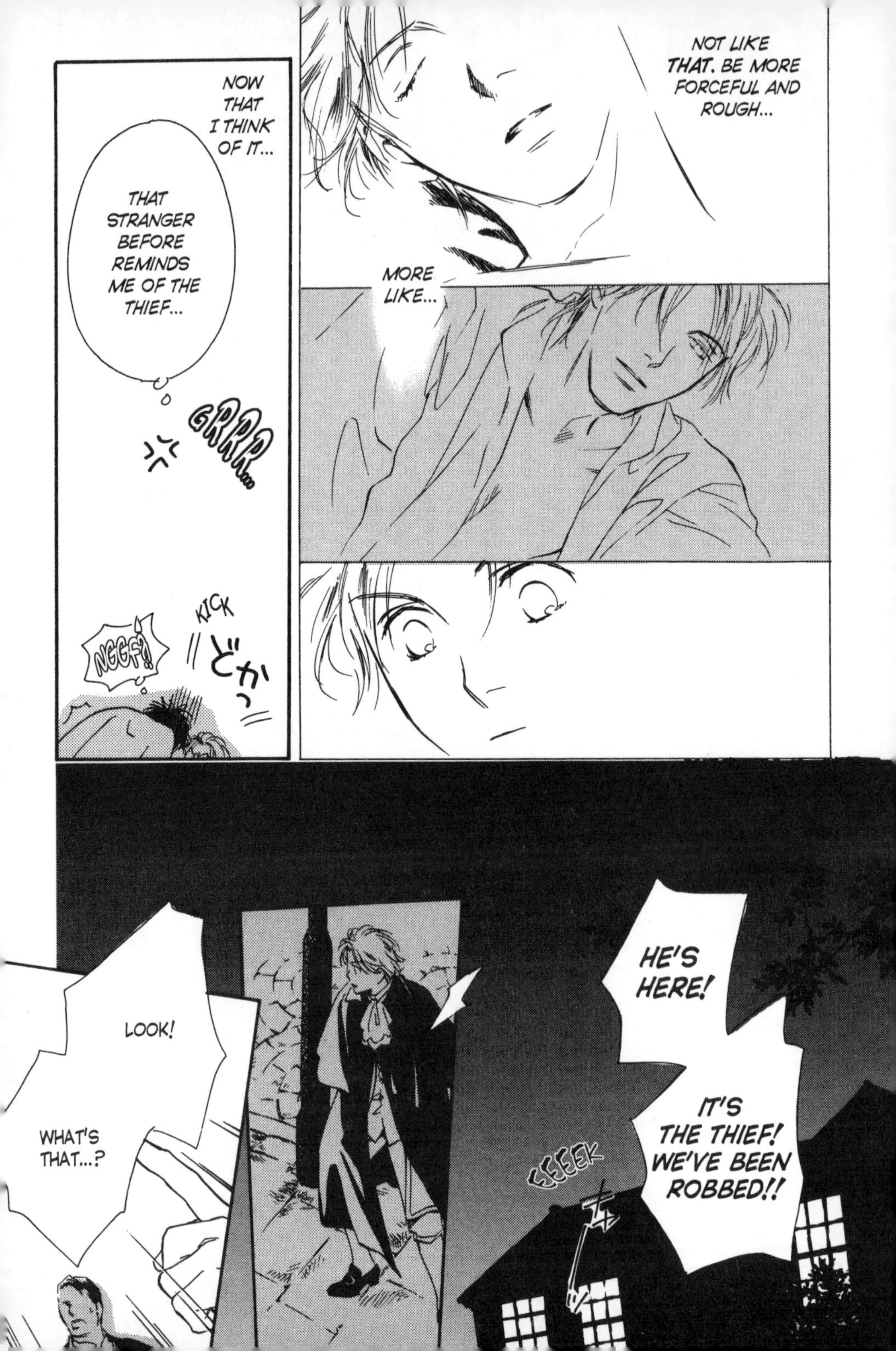
NOT LIKE THAT. BE MORE FORCEFUL AND ROUGH...
MORE LIKE...
NOW THAT I THINK OF IT...
THAT STRANGER BEFORE REMINDS ME OF THE THIEF...
GRRR...
KICK
どかっ
NGGF?!
HE'S HERE!
IT'S THE THIEF! WE'VE BEEN ROBBED!!
EEEEK
LOOK!
WHAT'S THAT...?

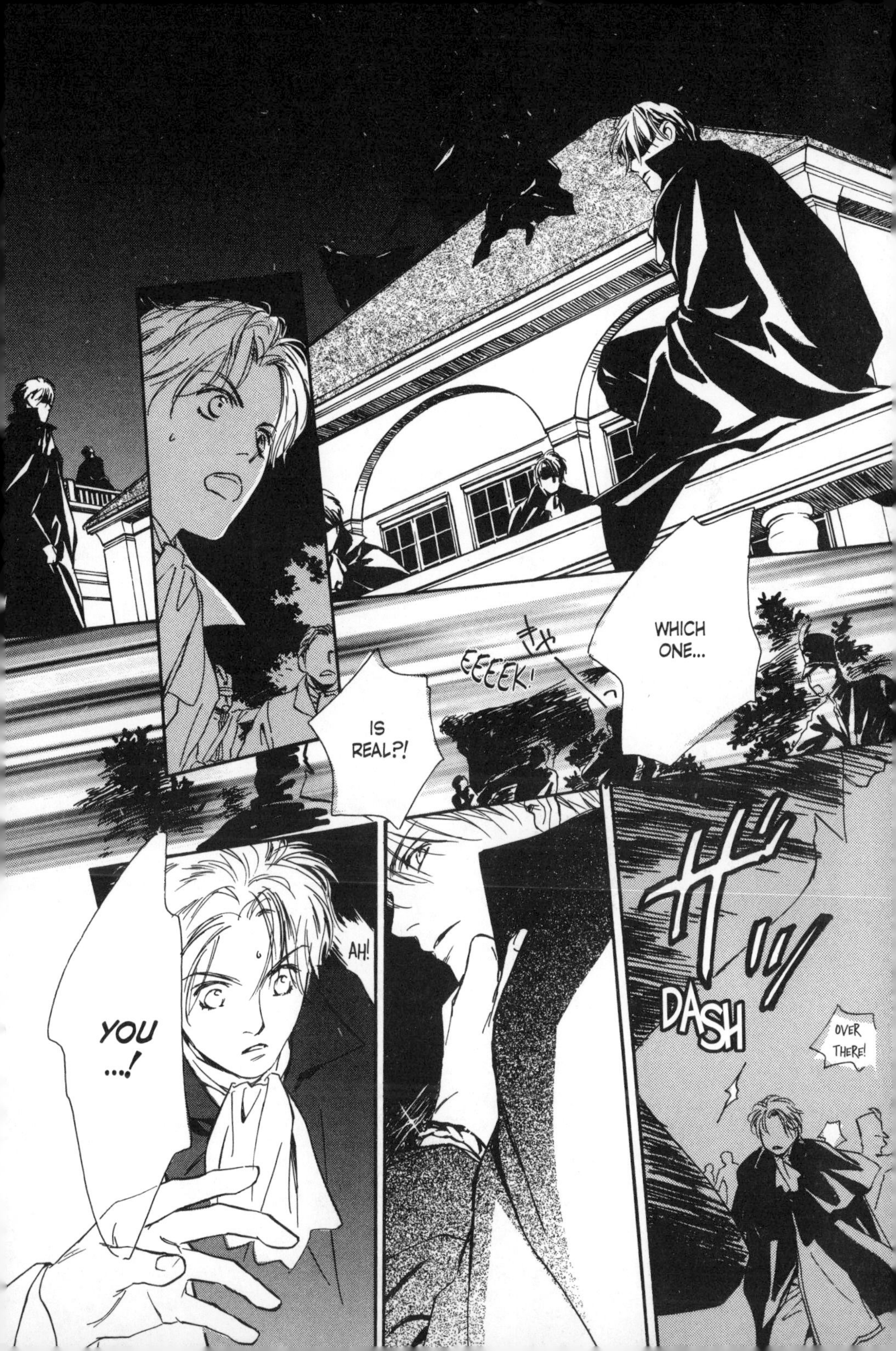
WHICH ONE...
IS REAL?!
きゃ
EEEEK!
ザッ
DASH
OVER THERE!
AH!
YOU ...!

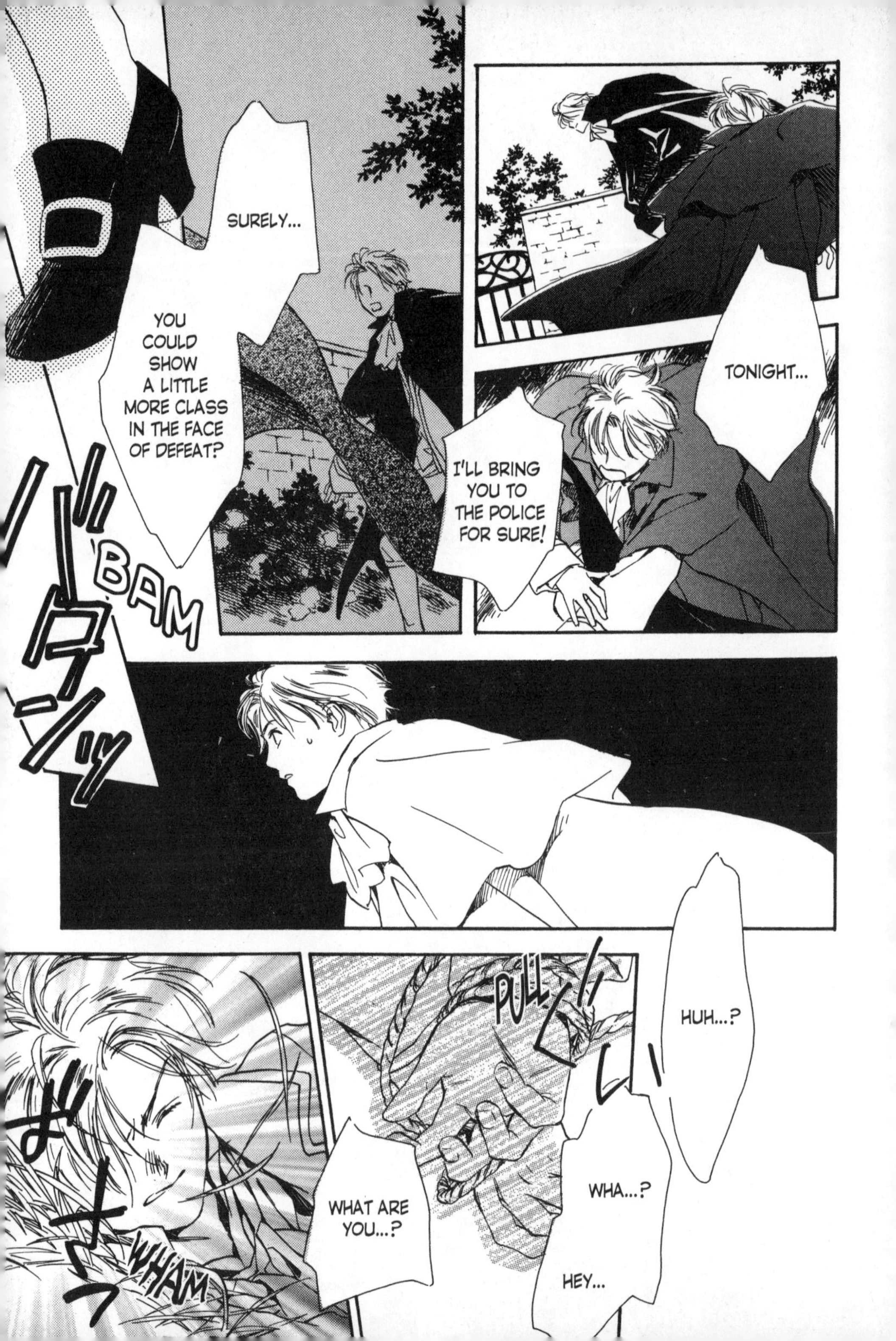
TONIGHT...
I'LL BRING YOU TO THE POLICE FOR SURE!
SURELY...
YOU COULD SHOW A LITTLE MORE CLASS IN THE FACE OF DEFEAT?
BAM
HUH...?
WHA...?
HEY...
PULL
WHAT ARE YOU...?
WHAM

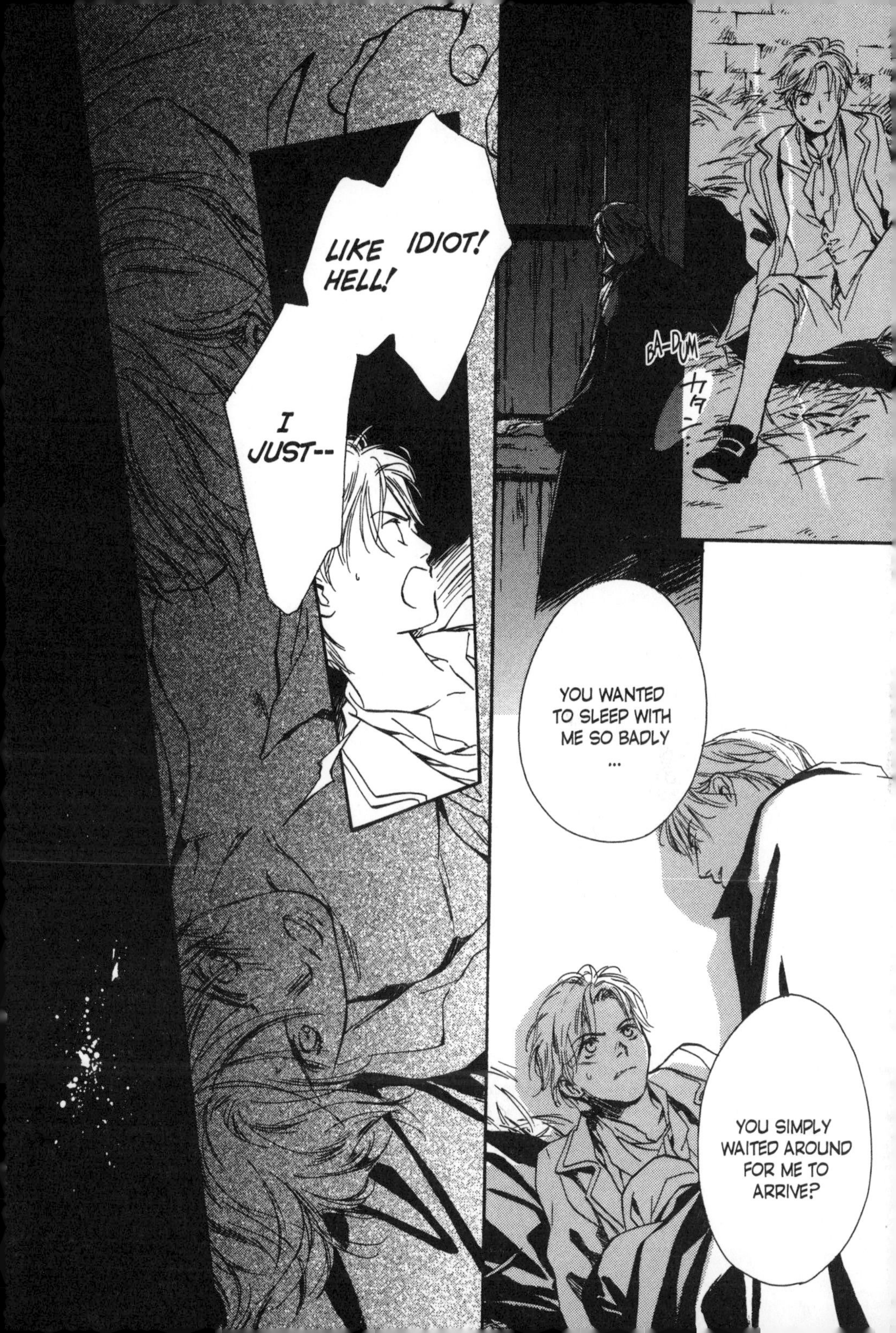
BA-DUM
カタ
YOU WANTED TO SLEEP WITH ME SO BADLY ...
YOU SIMPLY WAITED AROUND FOR ME TO ARRIVE?
IDIOT!
LIKE HELL!
I JUST--

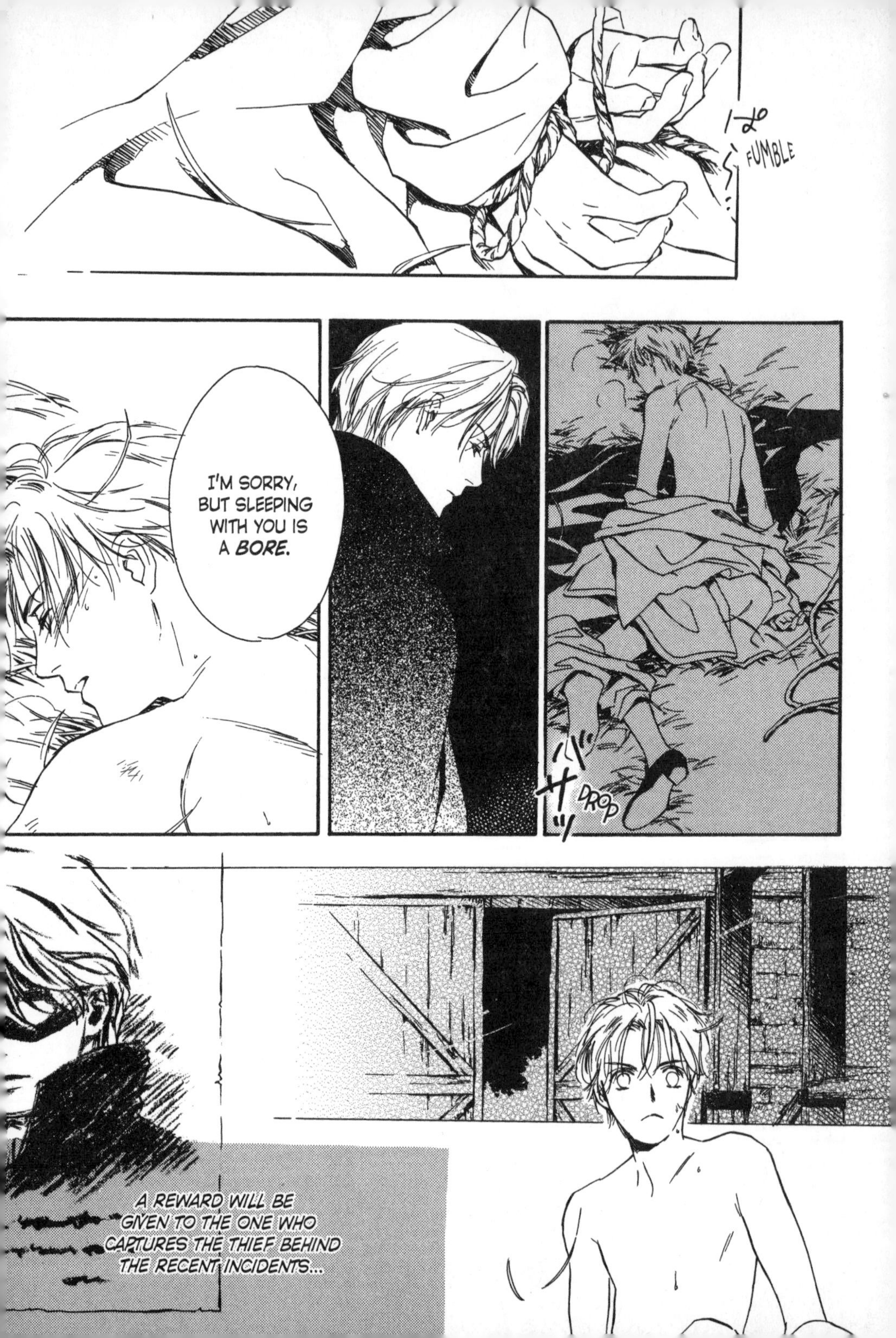
FUMBLE
DROP
I'M SORRY, BUT SLEEPING WITH YOU IS A *BORE*.
A REWARD WILL BE GIVEN TO THE ONE WHO CAPTURES THE THIEF BEHIND THE RECENT INCIDENTS...

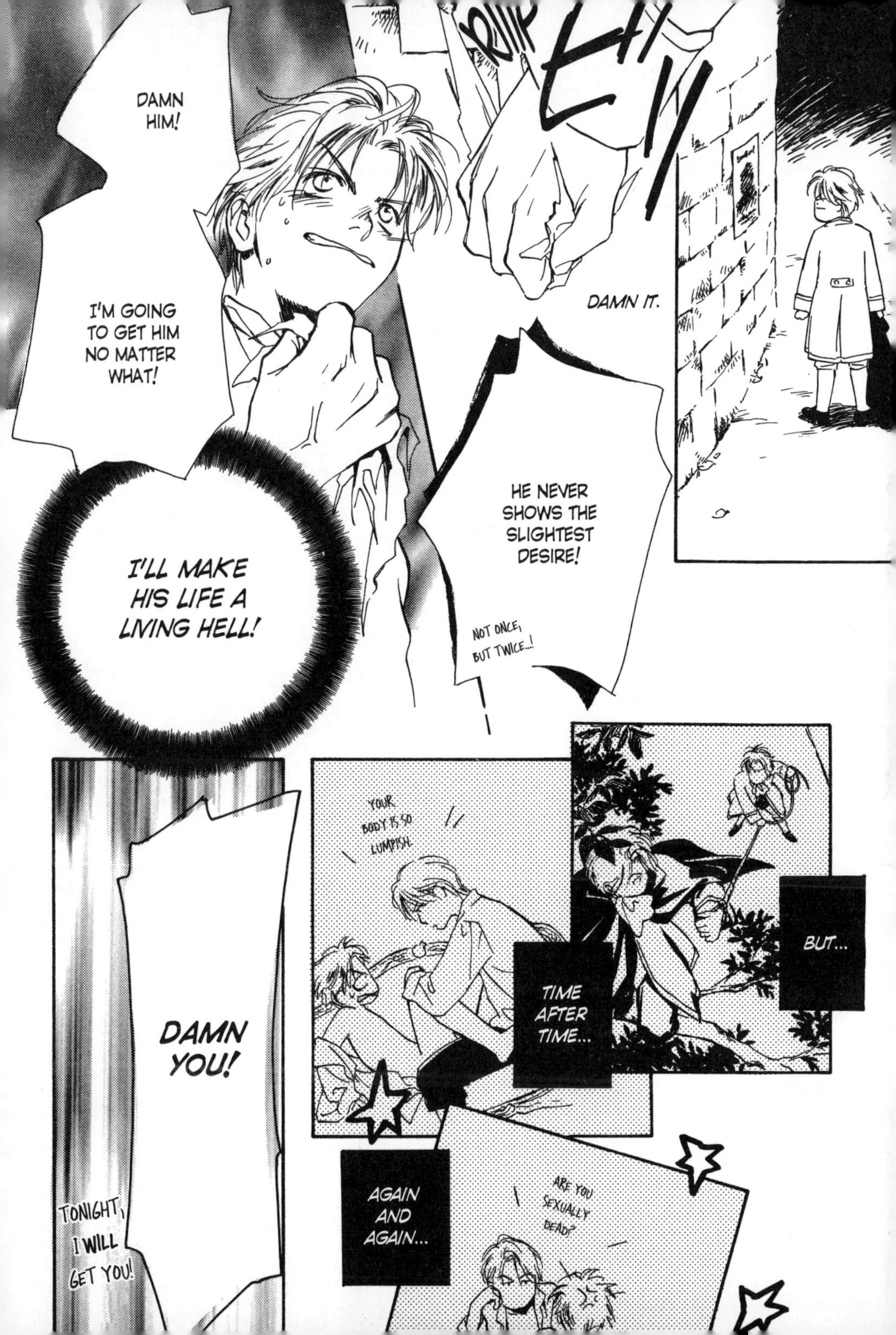
RIIIP
DAMN IT.
HE NEVER SHOWS THE SLIGHTEST DESIRE!
NOT ONCE, BUT TWICE...!
DAMN HIM!
I'M GOING TO GET HIM NO MATTER WHAT!
I'LL MAKE HIS LIFE A LIVING HELL!
BUT...
TIME AFTER TIME...
YOUR BODY IS SO LUMPISH.
AGAIN AND AGAIN...
ARE YOU SEXUALLY DEAD?
DAMN YOU!
TONIGHT, I WILL GET YOU!

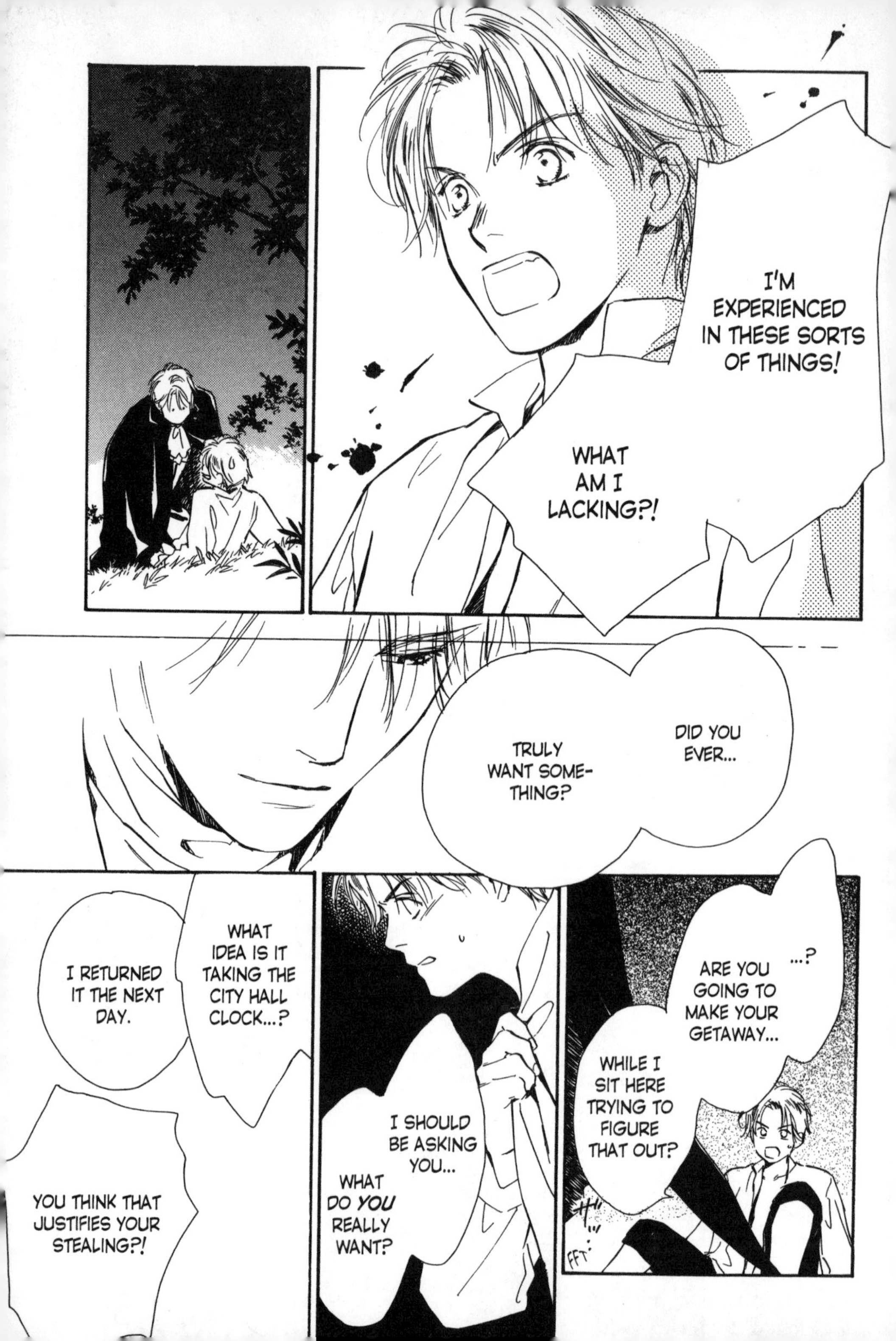
I'M EXPERIENCED IN THESE SORTS OF THINGS!
WHAT AM I LACKING?!
DID YOU EVER...
TRULY WANT SOME-THING?
...?
ARE YOU GOING TO MAKE YOUR GETAWAY...
WHILE I SIT HERE TRYING TO FIGURE THAT OUT?
FFT
I SHOULD BE ASKING YOU...
WHAT DO *YOU* REALLY WANT?
WHAT IDEA IS IT TAKING THE CITY HALL CLOCK...?
I RETURNED IT THE NEXT DAY.
YOU THINK THAT JUSTIFIES YOUR STEALING?!

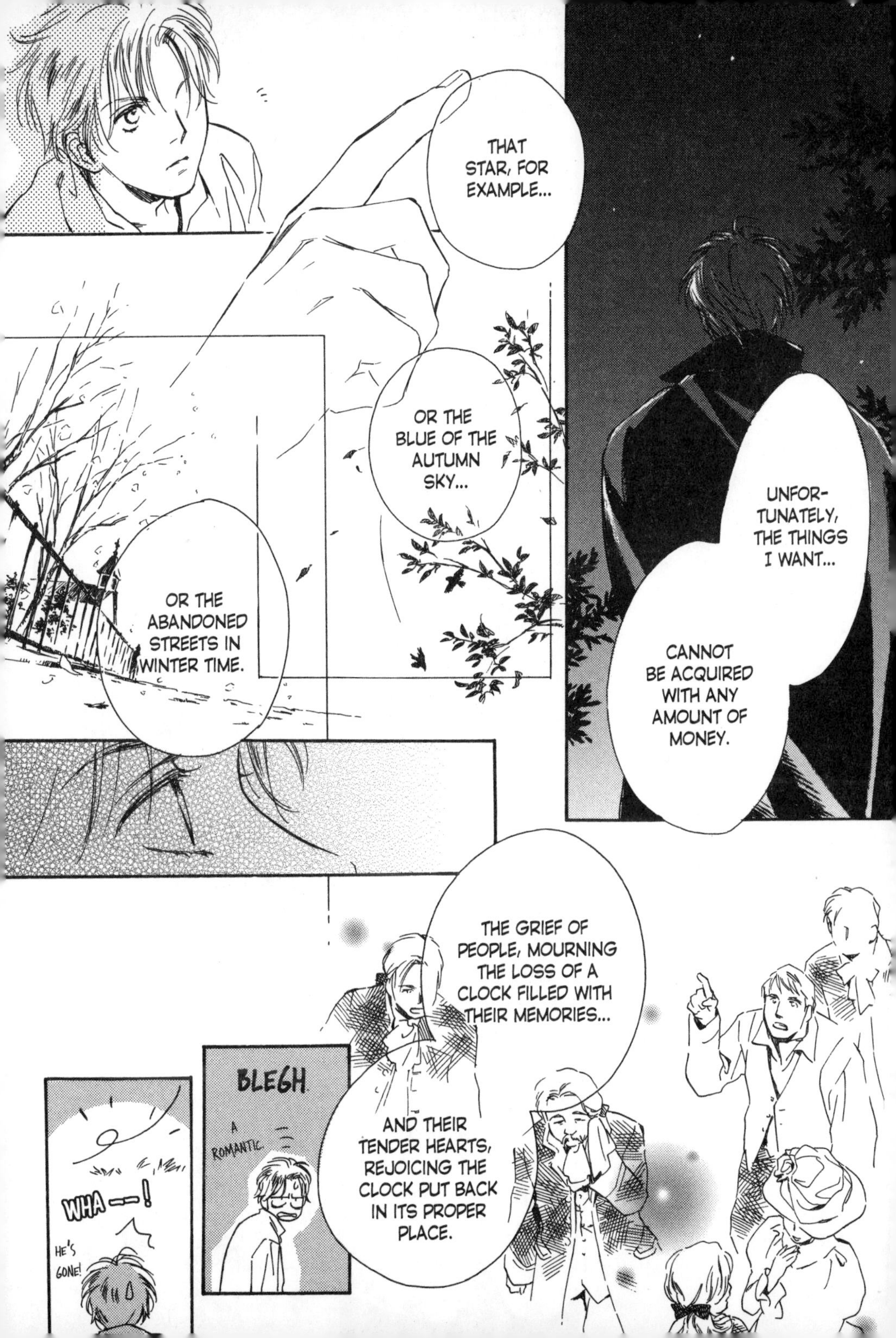
UNFORTUNATELY, THE THINGS I WANT...
CANNOT BE ACQUIRED WITH ANY AMOUNT OF MONEY.
THAT STAR, FOR EXAMPLE...
OR THE BLUE OF THE AUTUMN SKY...
OR THE ABANDONED STREETS IN WINTER TIME.
THE GRIEF OF PEOPLE, MOURNING THE LOSS OF A CLOCK FILLED WITH THEIR MEMORIES...
AND THEIR TENDER HEARTS, REJOICING THE CLOCK PUT BACK IN ITS PROPER PLACE.
BLEGH
A ROMANTIC.
WHA--!
HE'S GONE!

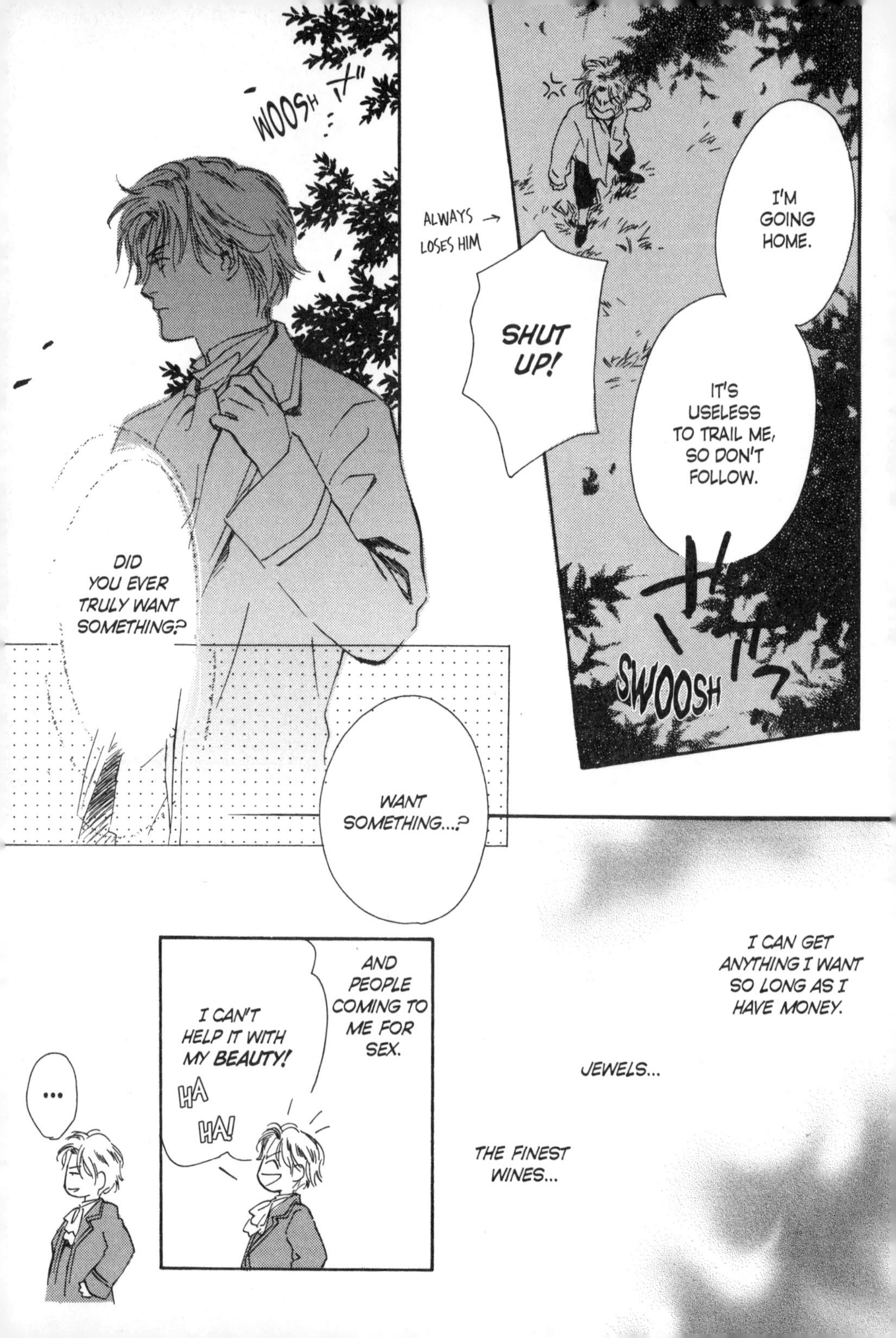

I'M GOING HOME.
IT'S USELESS TO TRAIL ME, SO DON'T FOLLOW.
SHUT UP!
ALWAYS → LOSES HIM
SWOOSH
WOOSH
DID YOU EVER TRULY WANT SOMETHING?
WANT SOMETHING...?
I CAN GET ANYTHING I WANT SO LONG AS I HAVE MONEY.
JEWELS...
THE FINEST WINES...
AND PEOPLE COMING TO ME FOR SEX.
I CAN'T HELP IT WITH MY BEAUTY!
HA HA!
...

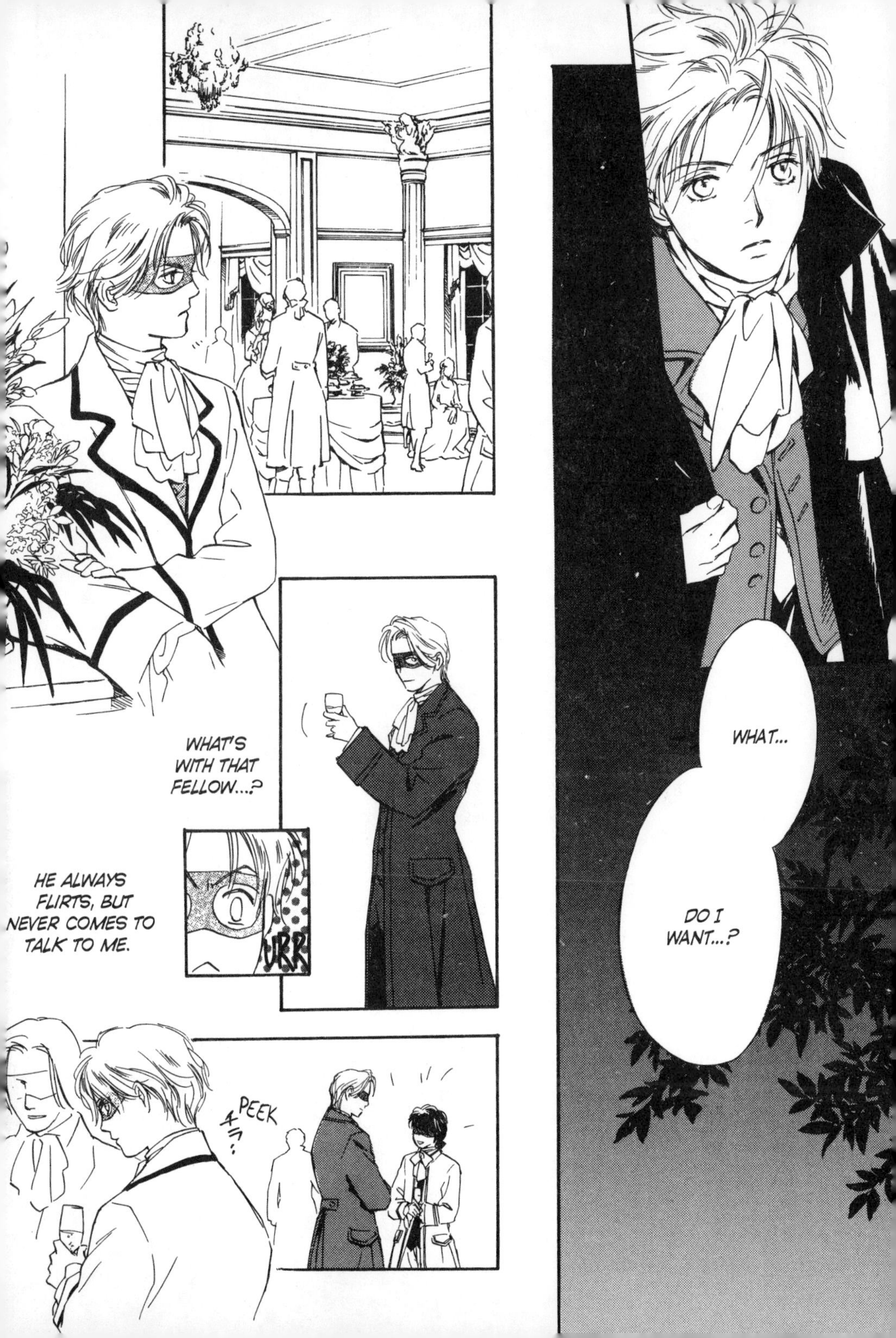
WHAT...
DO I WANT...?
WHAT'S WITH THAT FELLOW...?
HE ALWAYS FLIRTS, BUT NEVER COMES TO TALK TO ME.
URR
PEEK

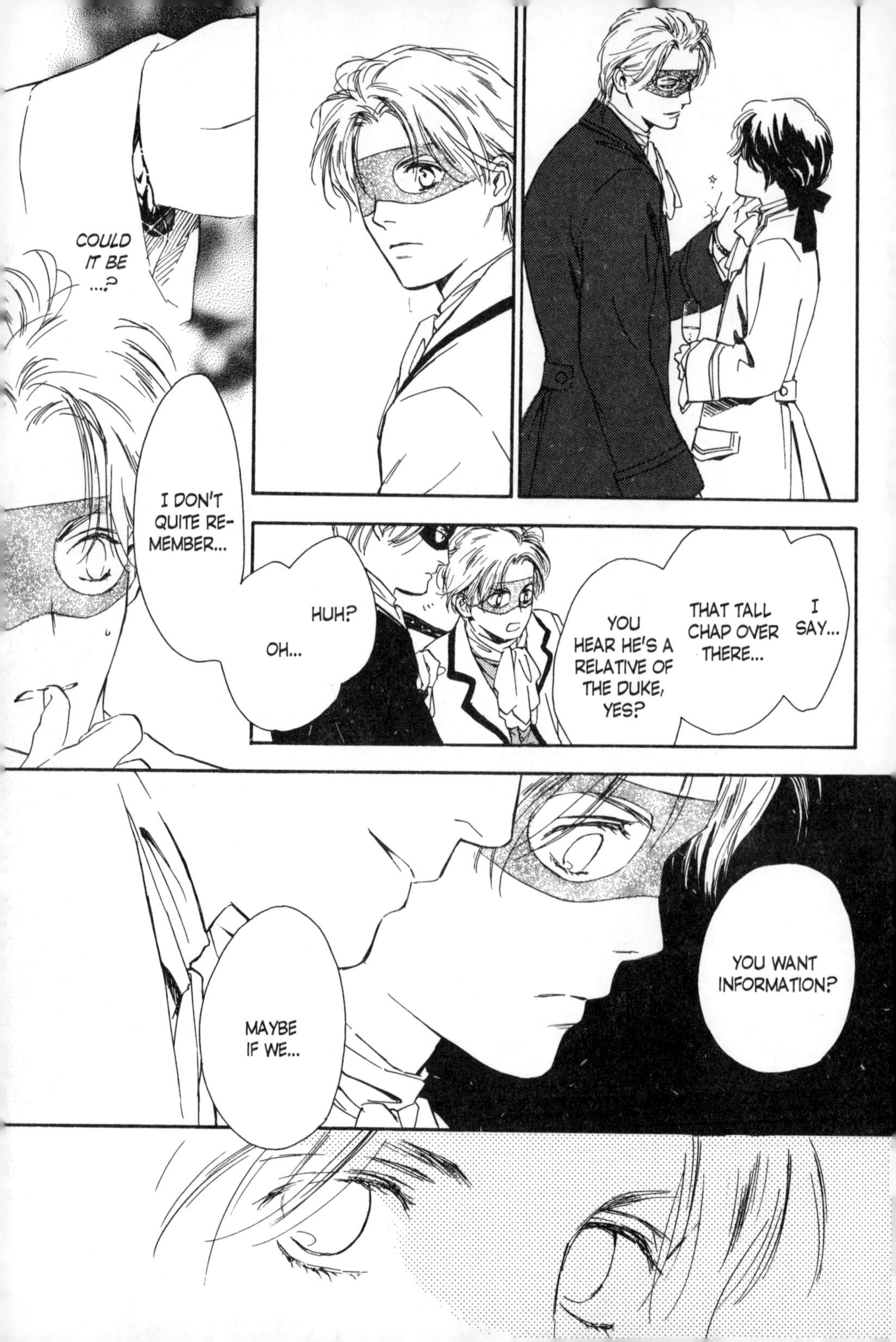
I SAY...
THAT TALL CHAP OVER THERE...
YOU HEAR HE'S A RELATIVE OF THE DUKE, YES?
HUH?
OH...
COULD IT BE ...?
I DON'T QUITE RE- MEMBER...
YOU WANT INFORMATION?
MAYBE IF WE...

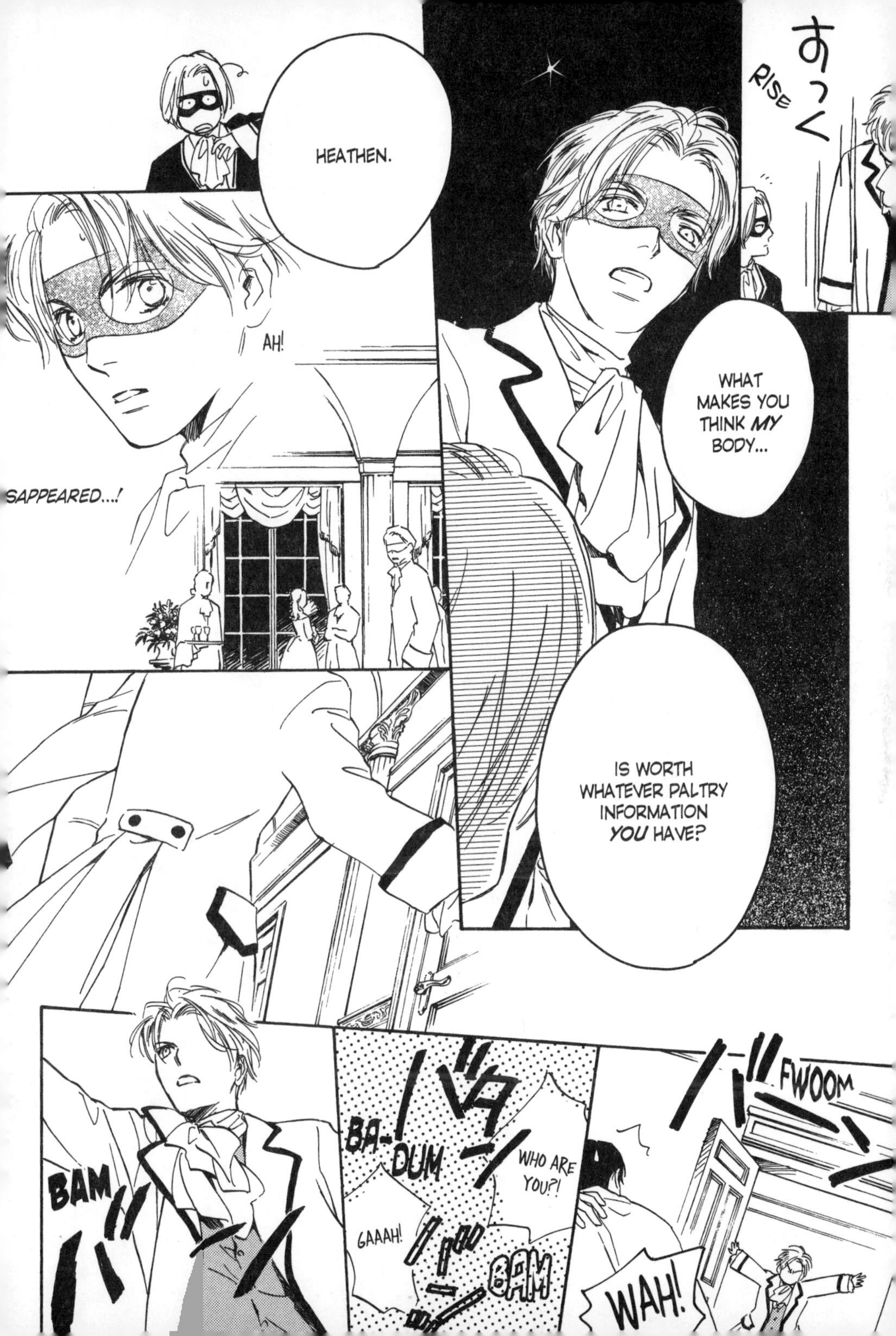
おっく
RISE
WHAT MAKES YOU THINK *MY* BODY...
IS WORTH WHATEVER PALTRY INFORMATION *YOU* HAVE?
HEATHEN.
AH!
SAPPEARED...!
FWOOM
WAH!
BA-DUM
WHO ARE YOU?!
GAAAH!
BAM
BAM

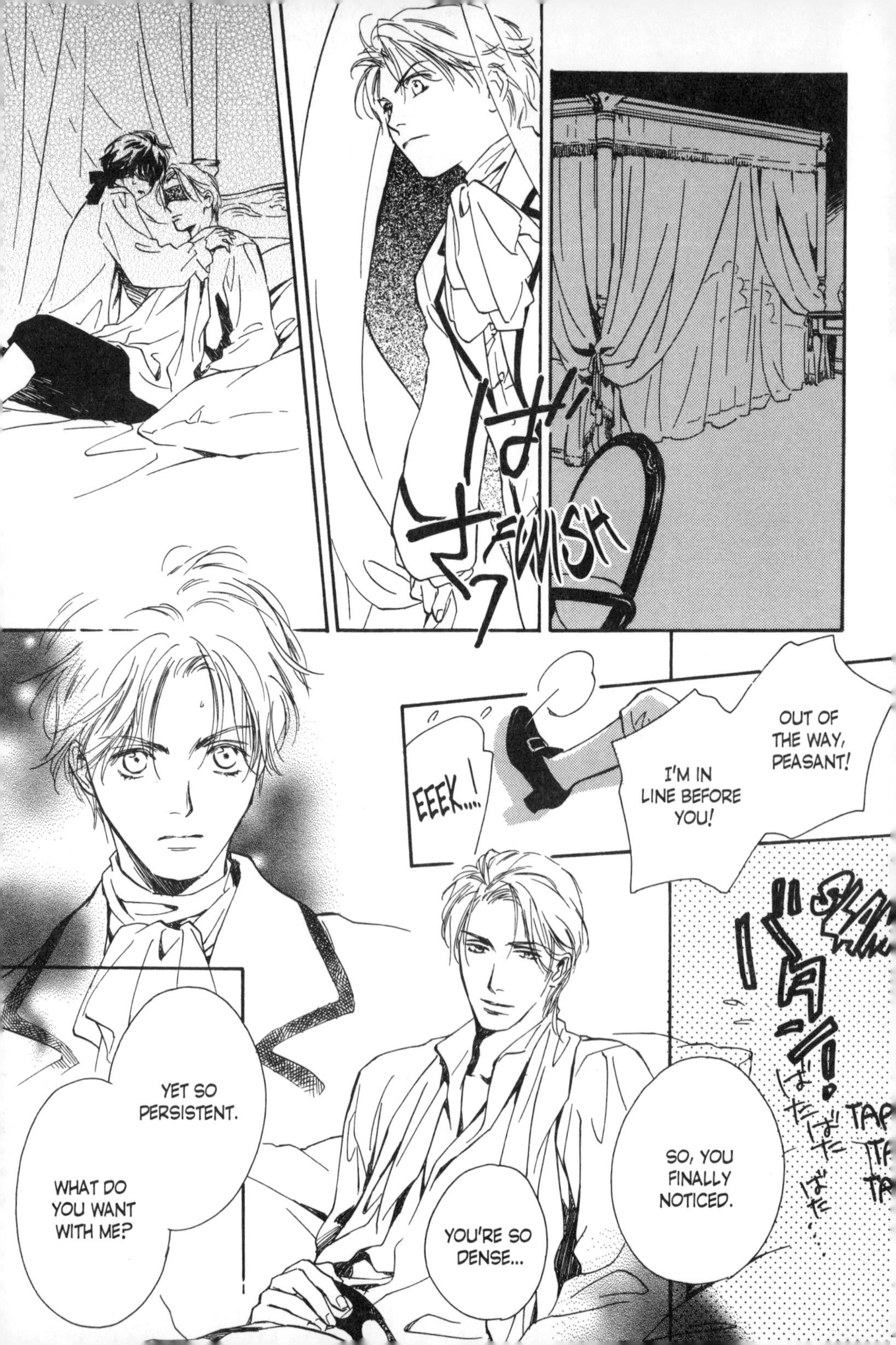
ばさっ
FWISH
OUT OF THE WAY, PEASANT!
I'M IN LINE BEFORE YOU!
EEEK...!
ばたばたばた…
TAP
SO, YOU FINALLY NOTICED.
YOU'RE SO DENSE...
YET SO PERSISTENT.
WHAT DO YOU WANT WITH ME?

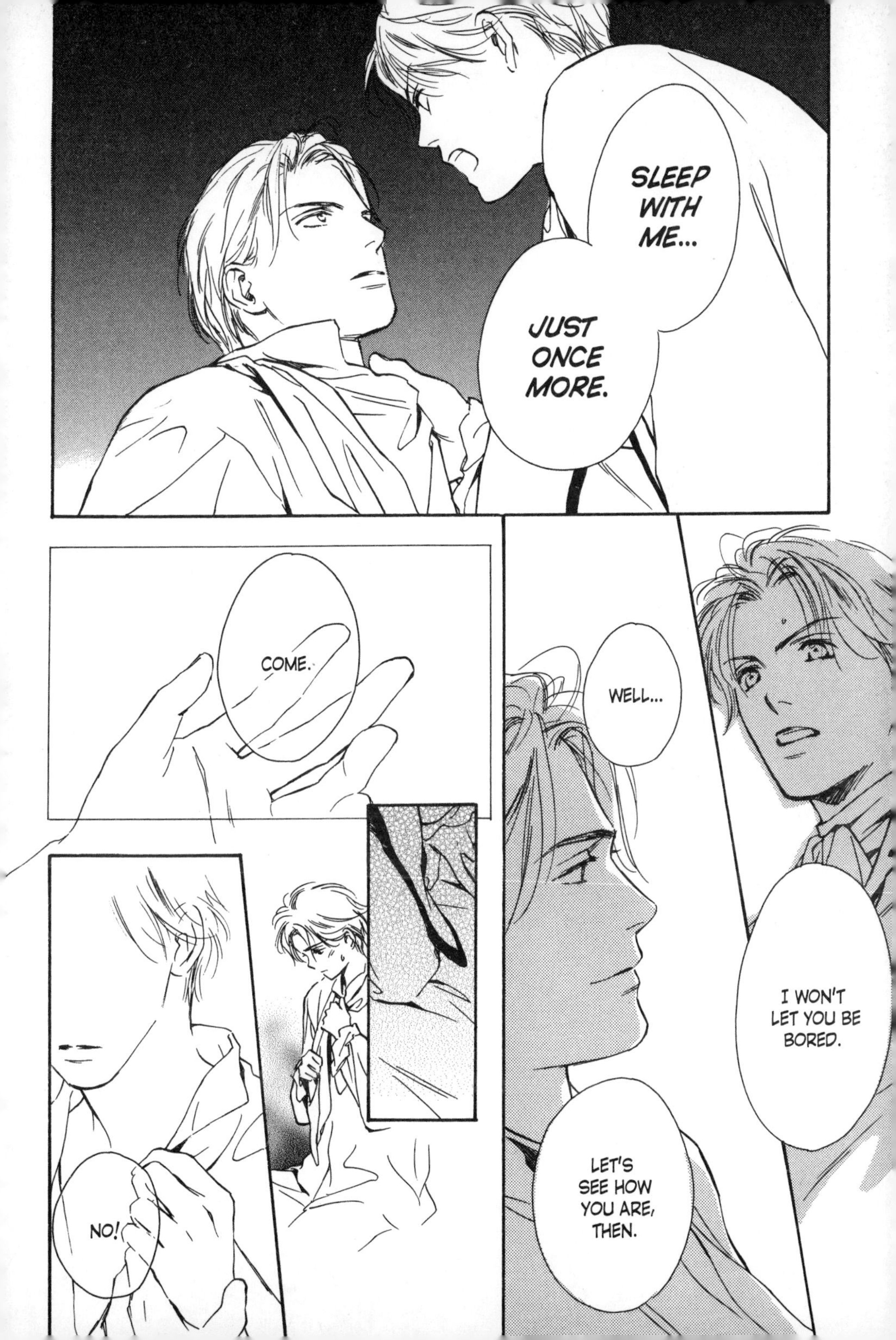
SLEEP WITH ME...
JUST ONCE MORE.
WELL...
I WON'T LET YOU BE BORED.
LET'S SEE HOW YOU ARE, THEN.
COME.
NO!

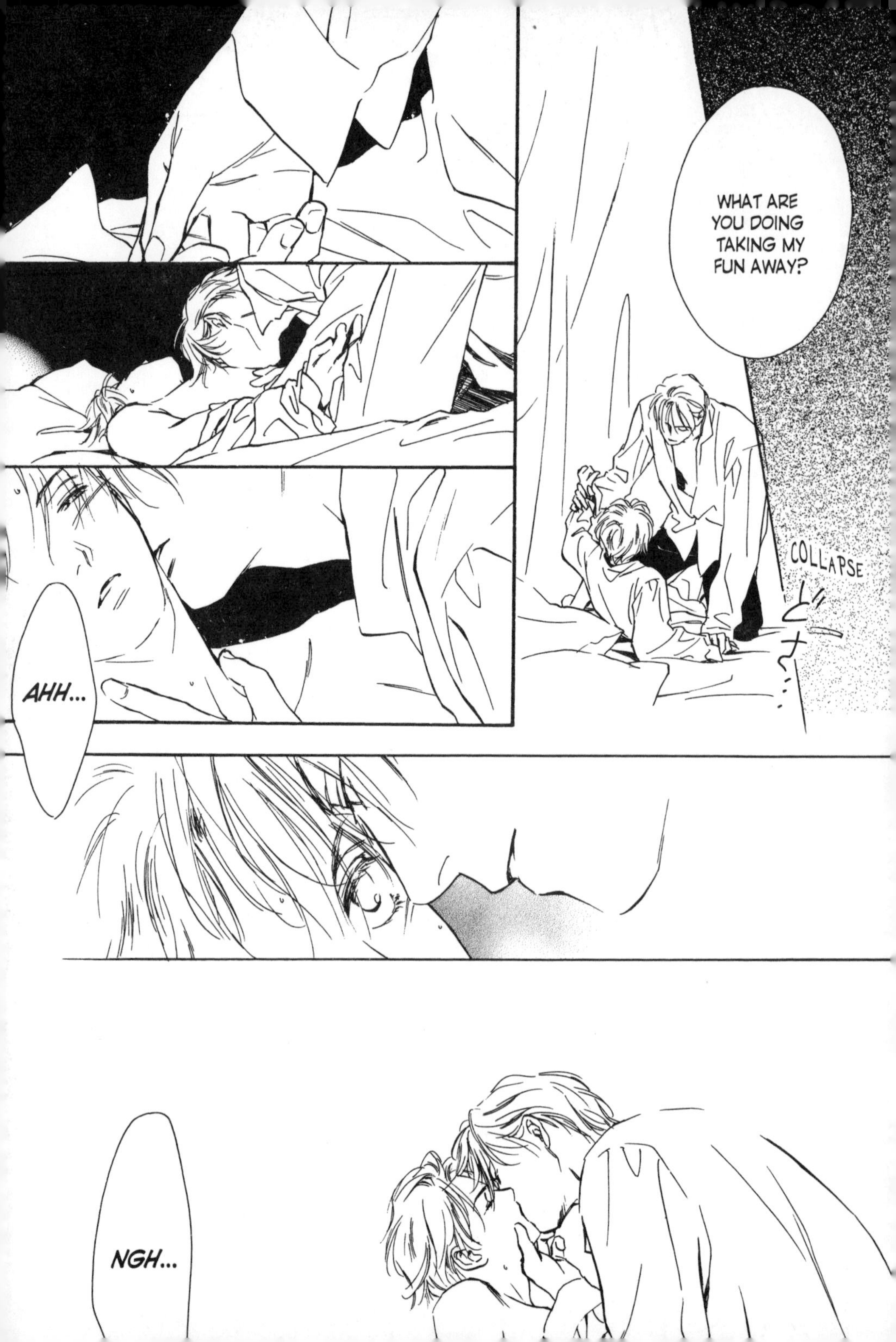
WHAT ARE YOU DOING TAKING MY FUN AWAY?
COLLAPSE
AHH...
NGH...

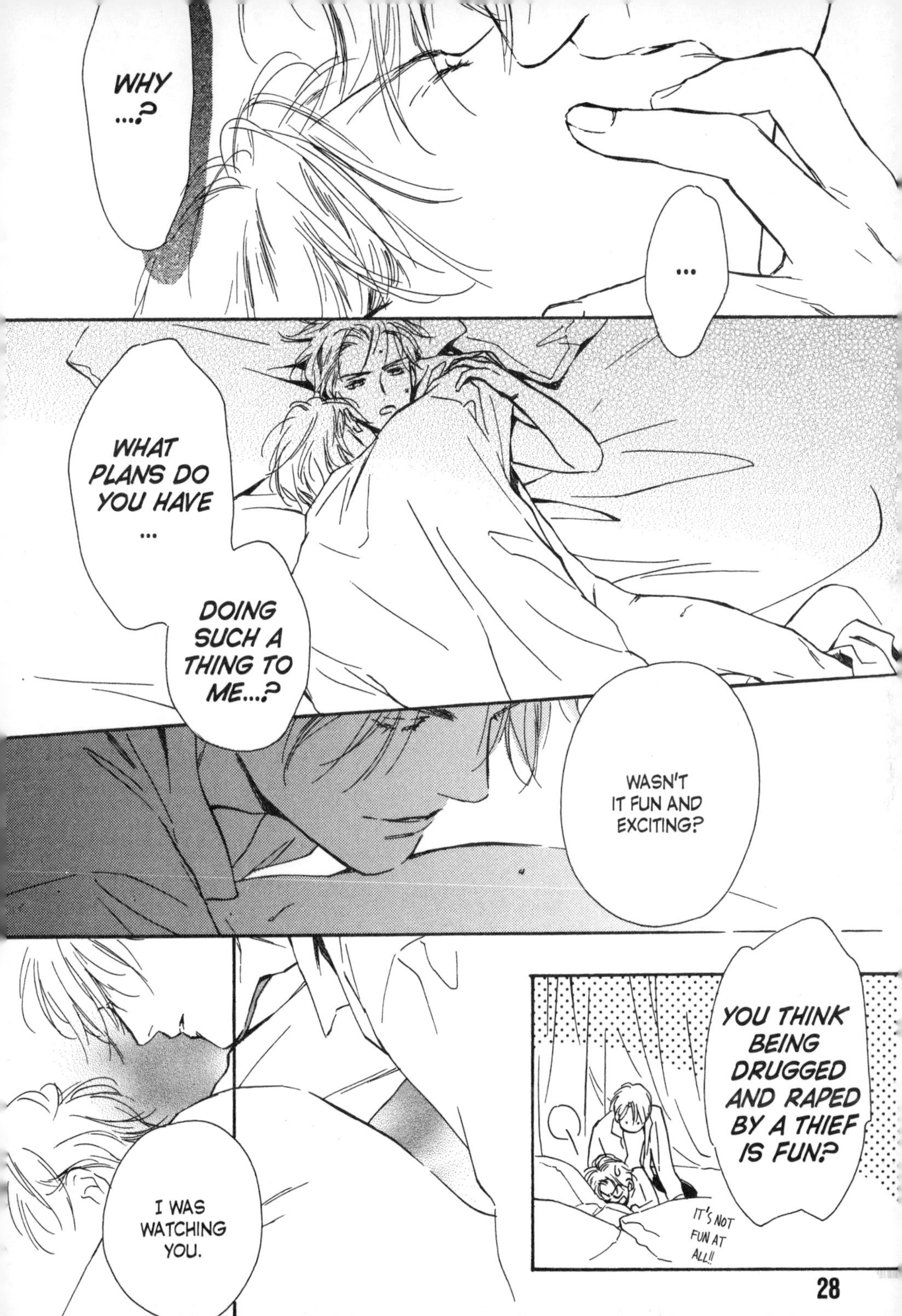
WHY ...?
...
WHAT PLANS DO YOU HAVE ...
DOING SUCH A THING TO ME...?
WASN'T IT FUN AND EXCITING?
YOU THINK BEING DRUGGED AND RAPED BY A THIEF IS FUN?
IT'S NOT FUN AT ALL!!
I WAS WATCHING YOU.

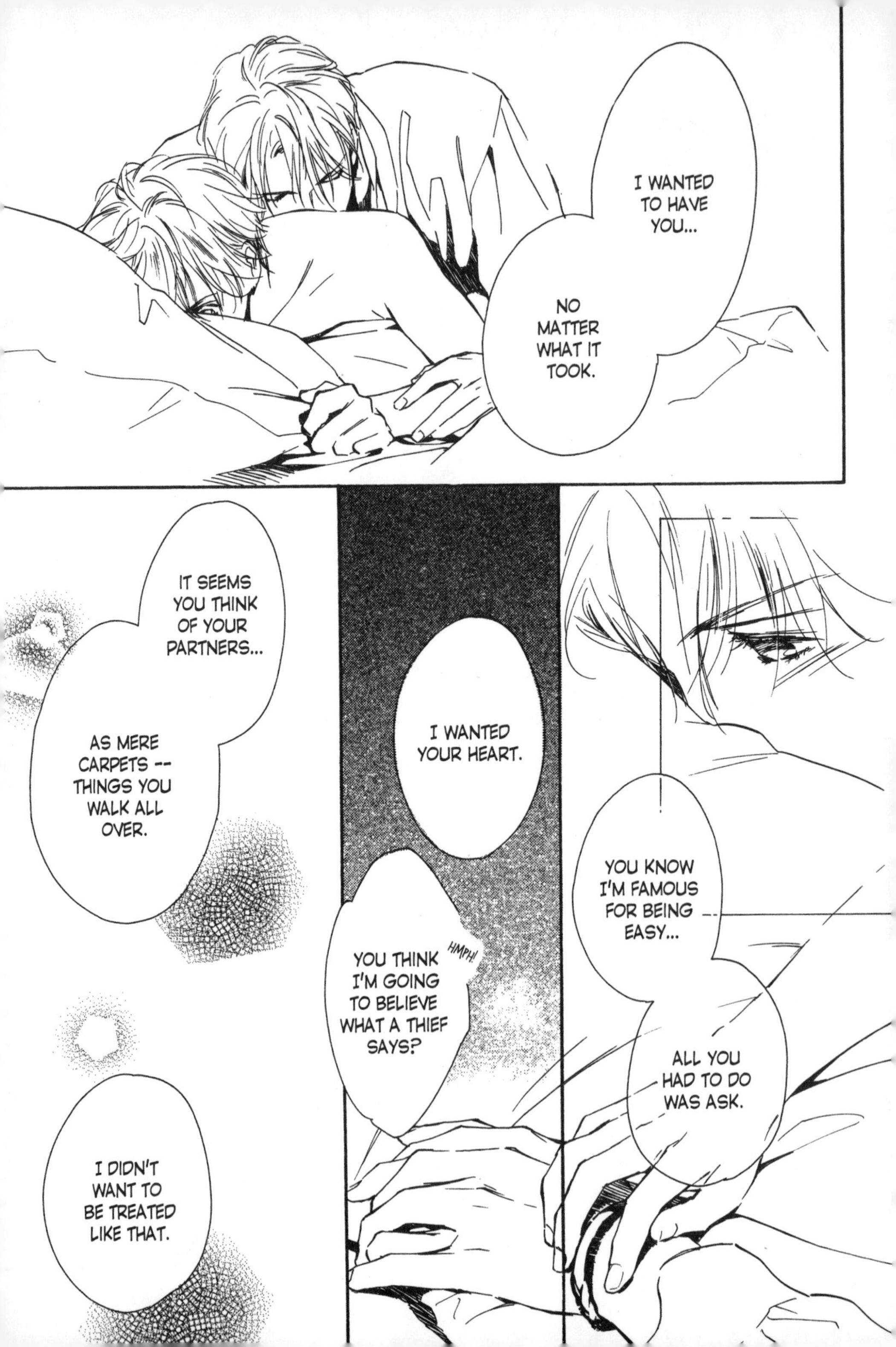
I WANTED TO HAVE YOU...
NO MATTER WHAT IT TOOK.
YOU KNOW I'M FAMOUS FOR BEING EASY...
ALL YOU HAD TO DO WAS ASK.
I WANTED YOUR HEART.
HMPH!
YOU THINK I'M GOING TO BELIEVE WHAT A THIEF SAYS?
IT SEEMS YOU THINK OF YOUR PARTNERS...
AS MERE CARPETS -- THINGS YOU WALK ALL OVER.
I DIDN'T WANT TO BE TREATED LIKE THAT.

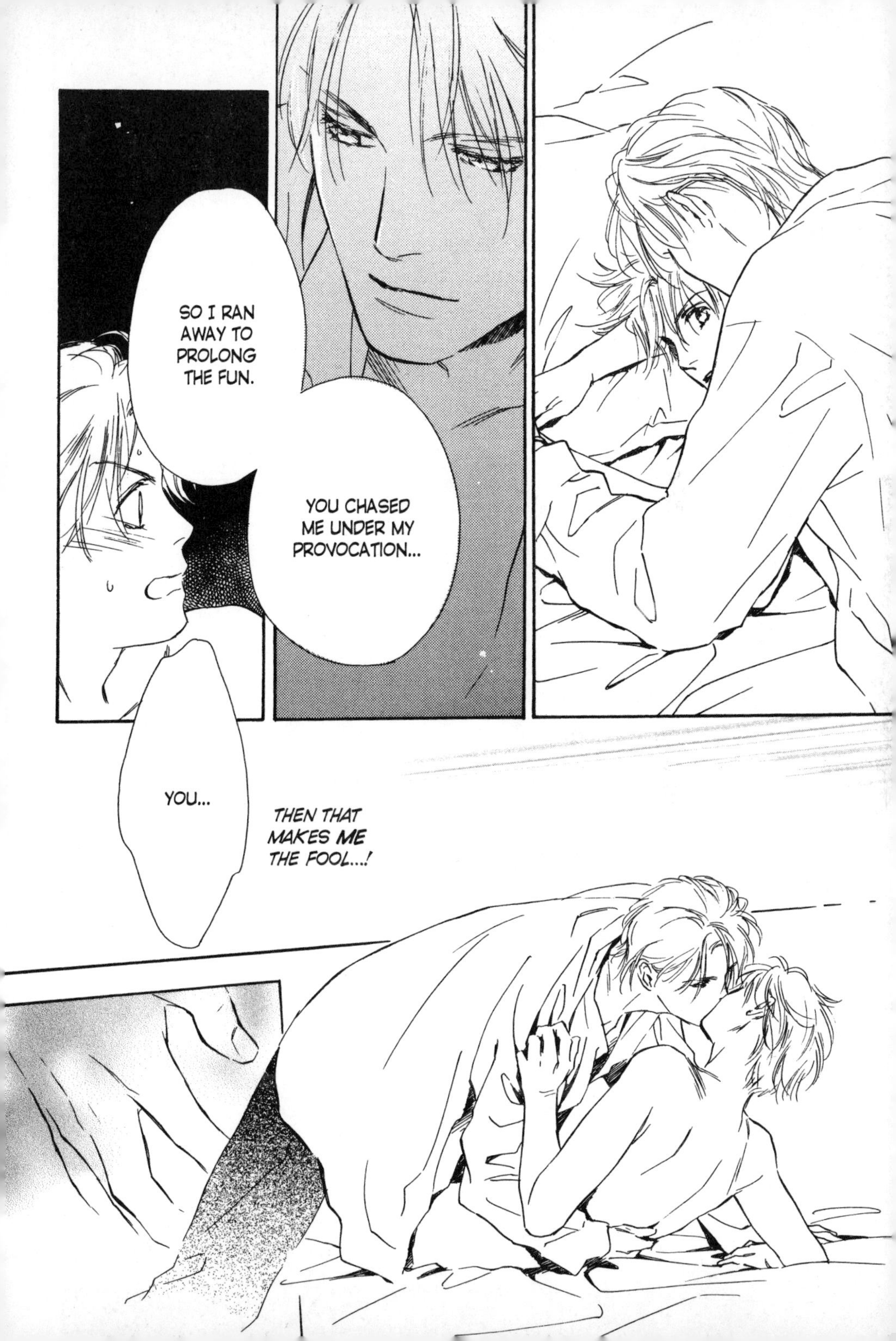
YOU CHASED ME UNDER MY PROVOCATION...
SO I RAN AWAY TO PROLONG THE FUN.
YOU...
THEN THAT MAKES **ME** THE FOOL...!

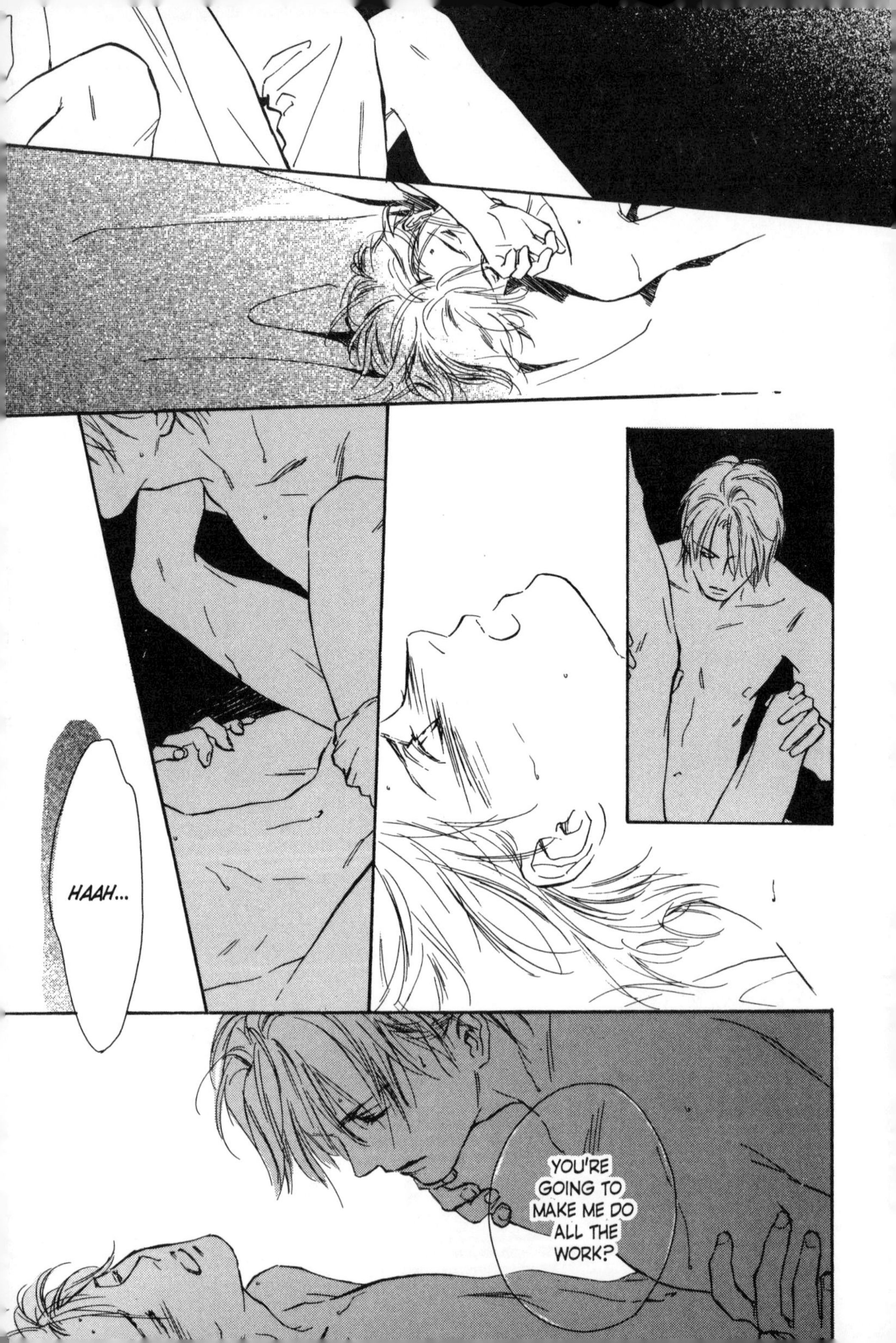
HAAH...
YOU'RE GOING TO MAKE ME DO ALL THE WORK?

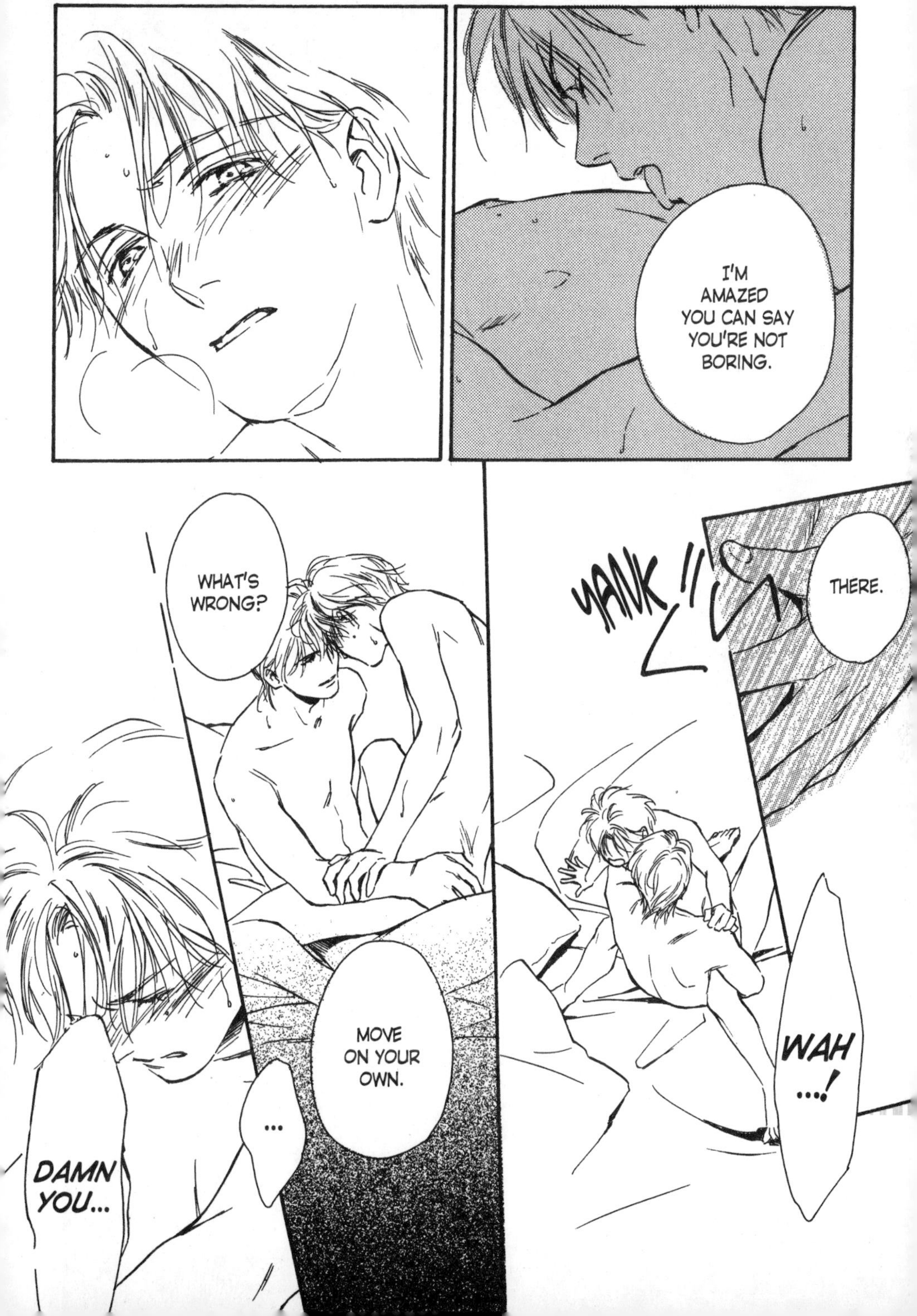
I'M AMAZED YOU CAN SAY YOU'RE NOT BORING.
THERE.
YANK
WAH ...!
WHAT'S WRONG?
MOVE ON YOUR OWN.
...
DAMN YOU...

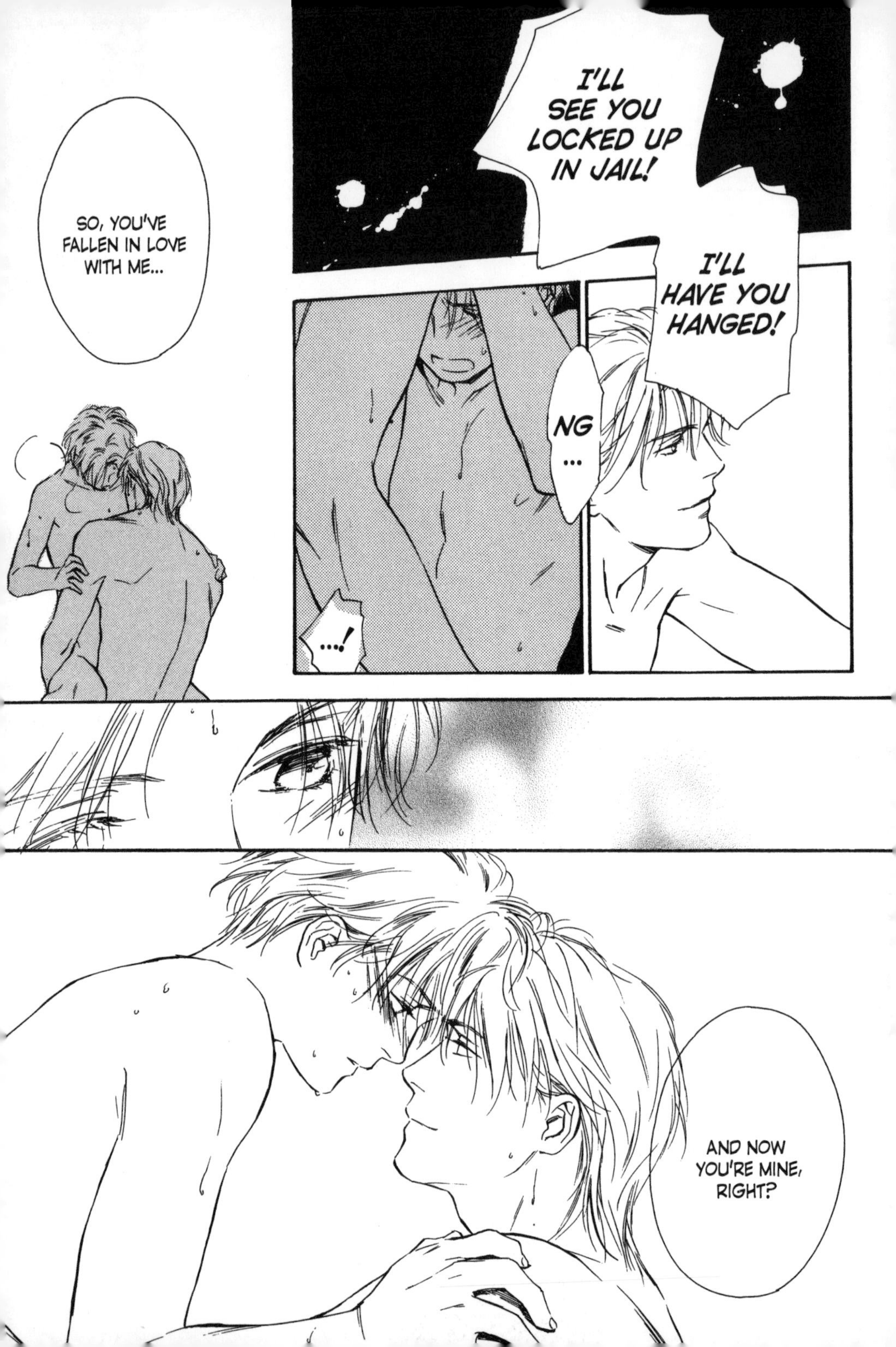
I'LL SEE YOU LOCKED UP IN JAIL!
I'LL HAVE YOU HANGED!
NG...
...!
SO, YOU'VE FALLEN IN LOVE WITH ME...
AND NOW YOU'RE MINE, RIGHT?

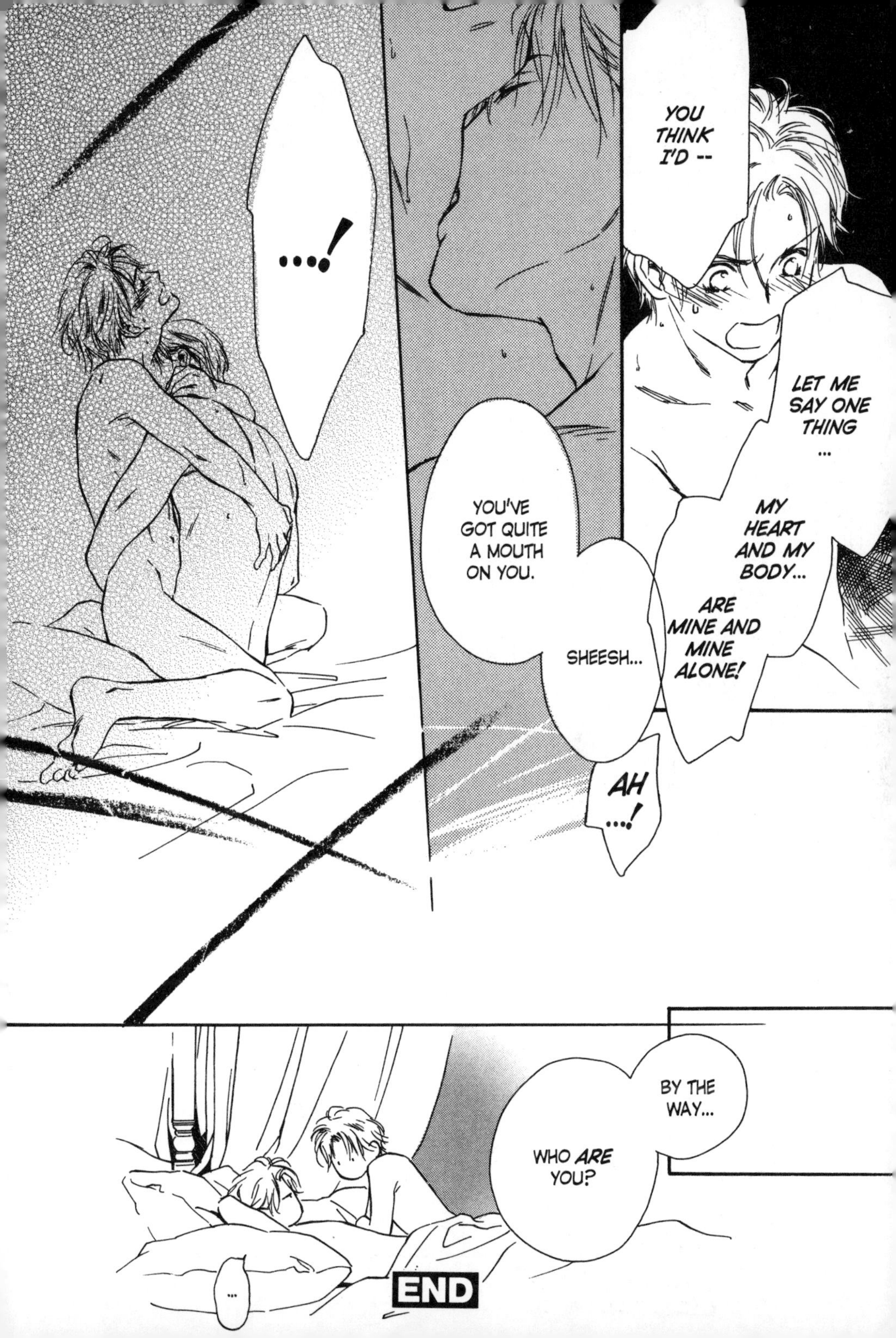
YOU THINK I'D --
LET ME SAY ONE THING ...
MY HEART AND MY BODY...
ARE MINE AND MINE ALONE!
YOU'VE GOT QUITE A MOUTH ON YOU.
SHEESH...
AH ...!
...!
BY THE WAY...
WHO ARE YOU?
...
END

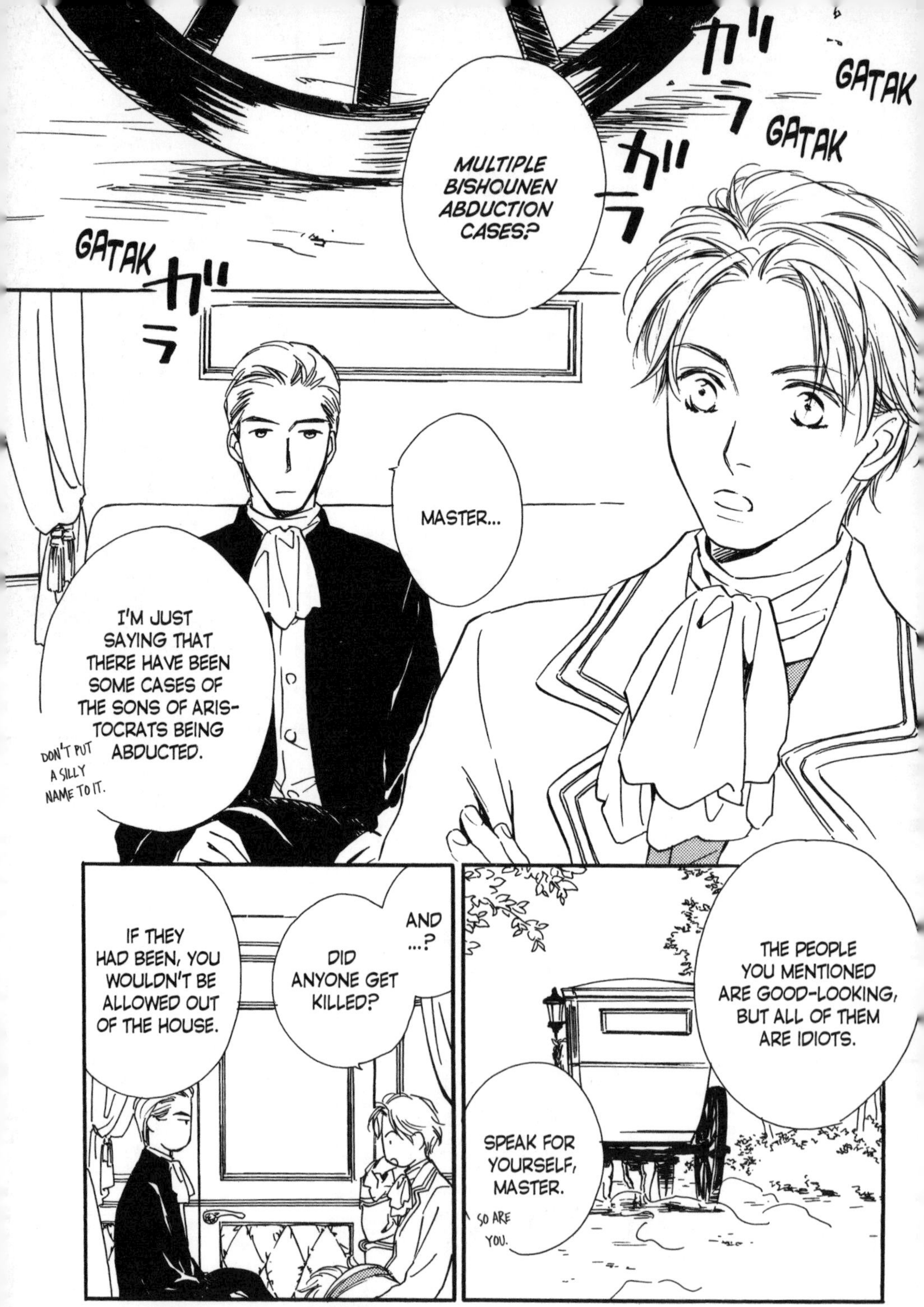
GATAK
GATAK
MULTIPLE BISHOUNEN ABDUCTION CASES?
GATAK
MASTER...
I'M JUST SAYING THAT THERE HAVE BEEN SOME CASES OF THE SONS OF ARIS-TOCRATS BEING ABDUCTED.
DON'T PUT A SILLY NAME TO IT.
THE PEOPLE YOU MENTIONED ARE GOOD-LOOKING, BUT ALL OF THEM ARE IDIOTS.
SPEAK FOR YOURSELF, MASTER.
SO ARE YOU.
AND ...?
DID ANYONE GET KILLED?
IF THEY HAD BEEN, YOU WOULDN'T BE ALLOWED OUT OF THE HOUSE.

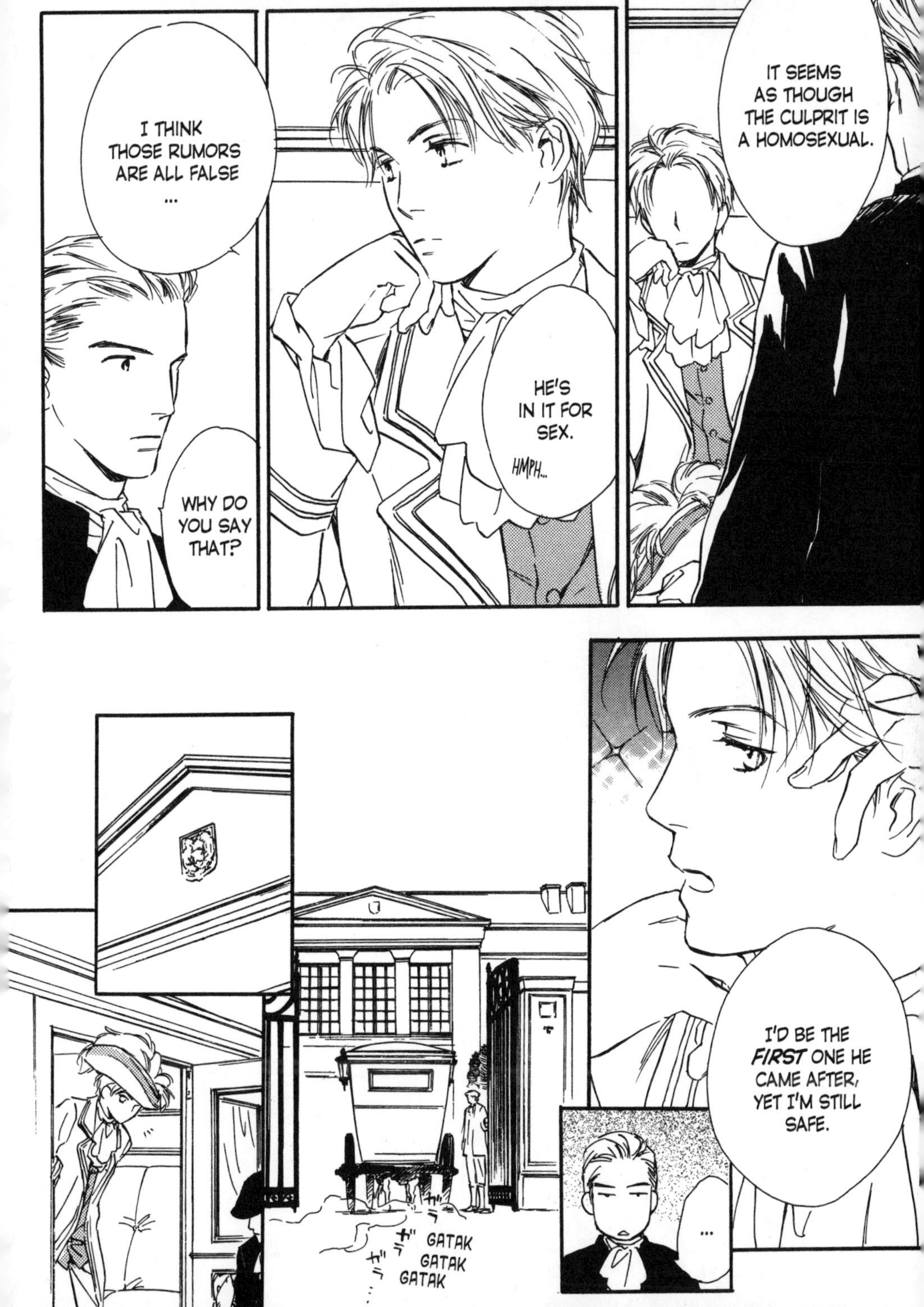

IT SEEMS AS THOUGH THE CULPRIT IS A HOMOSEXUAL.
HE'S IN IT FOR SEX.
HMPH...
I THINK THOSE RUMORS ARE ALL FALSE ...
WHY DO YOU SAY THAT?
I'D BE THE FIRST ONE HE CAME AFTER, YET I'M STILL SAFE.
...
GATAK GATAK GATAK

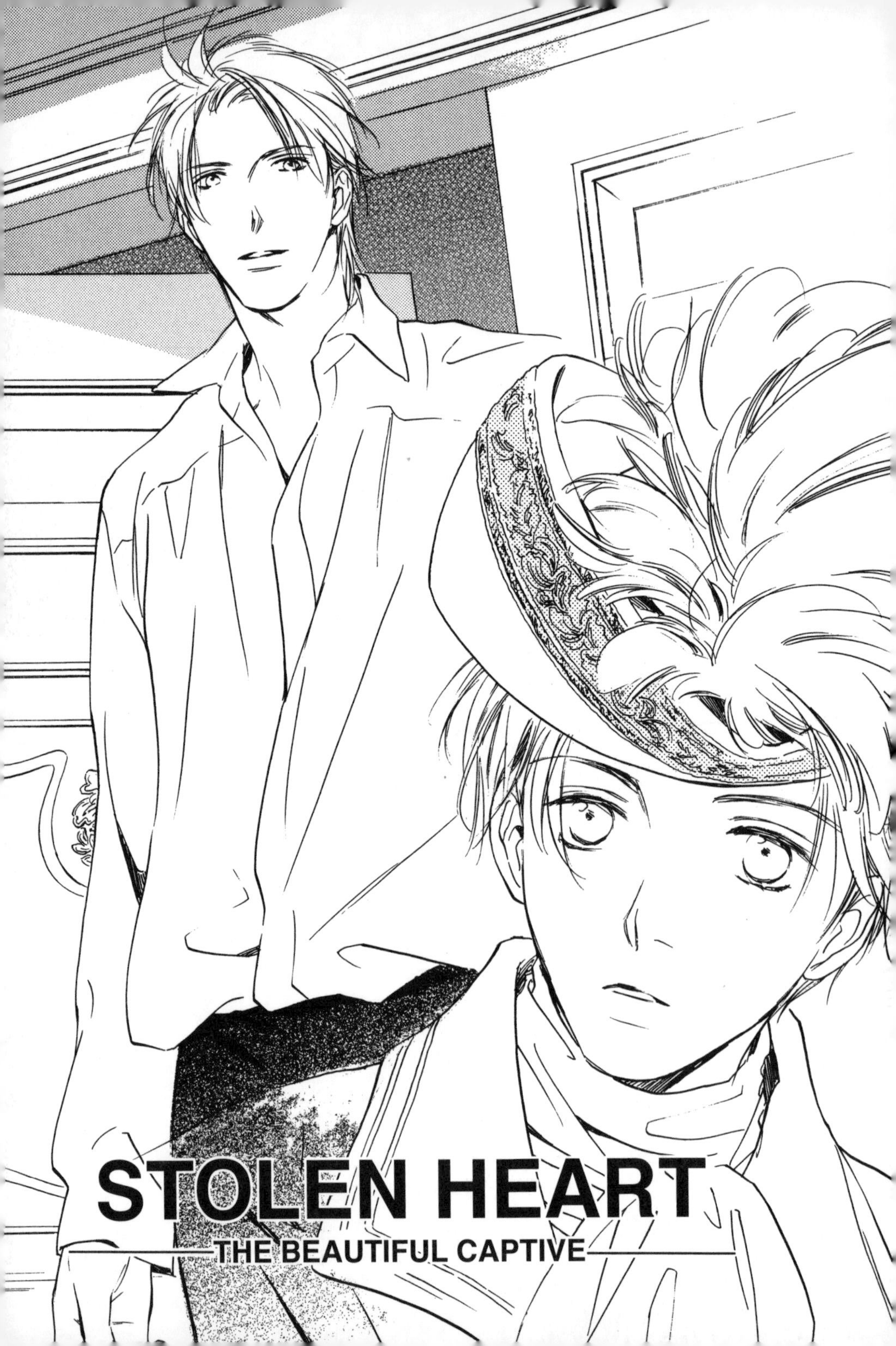
STOLEN HEART
THE BEAUTIFUL CAPTIVE

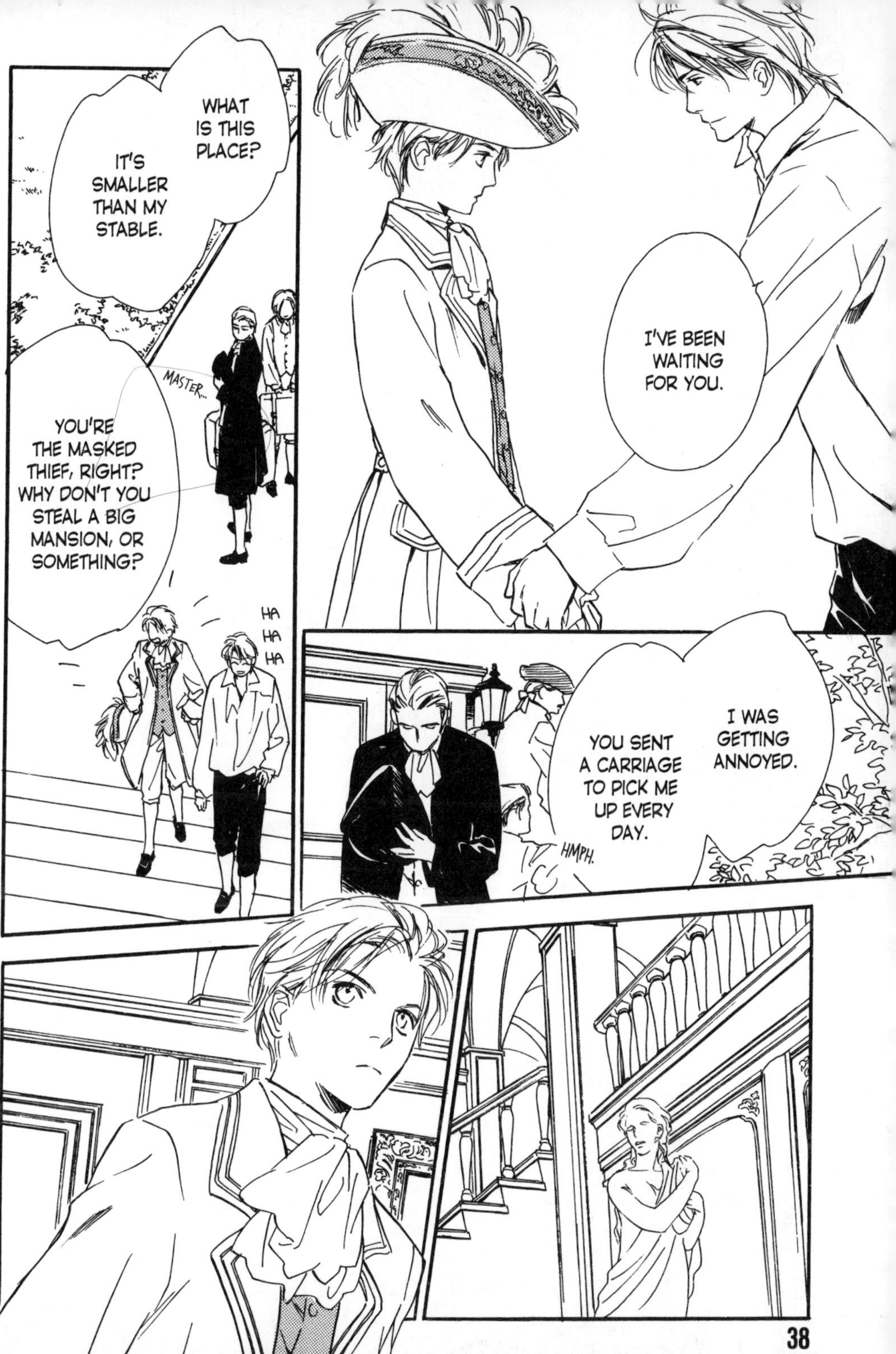
I'VE BEEN WAITING FOR YOU.
I WAS GETTING ANNOYED.
YOU SENT A CARRIAGE TO PICK ME UP EVERY DAY.
HMPH.
WHAT IS THIS PLACE?
IT'S SMALLER THAN MY STABLE.
MASTER...
YOU'RE THE MASKED THIEF, RIGHT? WHY DON'T YOU STEAL A BIG MANSION, OR SOMETHING?
HA HA HA

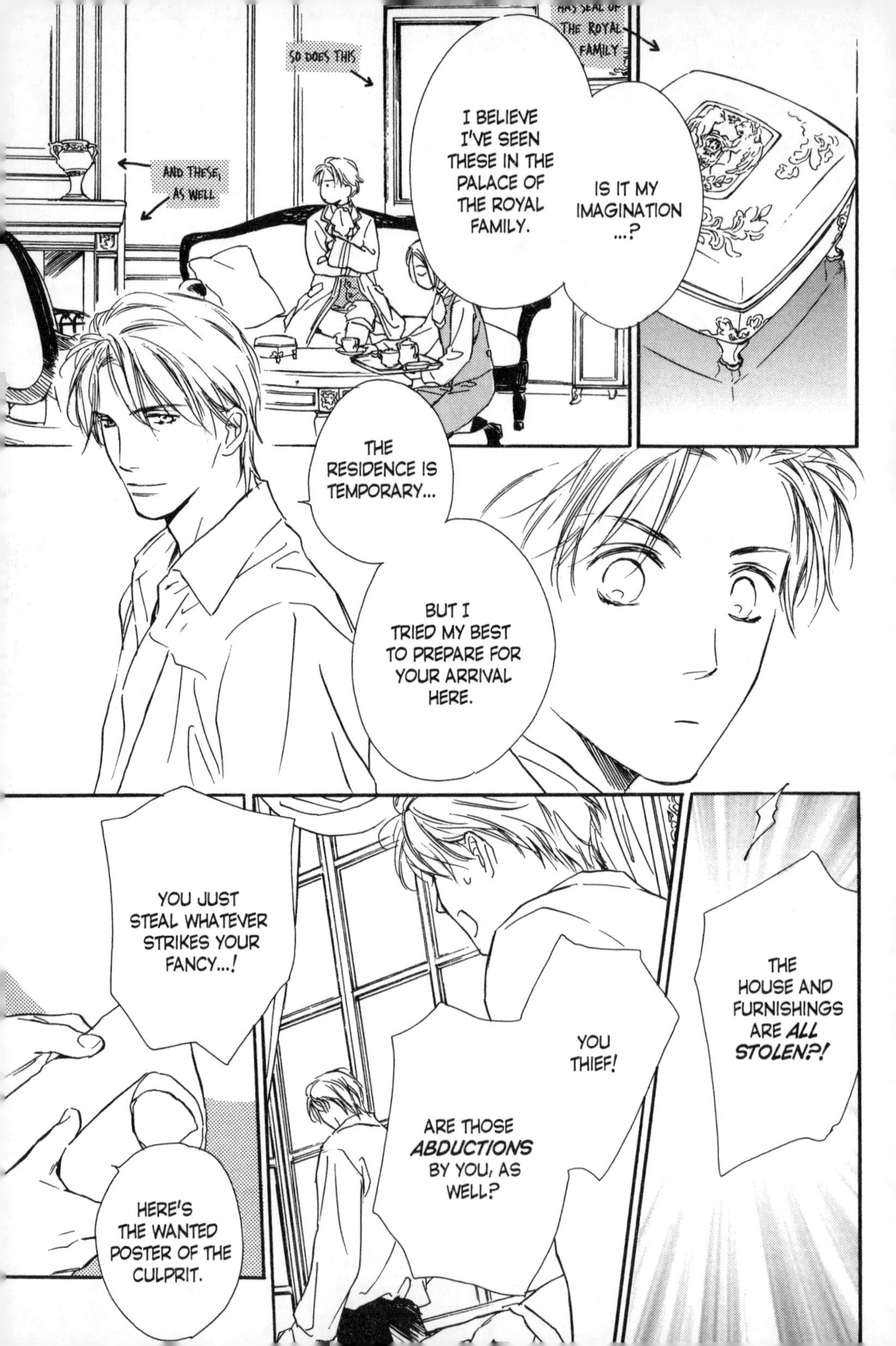
HAS SEAL OF THE ROYAL FAMILY
SO DOES THIS
AND THESE, AS WELL
I BELIEVE I'VE SEEN THESE IN THE PALACE OF THE ROYAL FAMILY.
IS IT MY IMAGINATION ...?
THE RESIDENCE IS TEMPORARY...
BUT I TRIED MY BEST TO PREPARE FOR YOUR ARRIVAL HERE.
THE HOUSE AND FURNISHINGS ARE *ALL STOLEN?!*
YOU THIEF!
ARE THOSE *ABDUCTIONS* BY YOU, AS WELL?
YOU JUST STEAL WHATEVER STRIKES YOUR FANCY...!
HERE'S THE WANTED POSTER OF THE CULPRIT.

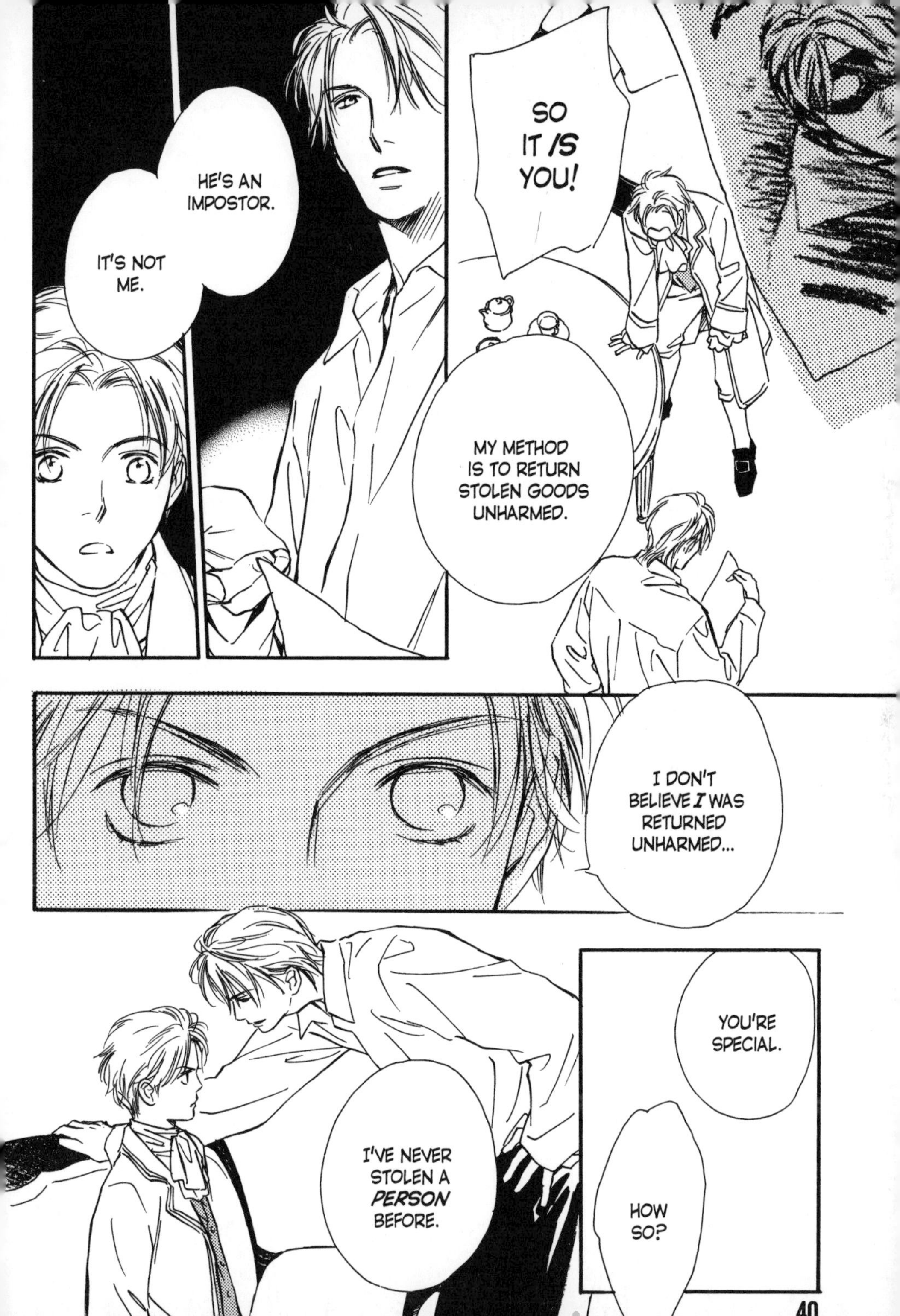
SO IT *IS* YOU!
MY METHOD IS TO RETURN STOLEN GOODS UNHARMED.
HE'S AN IMPOSTOR.
IT'S NOT ME.
I DON'T BELIEVE *I* WAS RETURNED UNHARMED...
YOU'RE SPECIAL.
HOW SO?
I'VE NEVER STOLEN A ***PERSON*** BEFORE.

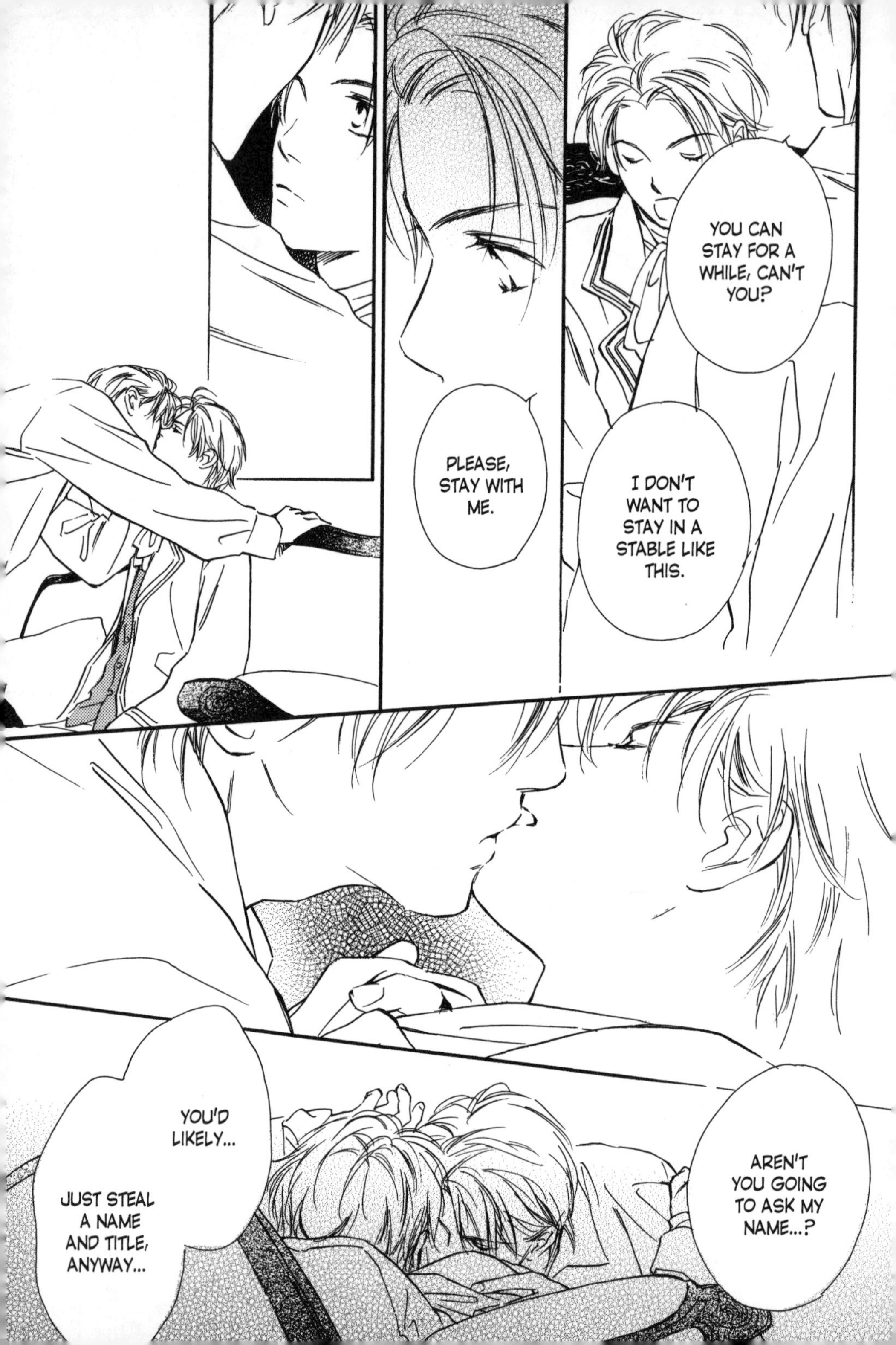
YOU CAN STAY FOR A WHILE, CAN'T YOU?
I DON'T WANT TO STAY IN A STABLE LIKE THIS.
PLEASE, STAY WITH ME.
AREN'T YOU GOING TO ASK MY NAME...?
YOU'D LIKELY...
JUST STEAL A NAME AND TITLE, ANYWAY...

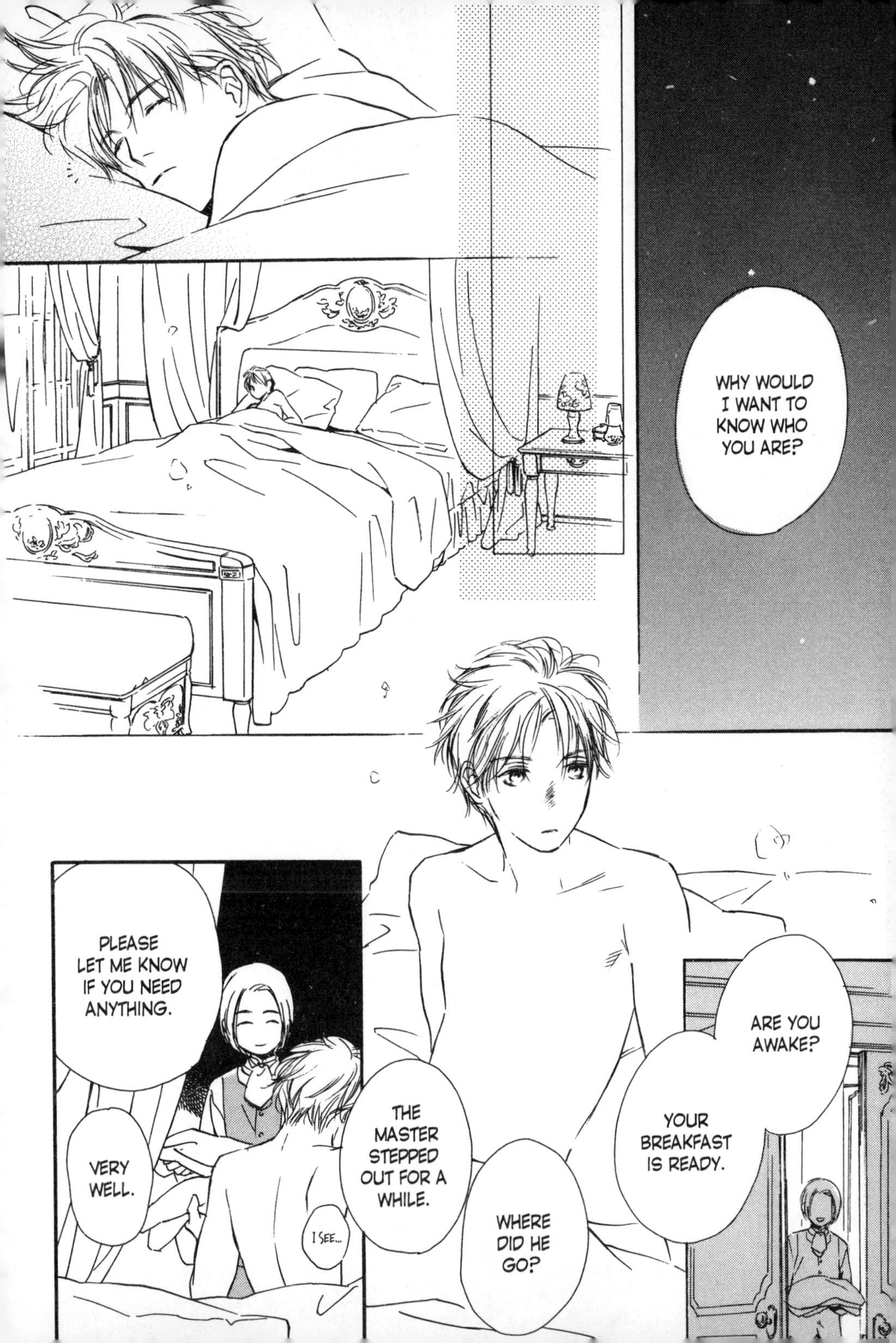
WHY WOULD I WANT TO KNOW WHO YOU ARE?
ARE YOU AWAKE?
YOUR BREAKFAST IS READY.
WHERE DID HE GO?
THE MASTER STEPPED OUT FOR A WHILE.
I SEE...
PLEASE LET ME KNOW IF YOU NEED ANYTHING.
VERY WELL.

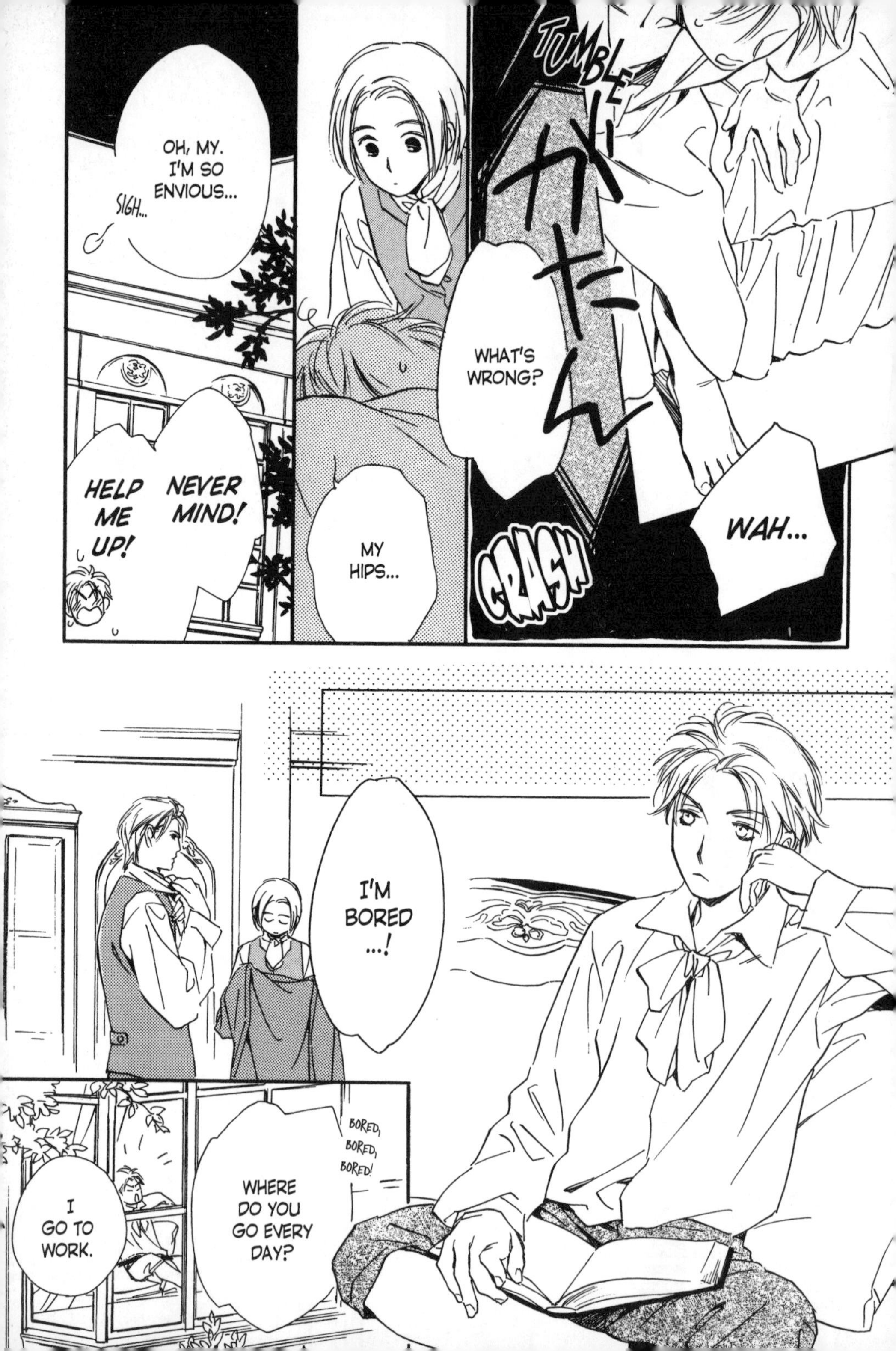
TUMBLE
ガターン
WHAT'S WRONG?
WAH...
CRASH
MY HIPS...
OH, MY. I'M SO ENVIOUS...
SIGH...
NEVER MIND!
HELP ME UP!
I'M BORED ...!
BORED, BORED, BORED!
WHERE DO YOU GO EVERY DAY?
I GO TO WORK.

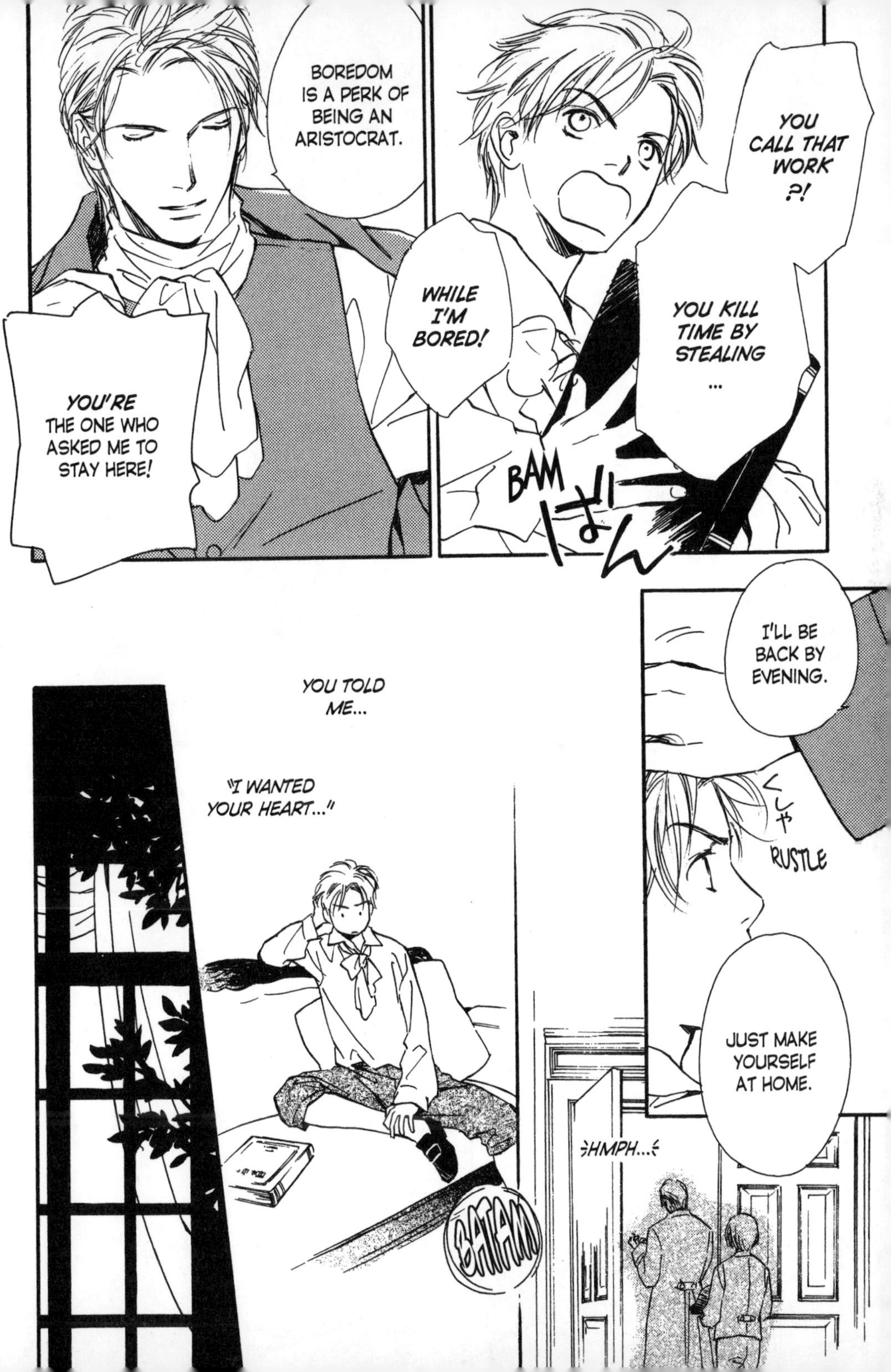
YOU CALL THAT WORK ?!
YOU KILL TIME BY STEALING ...
WHILE I'M BORED!
BAM
ばん
BOREDOM IS A PERK OF BEING AN ARISTOCRAT.
YOU'RE THE ONE WHO ASKED ME TO STAY HERE!
I'LL BE BACK BY EVENING.
くしゃ
RUSTLE
JUST MAKE YOURSELF AT HOME.
HMPH...
BATAN
YOU TOLD ME...
"I WANTED YOUR HEART..."

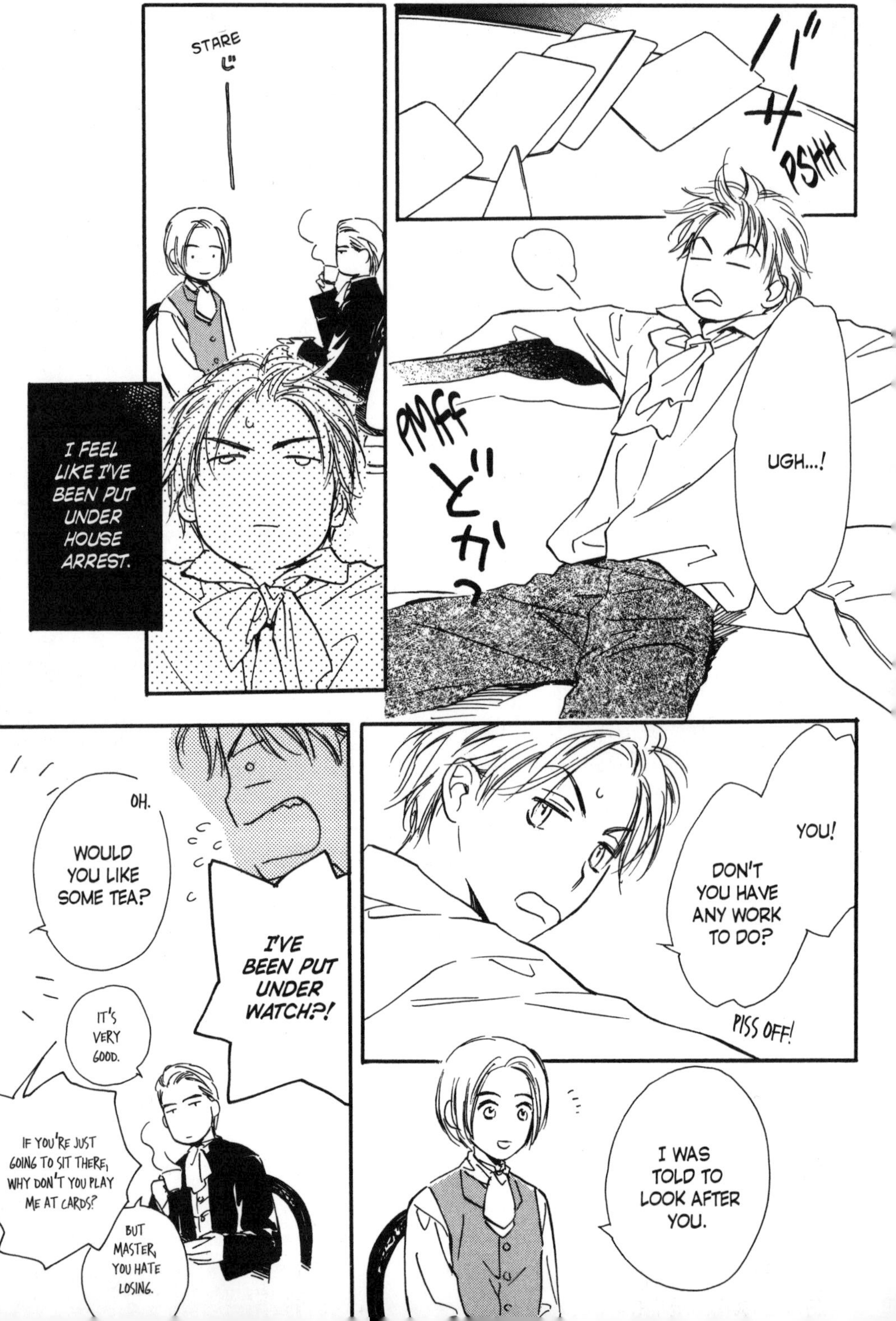
バッ
PSHH
どかっ
PMFF
UGH...!
STARE
じー
I FEEL LIKE I'VE BEEN PUT UNDER HOUSE ARREST.
YOU!
DON'T YOU HAVE ANY WORK TO DO?
PISS OFF!
I WAS TOLD TO LOOK AFTER YOU.
OH.
WOULD YOU LIKE SOME TEA?
I'VE BEEN PUT UNDER WATCH?!
IT'S VERY GOOD.
IF YOU'RE JUST GOING TO SIT THERE, WHY DON'T YOU PLAY ME AT CARDS?
BUT MASTER, YOU HATE LOSING.

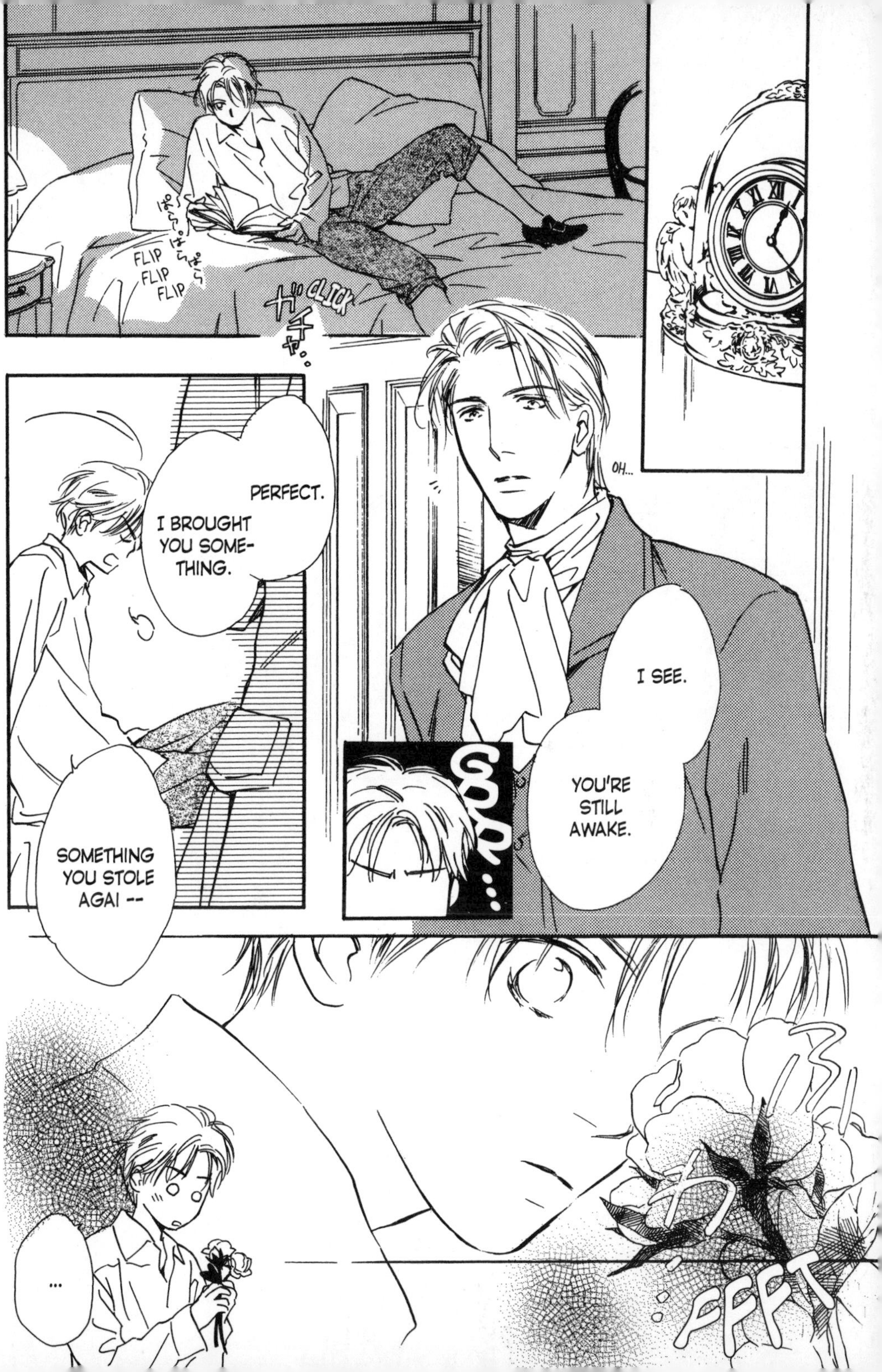
ぱらぱらぱらぱら
FLIP
FLIP
FLIP
ガチャ。。
CLICK
OH...
I SEE.
YOU'RE STILL AWAKE.
GRR...
PERFECT.
I BROUGHT YOU SOME-THING.
SOMETHING YOU STOLE AGAI --
...
ふわ
FFFT

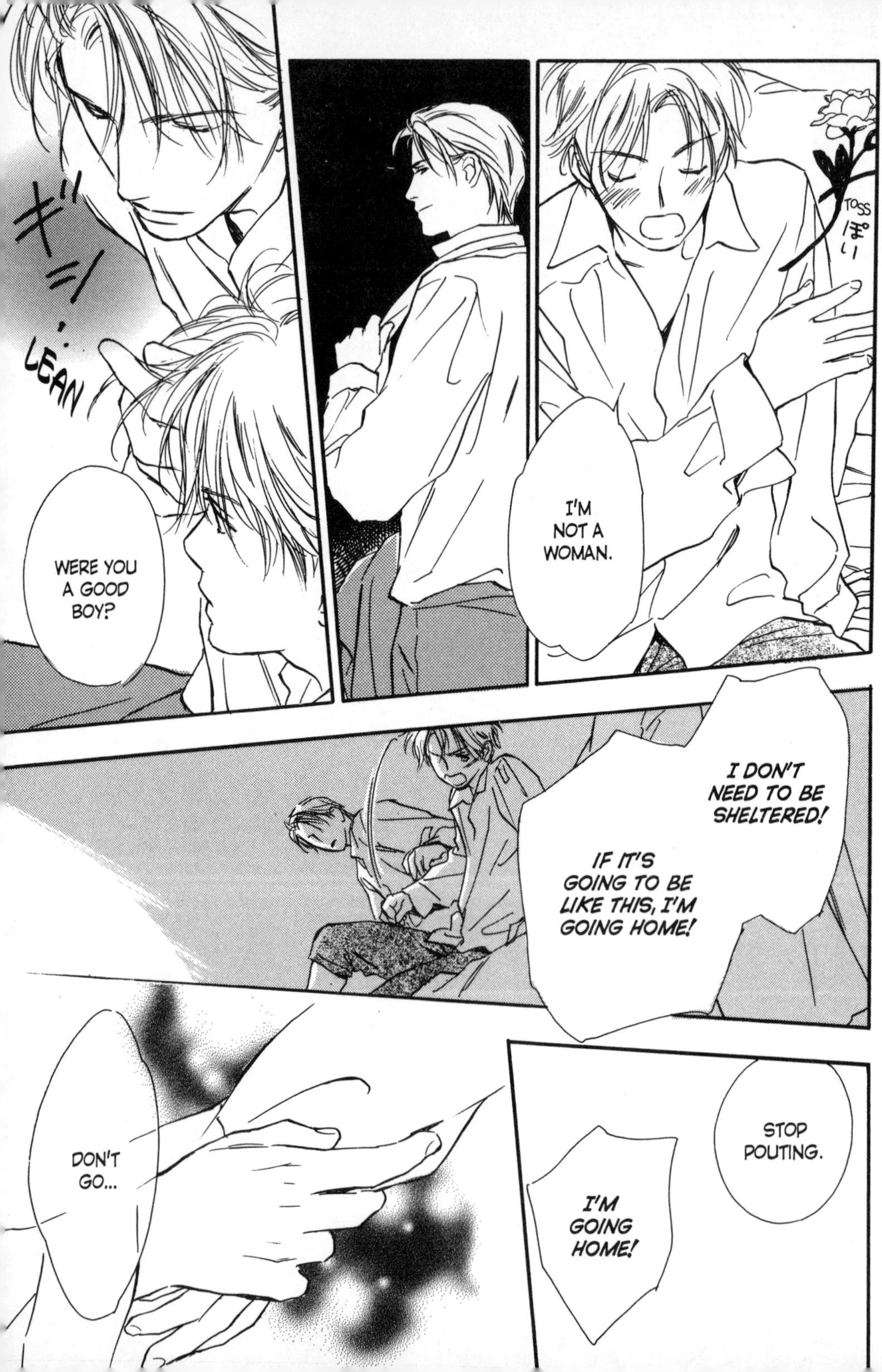
TOSS
ぽい
I'M NOT A WOMAN.
ギシ
LEAN
WERE YOU A GOOD BOY?
I DON'T NEED TO BE SHELTERED!
IF IT'S GOING TO BE LIKE THIS, I'M GOING HOME!
STOP POUTING.
I'M GOING HOME!
DON'T GO...

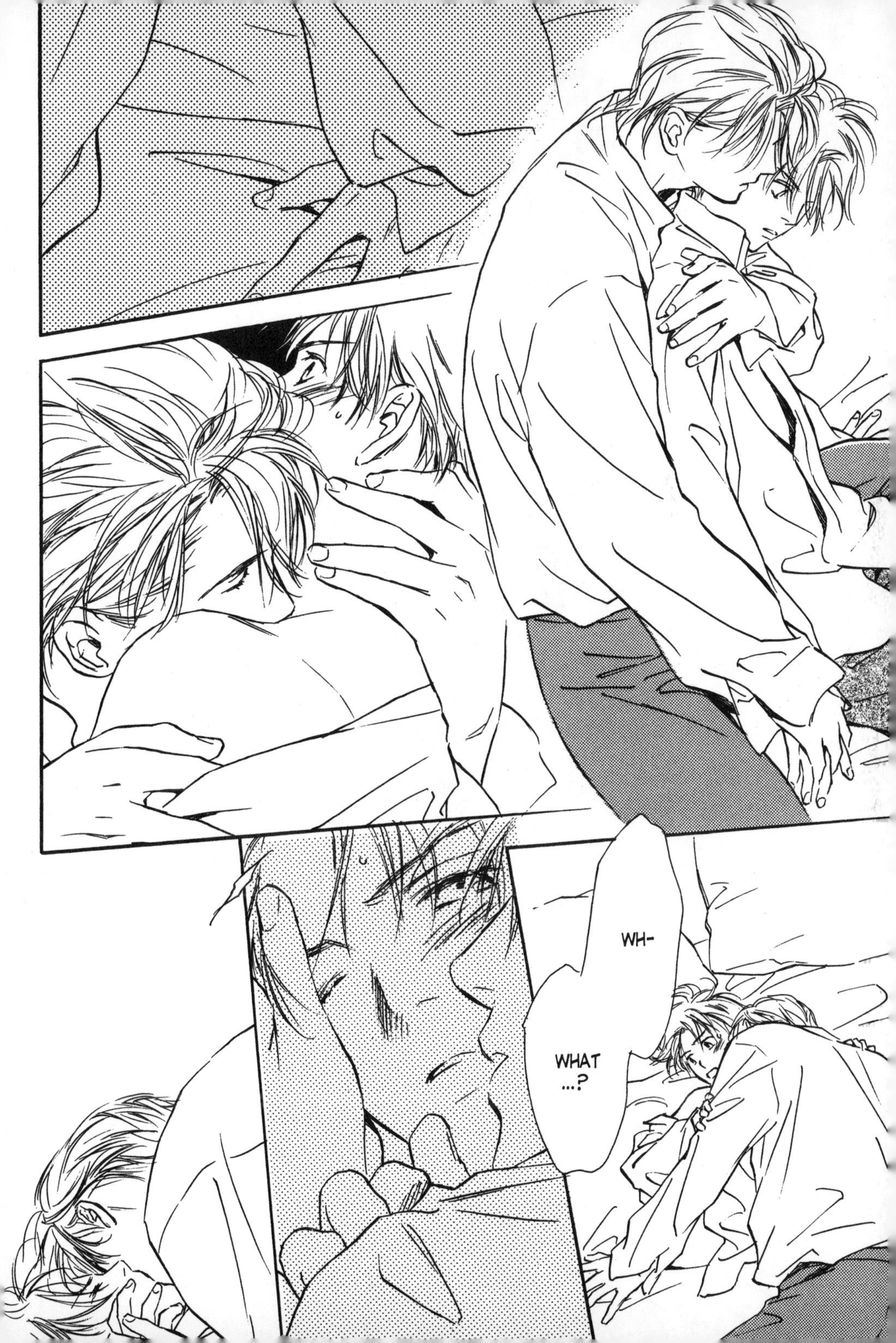
WH-
WHAT ...?

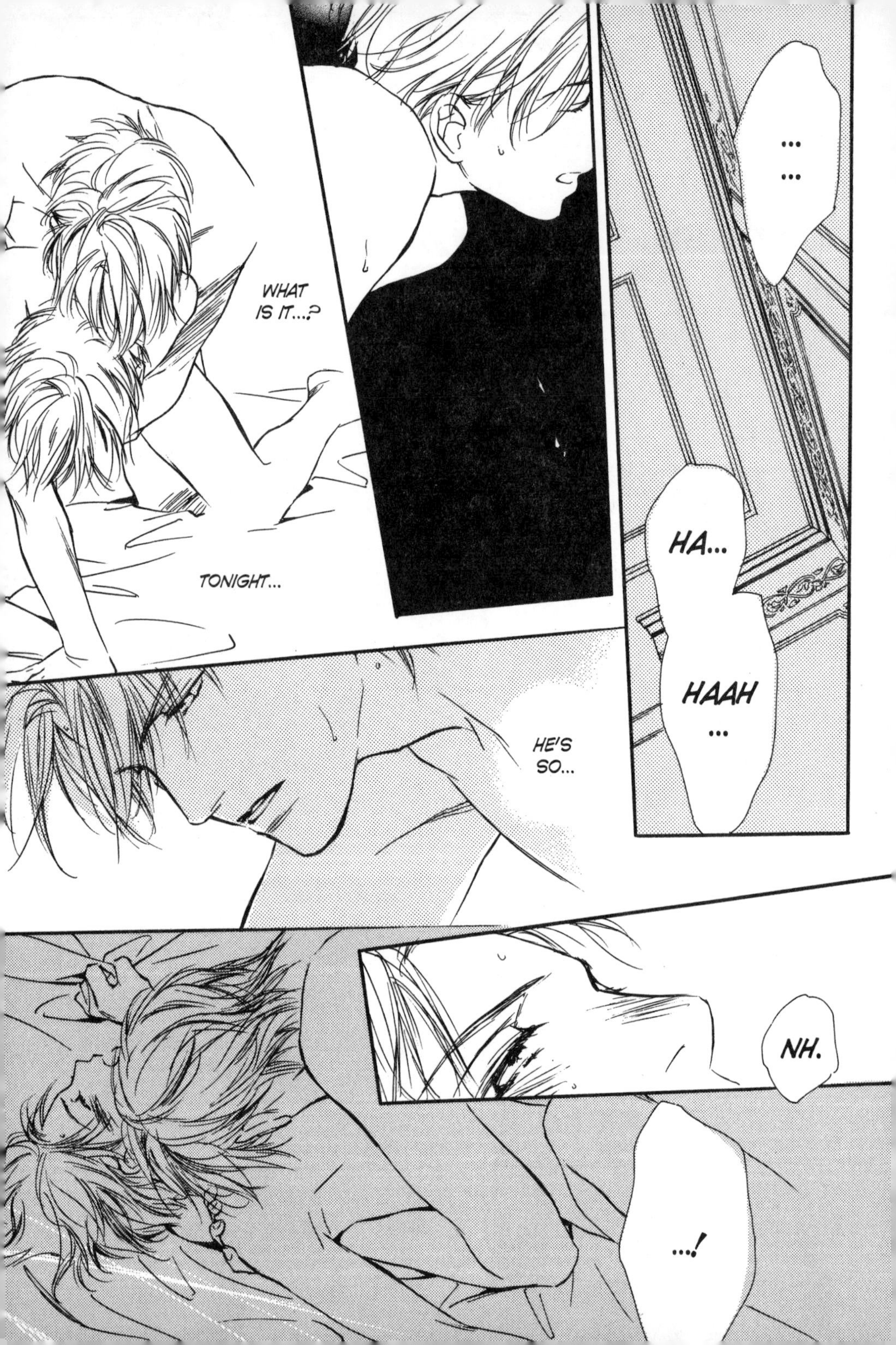
...
...
HA...
HAAH
...
WHAT IS IT...?
TONIGHT...
HE'S SO...
NH.
...!

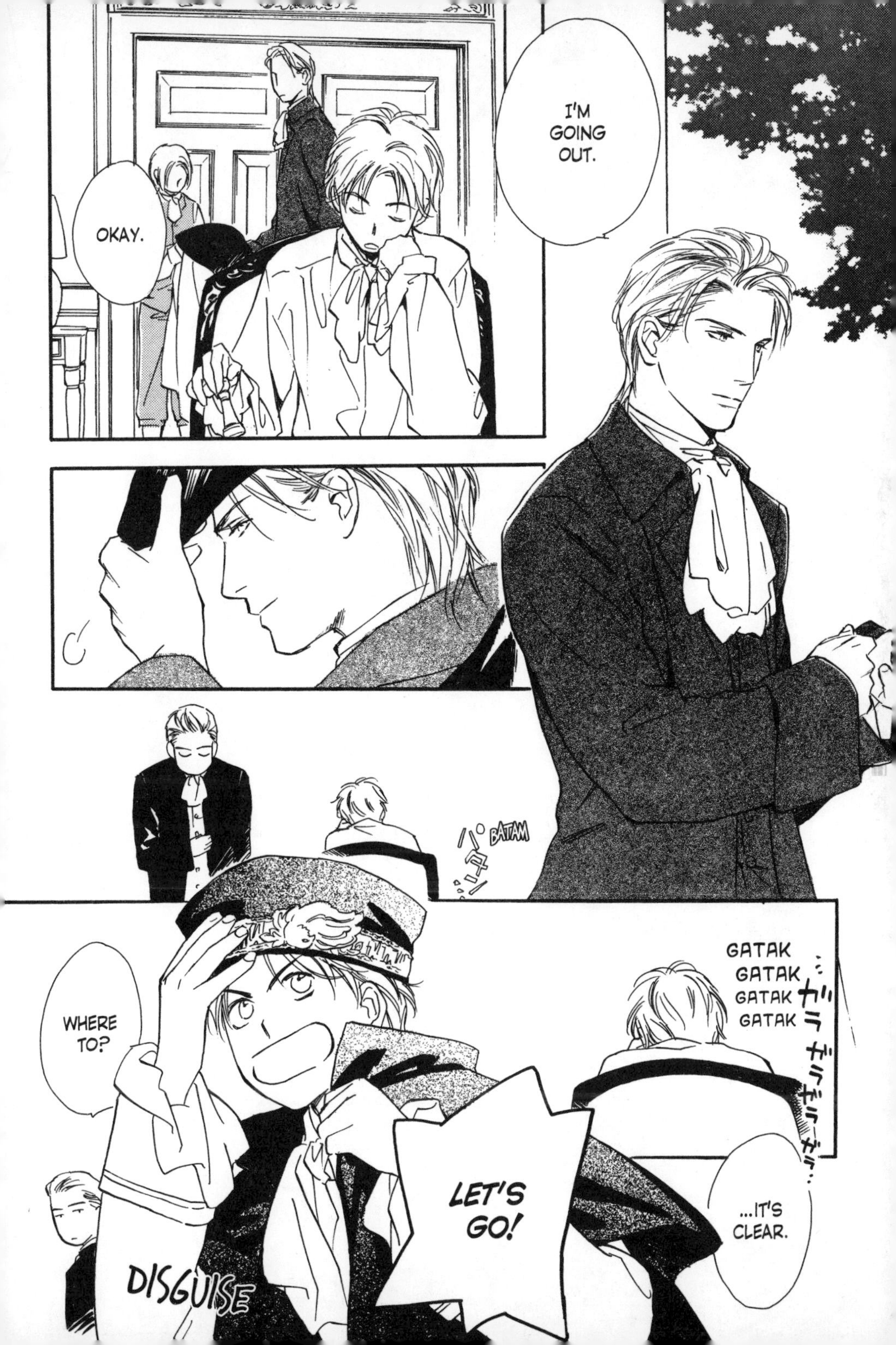
I'M GOING OUT.
OKAY.
パタン
BATAM
ガラガラガラ
GATAK GATAK GATAK GATAK
...IT'S CLEAR.
LET'S GO!
WHERE TO?
DISGUISE

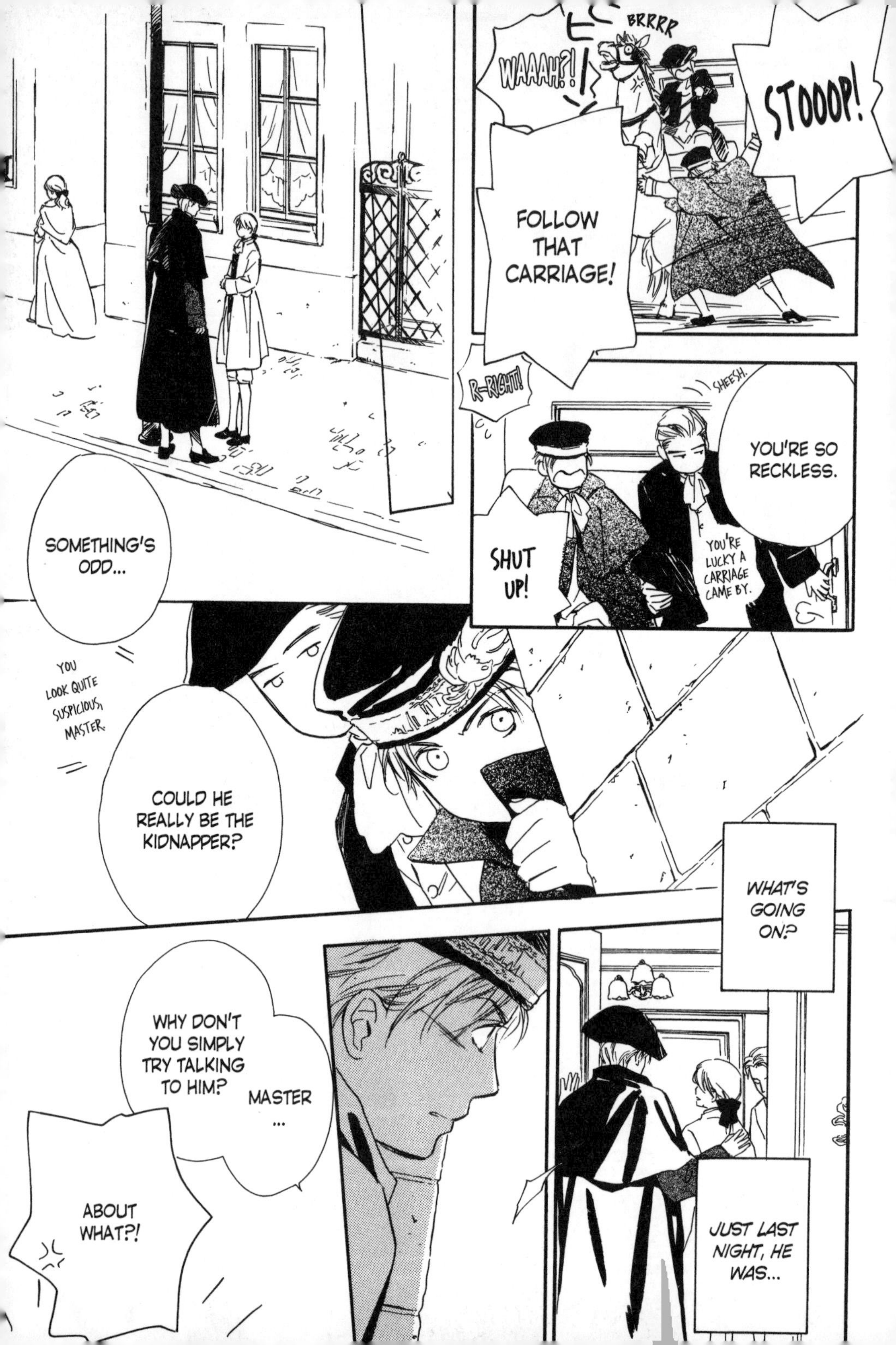
STOOOP!
WAAAH?!
BRRRR
FOLLOW THAT CARRIAGE!
R-RIGHT!
SHEESH.
YOU'RE SO RECKLESS.
YOU'RE LUCKY A CARRIAGE CAME BY.
SHUT UP!
SOMETHING'S ODD...
COULD HE REALLY BE THE KIDNAPPER?
YOU LOOK QUITE SUSPICIOUS, MASTER.
WHAT'S GOING ON?
JUST LAST NIGHT, HE WAS...
MASTER ...
WHY DON'T YOU SIMPLY TRY TALKING TO HIM?
ABOUT WHAT?!

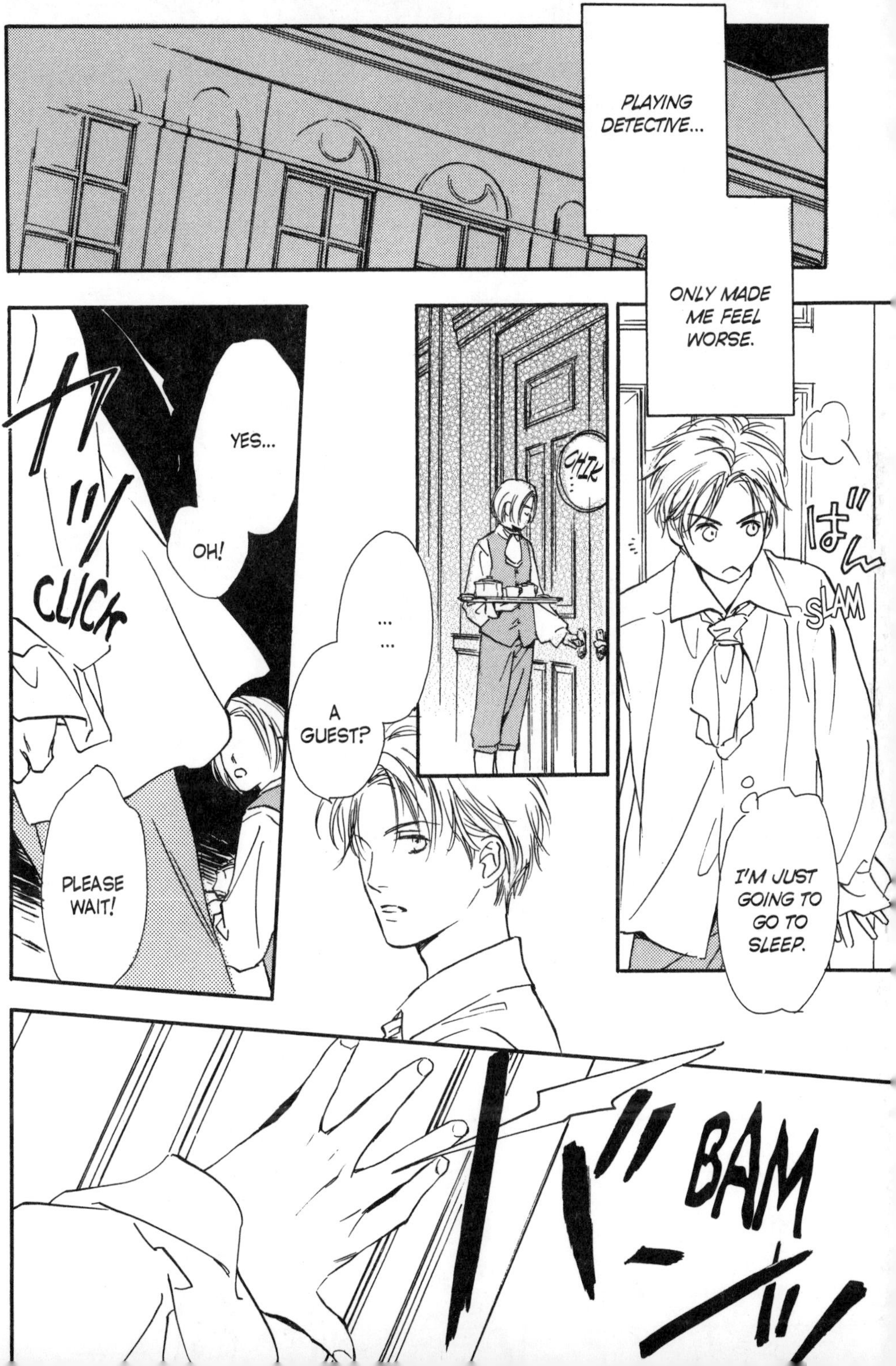
PLAYING DETECTIVE...
ONLY MADE ME FEEL WORSE.
ばん
SLAM
I'M JUST GOING TO GO TO SLEEP.
CHIK
... ...
A GUEST?
カチ
CLICK
YES...
OH!
PLEASE WAIT!
バーン
BAM

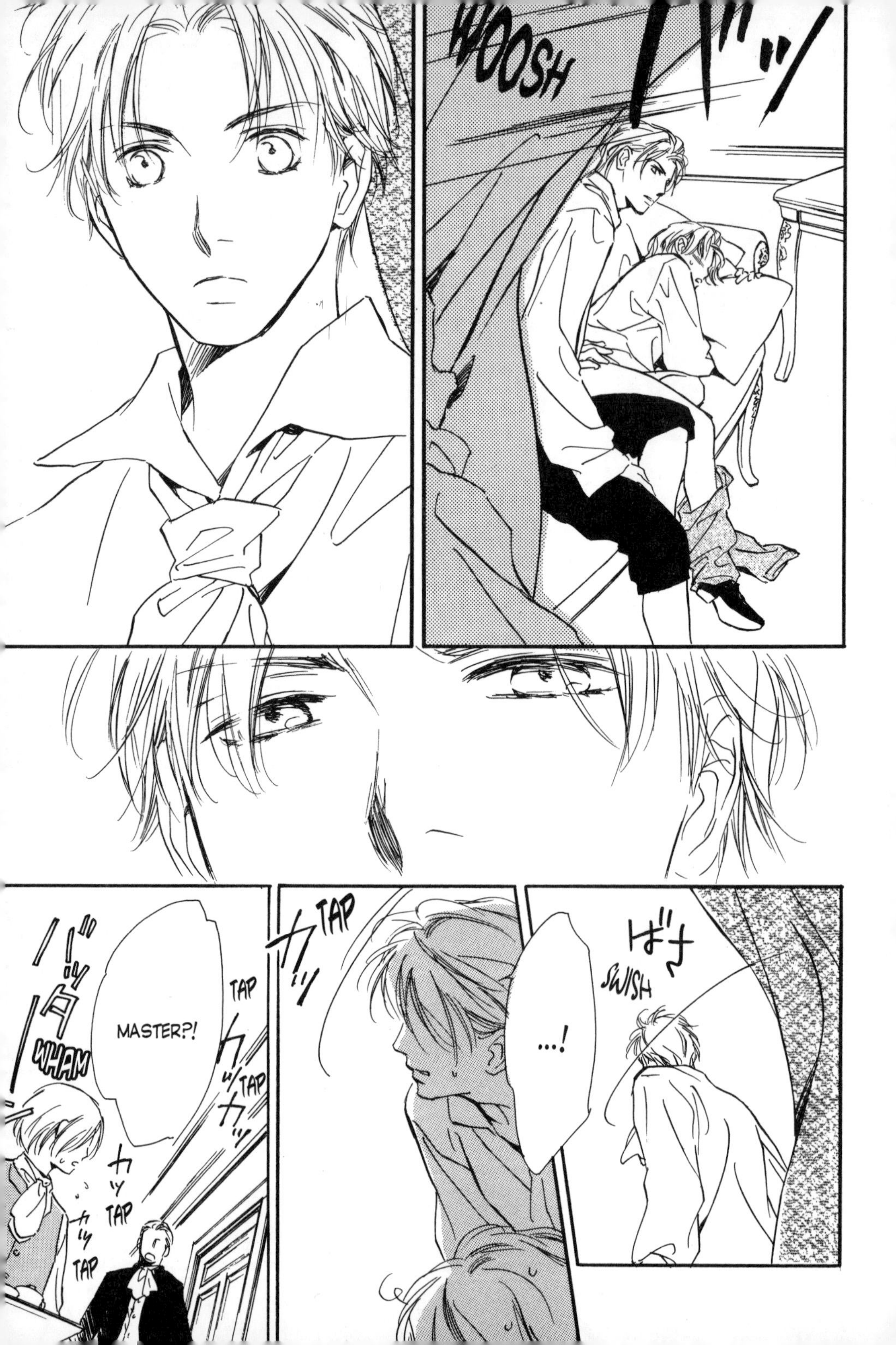

WOOSH
バッ
ばさ
SWISH
...!
カッ
TAP
MASTER?!
WHAM
TAP
TAP
TAP
TAP

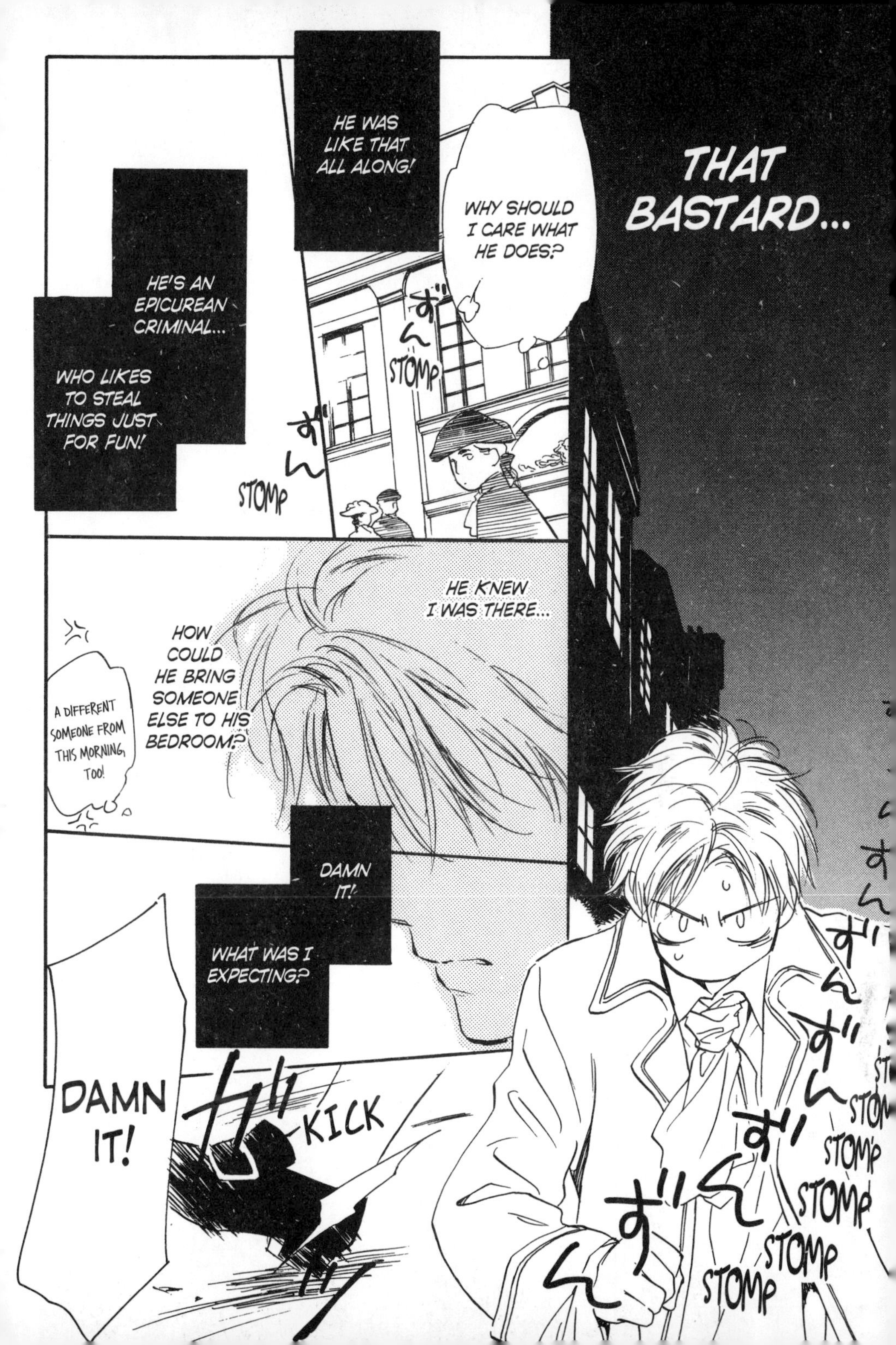
THAT BASTARD...
ずん
STOMP
ずん
STOMP
ずん
STOMP
ずん
STOMP
HE WAS LIKE THAT ALL ALONG!
WHY SHOULD I CARE WHAT HE DOES?
HE'S AN EPICUREAN CRIMINAL...
WHO LIKES TO STEAL THINGS JUST FOR FUN!
ずん
STOMP
ずん
STOMP
HE KNEW I WAS THERE...
HOW COULD HE BRING SOMEONE ELSE TO HIS BEDROOM?
A DIFFERENT SOMEONE FROM THIS MORNING, TOO!
DAMN IT!
WHAT WAS I EXPECTING?
ガッ
KICK
DAMN IT!

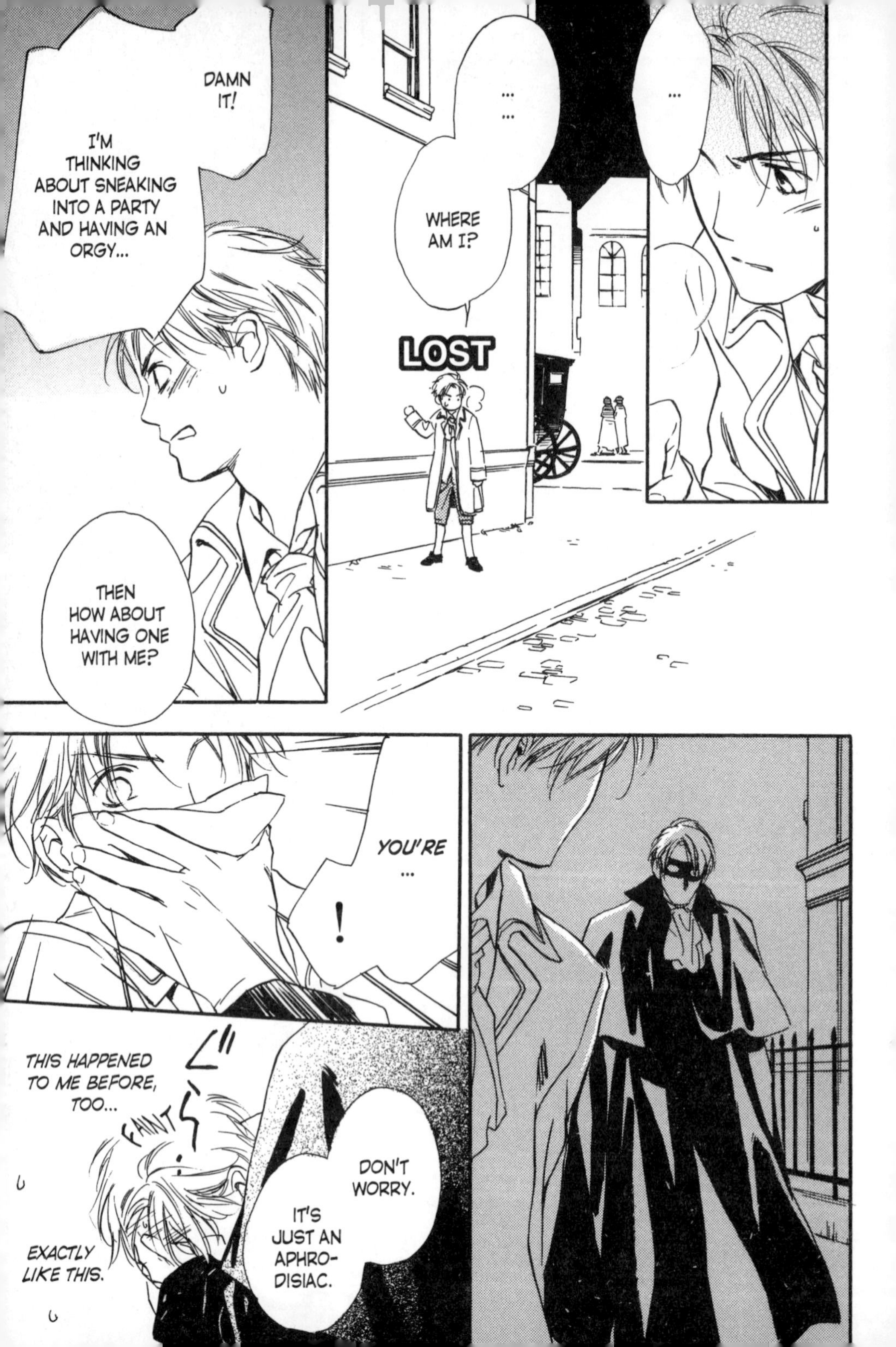
...
... ...
WHERE AM I?
LOST
DAMN IT!
I'M THINKING ABOUT SNEAKING INTO A PARTY AND HAVING AN ORGY...
THEN HOW ABOUT HAVING ONE WITH ME?
YOU'RE ...
!
THIS HAPPENED TO ME BEFORE, TOO...
FAINT
DON'T WORRY.
IT'S JUST AN APHRODISIAC.
EXACTLY LIKE THIS.

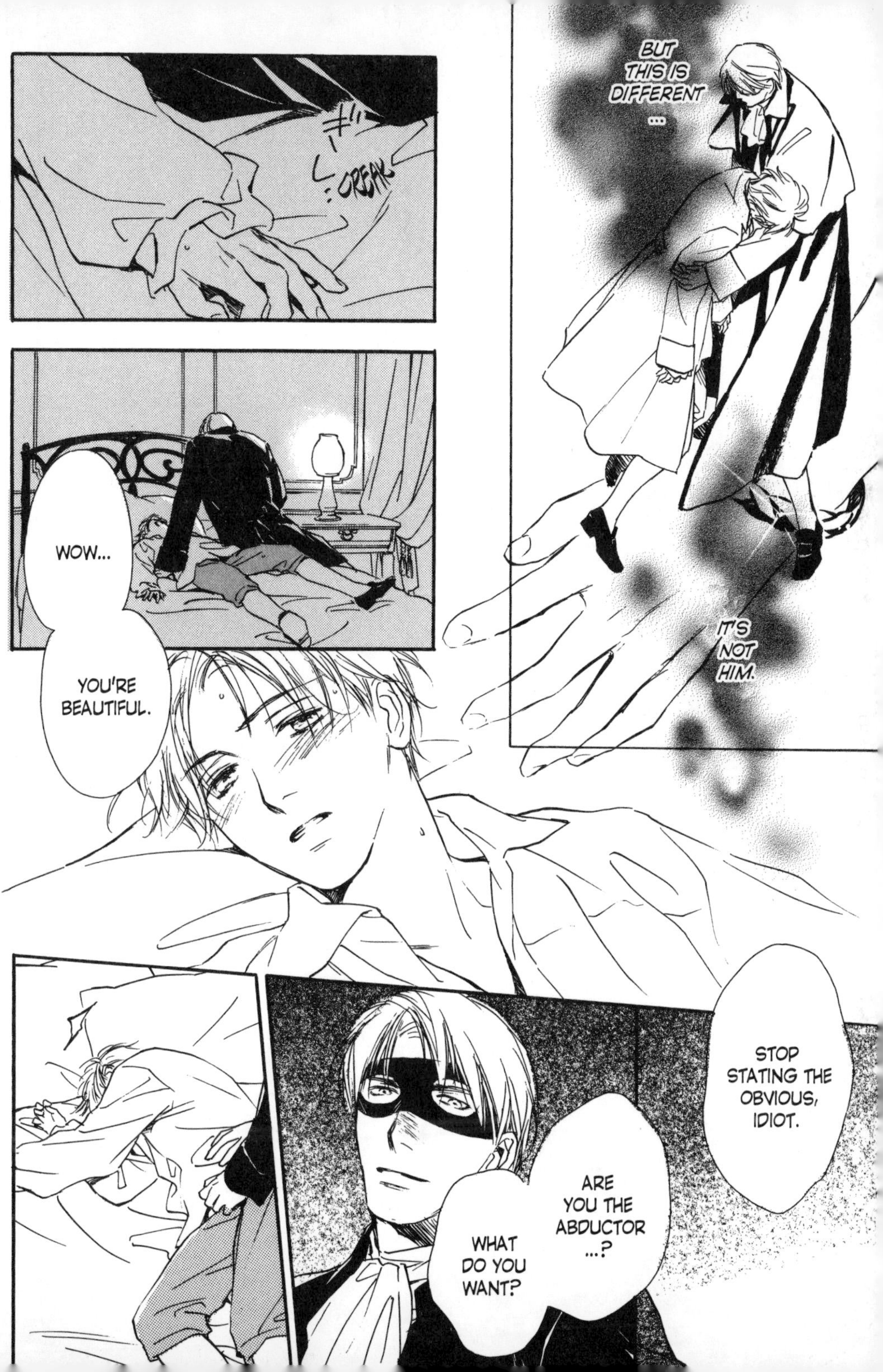
BUT THIS IS DIFFERENT ...
IT'S NOT HIM.
CREAK
WOW...
YOU'RE BEAUTIFUL.
STOP STATING THE OBVIOUS, IDIOT.
ARE YOU THE ABDUCTOR ...?
WHAT DO YOU WANT?

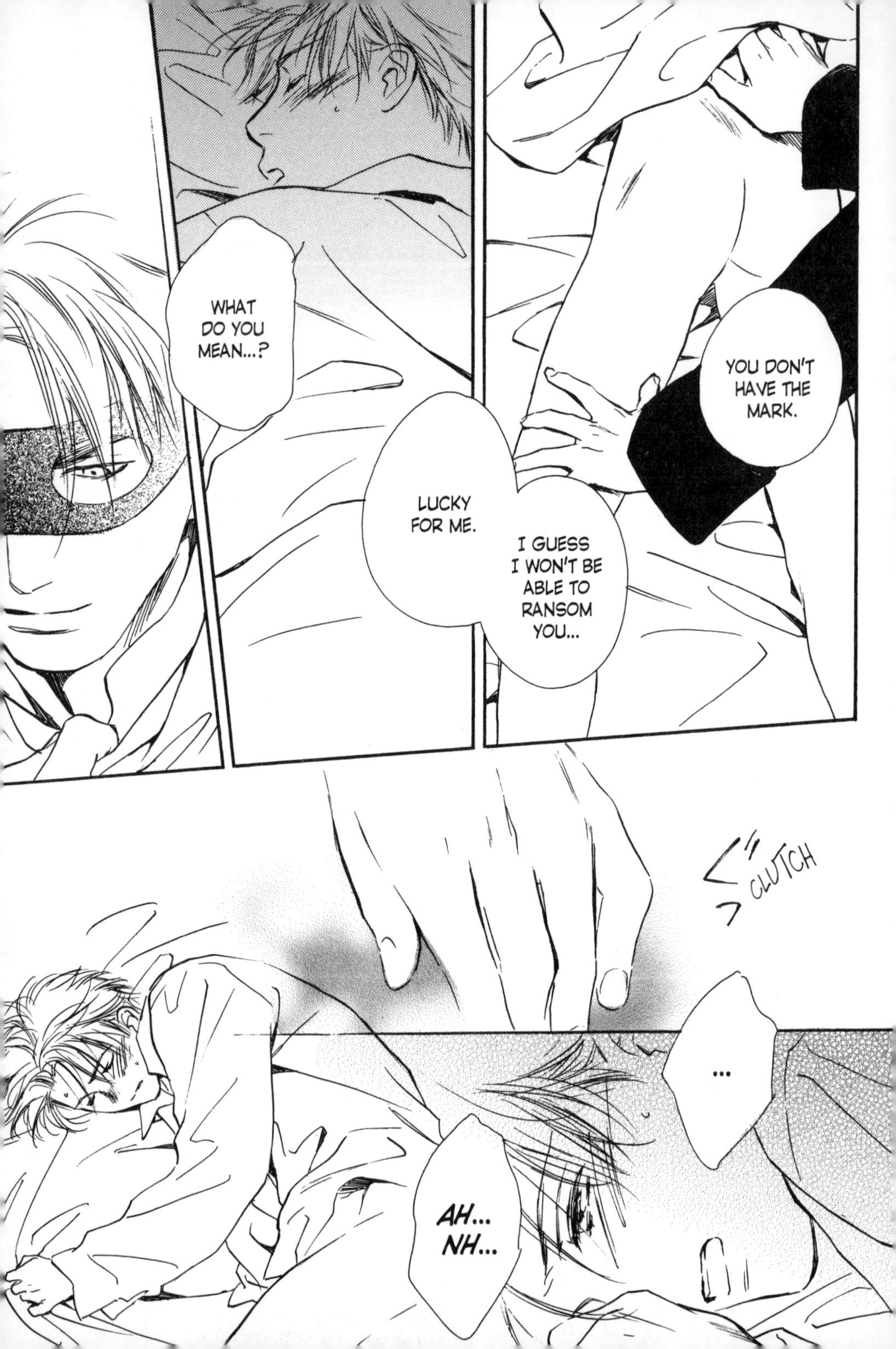
YOU DON'T HAVE THE MARK.
I GUESS I WON'T BE ABLE TO RANSOM YOU...
LUCKY FOR ME.
WHAT DO YOU MEAN...?
CLUTCH
...
AH... NH...

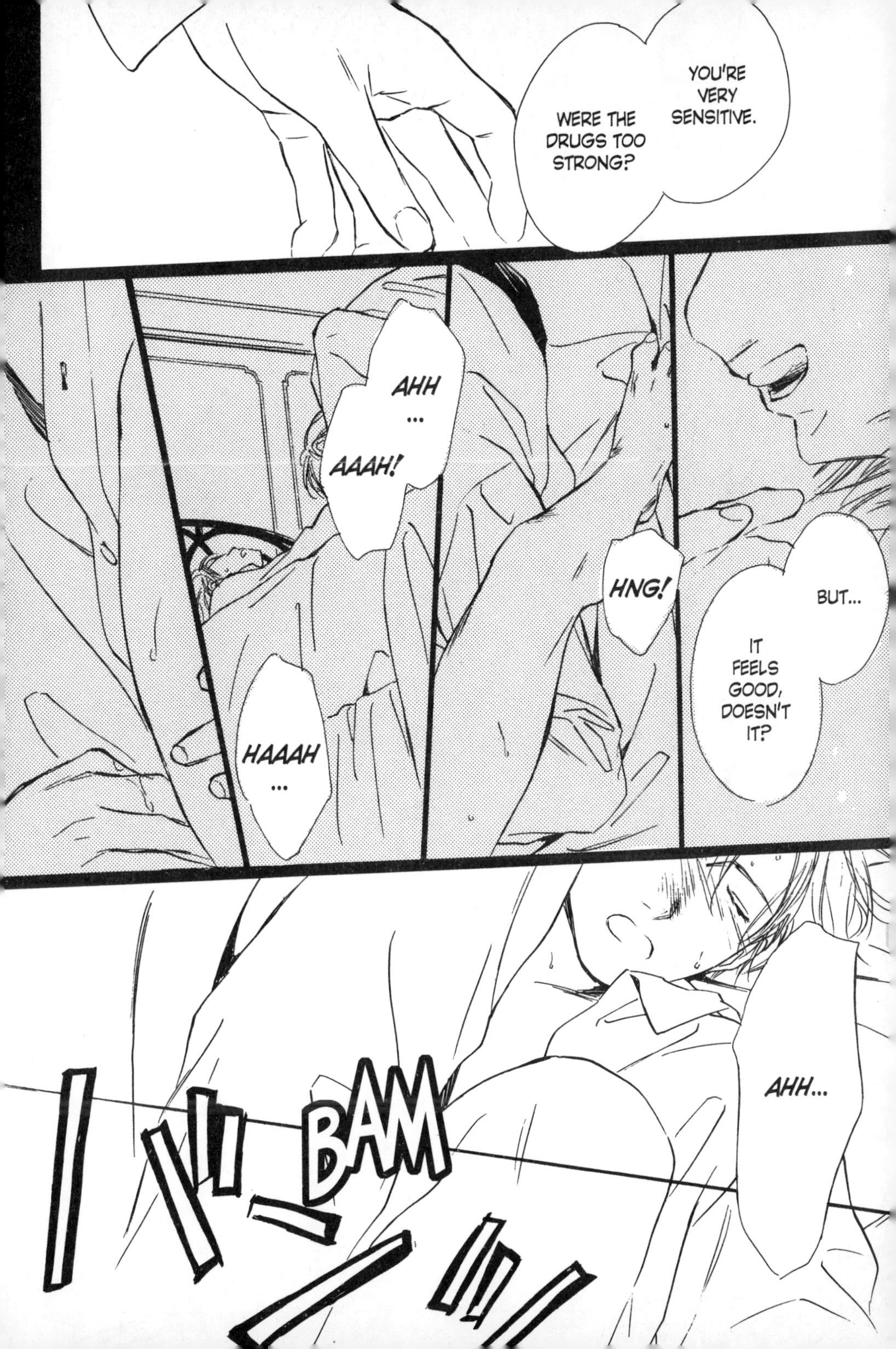
YOU'RE VERY SENSITIVE.
WERE THE DRUGS TOO STRONG?
BUT...
IT FEELS GOOD, DOESN'T IT?
HNG!
AHH ... AAAH!
HAAAH ...
AHH...
BAM

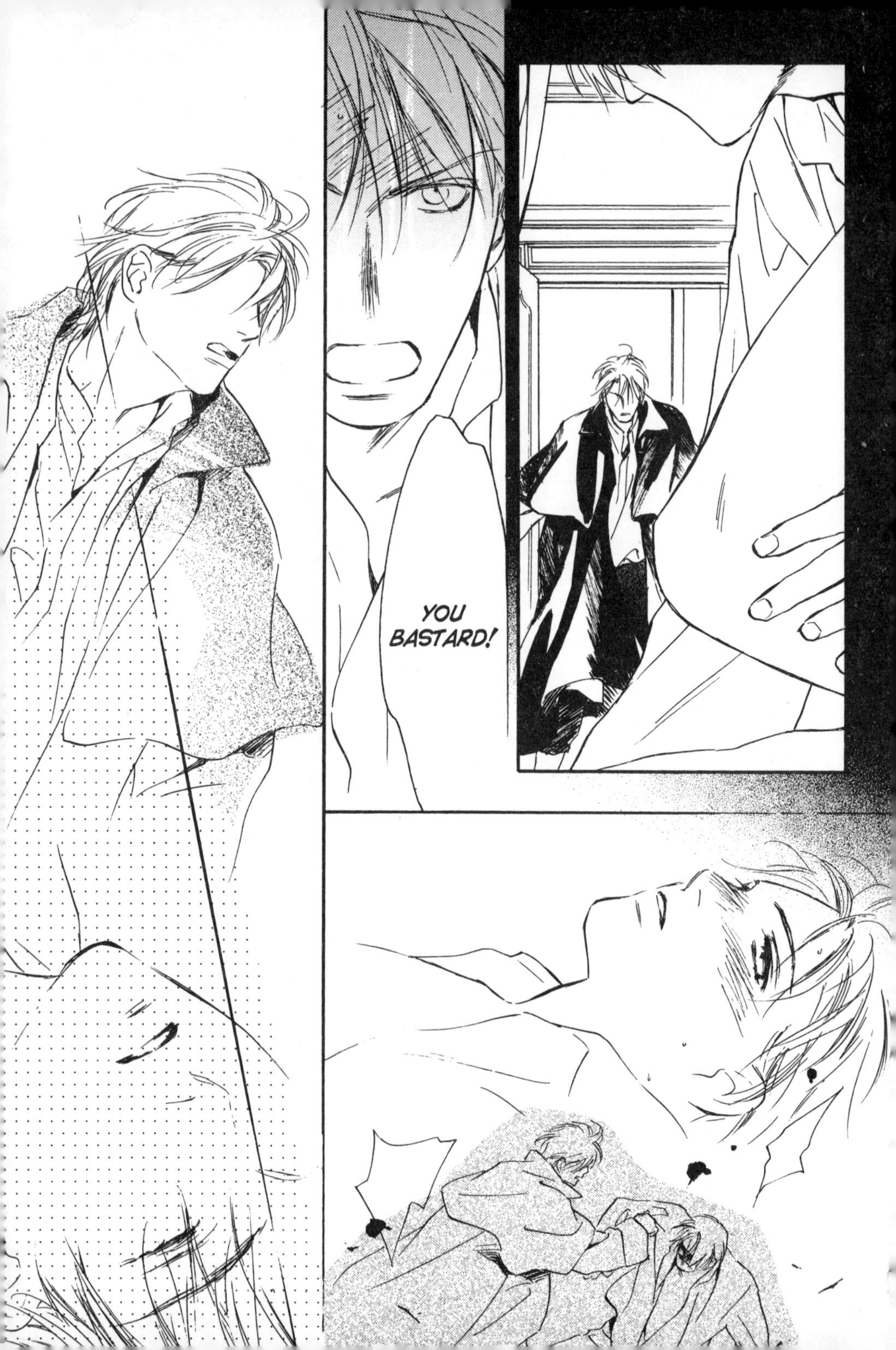
YOU BASTARD!

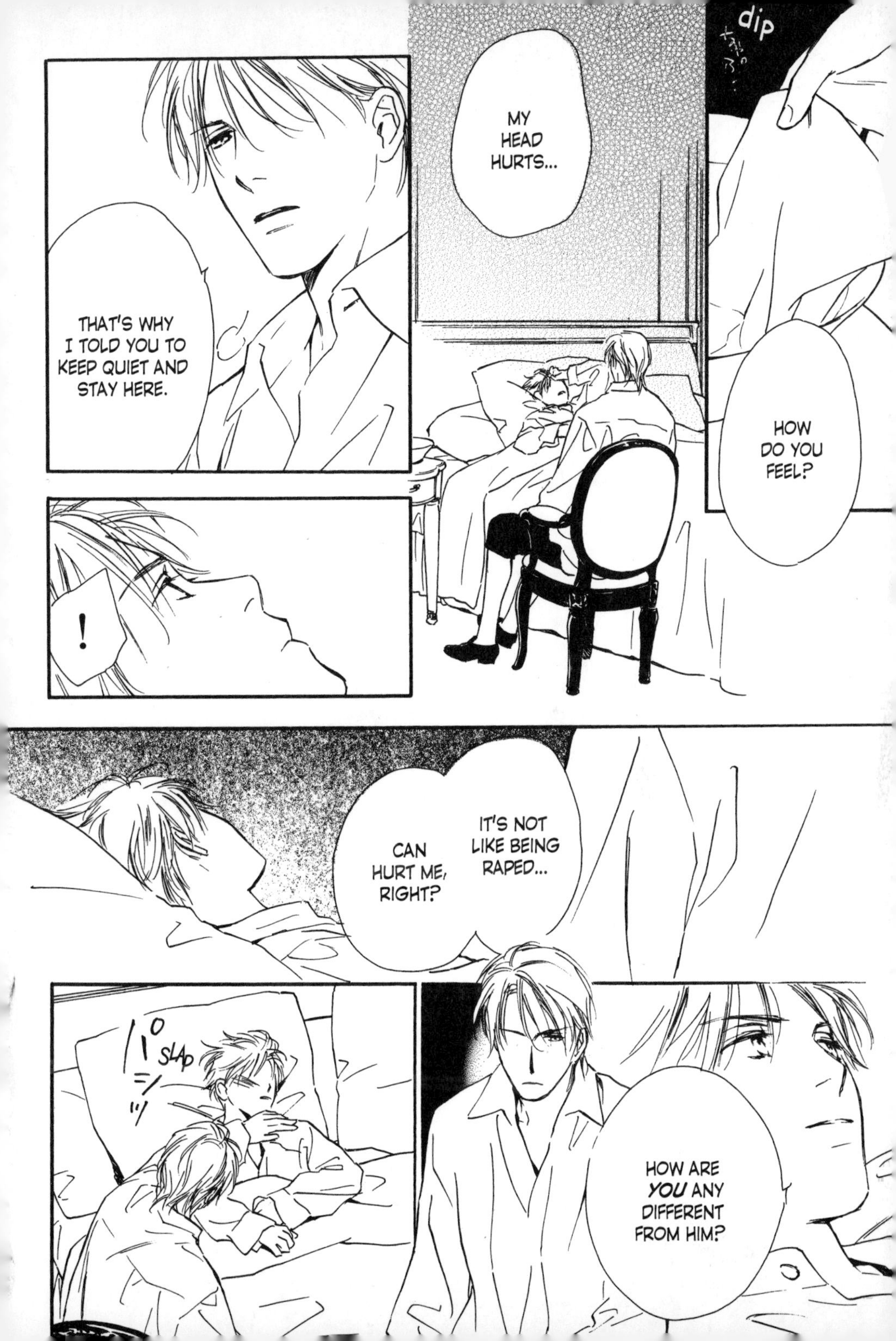
dip
HOW DO YOU FEEL?
MY HEAD HURTS...
THAT'S WHY I TOLD YOU TO KEEP QUIET AND STAY HERE.
!
IT'S NOT LIKE BEING RAPED...
CAN HURT ME, RIGHT?
HOW ARE *YOU* ANY DIFFERENT FROM HIM?
SLAP

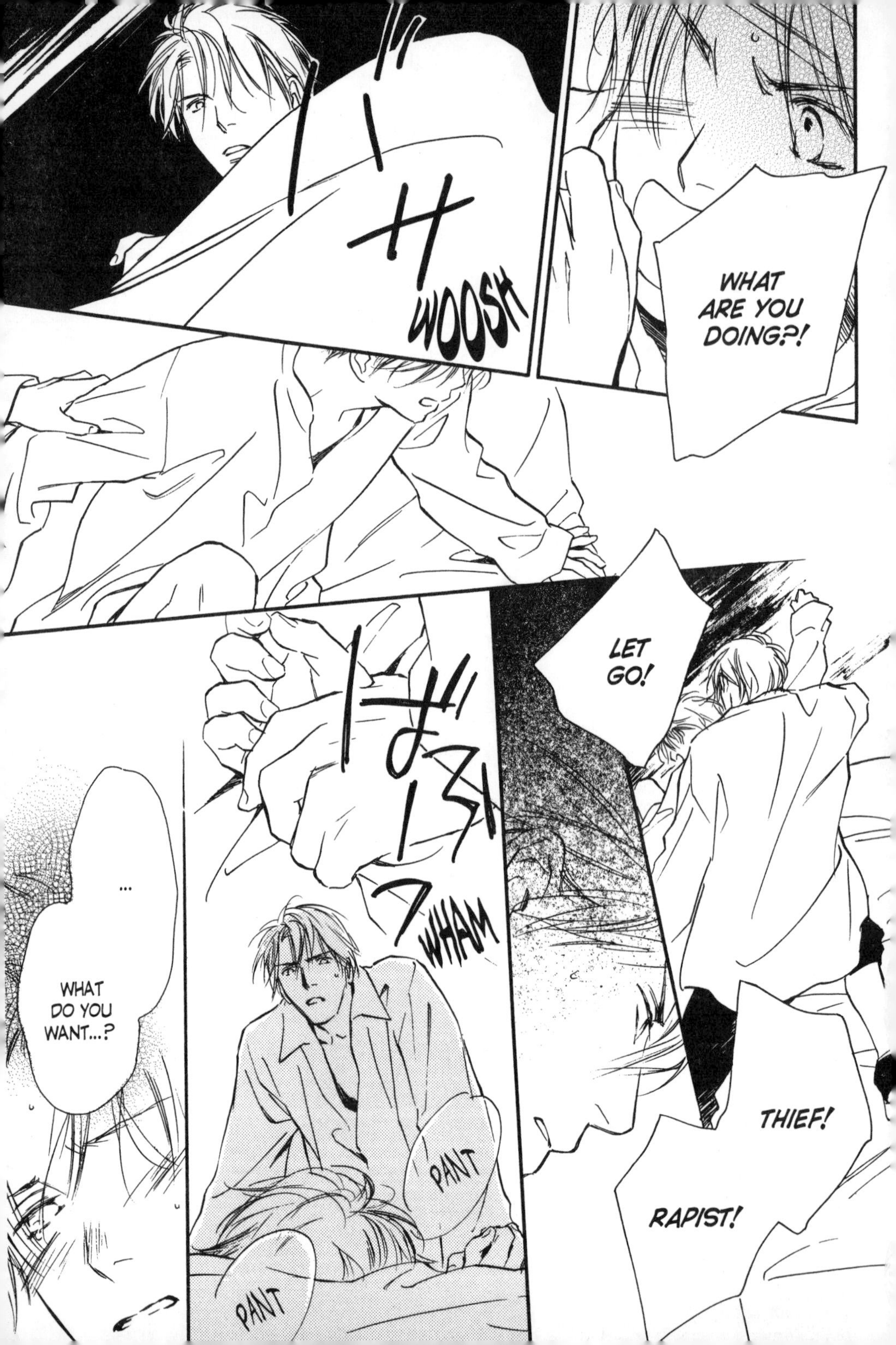
WHAT ARE YOU DOING?!
ザッ
WOOSH
LET GO!
THIEF!
RAPIST!
WHAM
PANT
PANT
...
WHAT DO YOU WANT...?

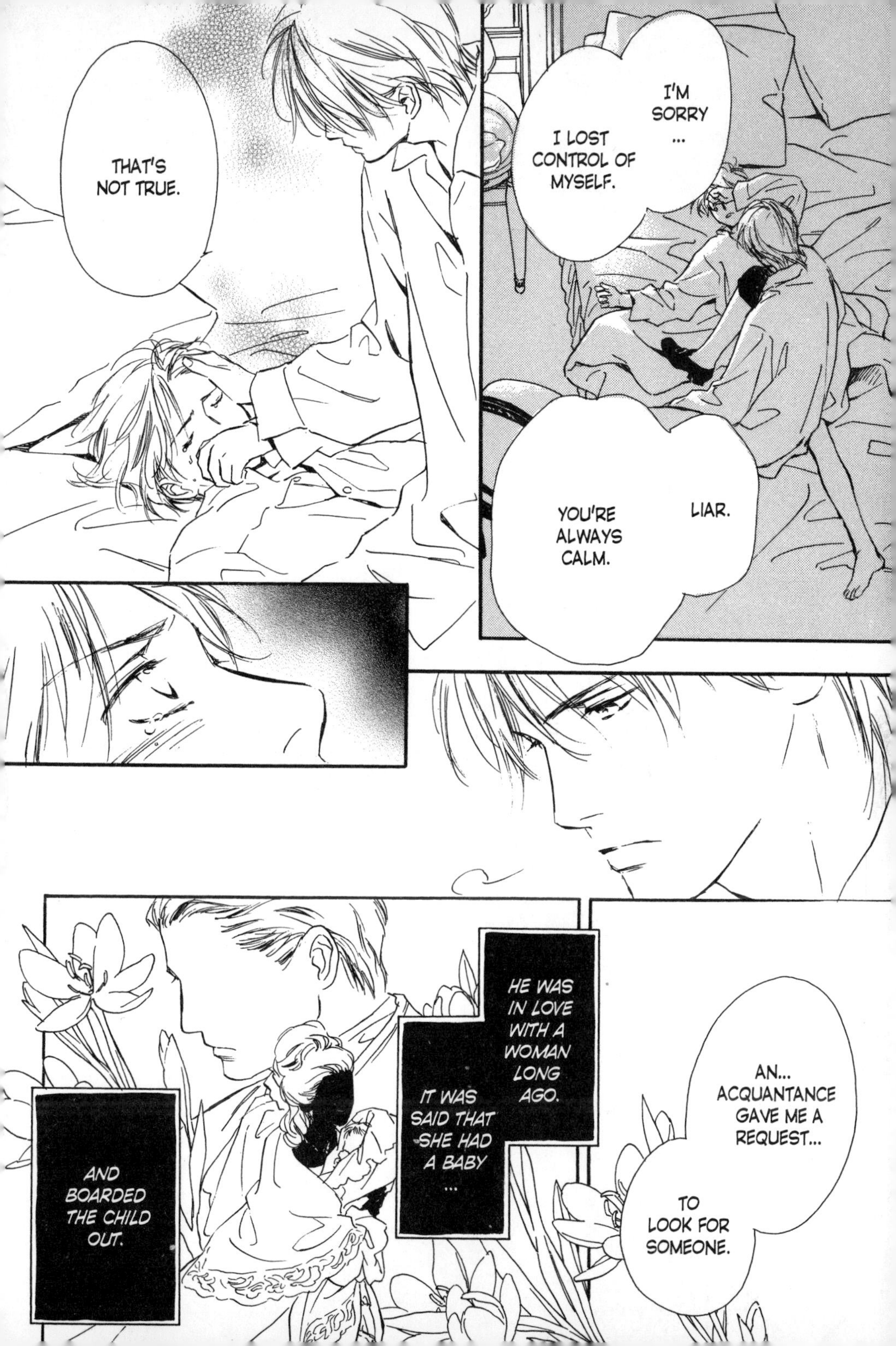
I'M SORRY ... I LOST CONTROL OF MYSELF.
LIAR. YOU'RE ALWAYS CALM.
THAT'S NOT TRUE.
AN... ACQUANTANCE GAVE ME A REQUEST...
TO LOOK FOR SOMEONE.
HE WAS IN LOVE WITH A WOMAN LONG AGO.
IT WAS SAID THAT SHE HAD A BABY ...
AND BOARDED THE CHILD OUT.

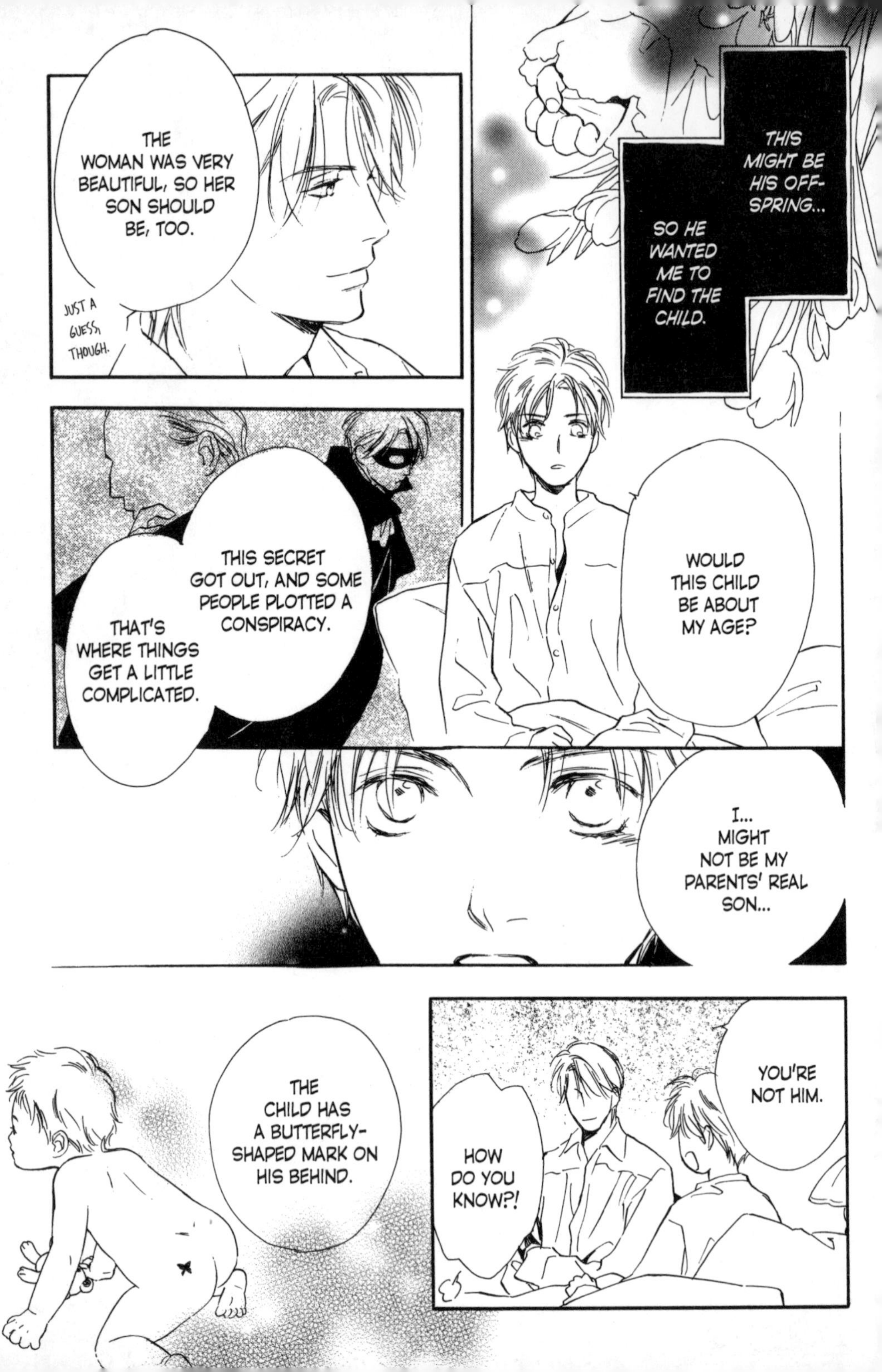
THIS MIGHT BE HIS OFF-SPRING...
SO HE WANTED ME TO FIND THE CHILD.
WOULD THIS CHILD BE ABOUT MY AGE?
THE WOMAN WAS VERY BEAUTIFUL, SO HER SON SHOULD BE, TOO.
JUST A GUESS, THOUGH.
THIS SECRET GOT OUT, AND SOME PEOPLE PLOTTED A CONSPIRACY.
THAT'S WHERE THINGS GET A LITTLE COMPLICATED.
I... MIGHT NOT BE MY PARENTS' REAL SON...
YOU'RE NOT HIM.
HOW DO YOU KNOW?!
THE CHILD HAS A BUTTERFLY-SHAPED MARK ON HIS BEHIND.

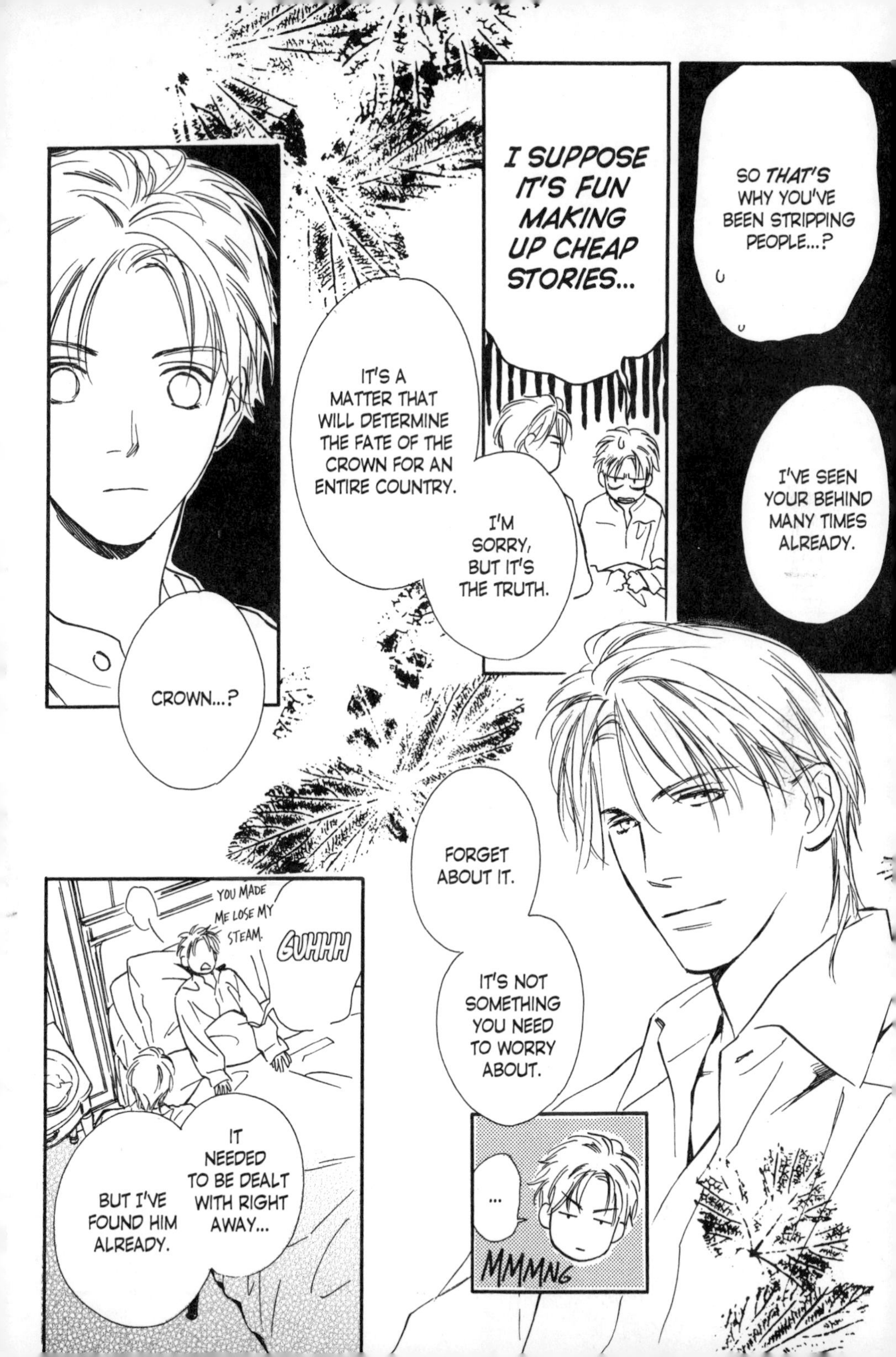
SO *THAT'S* WHY YOU'VE BEEN STRIPPING PEOPLE...?
I'VE SEEN YOUR BEHIND MANY TIMES ALREADY.
I SUPPOSE IT'S FUN MAKING UP CHEAP STORIES...
IT'S A MATTER THAT WILL DETERMINE THE FATE OF THE CROWN FOR AN ENTIRE COUNTRY.
I'M SORRY, BUT IT'S THE TRUTH.
CROWN...?
FORGET ABOUT IT.
IT'S NOT SOMETHING YOU NEED TO WORRY ABOUT.
...
MMMNG
GUHHH
YOU MADE ME LOSE MY STEAM.
IT NEEDED TO BE DEALT WITH RIGHT AWAY...
BUT I'VE FOUND HIM ALREADY.

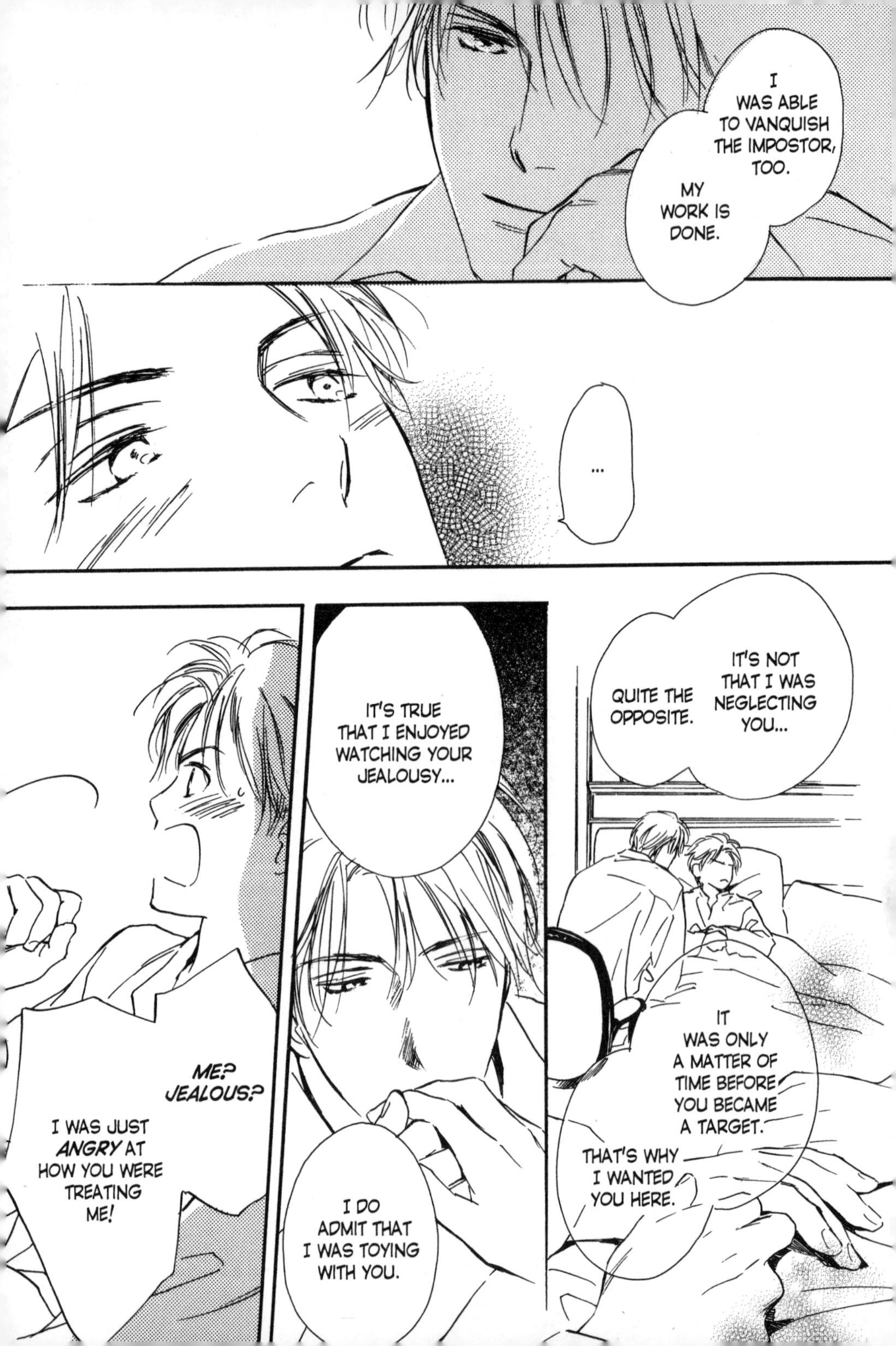
I WAS ABLE TO VANQUISH THE IMPOSTOR, TOO.
MY WORK IS DONE.
...
IT'S NOT THAT I WAS NEGLECTING YOU...
QUITE THE OPPOSITE.
IT WAS ONLY A MATTER OF TIME BEFORE YOU BECAME A TARGET.
THAT'S WHY I WANTED YOU HERE.
IT'S TRUE THAT I ENJOYED WATCHING YOUR JEALOUSY...
I DO ADMIT THAT I WAS TOYING WITH YOU.
ME? JEALOUS?
I WAS JUST *ANGRY* AT HOW YOU WERE TREATING ME!

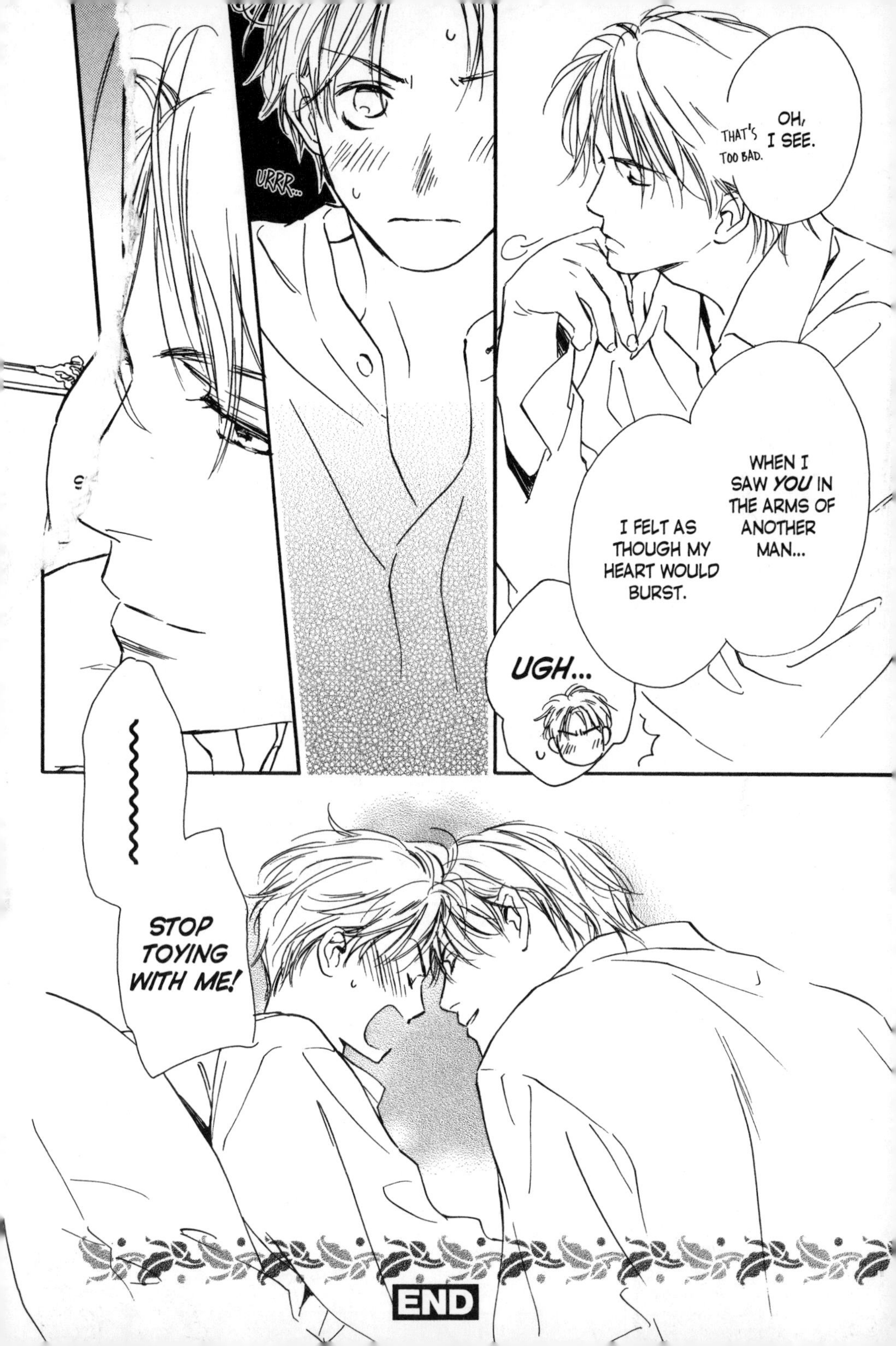

OH, I SEE.
THAT'S TOO BAD.
WHEN I SAW *YOU* IN THE ARMS OF ANOTHER MAN...
I FELT AS THOUGH MY HEART WOULD BURST.
UGH...
URRR...
STOP TOYING WITH ME!
END

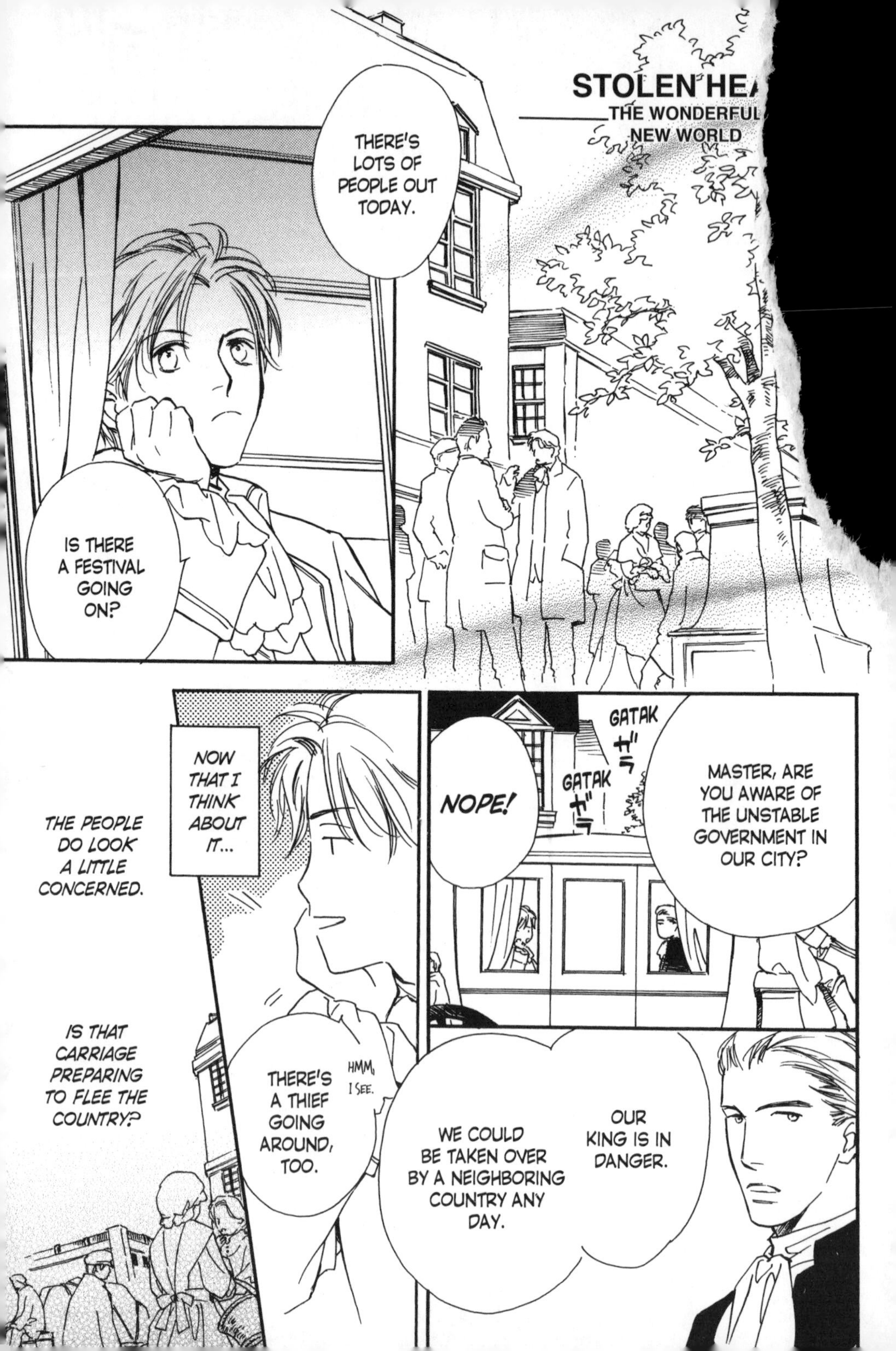
STOLEN HEA
THE WONDERFUL NEW WORLD
THERE'S LOTS OF PEOPLE OUT TODAY.
IS THERE A FESTIVAL GOING ON?
MASTER, ARE YOU AWARE OF THE UNSTABLE GOVERNMENT IN OUR CITY?
GATAK
GATAK
NOPE!
OUR KING IS IN DANGER.
WE COULD BE TAKEN OVER BY A NEIGHBORING COUNTRY ANY DAY.
NOW THAT I THINK ABOUT IT...
HMM, I SEE.
THERE'S A THIEF GOING AROUND, TOO.
THE PEOPLE DO LOOK A LITTLE CONCERNED.
IS THAT CARRIAGE PREPARING TO FLEE THE COUNTRY?

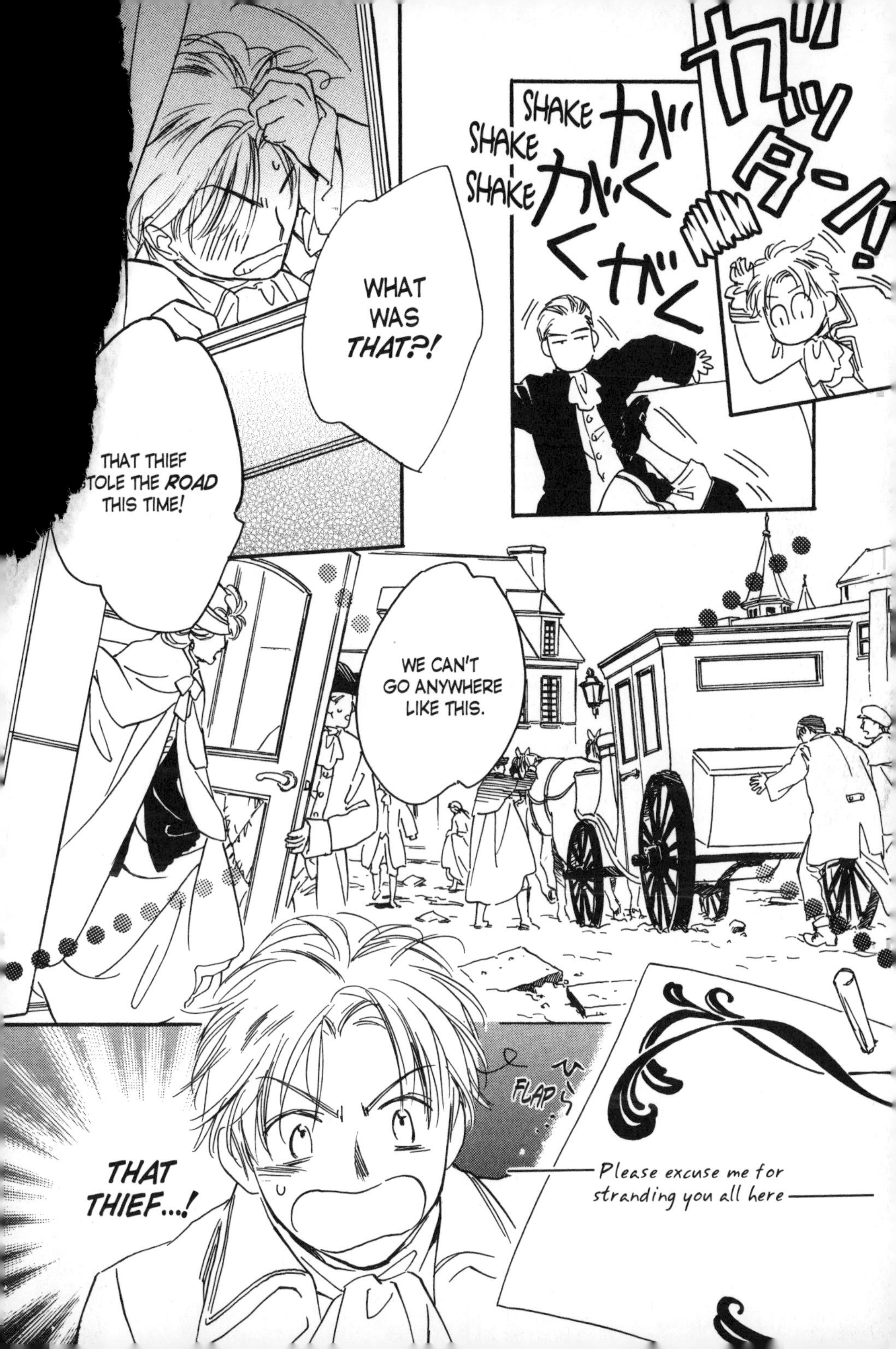
WHAM
SHAKE SHAKE SHAKE
WHAT WAS THAT?!
THAT THIEF STOLE THE ROAD THIS TIME!
WE CAN'T GO ANYWHERE LIKE THIS.
Please excuse me for stranding you all here
FLAP
THAT THIEF...!

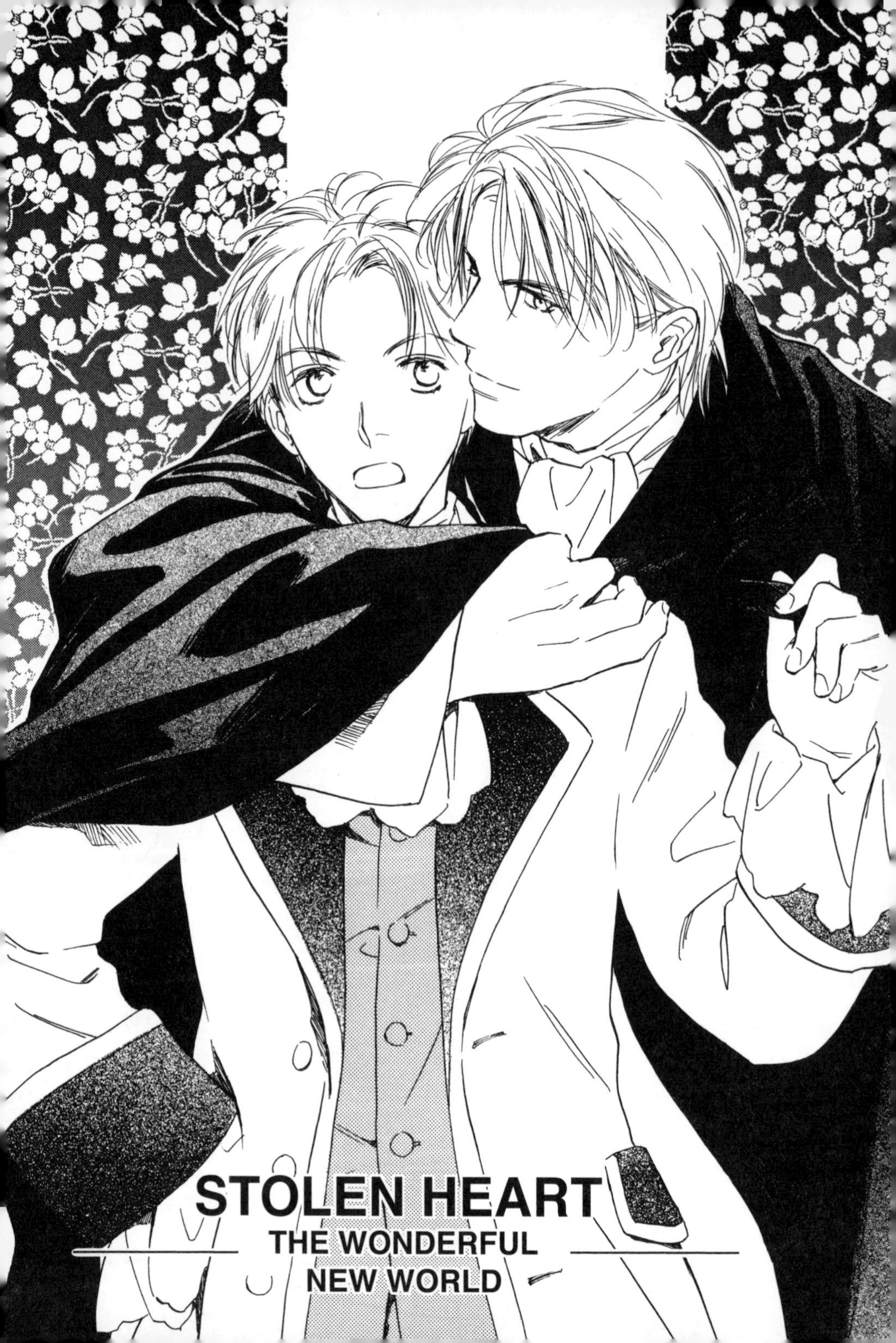
STOLEN HEART
THE WONDERFUL
NEW WORLD

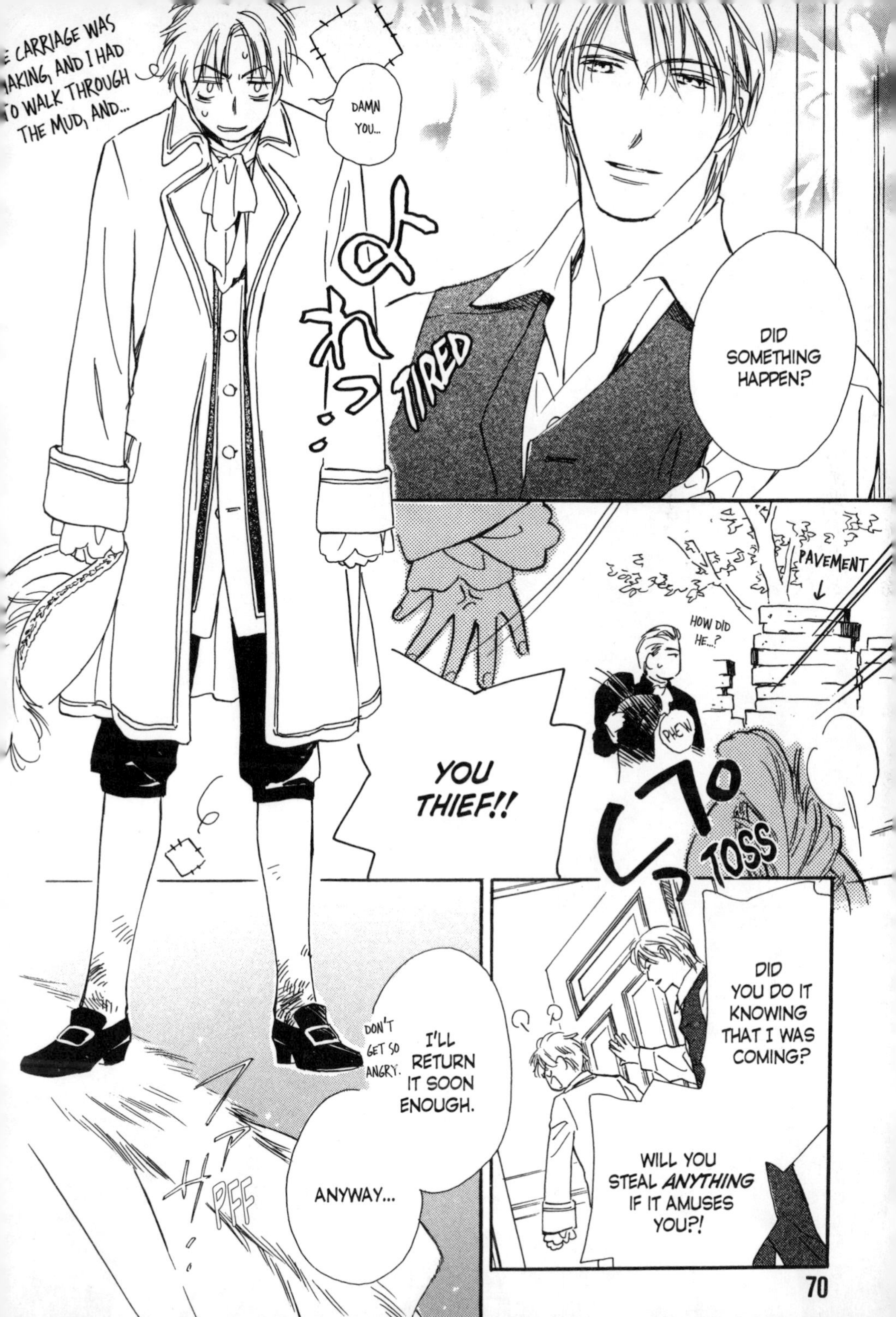
DID SOMETHING HAPPEN?
TIRED
...E CARRIAGE WAS ...AKING, AND I HAD ...O WALK THROUGH THE MUD, AND...
DAMN YOU...
PAVEMENT
HOW DID HE...?
PHEW
TOSS
YOU THIEF!!
DID YOU DO IT KNOWING THAT I WAS COMING?
WILL YOU STEAL *ANYTHING* IF IT AMUSES YOU?!
DON'T GET SO ANGRY.
I'LL RETURN IT SOON ENOUGH.
ANYWAY...
PFF

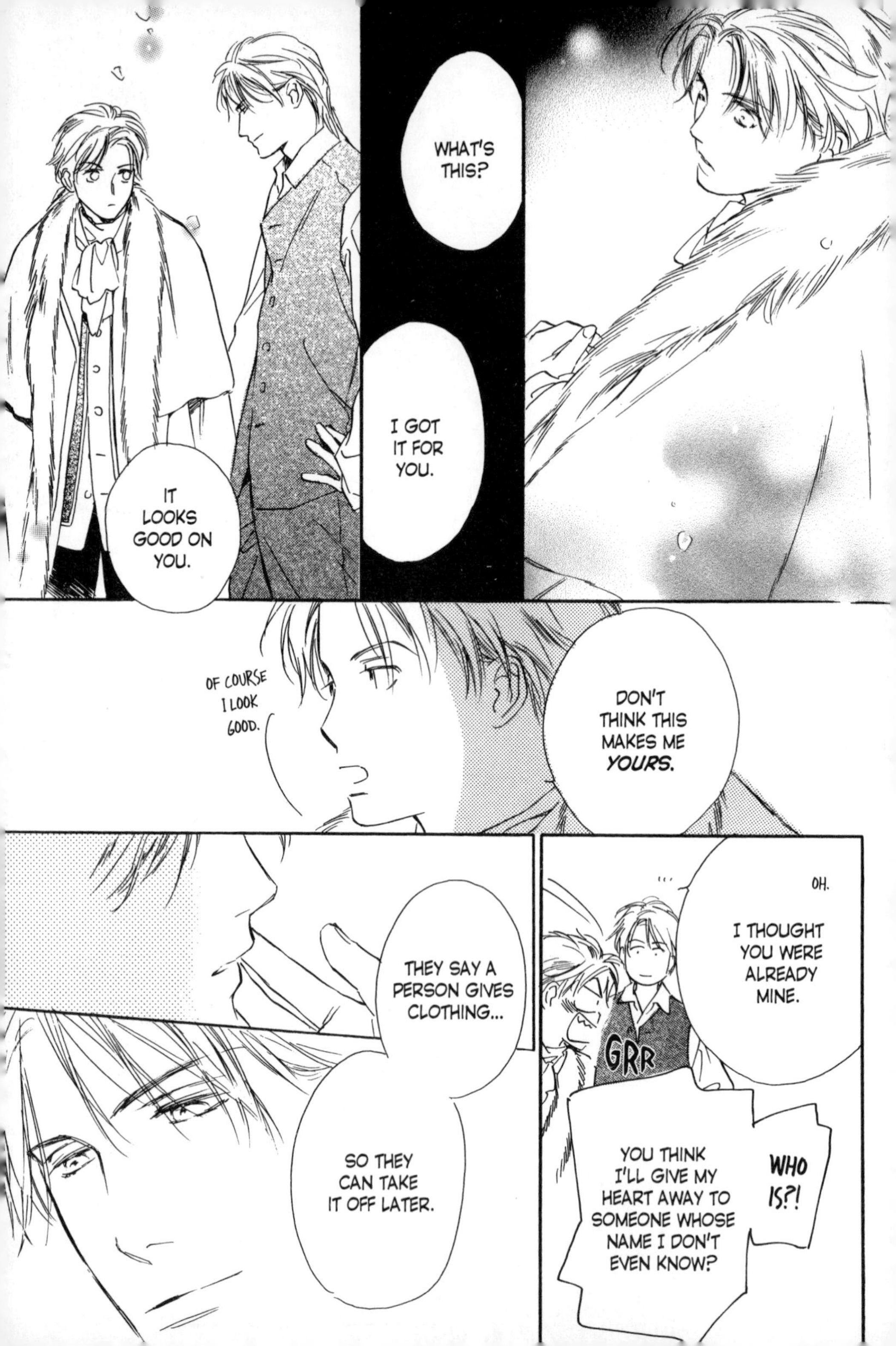
WHAT'S THIS?
I GOT IT FOR YOU.
IT LOOKS GOOD ON YOU.
DON'T THINK THIS MAKES ME ***YOURS.***
OF COURSE I LOOK GOOD.
...
OH.
I THOUGHT YOU WERE ALREADY MINE.
GRR
YOU THINK I'LL GIVE MY HEART AWAY TO SOMEONE WHOSE NAME I DON'T EVEN KNOW?
WHO IS?!
THEY SAY A PERSON GIVES CLOTHING...
SO THEY CAN TAKE IT OFF LATER.

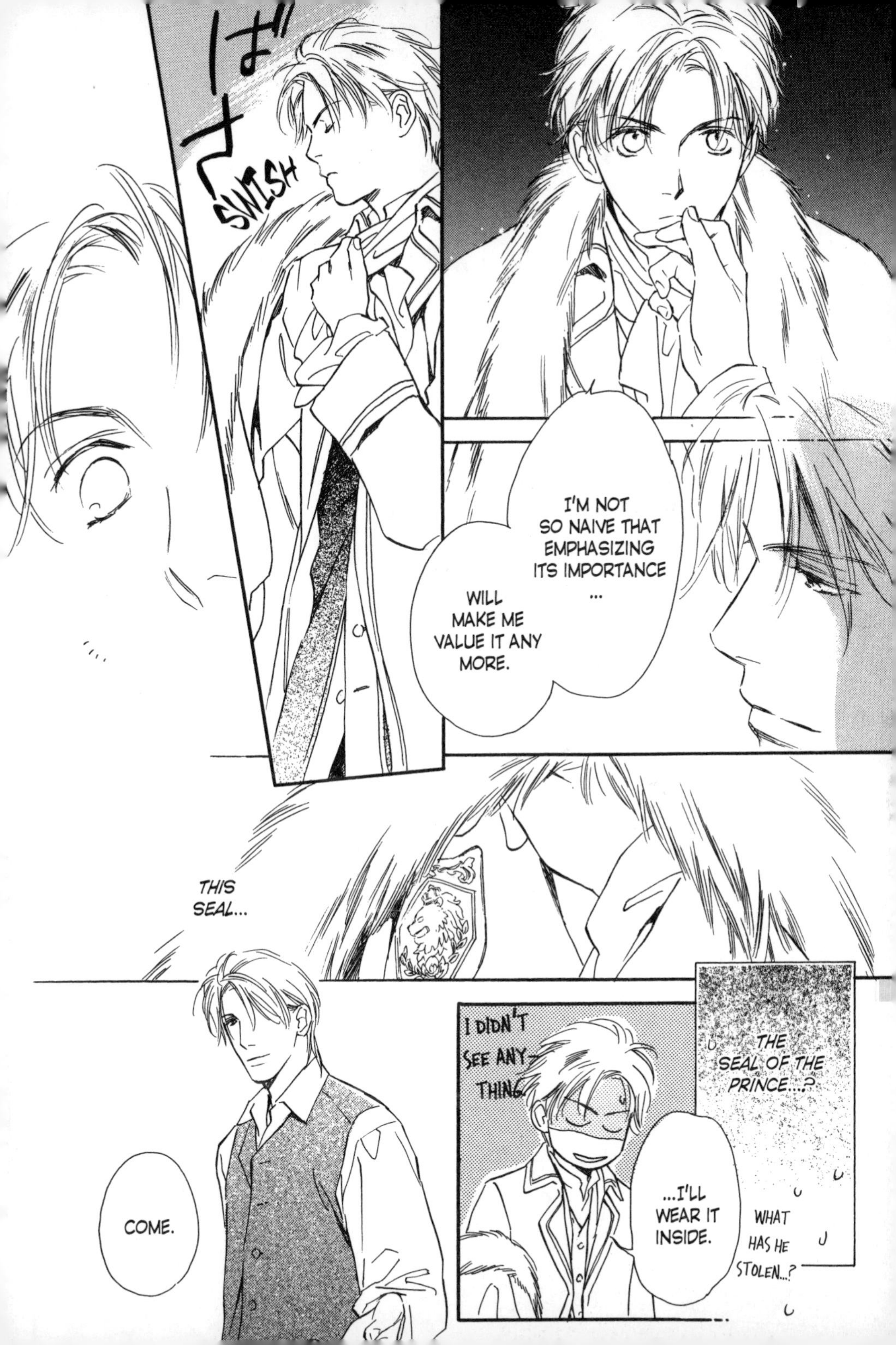
ばさ
SWISH
...
I'M NOT SO NAIVE THAT EMPHASIZING ITS IMPORTANCE...
WILL MAKE ME VALUE IT ANY MORE.
THIS SEAL...
THE SEAL OF THE PRINCE...?
WHAT HAS HE STOLEN...?
I DIDN'T SEE ANYTHING.
...I'LL WEAR IT INSIDE.
COME.

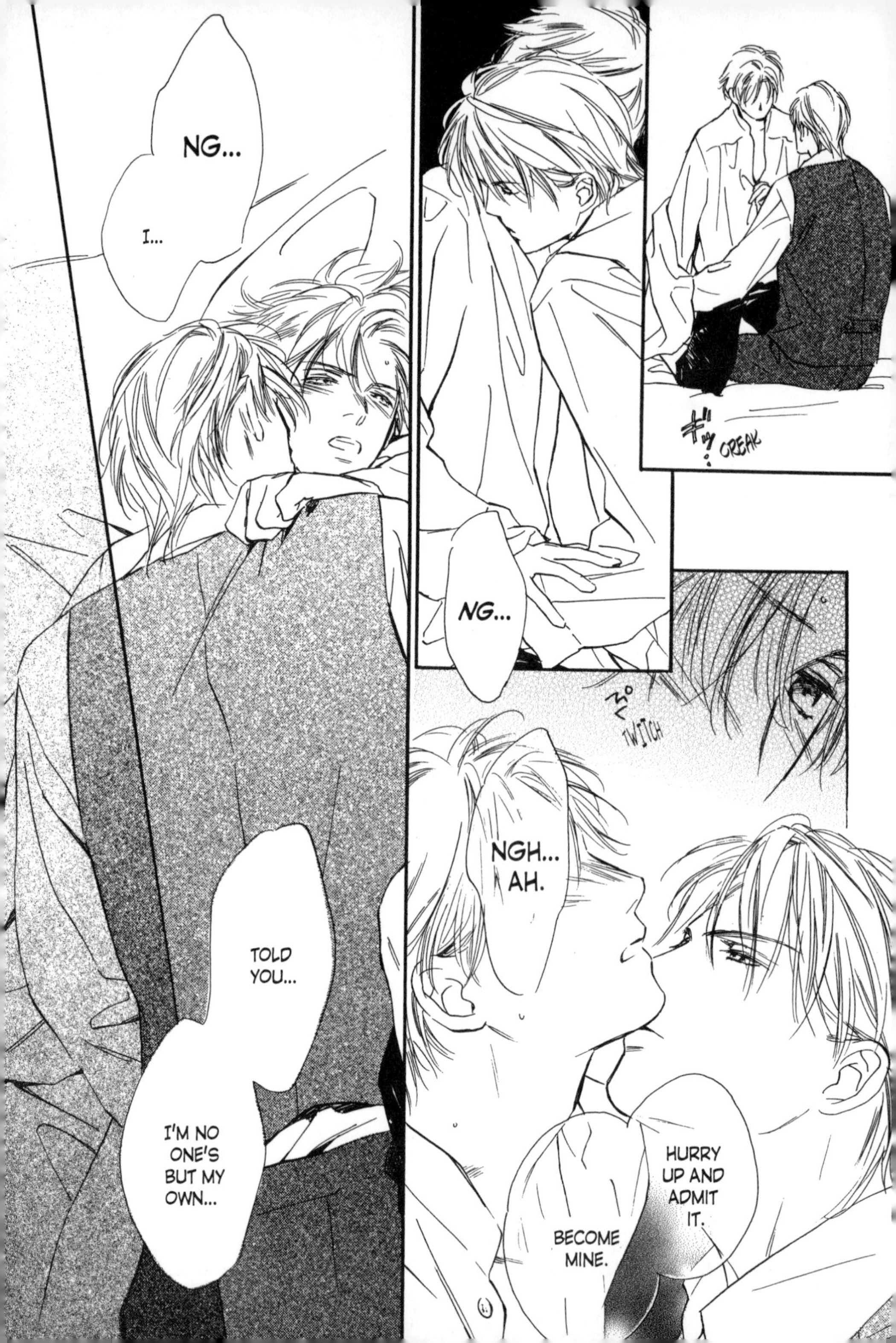
CREAK
NG...
TWITCH
NGH... AH.
HURRY UP AND ADMIT IT.
BECOME MINE.
NG...
I...
TOLD YOU...
I'M NO ONE'S BUT MY OWN...

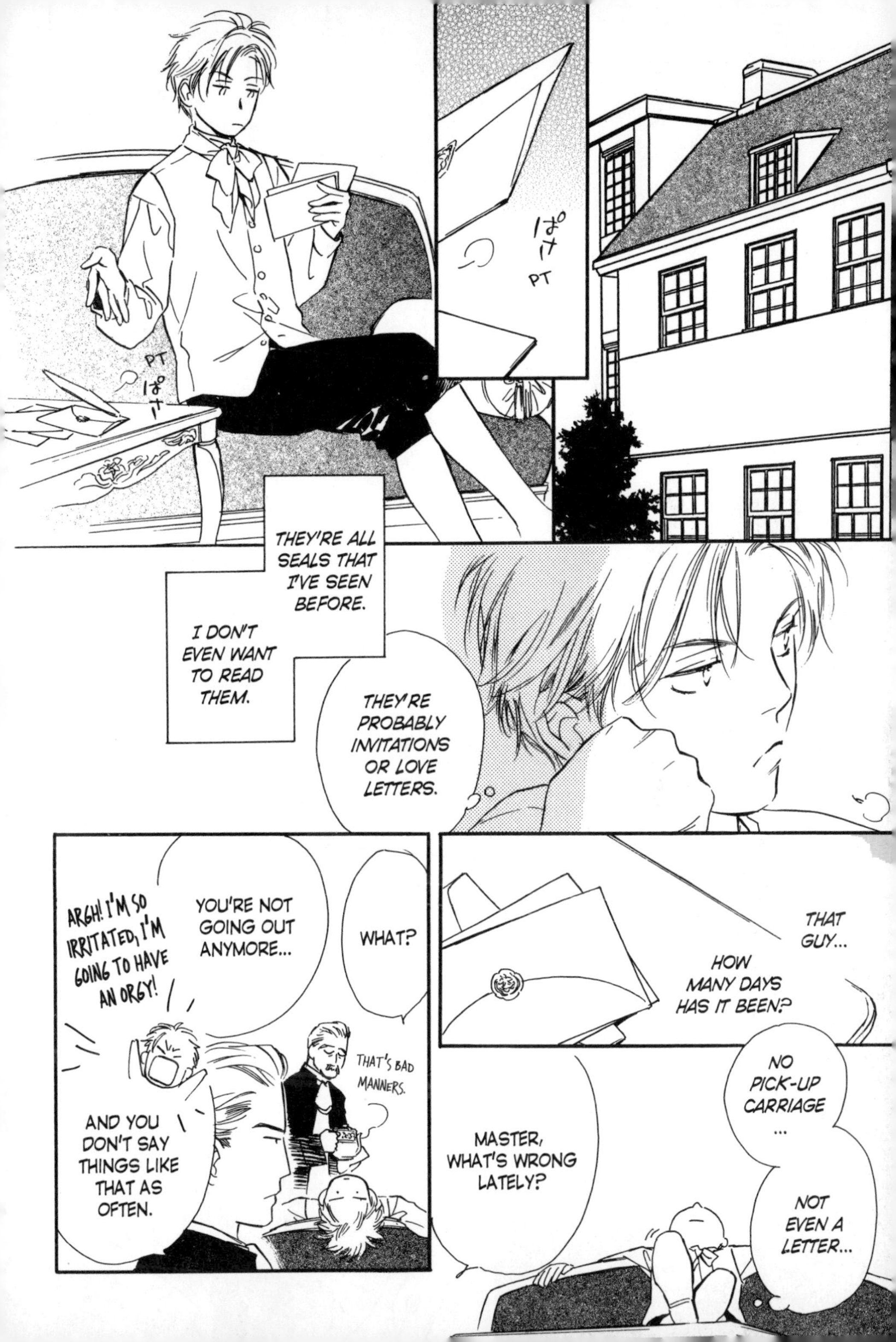
PT
PT
THEY'RE ALL SEALS THAT I'VE SEEN BEFORE.
I DON'T EVEN WANT TO READ THEM.
THEY'RE PROBABLY INVITATIONS OR LOVE LETTERS.
THAT GUY...
HOW MANY DAYS HAS IT BEEN?
NO PICK-UP CARRIAGE ...
NOT EVEN A LETTER...
MASTER, WHAT'S WRONG LATELY?
WHAT?
YOU'RE NOT GOING OUT ANYMORE...
ARGH! I'M SO IRRITATED, I'M GOING TO HAVE AN ORGY!
AND YOU DON'T SAY THINGS LIKE THAT AS OFTEN.
THAT'S BAD MANNERS.

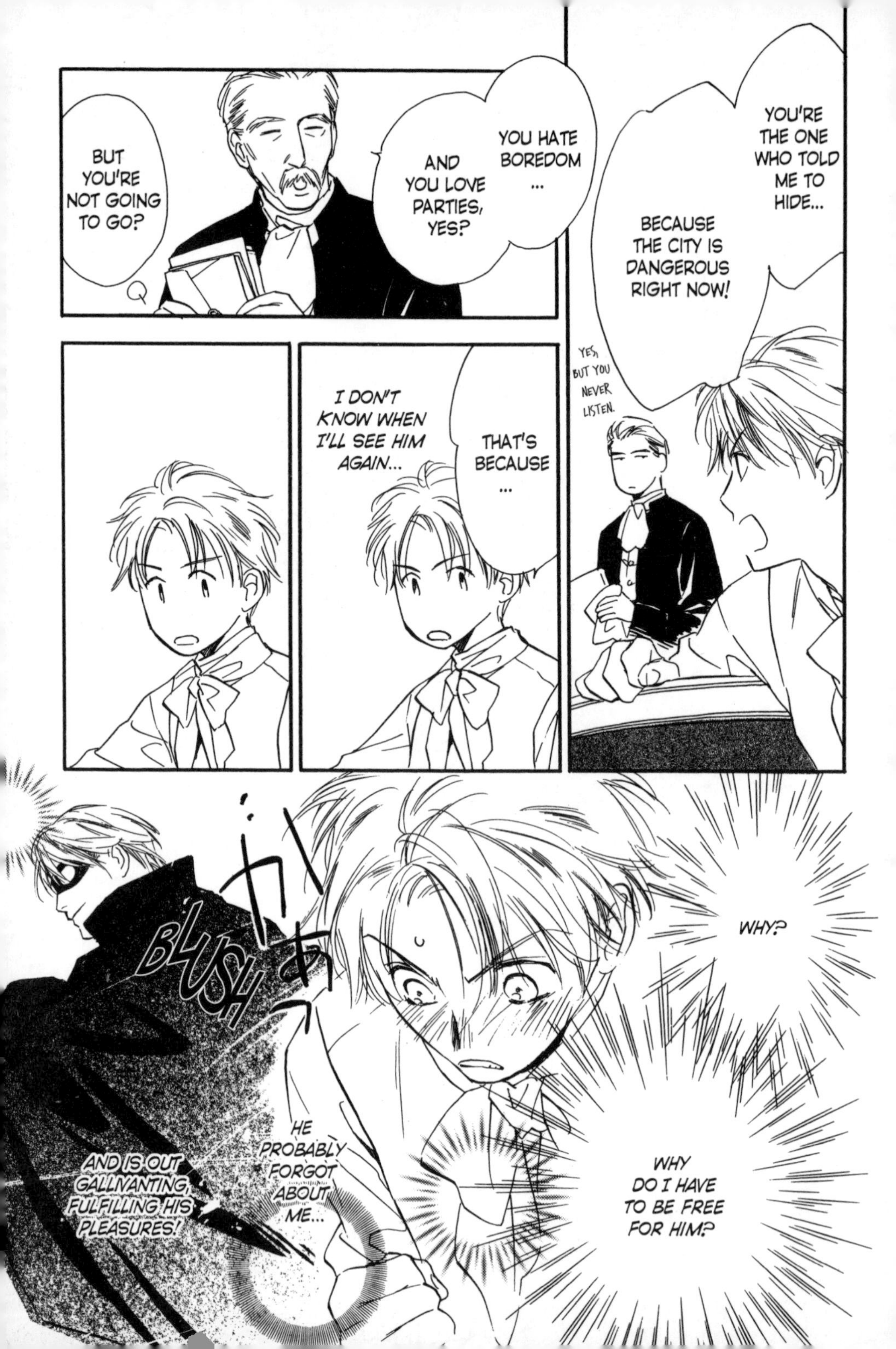
YOU'RE THE ONE WHO TOLD ME TO HIDE...
BECAUSE THE CITY IS DANGEROUS RIGHT NOW!
YES, BUT YOU NEVER LISTEN.
YOU HATE BOREDOM ...
AND YOU LOVE PARTIES, YES?
BUT YOU'RE NOT GOING TO GO?
THAT'S BECAUSE ...
I DON'T KNOW WHEN I'LL SEE HIM AGAIN...
WHY?
BLUSH
WHY DO I HAVE TO BE FREE FOR HIM?
HE PROBABLY FORGOT ABOUT ME...
AND IS OUT GALLIVANTING, FULFILLING HIS PLEASURES!

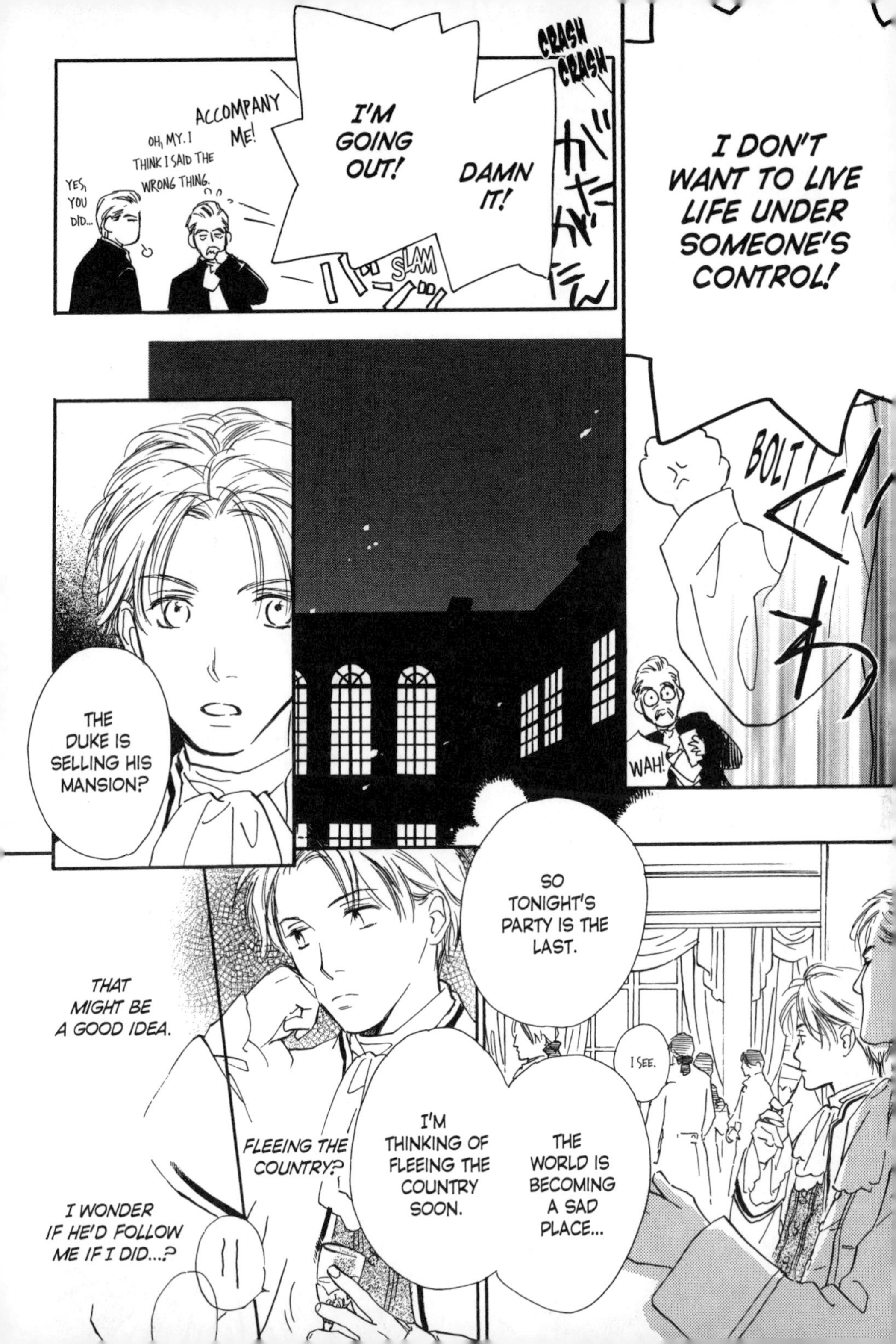
I DON'T WANT TO LIVE LIFE UNDER SOMEONE'S CONTROL!
CRASH CRASH
DAMN IT!
I'M GOING OUT!
SLAM
ACCOMPANY ME!
OH, MY. I THINK I SAID THE WRONG THING.
YES, YOU DID...
BOLT
WAH!
THE DUKE IS SELLING HIS MANSION?
SO TONIGHT'S PARTY IS THE LAST.
I SEE.
THE WORLD IS BECOMING A SAD PLACE...
I'M THINKING OF FLEEING THE COUNTRY SOON.
FLEEING THE COUNTRY?
THAT MIGHT BE A GOOD IDEA.
I WONDER IF HE'D FOLLOW ME IF I DID...?

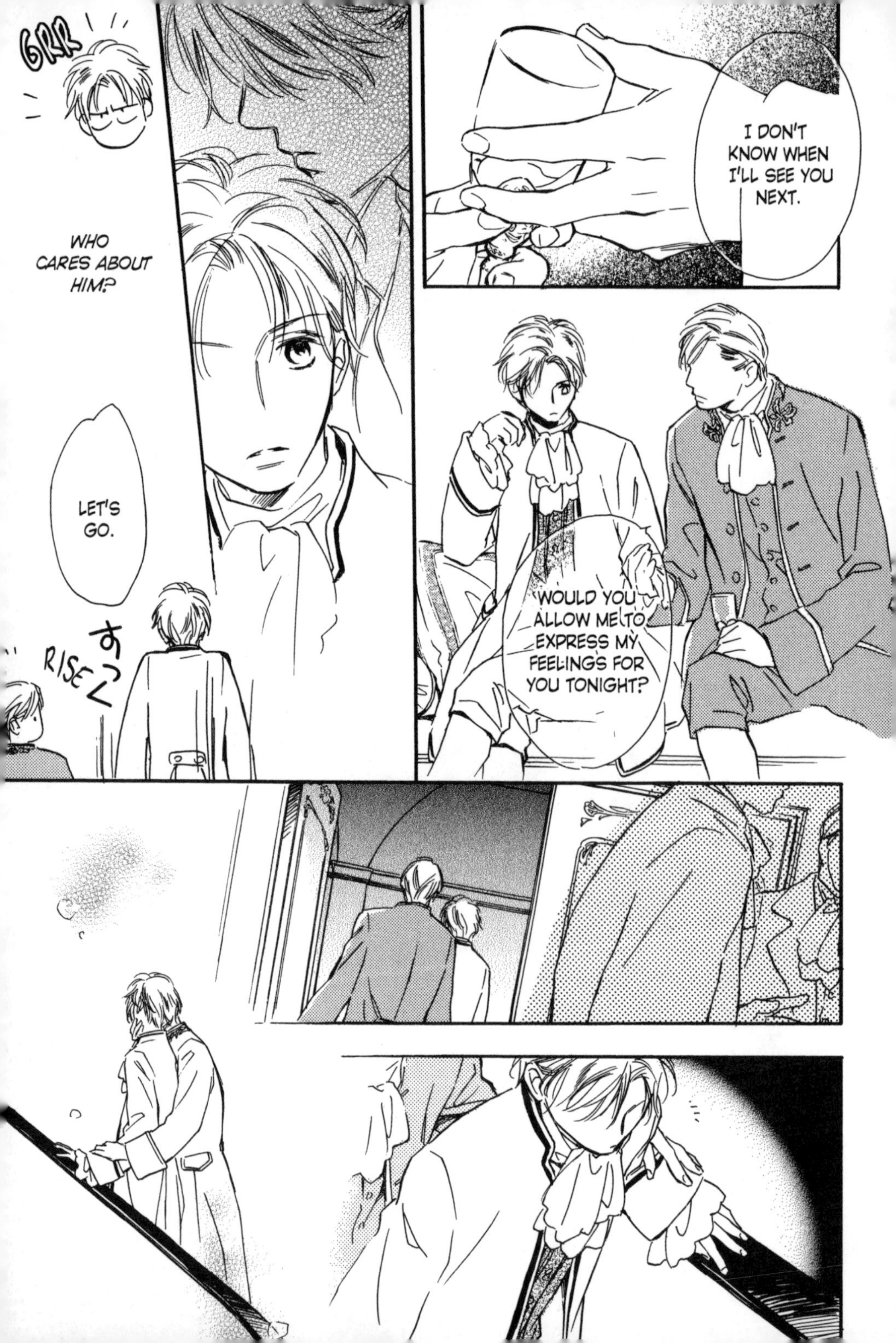
I DON'T KNOW WHEN I'LL SEE YOU NEXT.
WOULD YOU ALLOW ME TO EXPRESS MY FEELINGS FOR YOU TONIGHT?
GRR
WHO CARES ABOUT HIM?
LET'S GO.
すっく
RISE

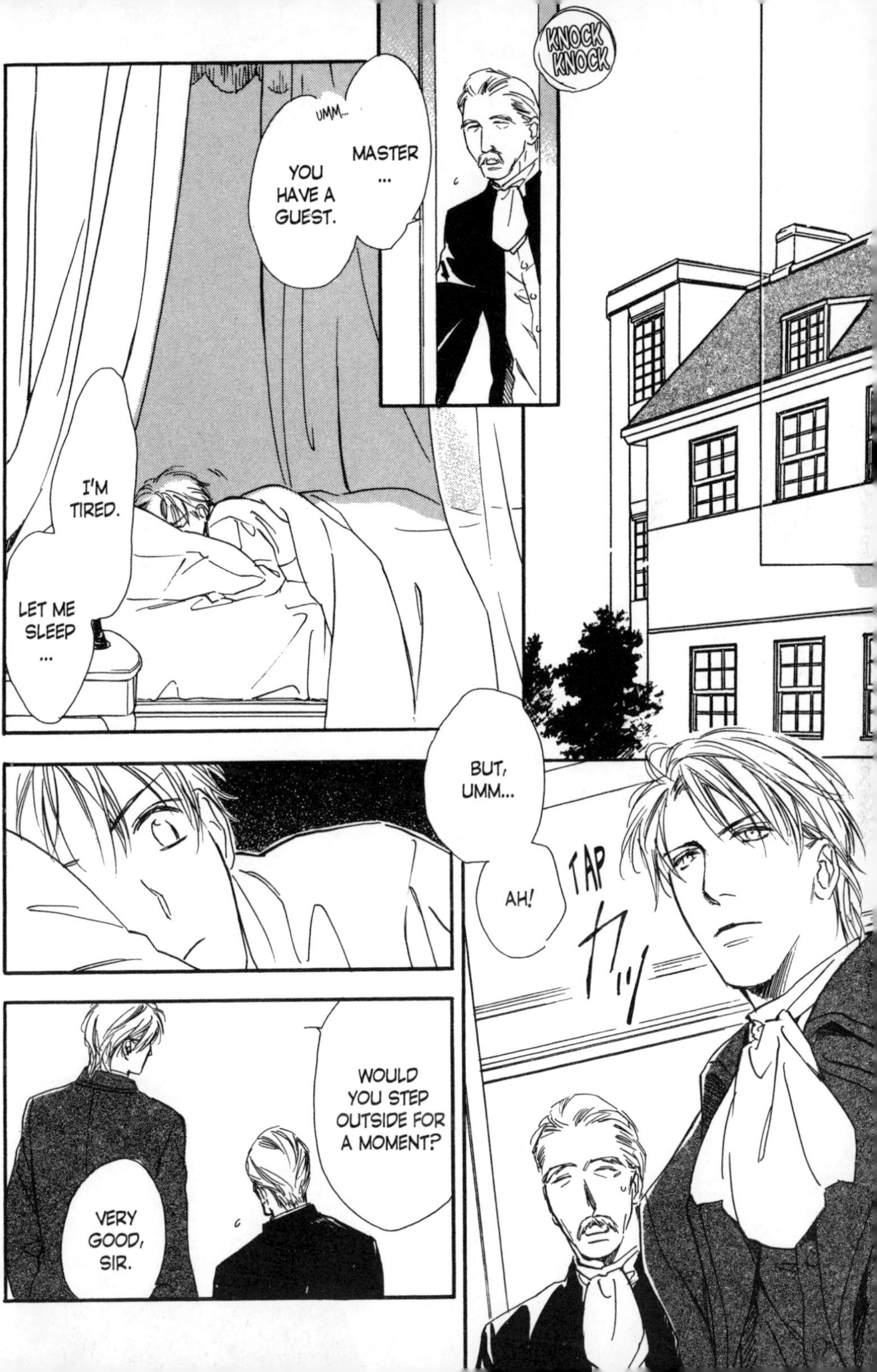
KNOCK KNOCK
UMM... MASTER ... YOU HAVE A GUEST.
I'M TIRED.
LET ME SLEEP ...
BUT, UMM...
AH!
TAP
カッ
WOULD YOU STEP OUTSIDE FOR A MOMENT?
VERY GOOD, SIR.

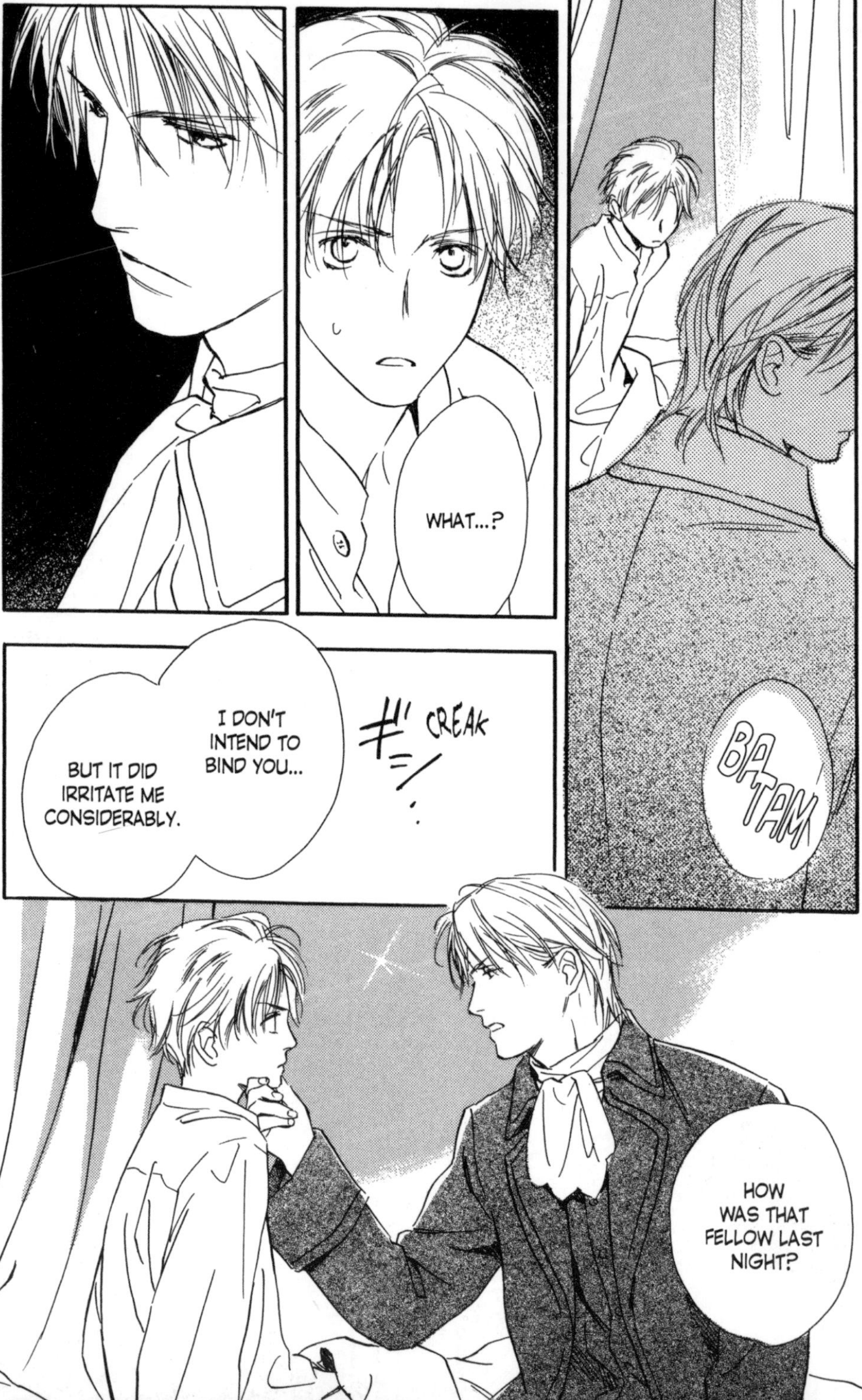
BA TAM
WHAT...?
CREAK
I DON'T INTEND TO BIND YOU...
BUT IT DID IRRITATE ME CONSIDERABLY.
HOW WAS THAT FELLOW LAST NIGHT?

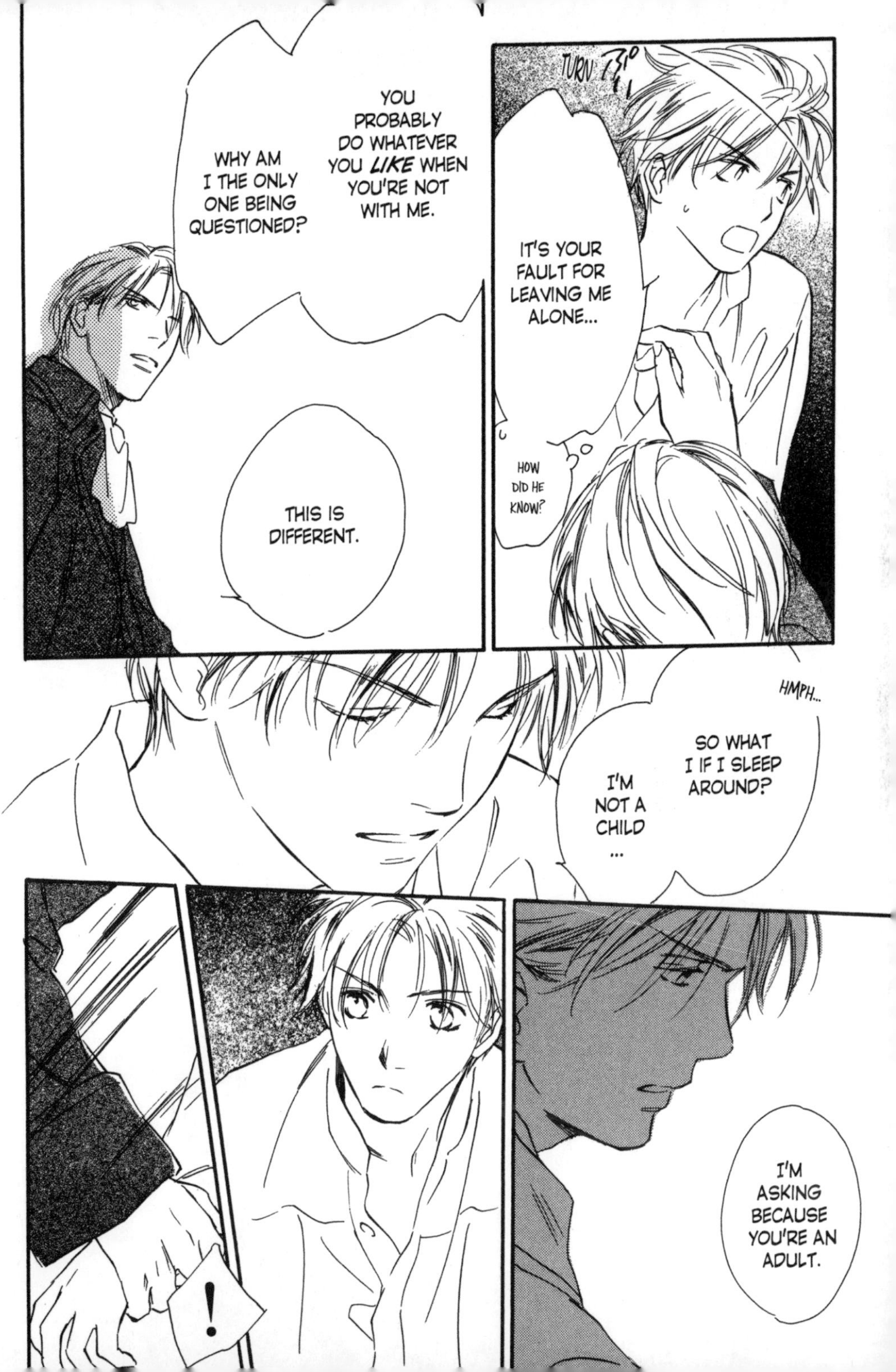
TURN
IT'S YOUR FAULT FOR LEAVING ME ALONE...
HOW DID HE KNOW?
YOU PROBABLY DO WHATEVER YOU *LIKE* WHEN YOU'RE NOT WITH ME.
WHY AM I THE ONLY ONE BEING QUESTIONED?
THIS IS DIFFERENT.
HMPH...
SO WHAT IF I SLEEP AROUND?
I'M NOT A CHILD ...
I'M ASKING BECAUSE YOU'RE AN ADULT.
!

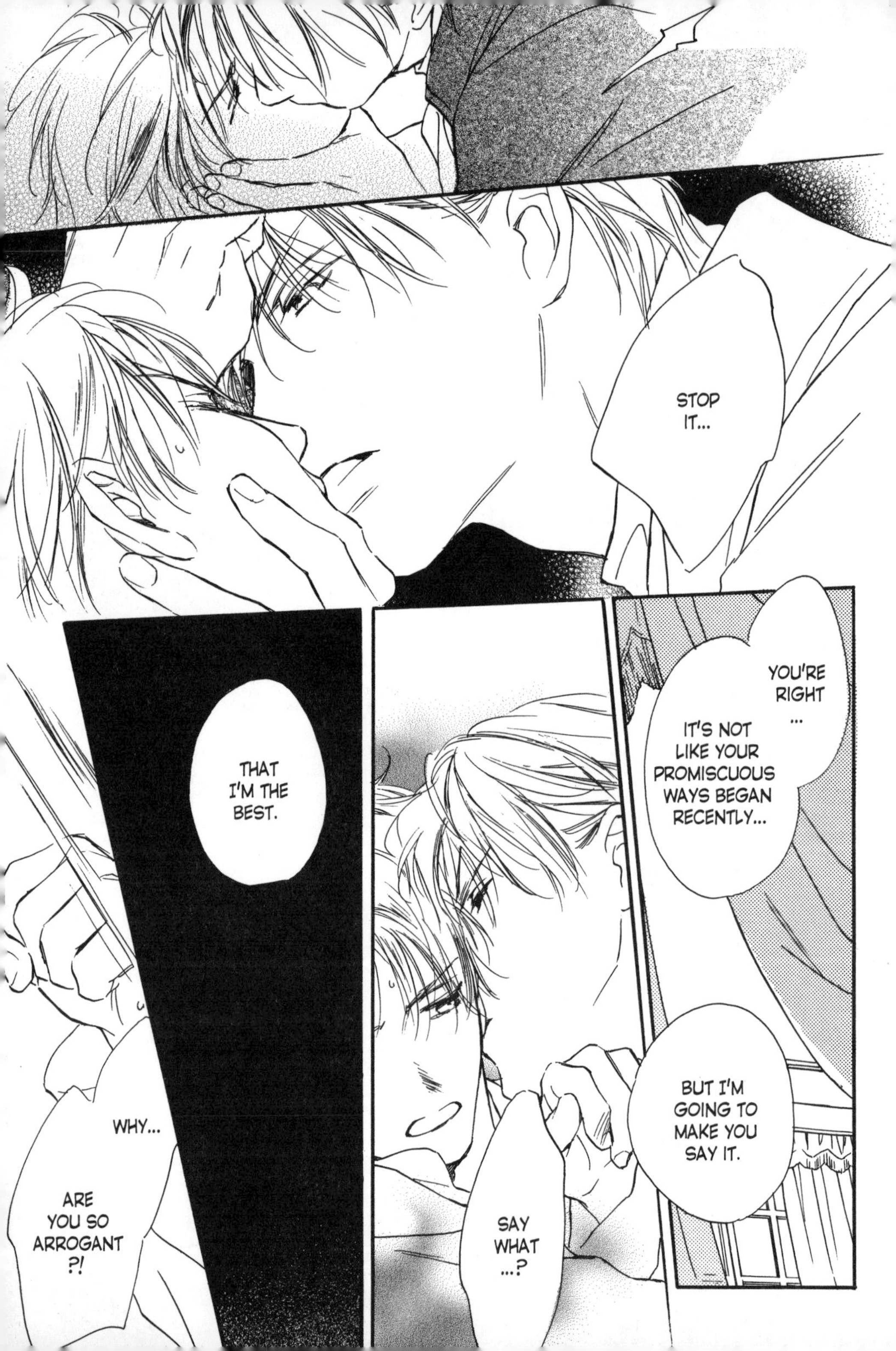
STOP IT...
YOU'RE RIGHT ...
IT'S NOT LIKE YOUR PROMISCUOUS WAYS BEGAN RECENTLY...
BUT I'M GOING TO MAKE YOU SAY IT.
SAY WHAT ...?
THAT I'M THE BEST.
WHY...
ARE YOU SO ARROGANT ?!

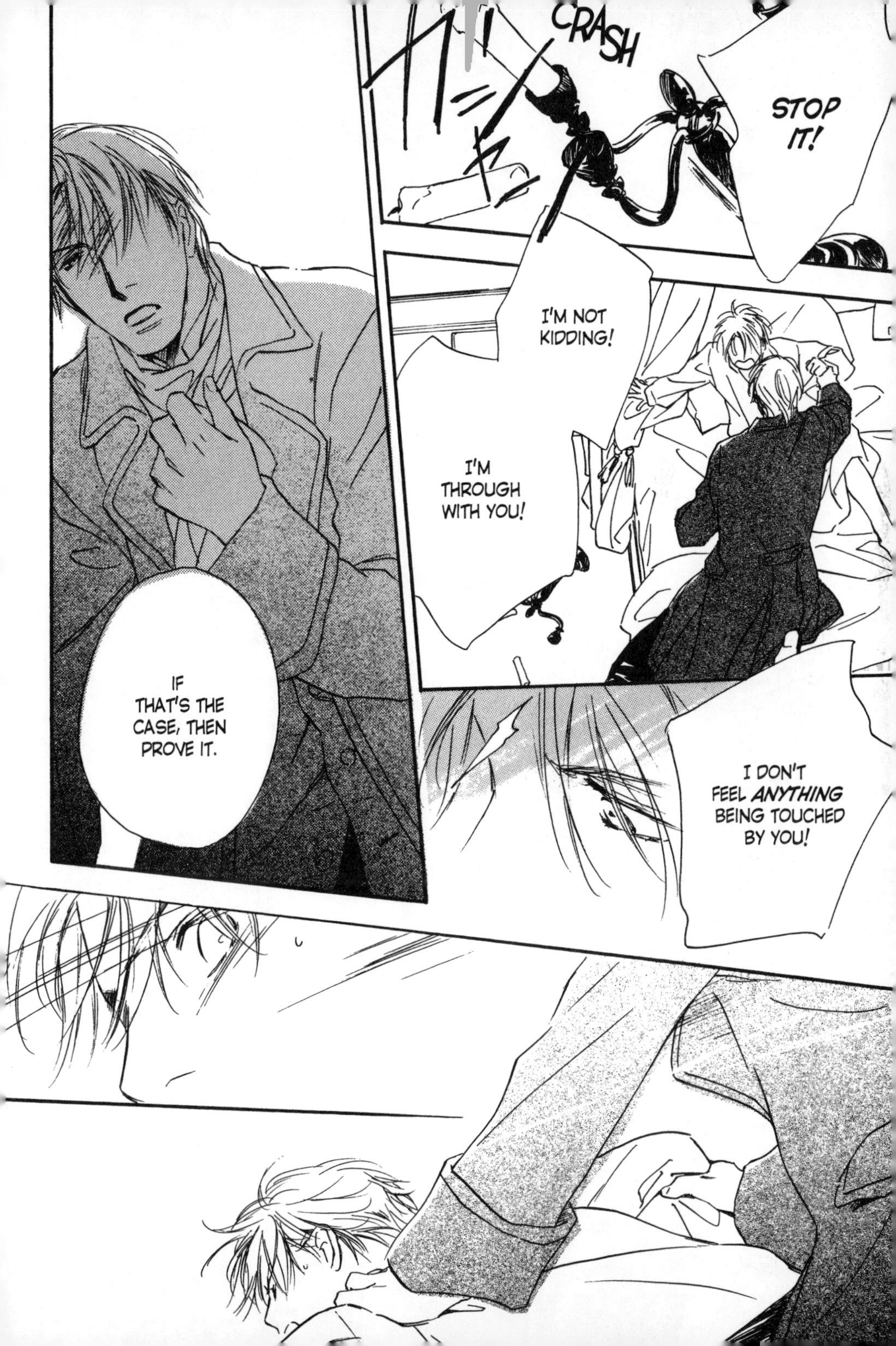
CRASH
STOP IT!
I'M NOT KIDDING!
I'M THROUGH WITH YOU!
I DON'T FEEL *ANYTHING* BEING TOUCHED BY YOU!
IF THAT'S THE CASE, THEN PROVE IT.

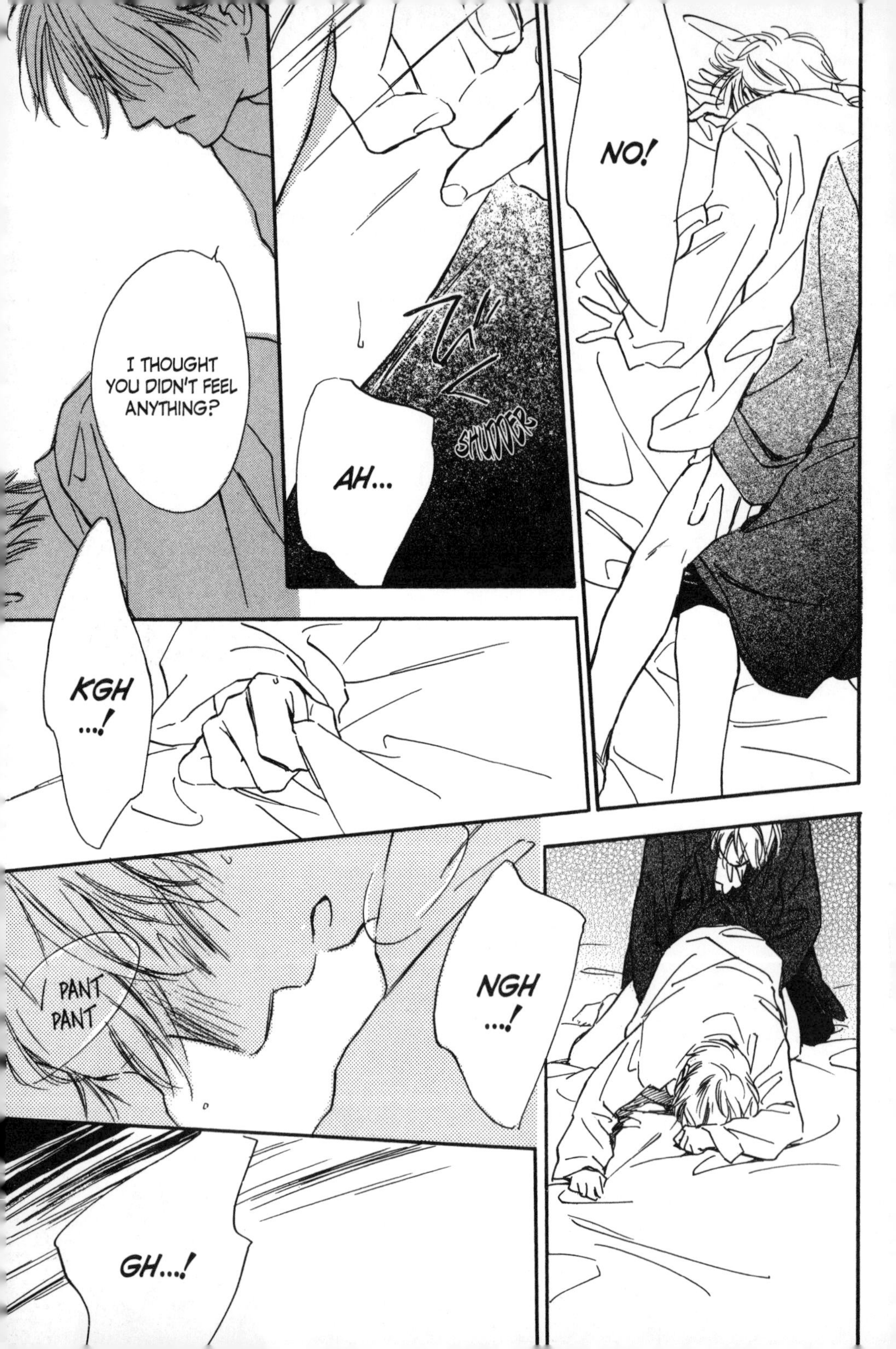
NO!
AH...
SHUDDER
I THOUGHT YOU DIDN'T FEEL ANYTHING?
KGH ...!
NGH ...!
PANT PANT
GH...!

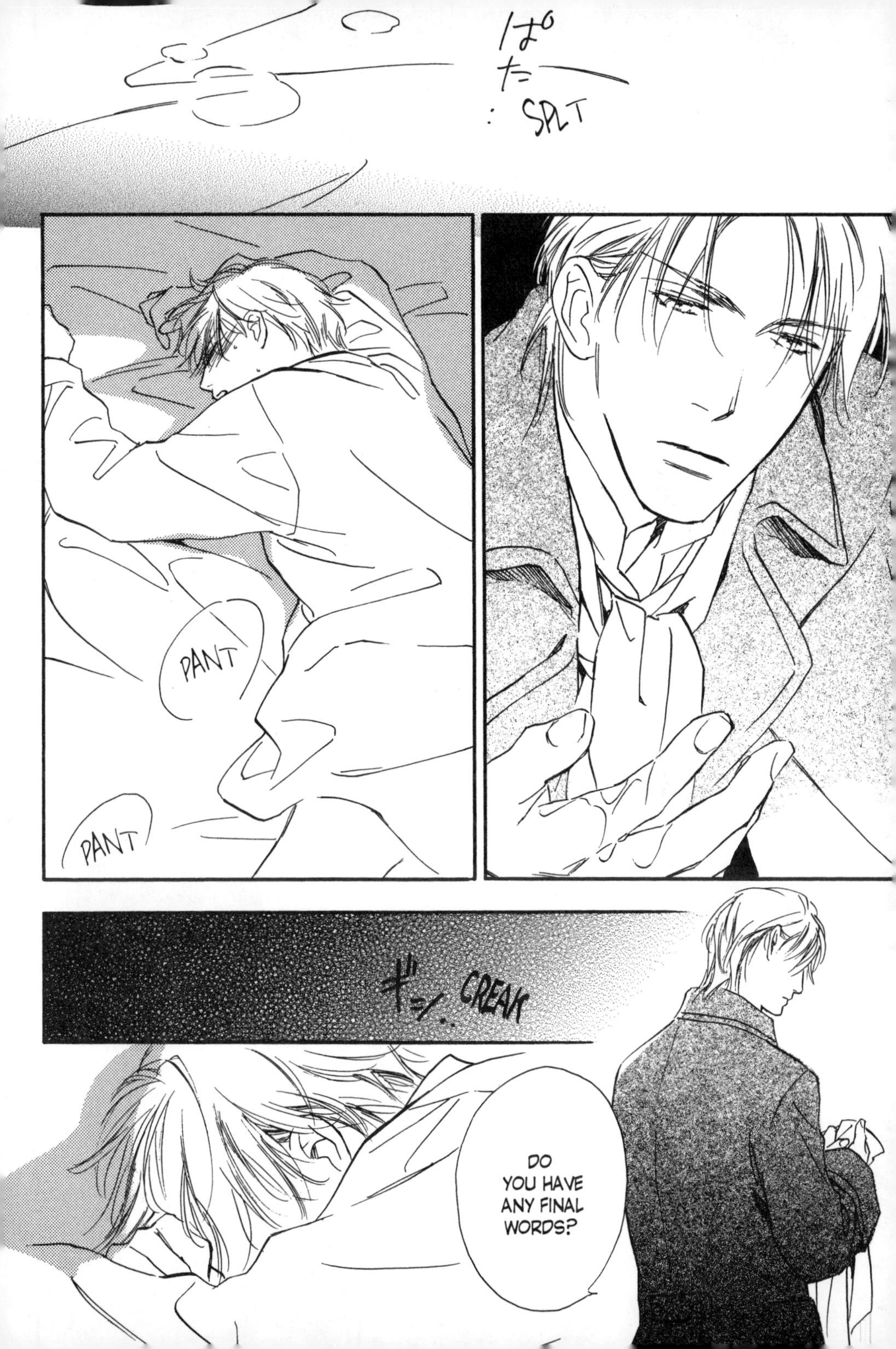
ぱた
: SPLT
PANT
PANT
ギィ.. CREAK
DO YOU HAVE ANY FINAL WORDS?

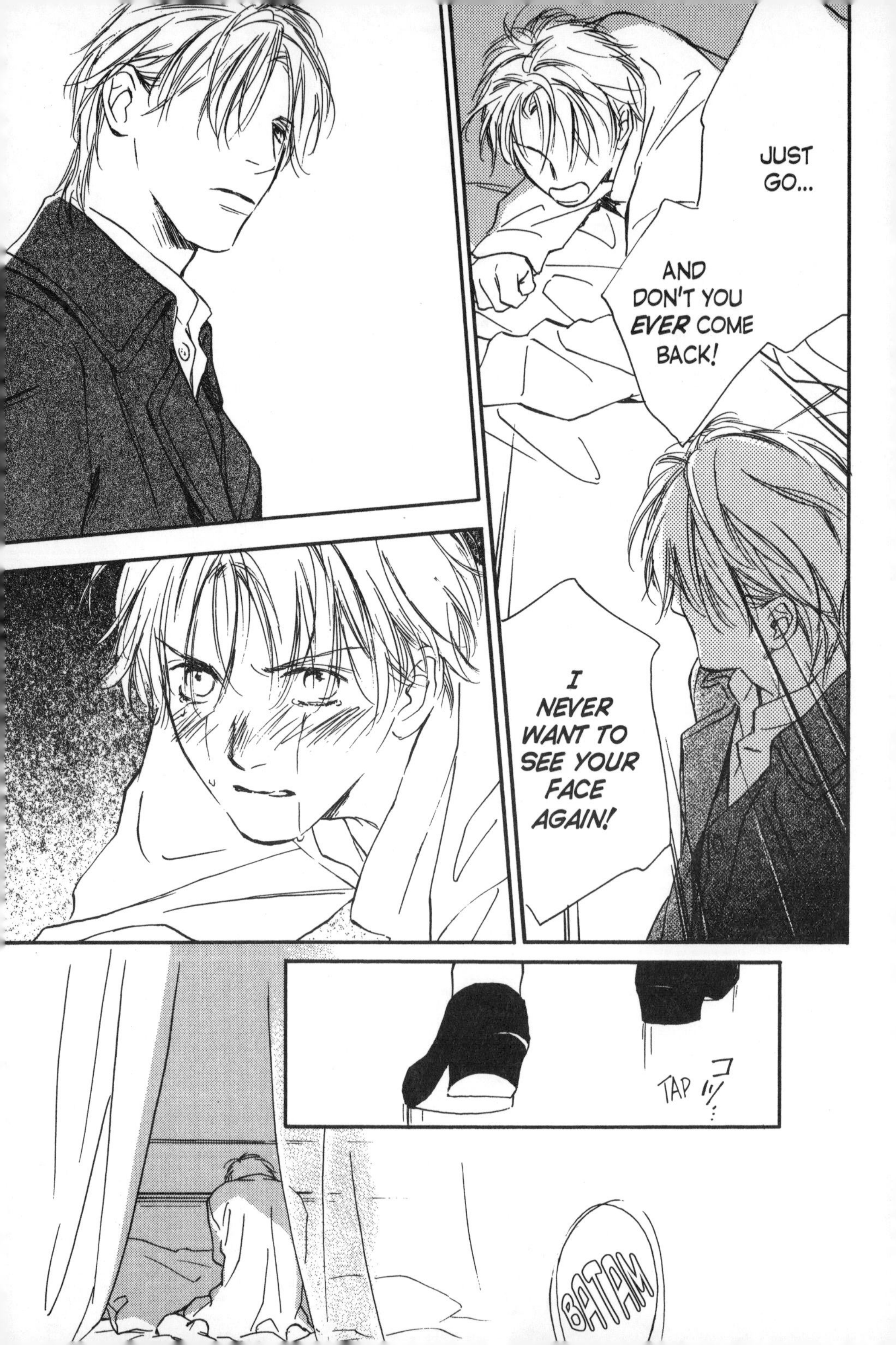
JUST GO...
AND DON'T YOU *EVER* COME BACK!
I NEVER WANT TO SEE YOUR FACE AGAIN!
TAP
BATAM

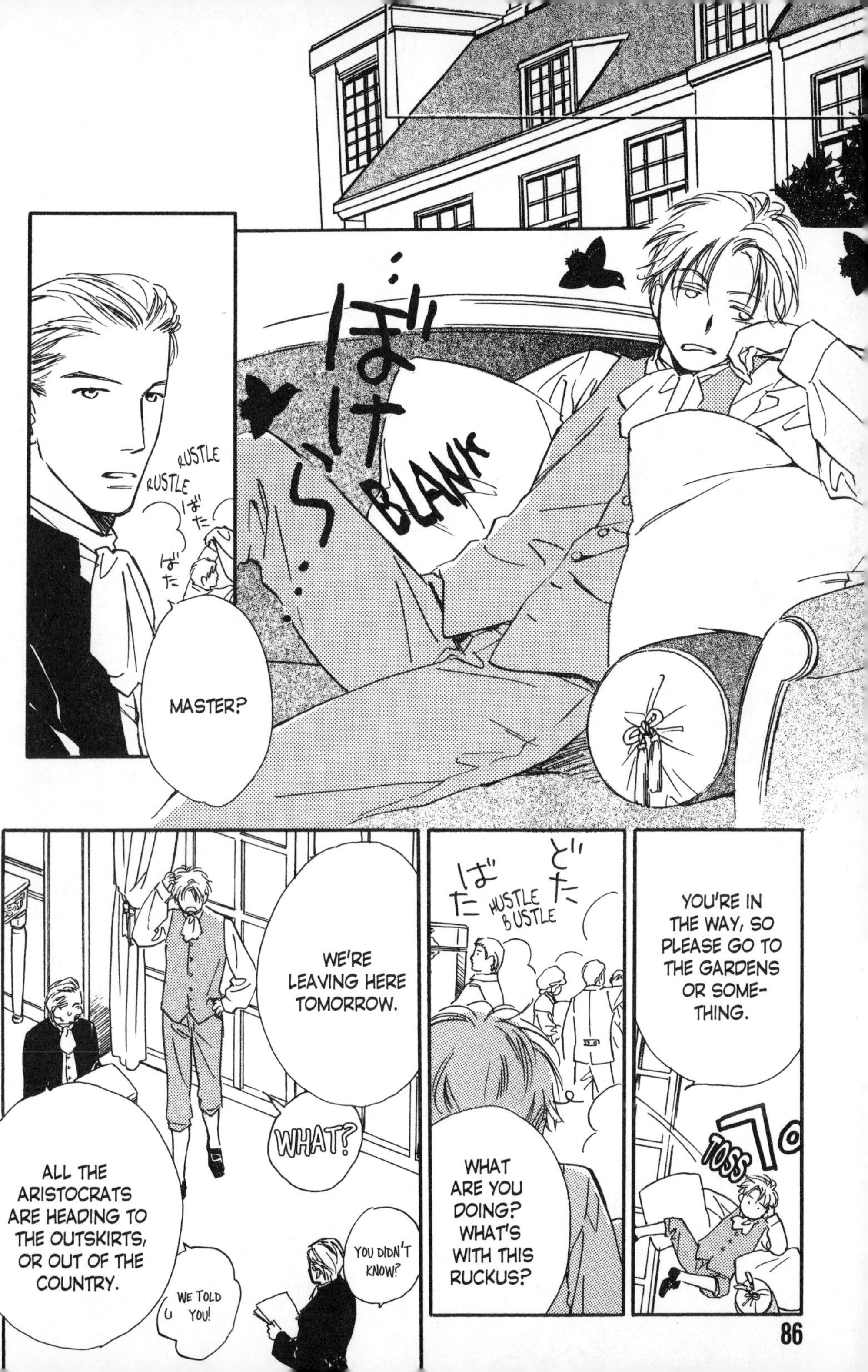
ぼけら
BLANK
RUSTLE
RUSTLE
ばた
ばた
MASTER?
YOU'RE IN THE WAY, SO PLEASE GO TO THE GARDENS OR SOME-THING.
TOSS
どた
ばた
HUSTLE BUSTLE
WHAT ARE YOU DOING? WHAT'S WITH THIS RUCKUS?
WE'RE LEAVING HERE TOMORROW.
WHAT?
ALL THE ARISTOCRATS ARE HEADING TO THE OUTSKIRTS, OR OUT OF THE COUNTRY.
YOU DIDN'T KNOW?
WE TOLD YOU!

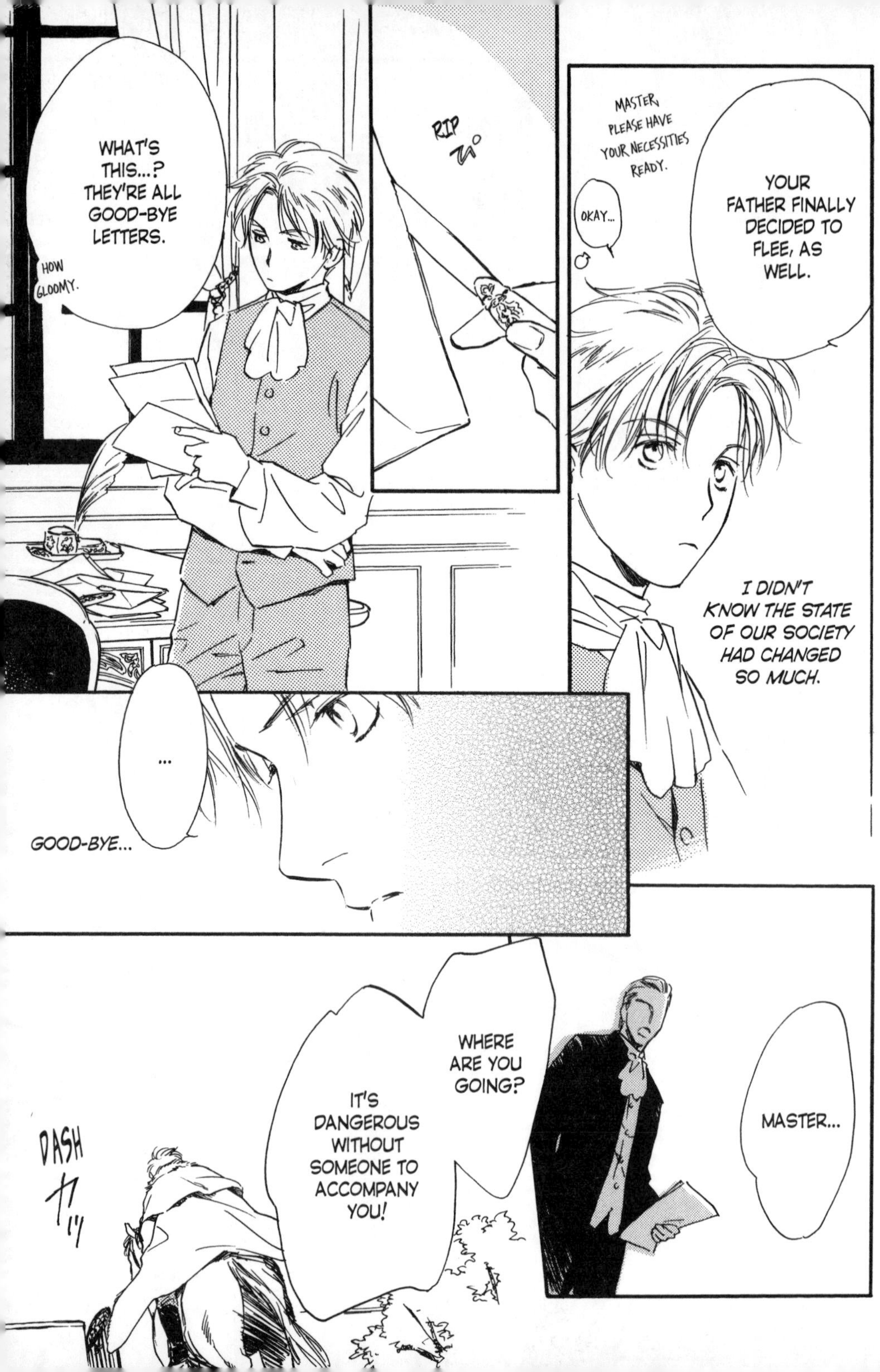
YOUR FATHER FINALLY DECIDED TO FLEE, AS WELL.
MASTER, PLEASE HAVE YOUR NECESSITIES READY.
OKAY...
I DIDN'T KNOW THE STATE OF OUR SOCIETY HAD CHANGED SO MUCH.
RIP
WHAT'S THIS...? THEY'RE ALL GOOD-BYE LETTERS.
HOW GLOOMY.
...
GOOD-BYE...
MASTER...
WHERE ARE YOU GOING?
IT'S DANGEROUS WITHOUT SOMEONE TO ACCOMPANY YOU!
DASH

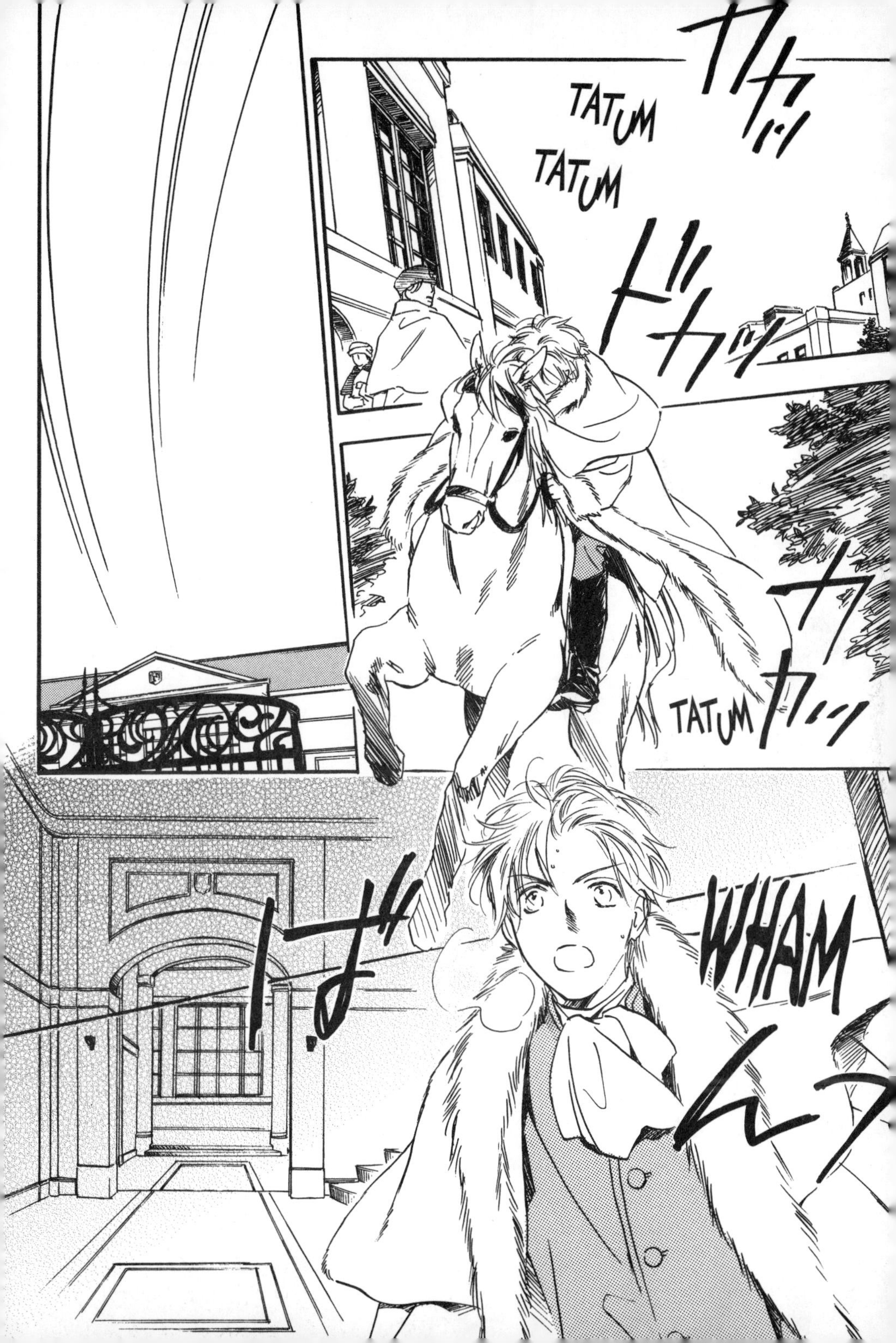
カカッ
TATUM TATUM
ドカッ
カカッ
TATUM
WHAM
ば

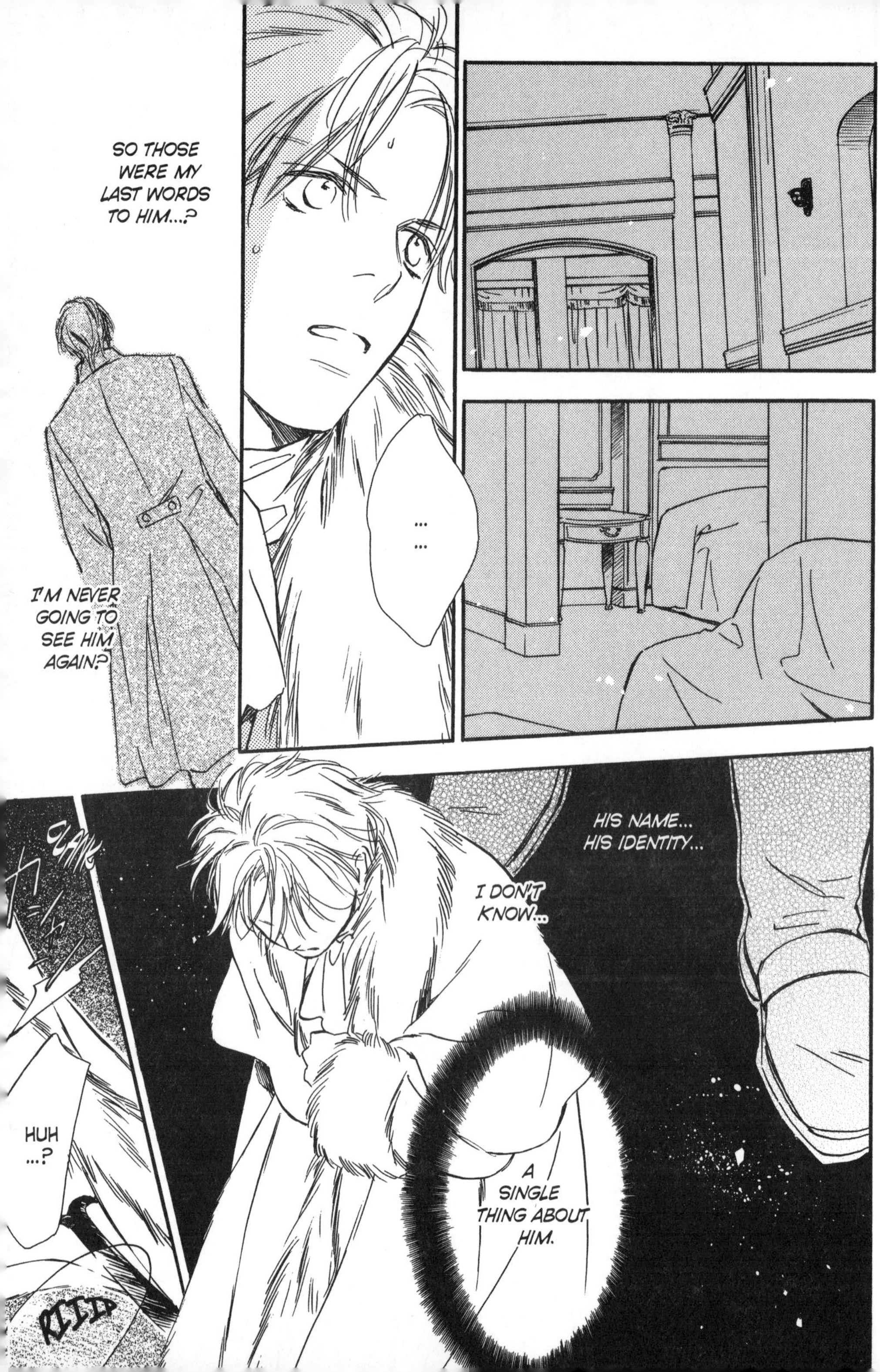
SO THOSE WERE MY LAST WORDS TO HIM...?
...
...
I'M NEVER GOING TO SEE HIM AGAIN?
HIS NAME... HIS IDENTITY...
I DON'T KNOW...
A SINGLE THING ABOUT HIM.
CLANK
HUH ...?
RIIP

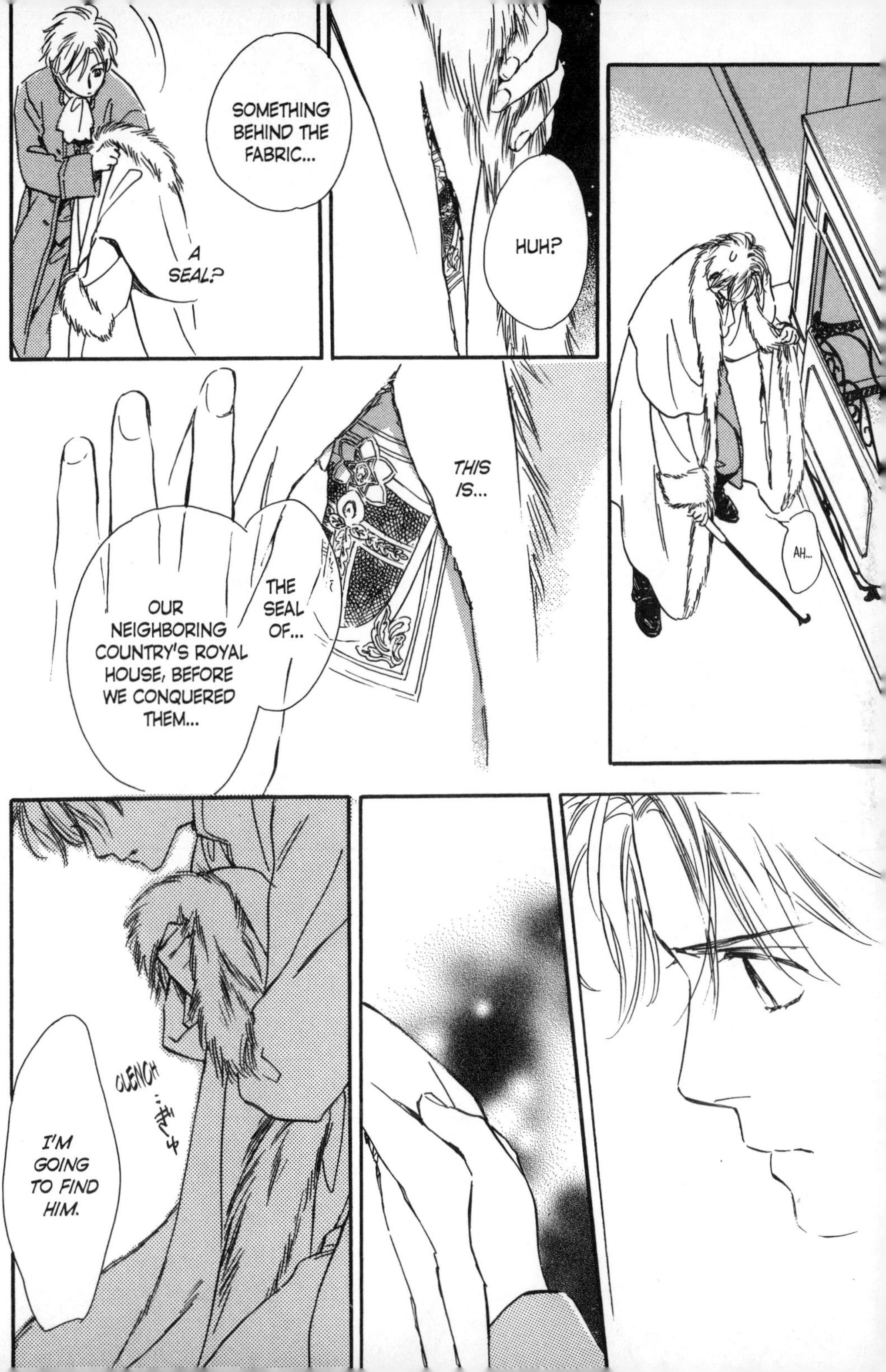
AH...
HUH?
SOMETHING BEHIND THE FABRIC...
A SEAL?
THIS IS...
THE SEAL OF...
OUR NEIGHBORING COUNTRY'S ROYAL HOUSE, BEFORE WE CONQUERED THEM...
CLENCH
I'M GOING TO FIND HIM.

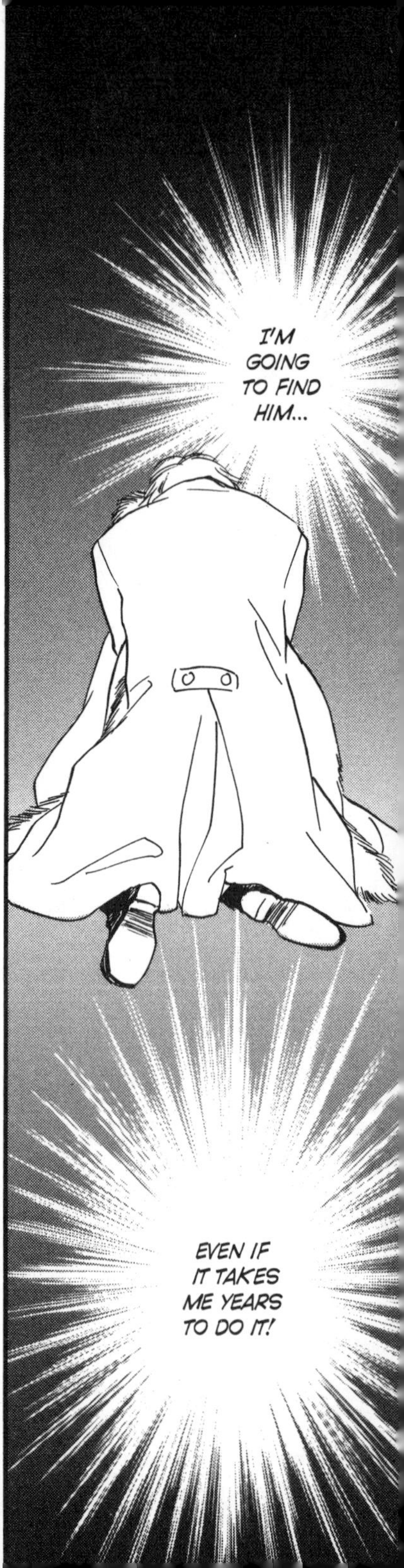
I'M GOING TO FIND HIM...
EVEN IF IT TAKES ME YEARS TO DO IT!
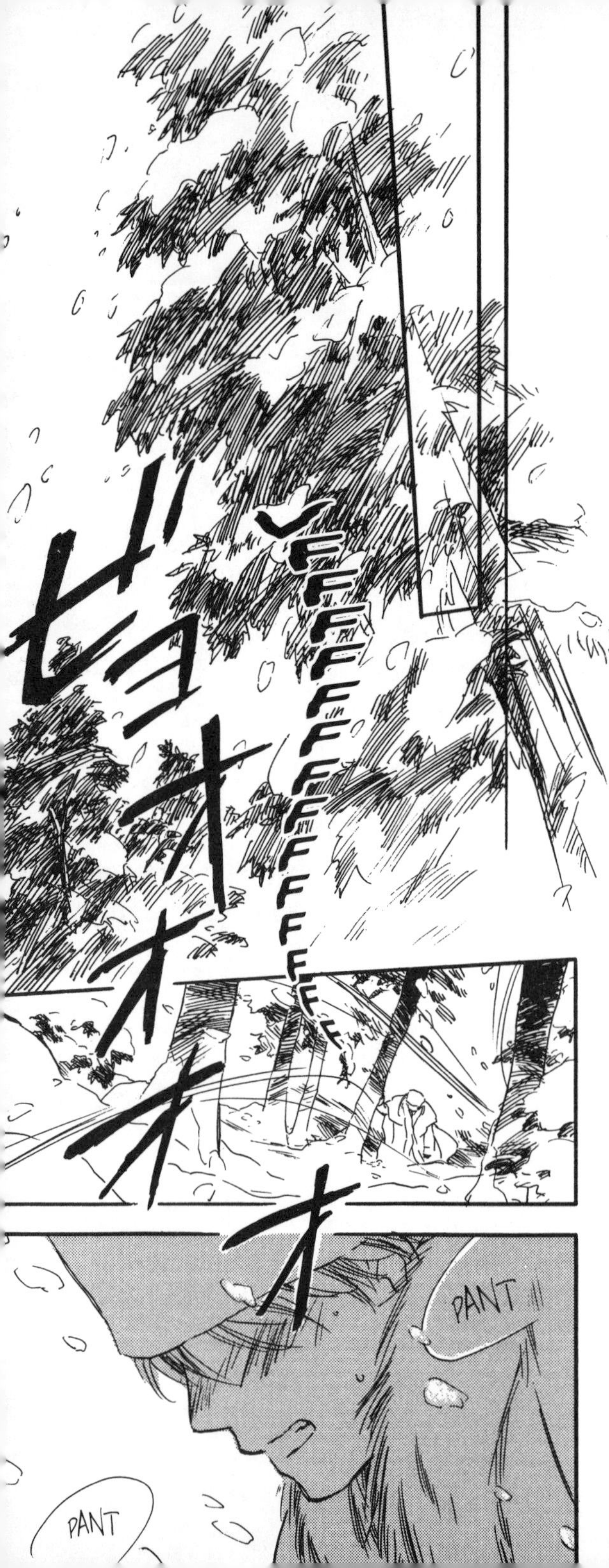
ビョオオオオ
VFFFFFFFFFFFFFF
PANT
PANT

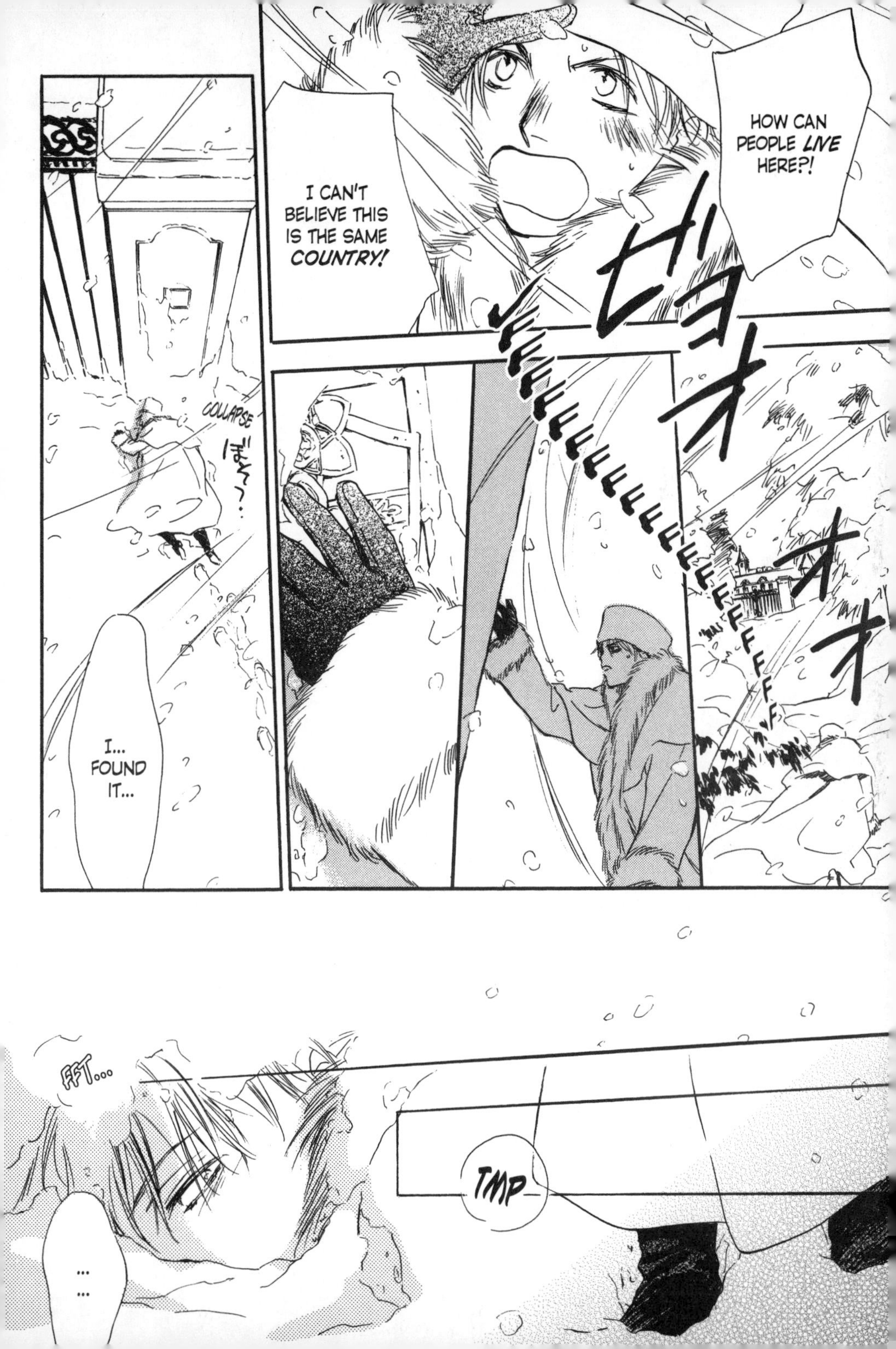

HOW CAN PEOPLE LIVE HERE?!
I CAN'T BELIEVE THIS IS THE SAME COUNTRY!
FFFFFFFFFFFFFFFFFF
COLLAPSE
ぼてっ
I... FOUND IT...
TMP
FFT...
...
...

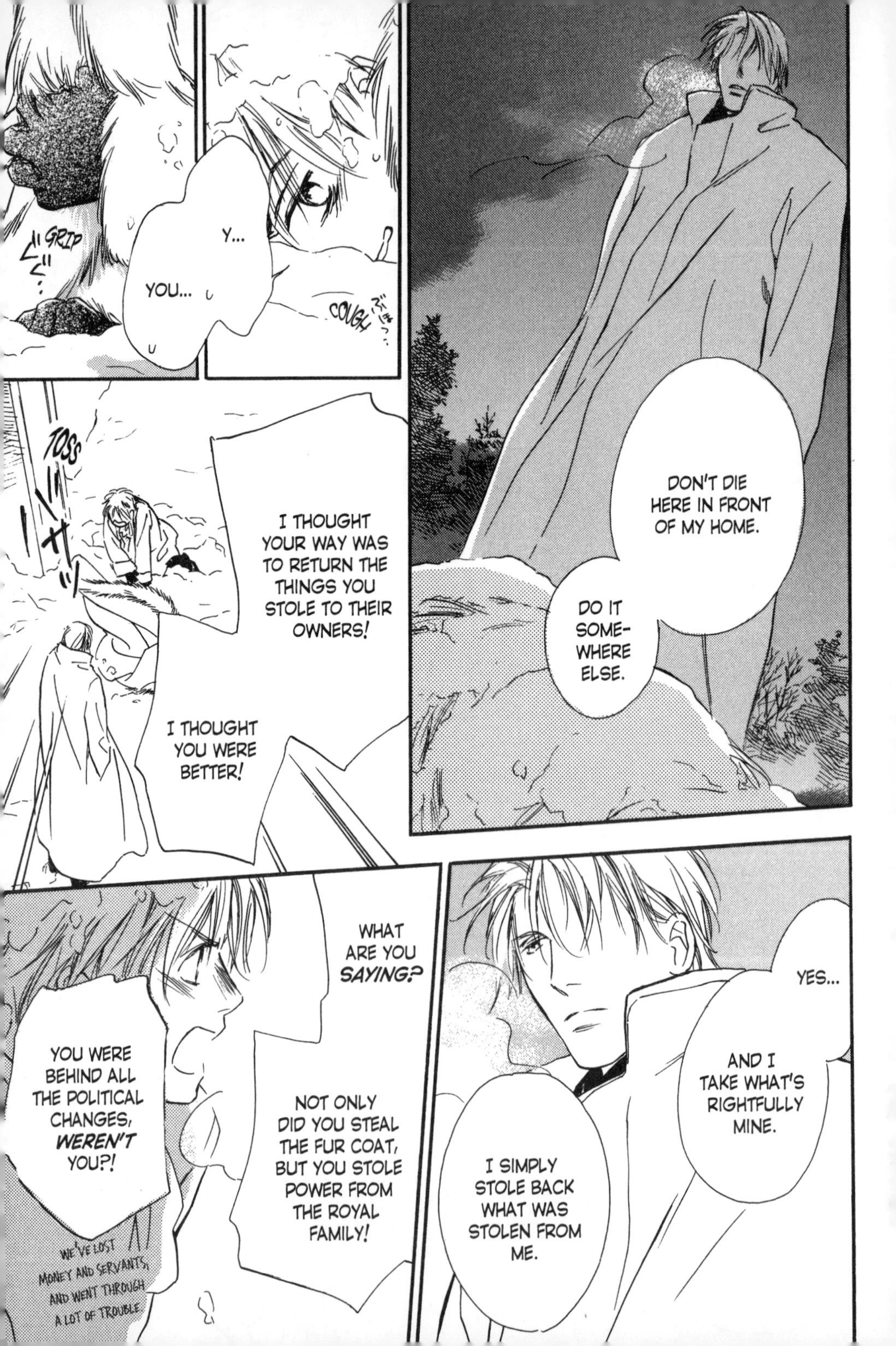
DON'T DIE HERE IN FRONT OF MY HOME.
DO IT SOME-WHERE ELSE.
Y...
YOU...
COUGH
GRIP
TOSS
I THOUGHT YOUR WAY WAS TO RETURN THE THINGS YOU STOLE TO THEIR OWNERS!
I THOUGHT YOU WERE BETTER!
YES...
AND I TAKE WHAT'S RIGHTFULLY MINE.
I SIMPLY STOLE BACK WHAT WAS STOLEN FROM ME.
WHAT ARE YOU *SAYING?*
NOT ONLY DID YOU STEAL THE FUR COAT, BUT YOU STOLE POWER FROM THE ROYAL FAMILY!
YOU WERE BEHIND ALL THE POLITICAL CHANGES, ***WEREN'T*** YOU?!
WE'VE LOST MONEY AND SERVANTS, AND WENT THROUGH A LOT OF TROUBLE.

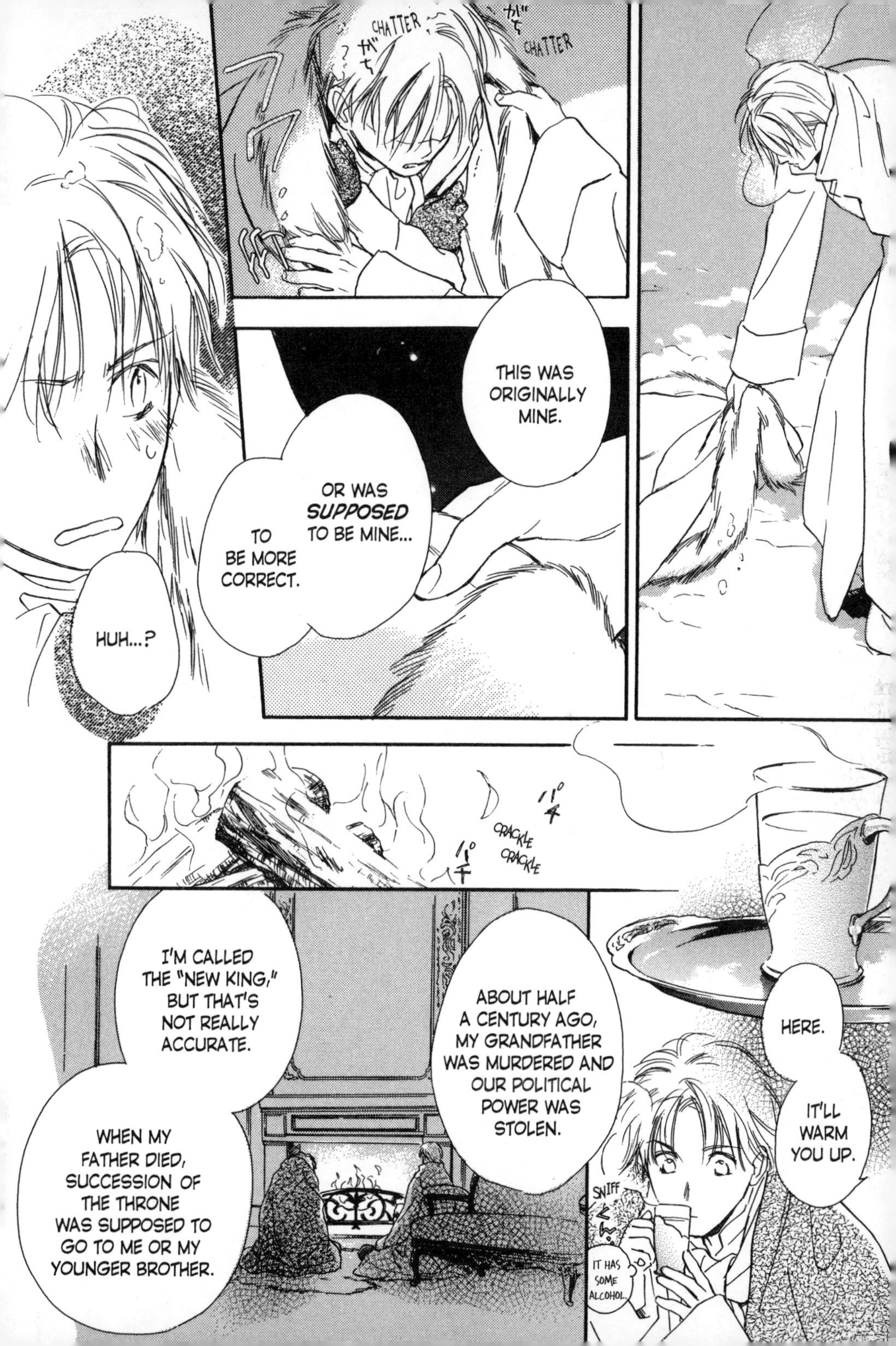
CHATTER
CHATTER
THIS WAS ORIGINALLY MINE.
OR WAS *SUPPOSED* TO BE MINE...
TO BE MORE CORRECT.
HUH...?
—
CRACKLE
CRACKLE
HERE.
IT'LL WARM YOU UP.
SNIFF
IT HAS SOME ALCOHOL.
ABOUT HALF A CENTURY AGO, MY GRANDFATHER WAS MURDERED AND OUR POLITICAL POWER WAS STOLEN.
I'M CALLED THE "NEW KING," BUT THAT'S NOT REALLY ACCURATE.
WHEN MY FATHER DIED, SUCCESSION OF THE THRONE WAS SUPPOSED TO GO TO ME OR MY YOUNGER BROTHER.

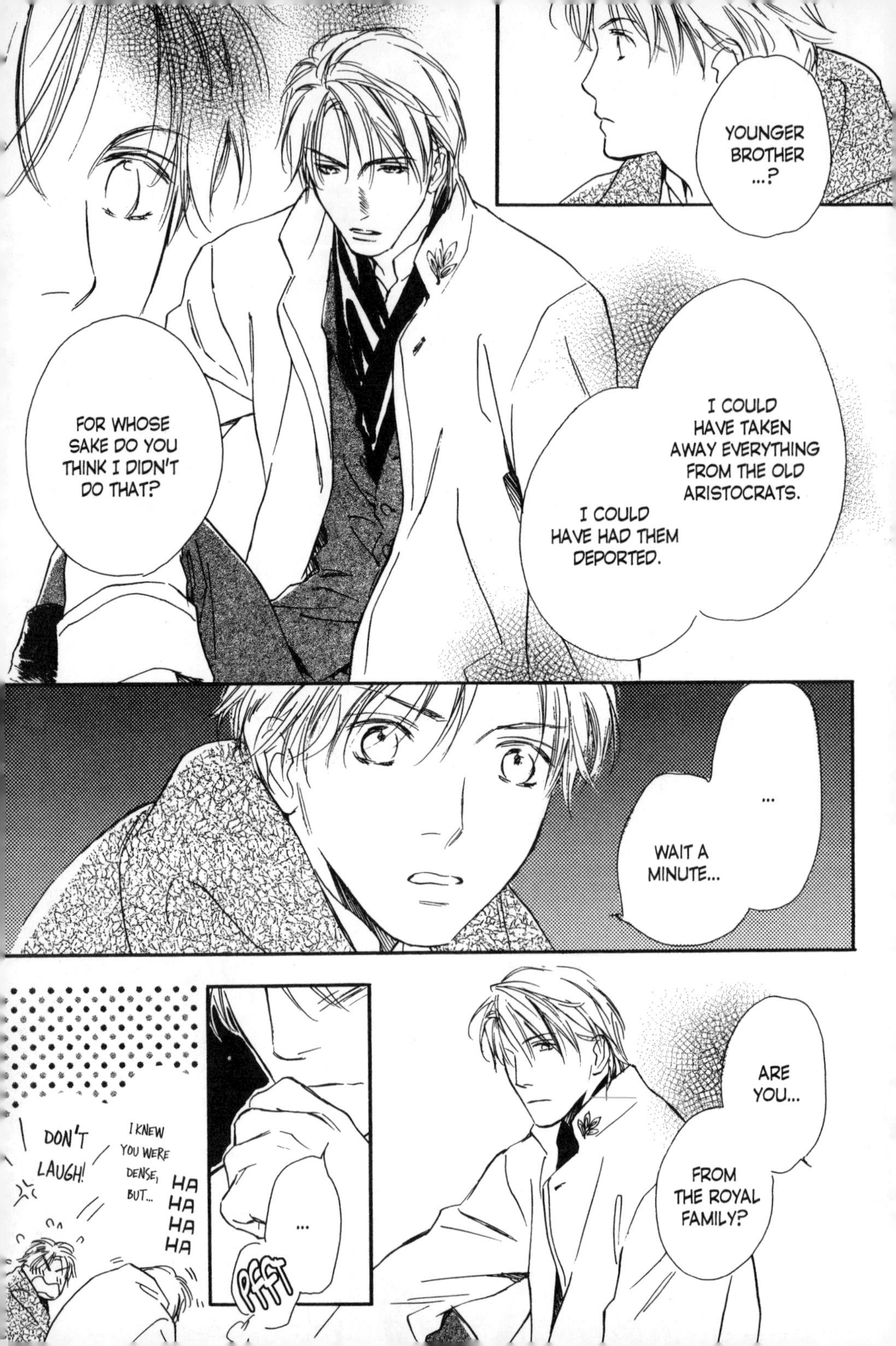
YOUNGER BROTHER ...?
I COULD HAVE TAKEN AWAY EVERYTHING FROM THE OLD ARISTOCRATS.
I COULD HAVE HAD THEM DEPORTED.
FOR WHOSE SAKE DO YOU THINK I DIDN'T DO THAT?
...
WAIT A MINUTE...
ARE YOU...
FROM THE ROYAL FAMILY?
...
PFFT
HA HA HA HA
I KNEW YOU WERE DENSE, BUT...
DON'T LAUGH!

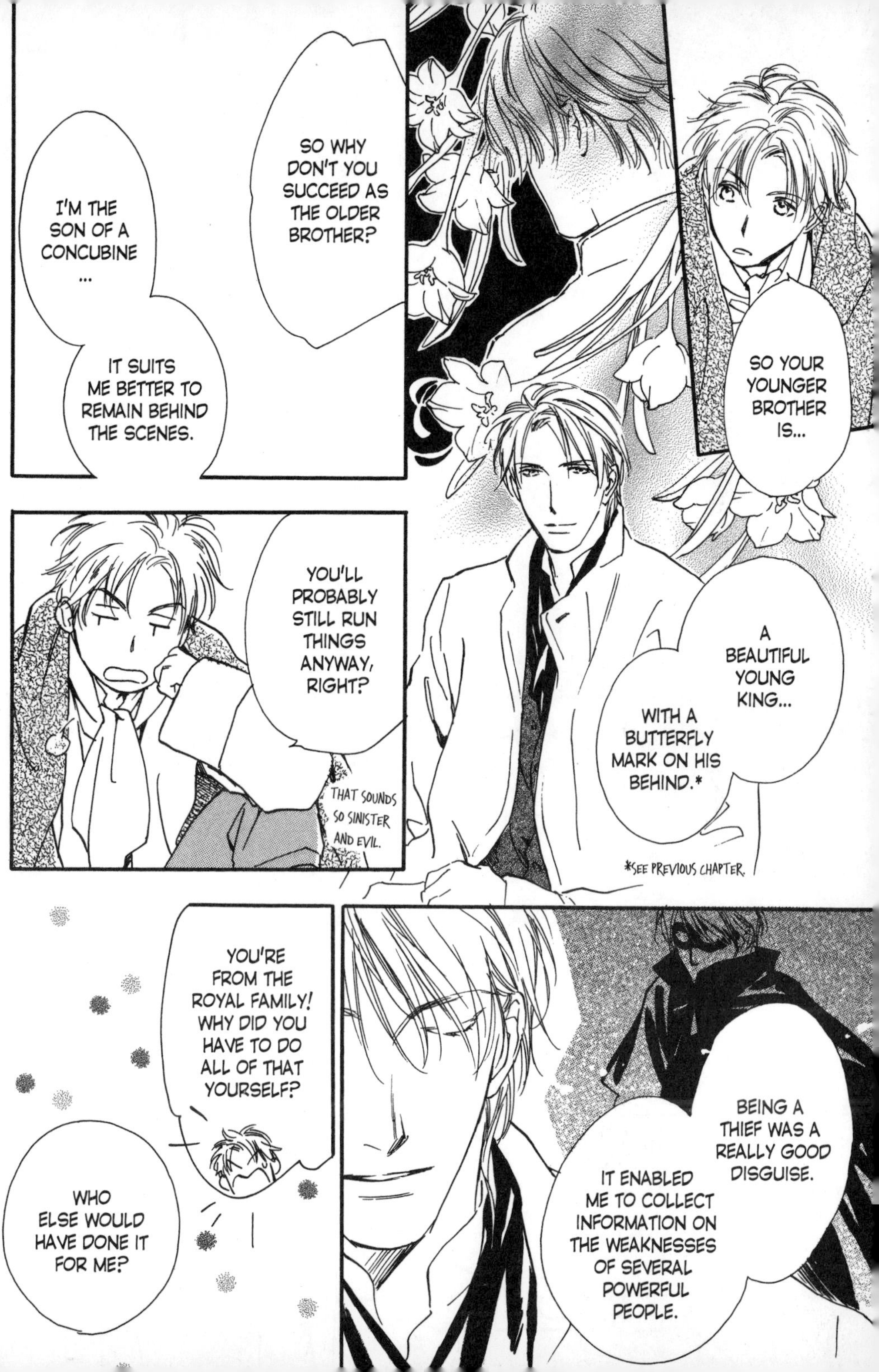
SO YOUR YOUNGER BROTHER IS...
A BEAUTIFUL YOUNG KING...
WITH A BUTTERFLY MARK ON HIS BEHIND.*
*SEE PREVIOUS CHAPTER.
SO WHY DON'T YOU SUCCEED AS THE OLDER BROTHER?
I'M THE SON OF A CONCUBINE ...
IT SUITS ME BETTER TO REMAIN BEHIND THE SCENES.
YOU'LL PROBABLY STILL RUN THINGS ANYWAY, RIGHT?
THAT SOUNDS SO SINISTER AND EVIL.
BEING A THIEF WAS A REALLY GOOD DISGUISE.
IT ENABLED ME TO COLLECT INFORMATION ON THE WEAKNESSES OF SEVERAL POWERFUL PEOPLE.
YOU'RE FROM THE ROYAL FAMILY! WHY DID YOU HAVE TO DO ALL OF THAT YOURSELF?
WHO ELSE WOULD HAVE DONE IT FOR ME?

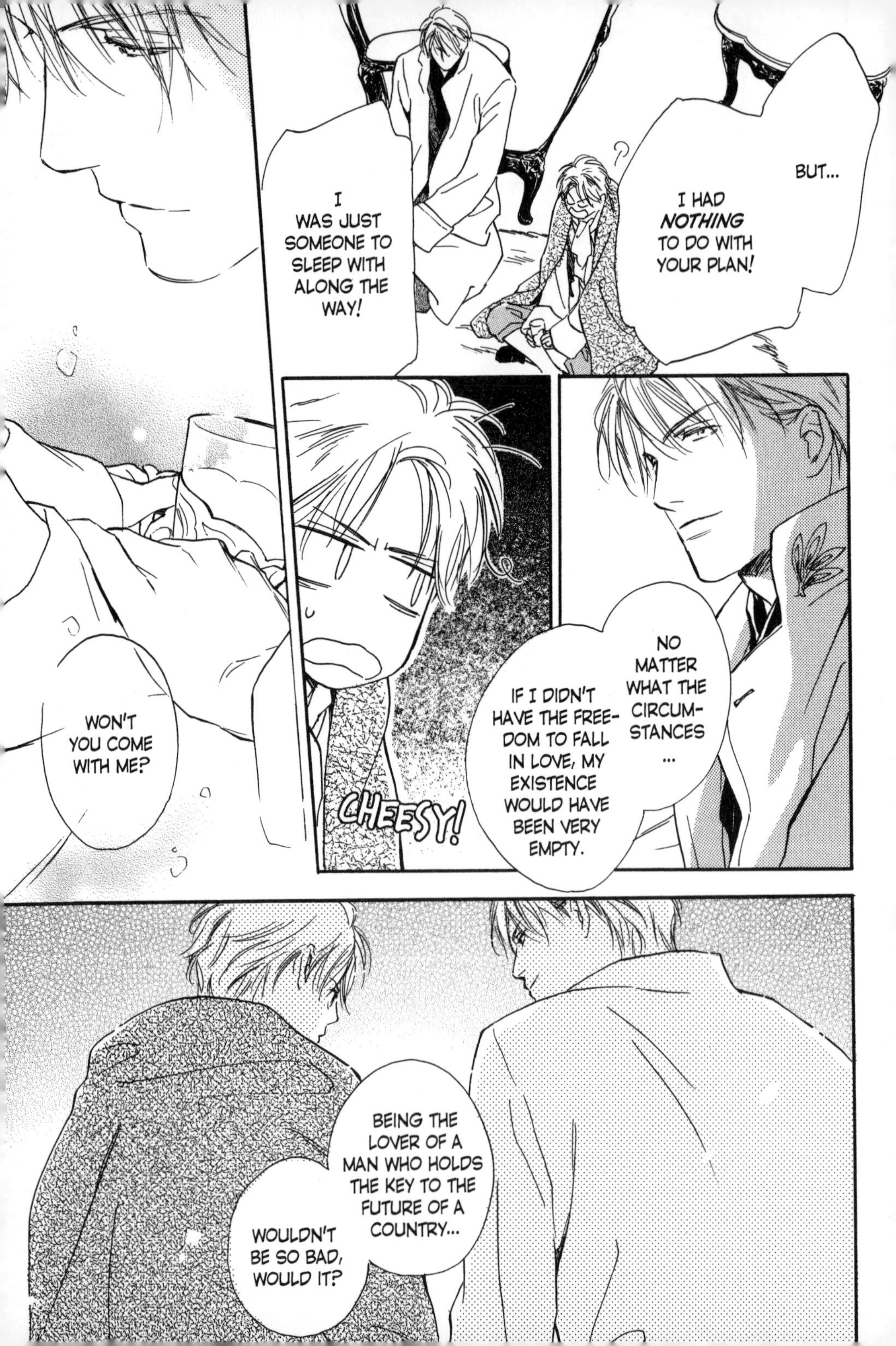
BUT...
I HAD *NOTHING* TO DO WITH YOUR PLAN!
I WAS JUST SOMEONE TO SLEEP WITH ALONG THE WAY!
NO MATTER WHAT THE CIRCUMSTANCES...
IF I DIDN'T HAVE THE FREEDOM TO FALL IN LOVE, MY EXISTENCE WOULD HAVE BEEN VERY EMPTY.
CHEESY!
WON'T YOU COME WITH ME?
BEING THE LOVER OF A MAN WHO HOLDS THE KEY TO THE FUTURE OF A COUNTRY...
WOULDN'T BE SO BAD, WOULD IT?

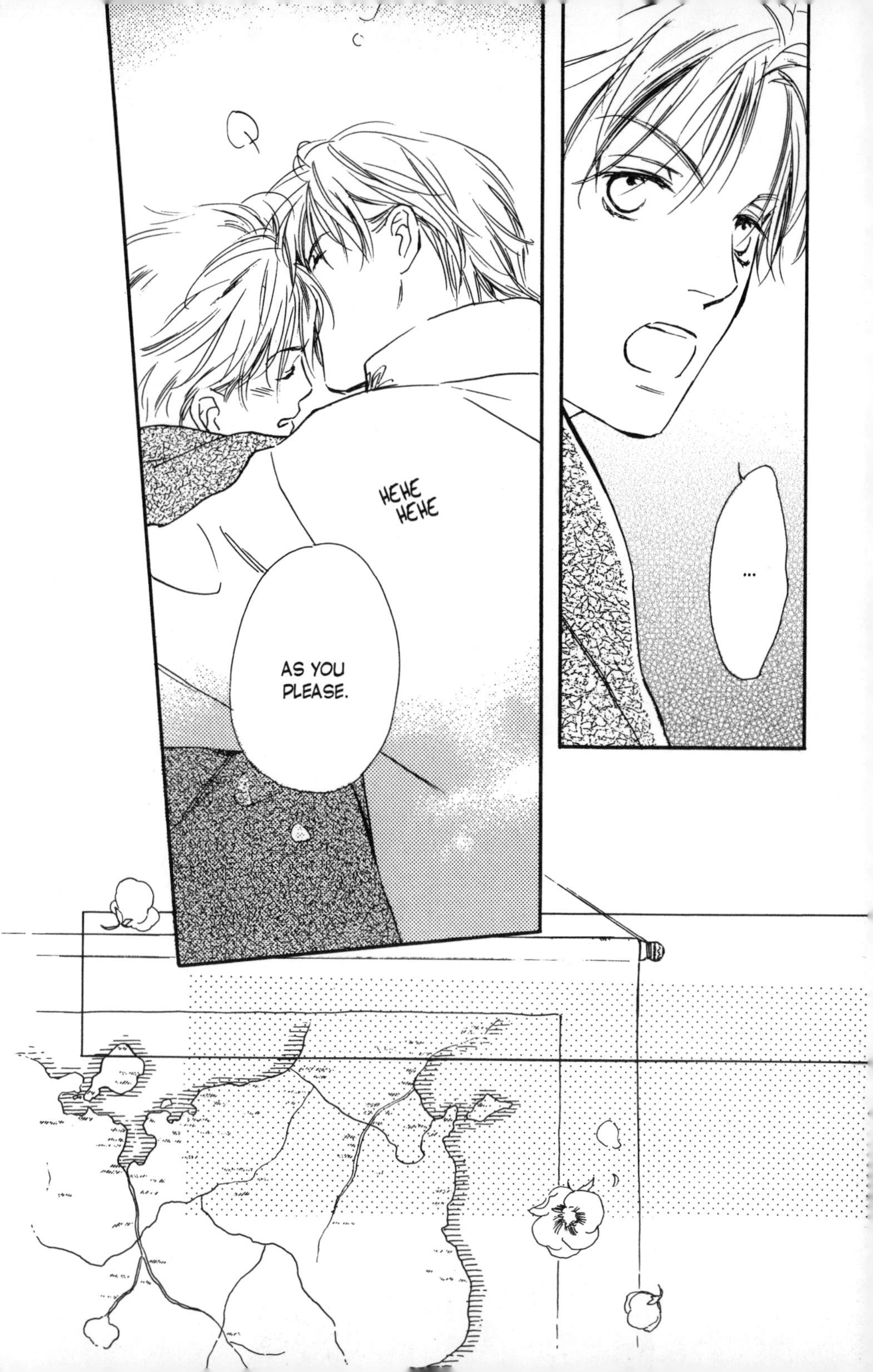
...
HEHE HEHE
AS YOU PLEASE.

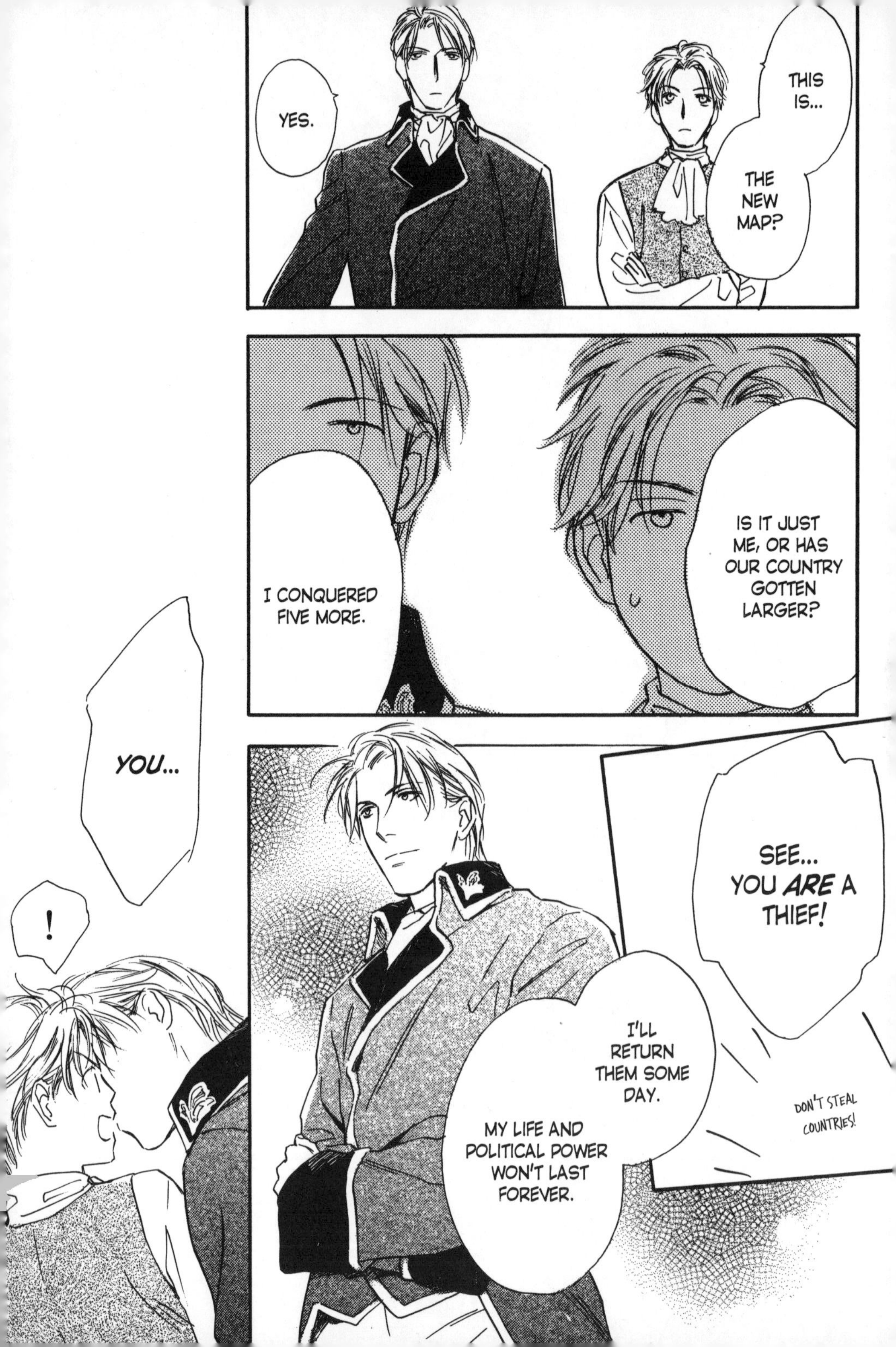
THIS IS...
THE NEW MAP?
YES.
IS IT JUST ME, OR HAS OUR COUNTRY GOTTEN LARGER?
I CONQUERED FIVE MORE.
SEE... YOU *ARE* A THIEF!
DON'T STEAL COUNTRIES!
I'LL RETURN THEM SOME DAY.
MY LIFE AND POLITICAL POWER WON'T LAST FOREVER.
YOU...
!

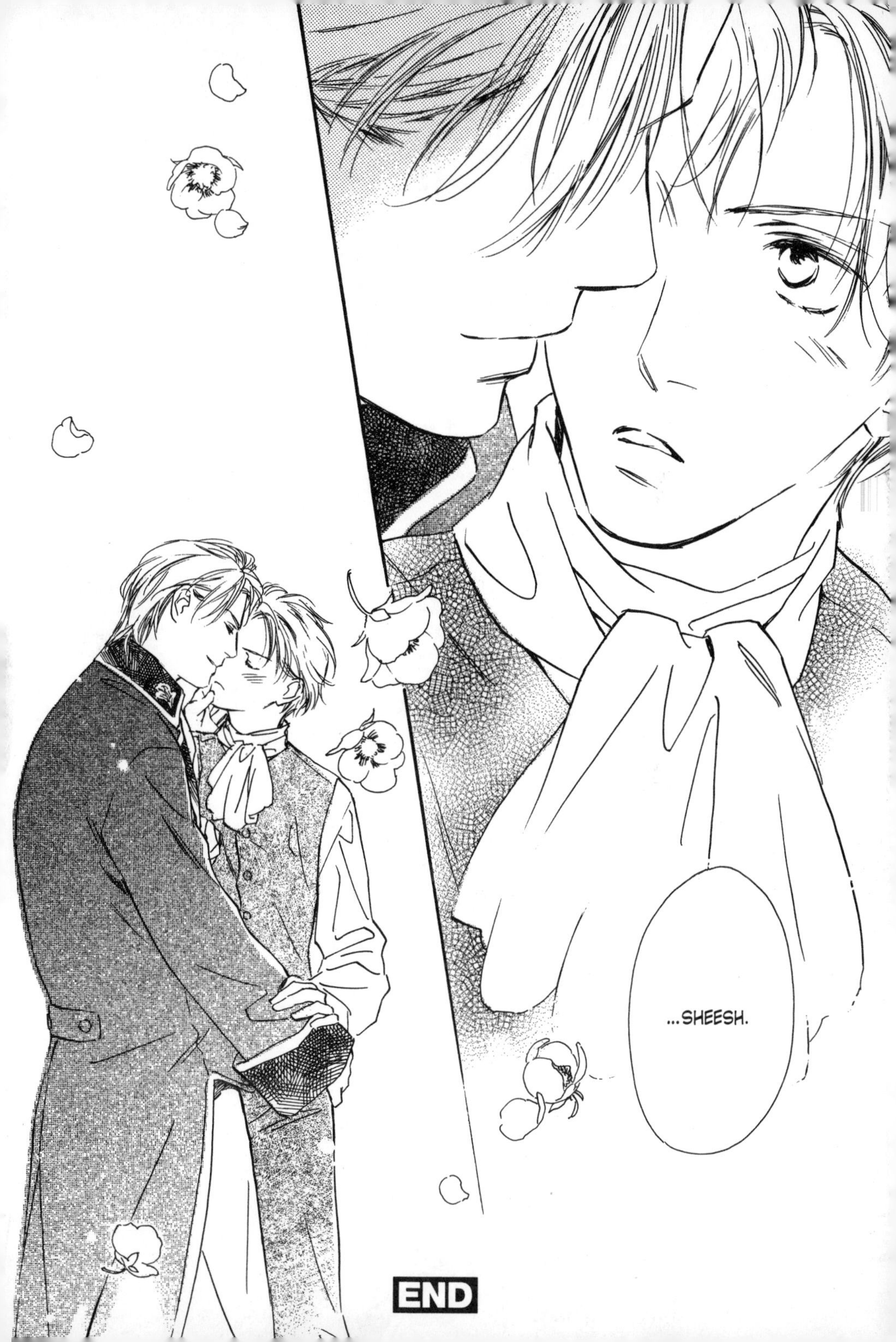
...SHEESH.
END

be nice

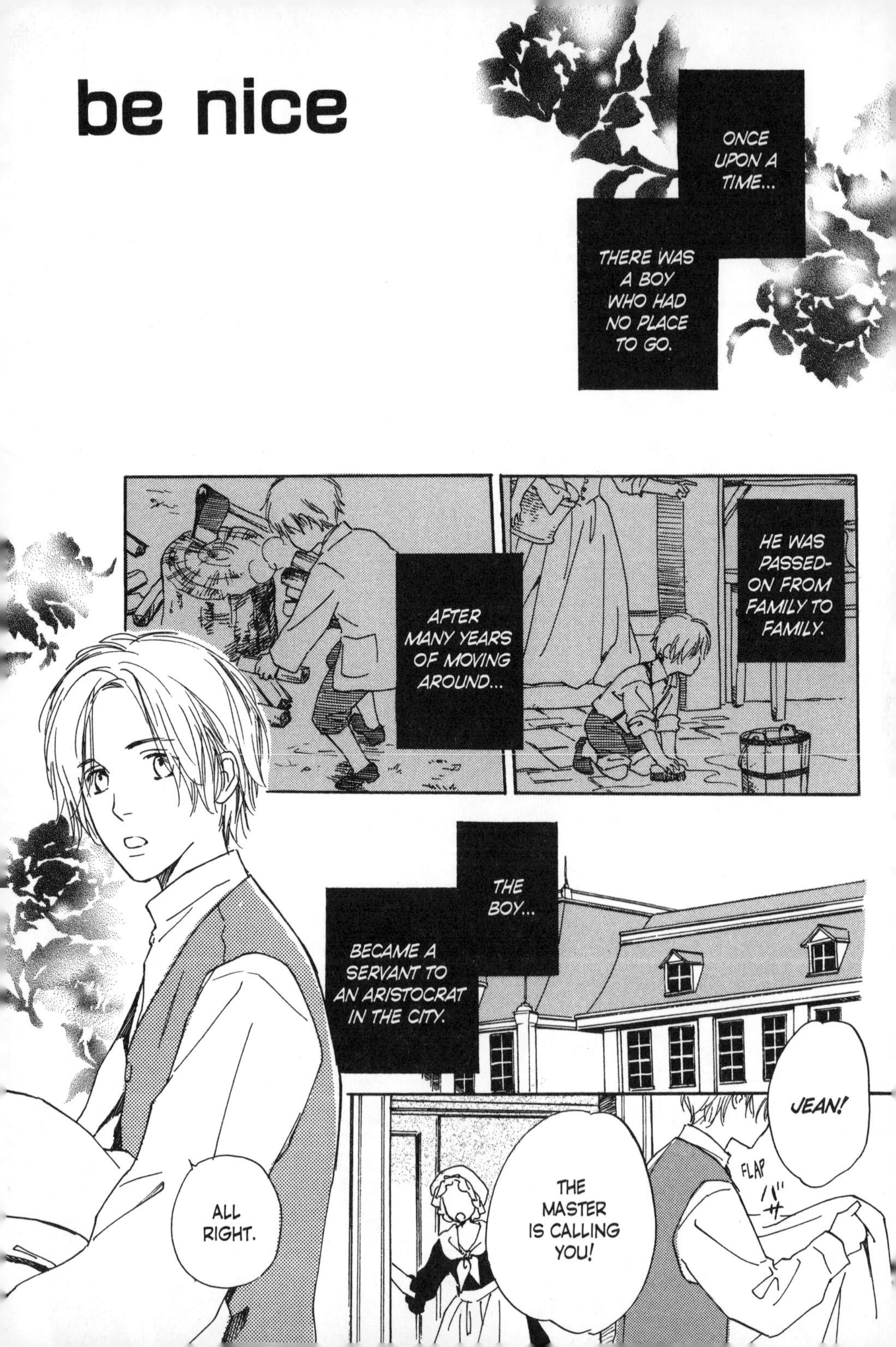
ONCE UPON A TIME...
THERE WAS A BOY WHO HAD NO PLACE TO GO.
HE WAS PASSED-ON FROM FAMILY TO FAMILY.
AFTER MANY YEARS OF MOVING AROUND...
THE BOY...
BECAME A SERVANT TO AN ARISTOCRAT IN THE CITY.
JEAN!
FLAP
THE MASTER IS CALLING YOU!
ALL RIGHT.

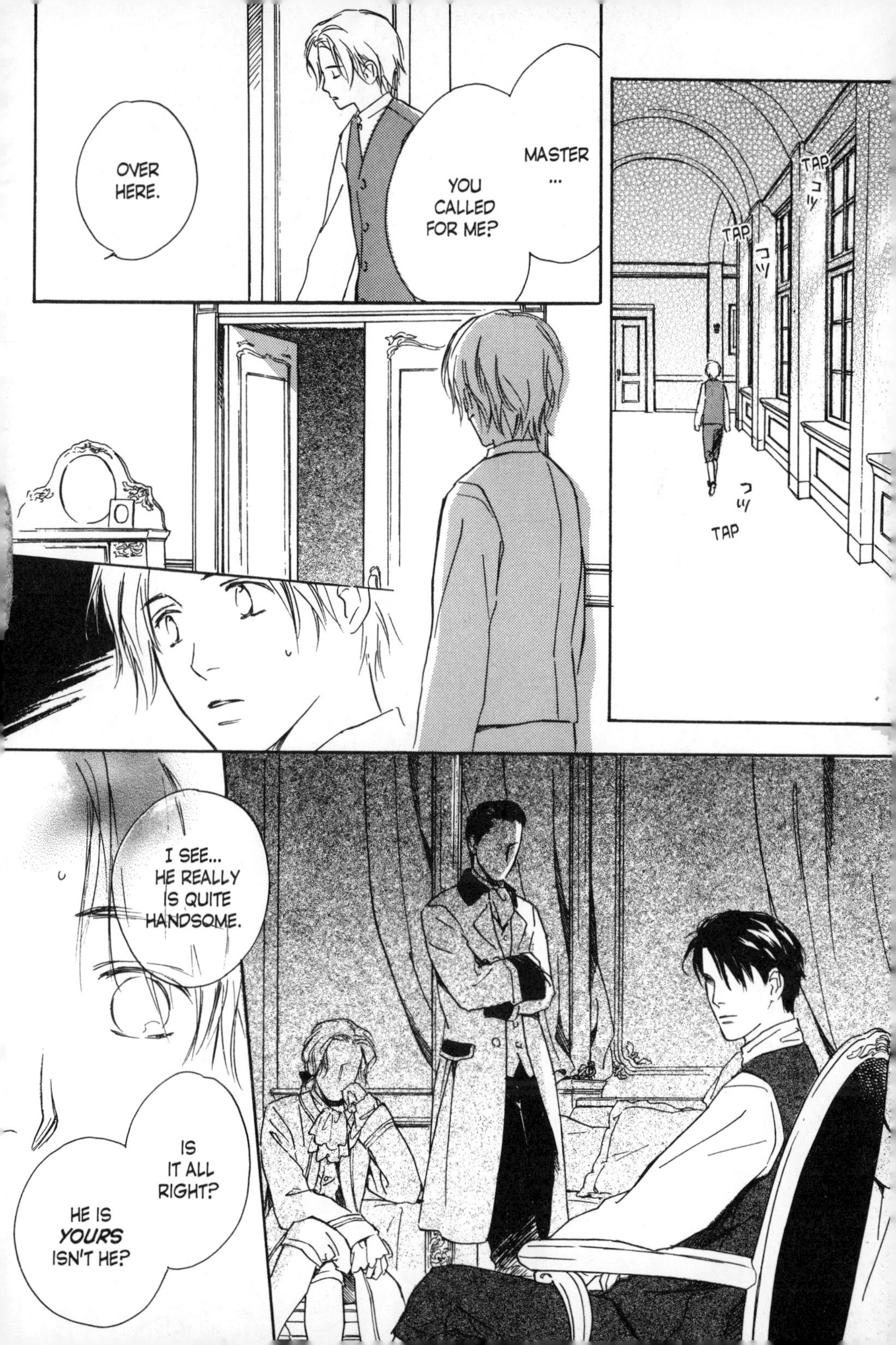
TAP
コツ
TAP
コツ
コツ
TAP
MASTER ...
YOU CALLED FOR ME?
OVER HERE.
I SEE... HE REALLY IS QUITE HANDSOME.
IS IT ALL RIGHT?
HE IS *YOURS* ISN'T HE?

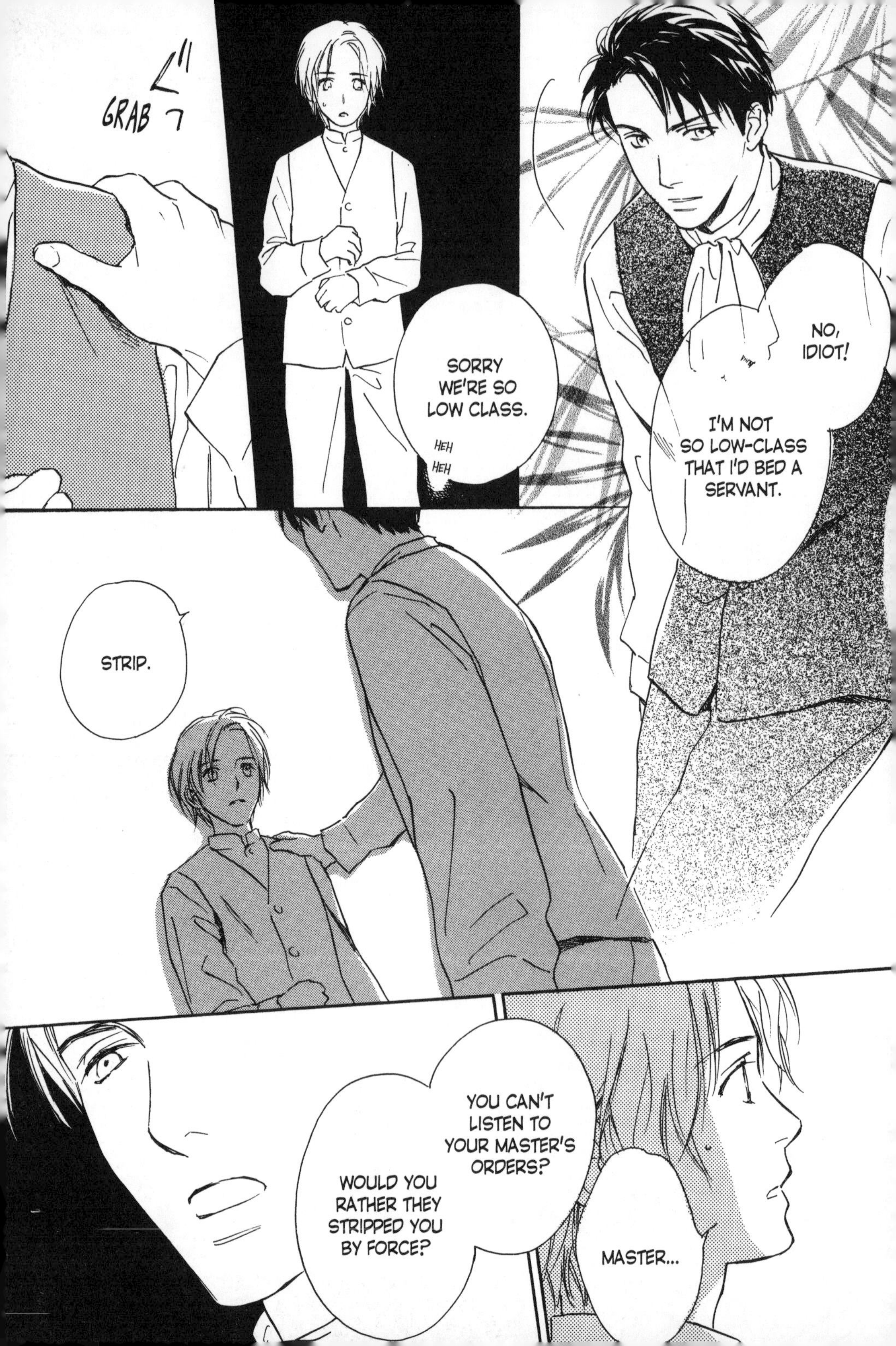
NO, IDIOT!
I'M NOT SO LOW-CLASS THAT I'D BED A SERVANT.
SORRY WE'RE SO LOW CLASS.
HEH HEH
GRAB
STRIP.
MASTER...
YOU CAN'T LISTEN TO YOUR MASTER'S ORDERS?
WOULD YOU RATHER THEY STRIPPED YOU BY FORCE?

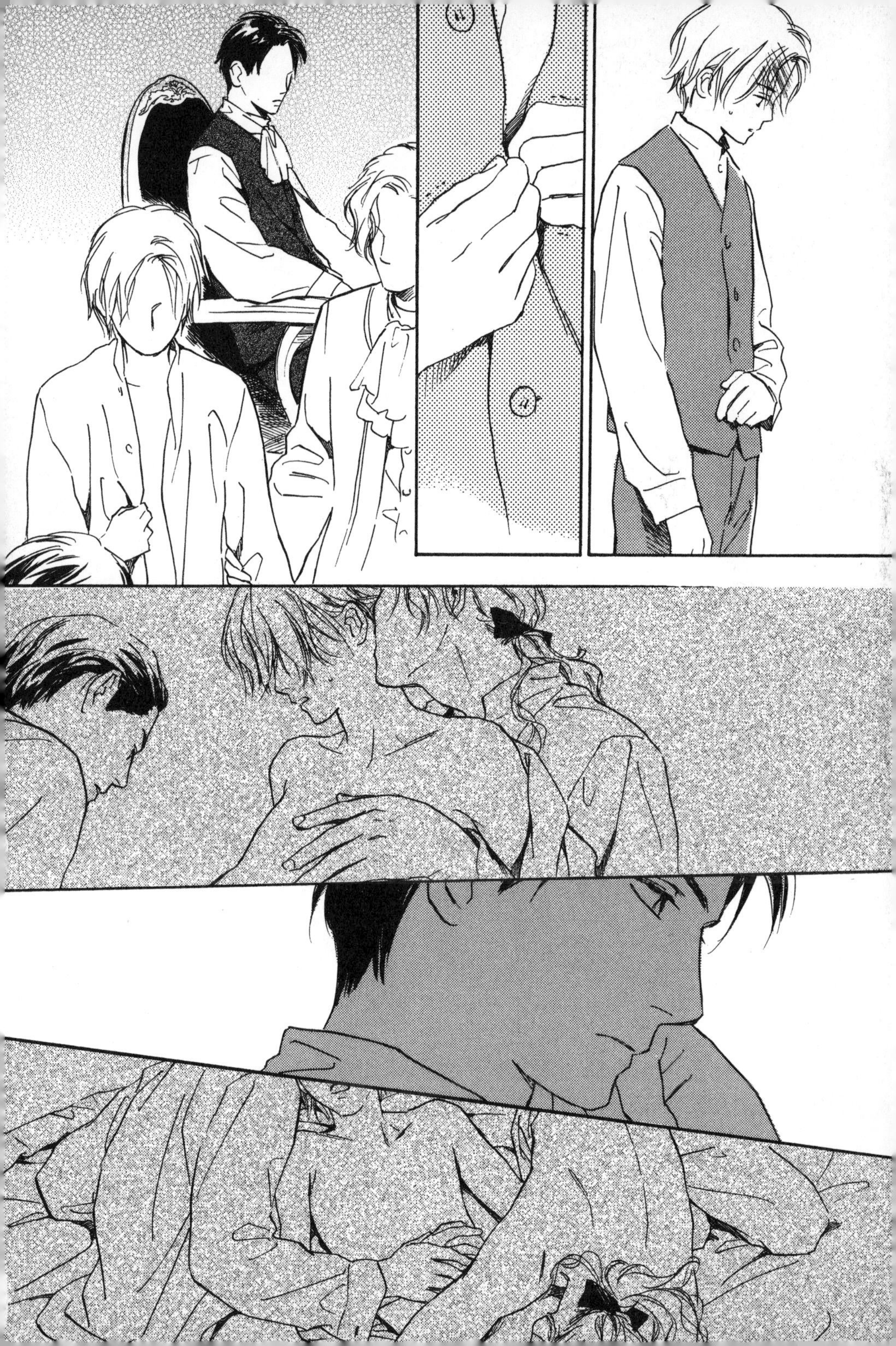

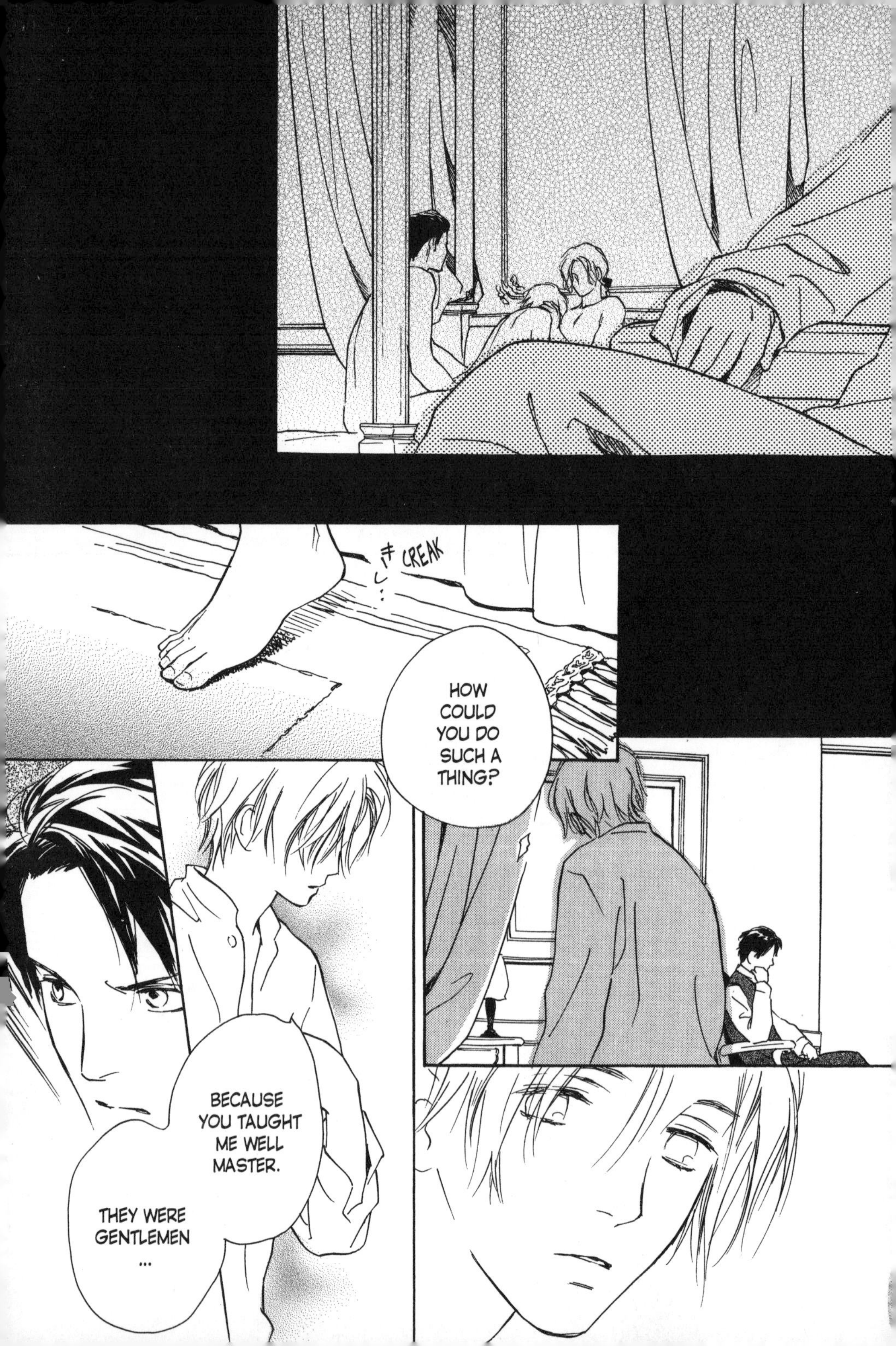
CREAK
HOW COULD YOU DO SUCH A THING?
BECAUSE YOU TAUGHT ME WELL MASTER.
THEY WERE GENTLEMEN ...

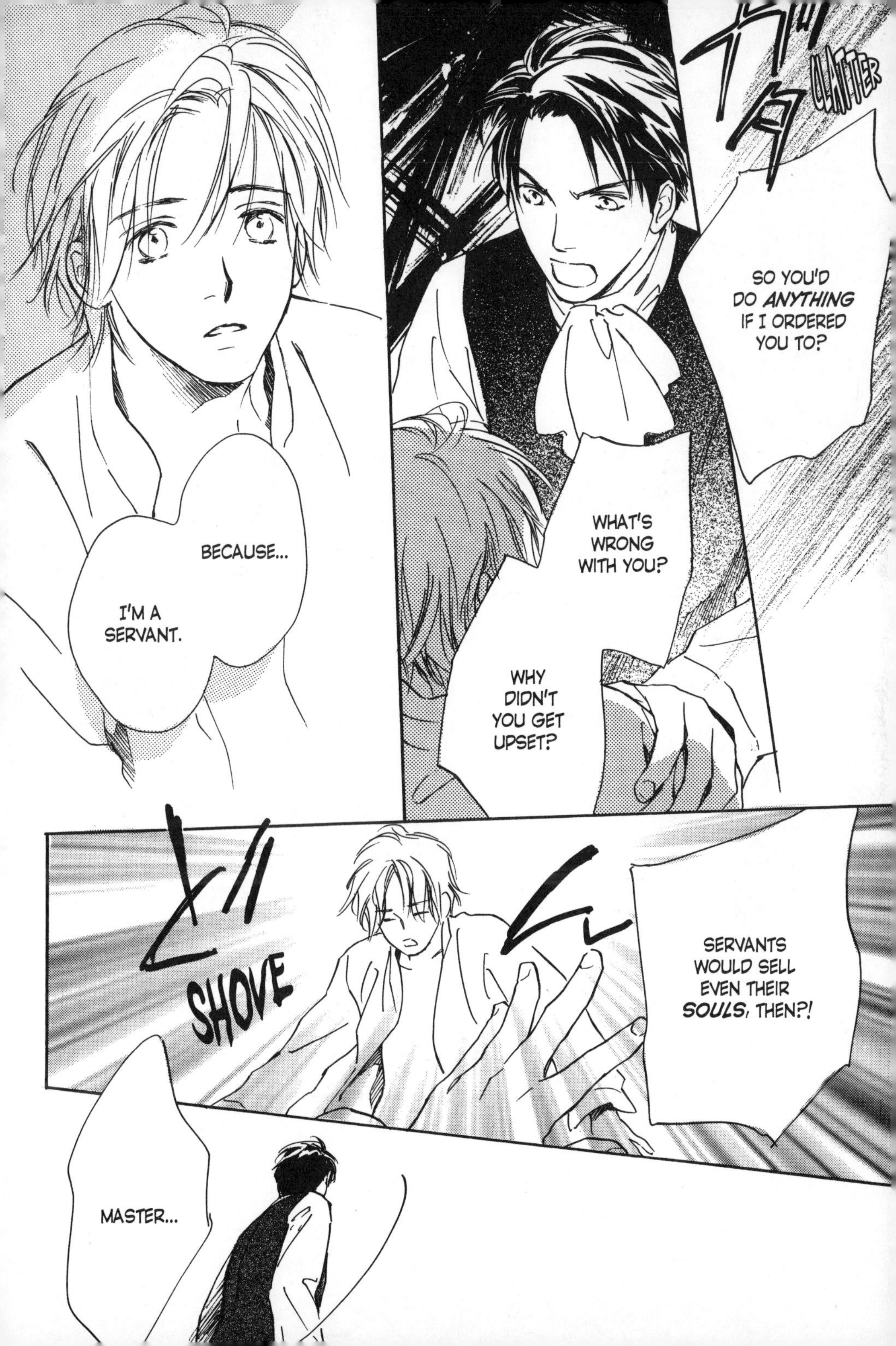
CLATTER
SO YOU'D DO *ANYTHING* IF I ORDERED YOU TO?
WHAT'S WRONG WITH YOU?
WHY DIDN'T YOU GET UPSET?
BECAUSE...
I'M A SERVANT.
SHOVE
SERVANTS WOULD SELL EVEN THEIR *SOULS*, THEN?!
MASTER...

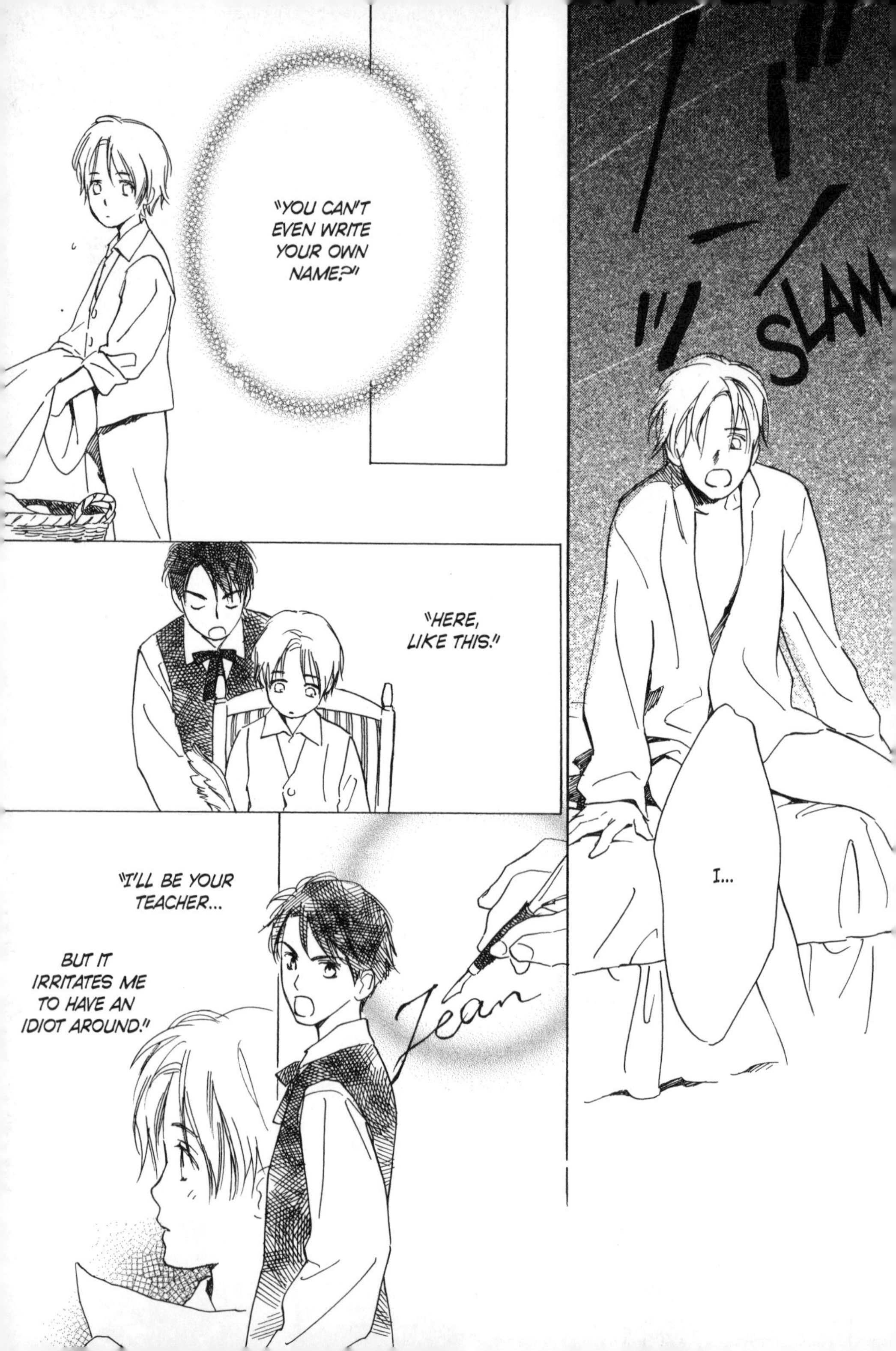
SLAM
I...
"YOU CAN'T EVEN WRITE YOUR OWN NAME?"
"HERE, LIKE THIS."
"I'LL BE YOUR TEACHER...
BUT IT IRRITATES ME TO HAVE AN IDIOT AROUND."
Jean

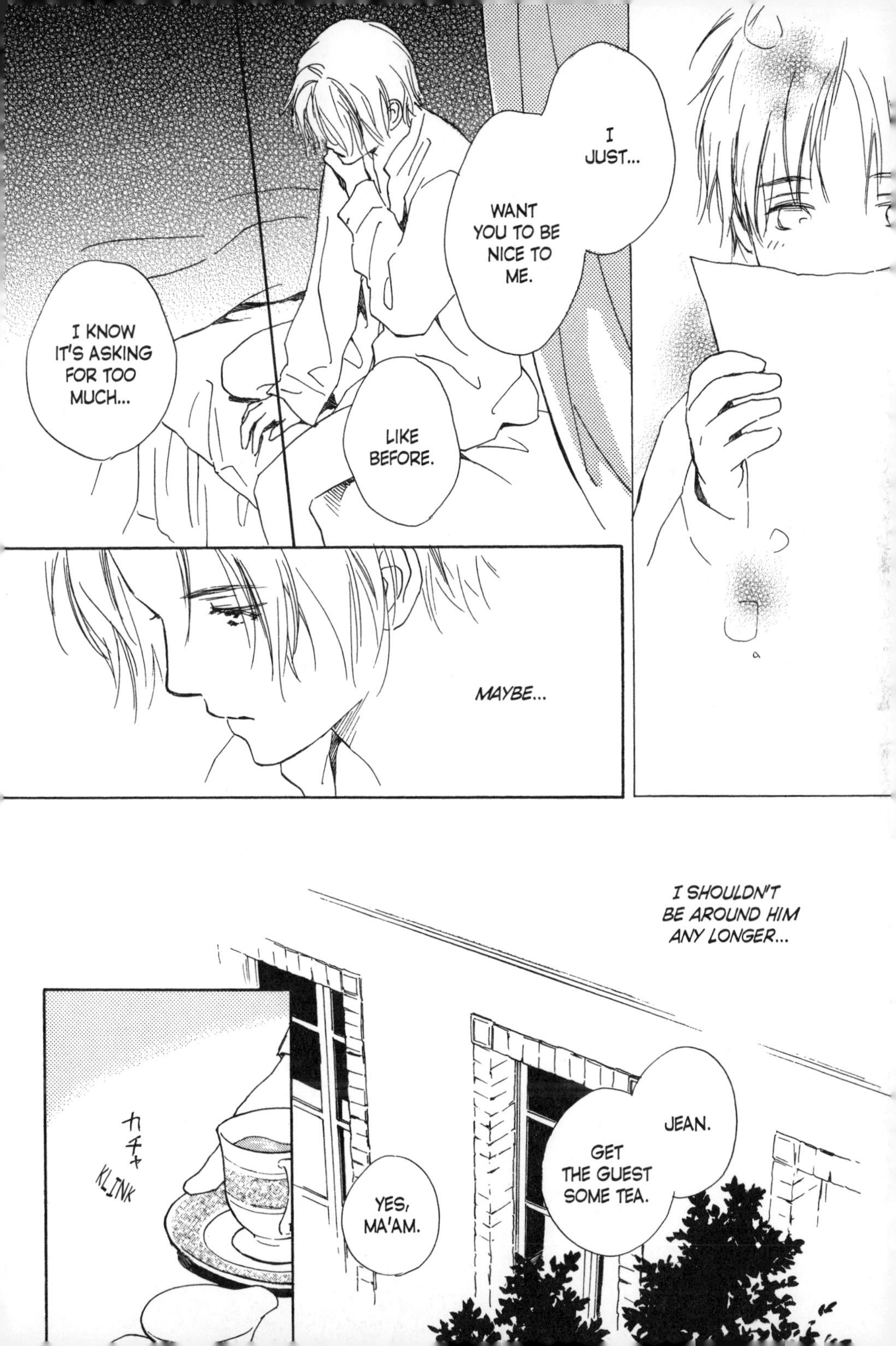
I JUST...
WANT YOU TO BE NICE TO ME.
LIKE BEFORE.
I KNOW IT'S ASKING FOR TOO MUCH...
MAYBE...
I SHOULDN'T BE AROUND HIM ANY LONGER...
JEAN.
GET THE GUEST SOME TEA.
YES, MA'AM.
カチャ
KLINK

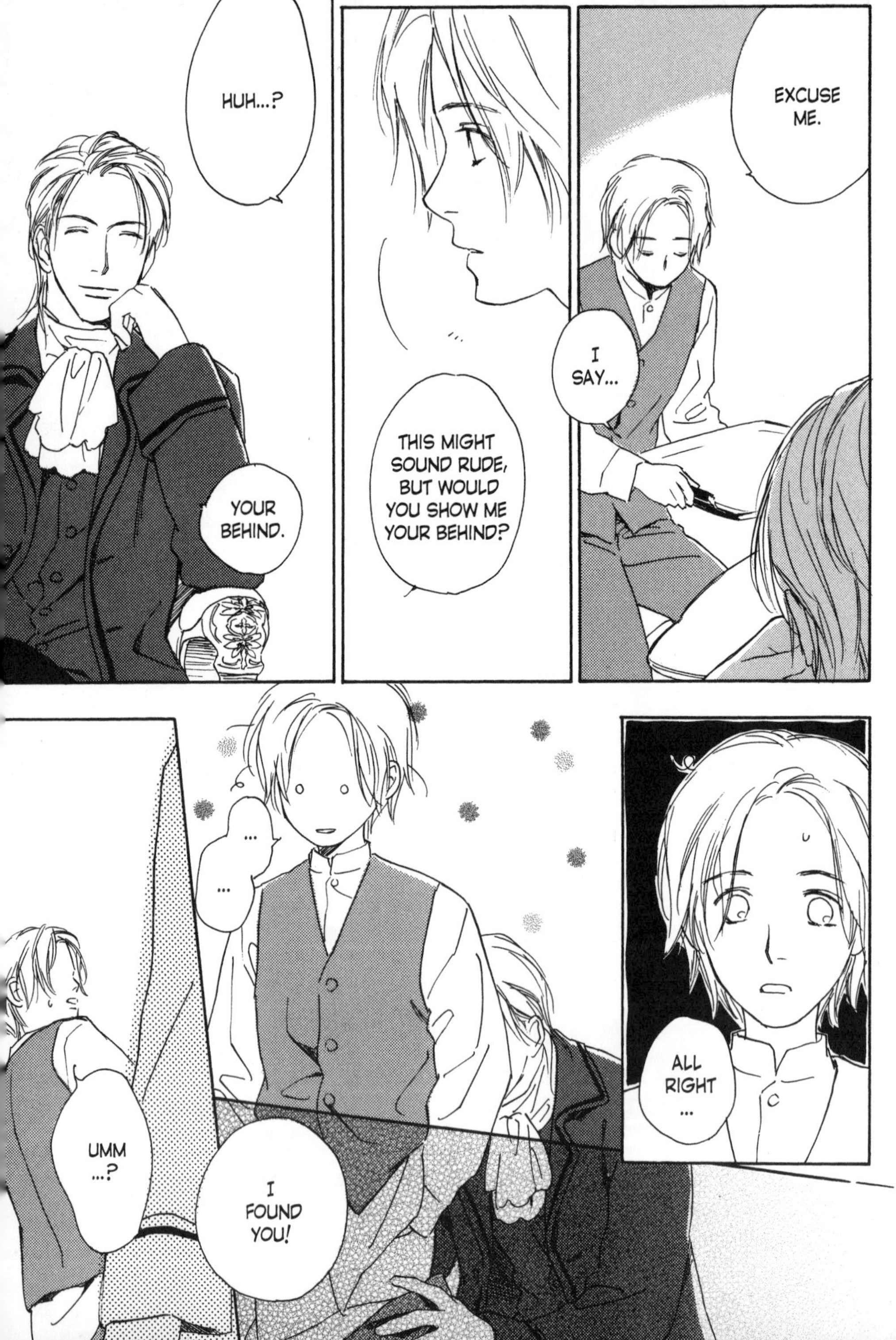
EXCUSE ME.
I SAY...
THIS MIGHT SOUND RUDE, BUT WOULD YOU SHOW ME YOUR BEHIND?
HUH...?
YOUR BEHIND.
ALL RIGHT ...
... ...
I FOUND YOU!
UMM ...?

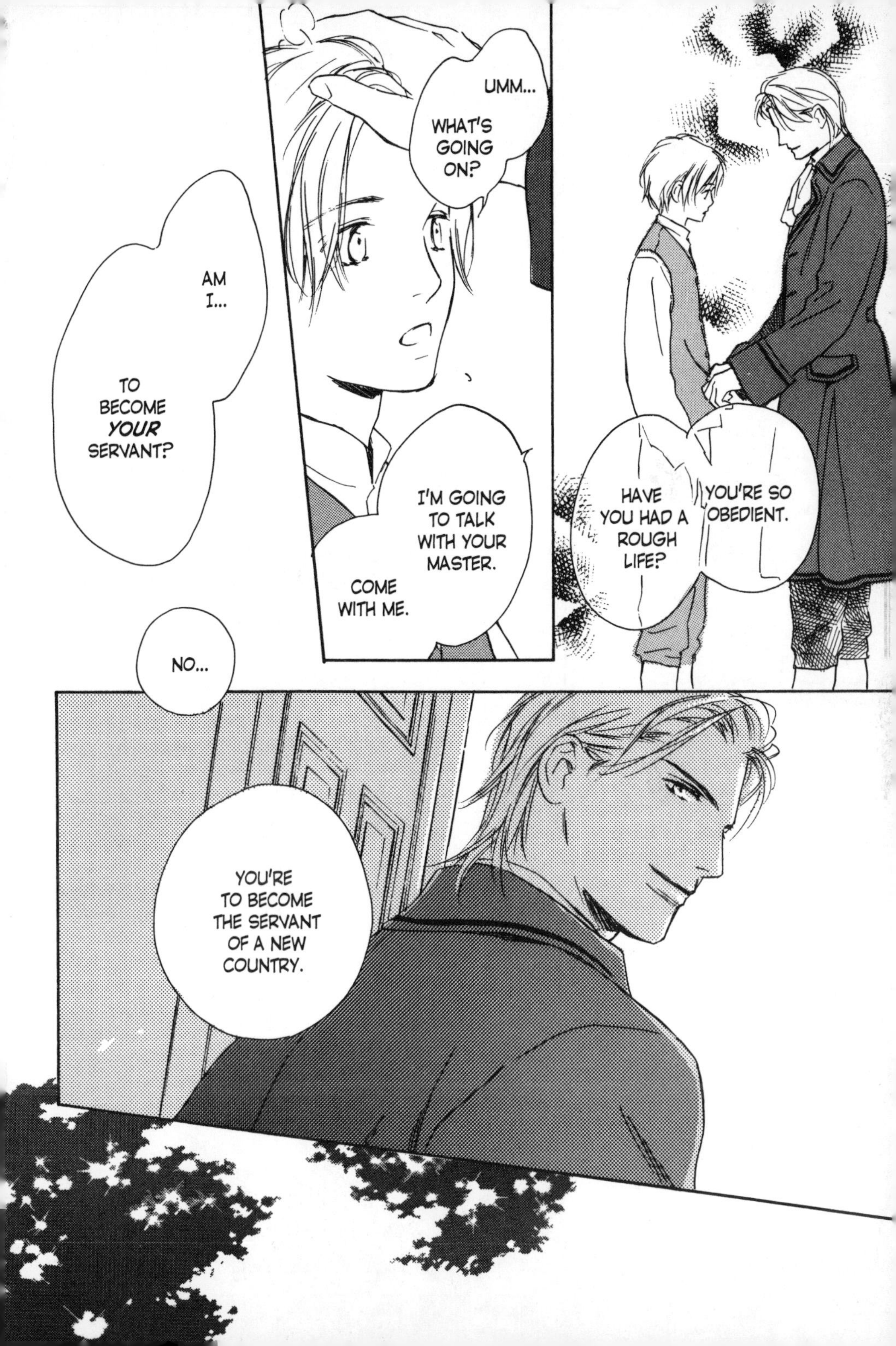
YOU'RE SO OBEDIENT.
HAVE YOU HAD A ROUGH LIFE?
UMM...
WHAT'S GOING ON?
I'M GOING TO TALK WITH YOUR MASTER.
COME WITH ME.
AM I...
TO BECOME *YOUR* SERVANT?
NO...
YOU'RE TO BECOME THE SERVANT OF A NEW COUNTRY.

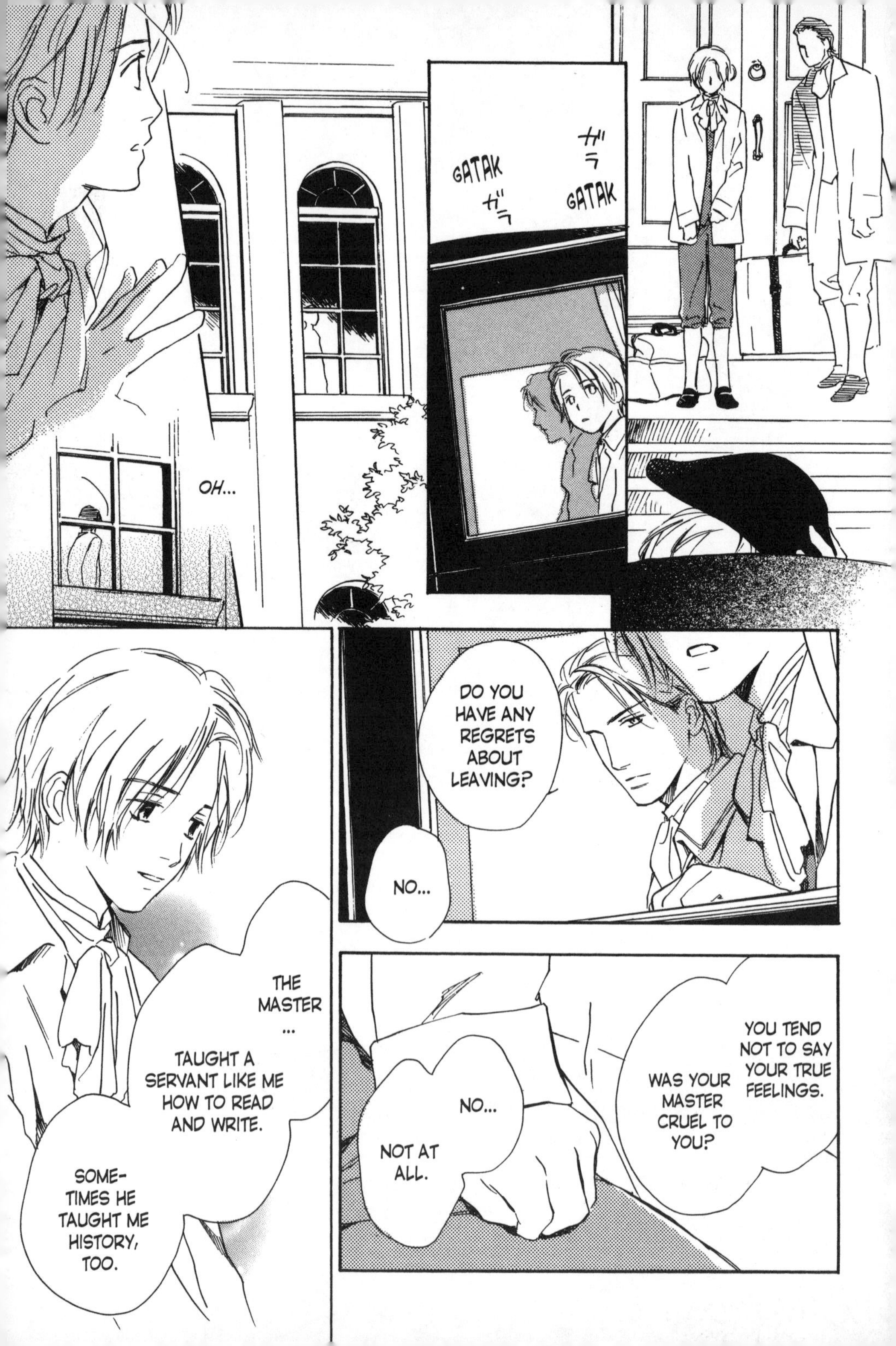
ガラ
GATAK
GATAK
ガラ
OH...
DO YOU HAVE ANY REGRETS ABOUT LEAVING?
NO...
YOU TEND NOT TO SAY YOUR TRUE FEELINGS.
WAS YOUR MASTER CRUEL TO YOU?
NO...
NOT AT ALL.
THE MASTER ...
TAUGHT A SERVANT LIKE ME HOW TO READ AND WRITE.
SOME-TIMES HE TAUGHT ME HISTORY, TOO.

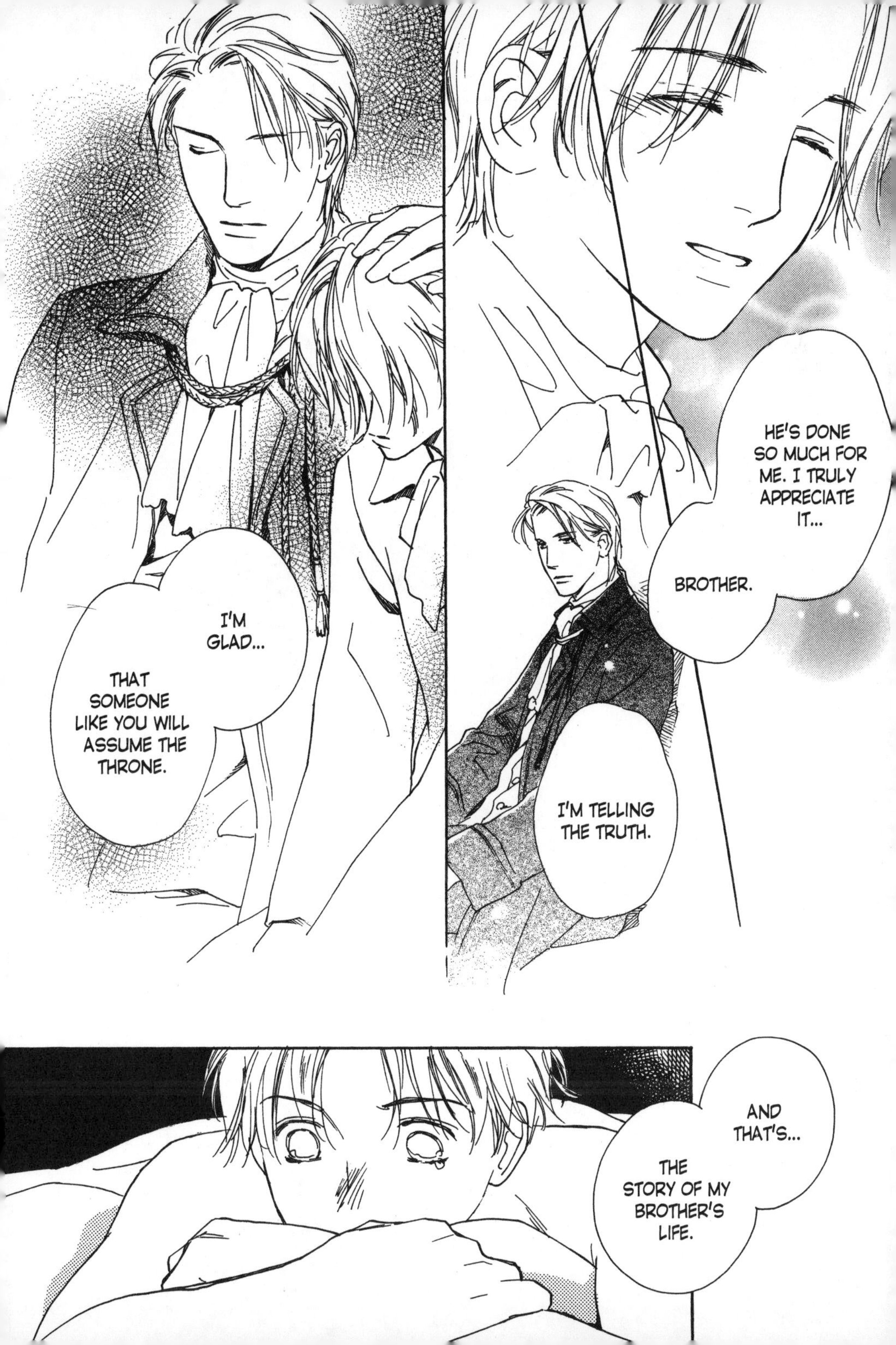
HE'S DONE SO MUCH FOR ME. I TRULY APPRECIATE IT...
BROTHER.
I'M TELLING THE TRUTH.
I'M GLAD...
THAT SOMEONE LIKE YOU WILL ASSUME THE THRONE.
AND THAT'S...
THE STORY OF MY BROTHER'S LIFE.

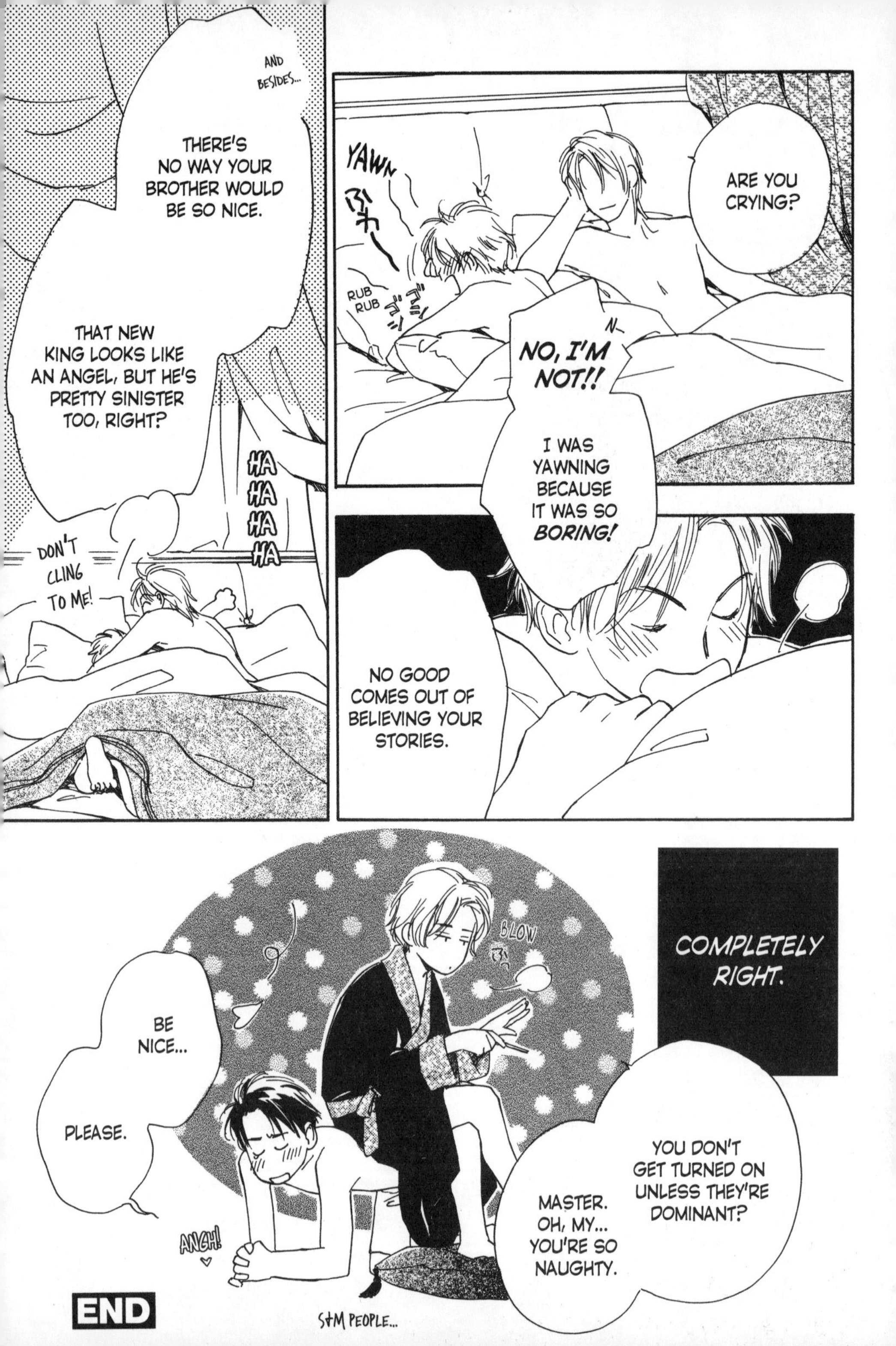

ARE YOU CRYING?
YAWN
RUB RUB
N-
NO, I'M NOT!!
I WAS YAWNING BECAUSE IT WAS SO BORING!
NO GOOD COMES OUT OF BELIEVING YOUR STORIES.
AND BESIDES...
THERE'S NO WAY YOUR BROTHER WOULD BE SO NICE.
THAT NEW KING LOOKS LIKE AN ANGEL, BUT HE'S PRETTY SINISTER TOO, RIGHT?
HA HA HA HA
DON'T CLING TO ME!
COMPLETELY RIGHT.
BLOW
YOU DON'T GET TURNED ON UNLESS THEY'RE DOMINANT?
MASTER. OH, MY... YOU'RE SO NAUGHTY.
BE NICE...
PLEASE.
ANGH!
S+M PEOPLE...
END

STOLEN HEART

FIRST AN INCIDENT OCCURS, AND THE SITUATION TAKES A TURN, AND ANOTHER... AND THEN IT TAKES MANY TWISTS AND TURNS... AND THEN THE RESOLUTION -- I WANTED TO MAKE IT A MYSTERY-TYPE STORY, BUT IF I PUT TOO MUCH ATTENTION INTO THE MYSTERY, THEN THE LOVE SCENES GET KIND OF LEFT BEHIND, AND MY EDITOR TANAKA GIVES ME A GOOD WHIPPING FOR THAT. ♥ I DID THE FIRST EPISODE THINKING IT WAS GOING TO BE A ONE-SHOT, BUT I HAD THE HONOR OF CONTINUING THE STORY, AND IT BECAME MORE AND MORE GRANDIOSE.

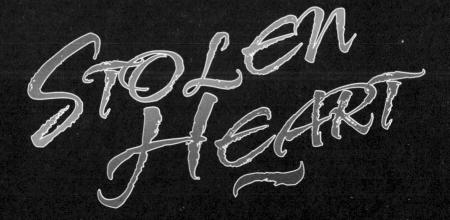

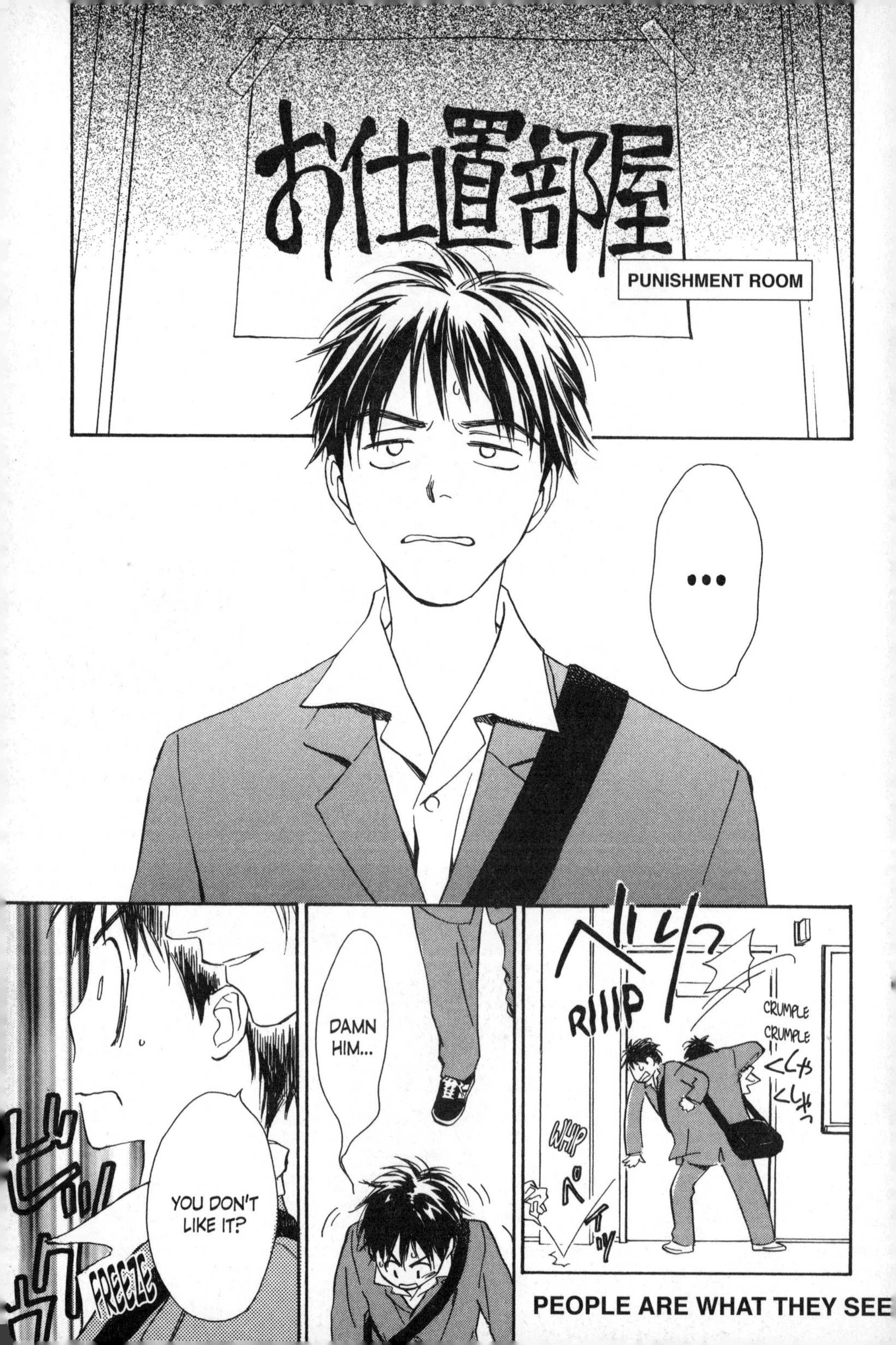
お仕置部屋
PUNISHMENT ROOM
...
ベリッ
RIIIP
CRUMPLE
CRUMPLE
くしゃ
くしゃっ
WHIP
ペイッ
DAMN HIM...
YOU DON'T LIKE IT?
ビクッ
FREEZE

PEOPLE ARE WHAT THEY SEE

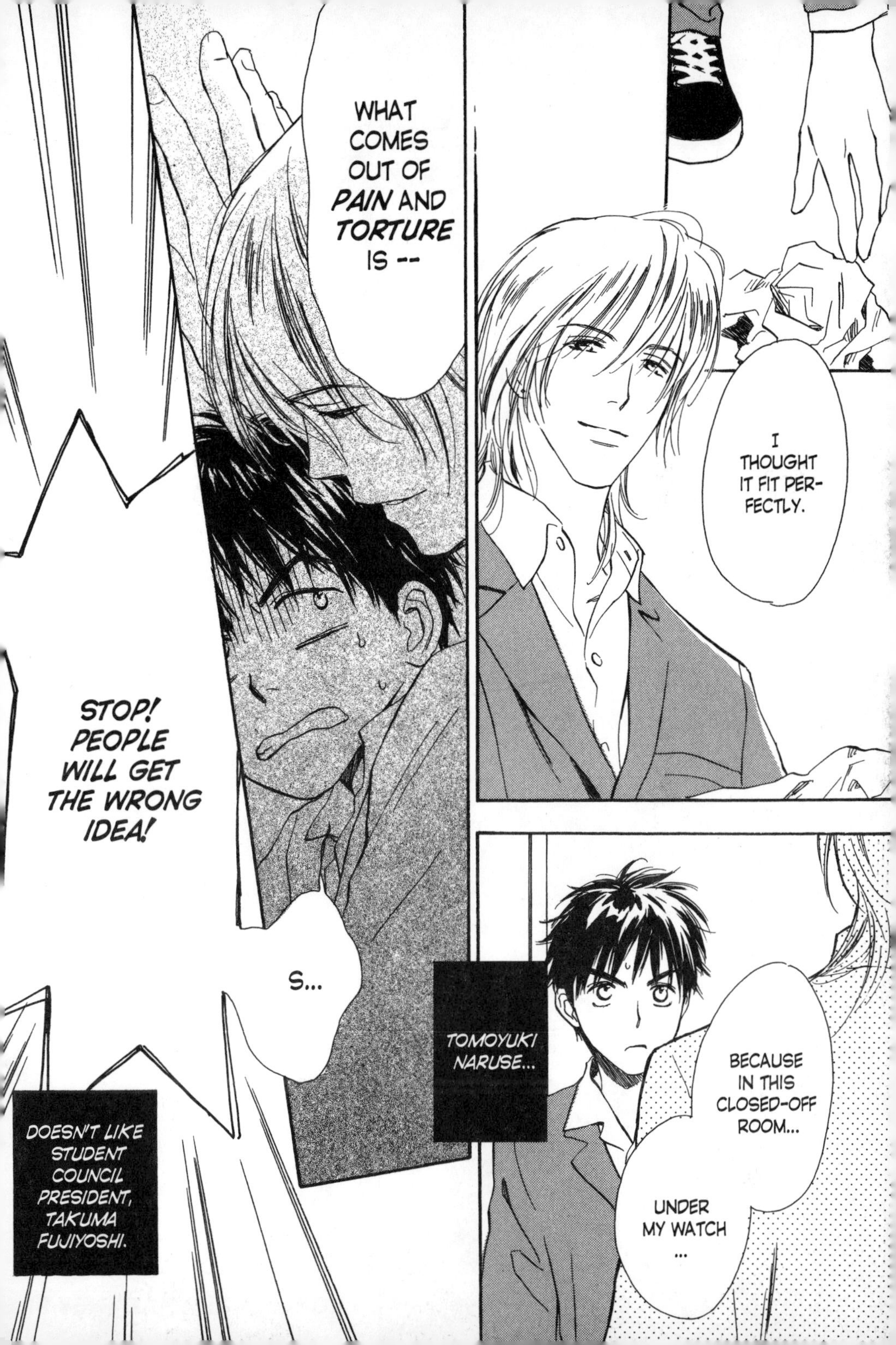
I THOUGHT IT FIT PERFECTLY.
BECAUSE IN THIS CLOSED-OFF ROOM...
UNDER MY WATCH ...
TOMOYUKI NARUSE...
WHAT COMES OUT OF PAIN AND TORTURE IS --
S...
STOP! PEOPLE WILL GET THE WRONG IDEA!
DOESN'T LIKE STUDENT COUNCIL PRESIDENT, TAKUMA FUJIYOSHI.

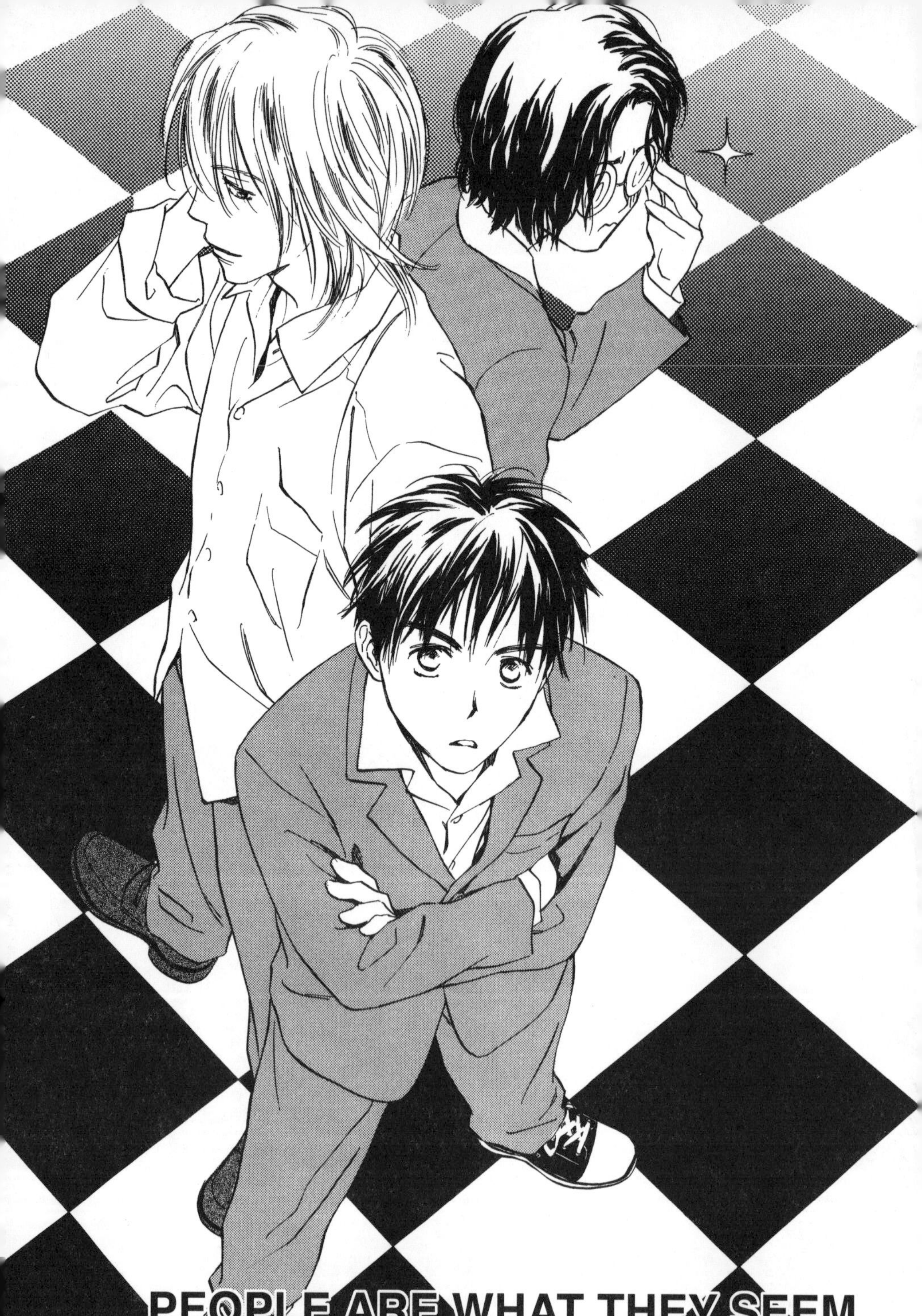

PEOPLE ARE WHAT THEY SEEM

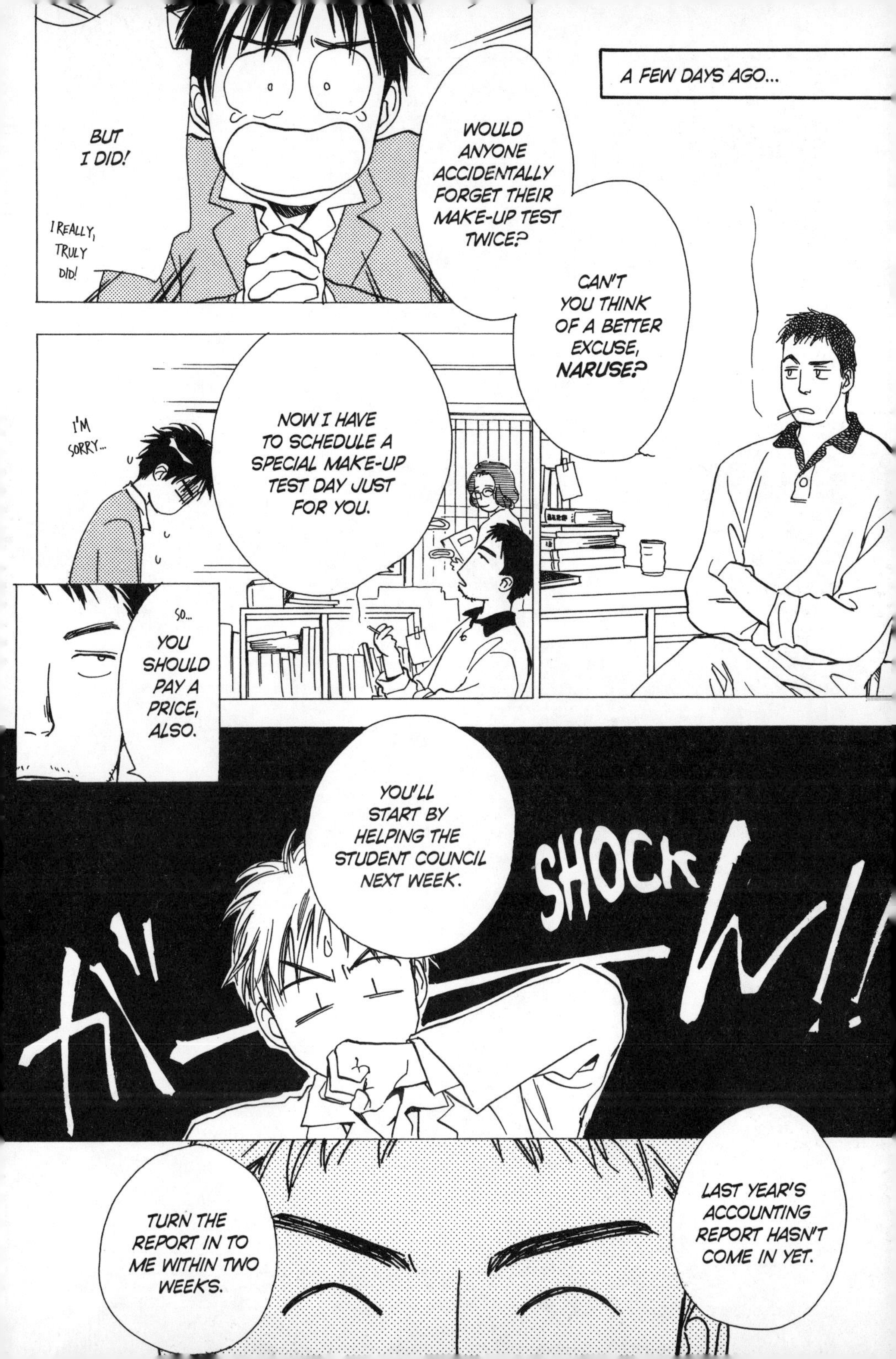

A FEW DAYS AGO...
WOULD ANYONE ACCIDENTALLY FORGET THEIR MAKE-UP TEST TWICE?
CAN'T YOU THINK OF A BETTER EXCUSE, NARUSE?
BUT I DID!
I REALLY, TRULY DID!
NOW I HAVE TO SCHEDULE A SPECIAL MAKE-UP TEST DAY JUST FOR YOU.
I'M SORRY...
SO...
YOU SHOULD PAY A PRICE, ALSO.
YOU'LL START BY HELPING THE STUDENT COUNCIL NEXT WEEK.
SHOCK
ガーン!!
LAST YEAR'S ACCOUNTING REPORT HASN'T COME IN YET.
TURN THE REPORT IN TO ME WITHIN TWO WEEKS.

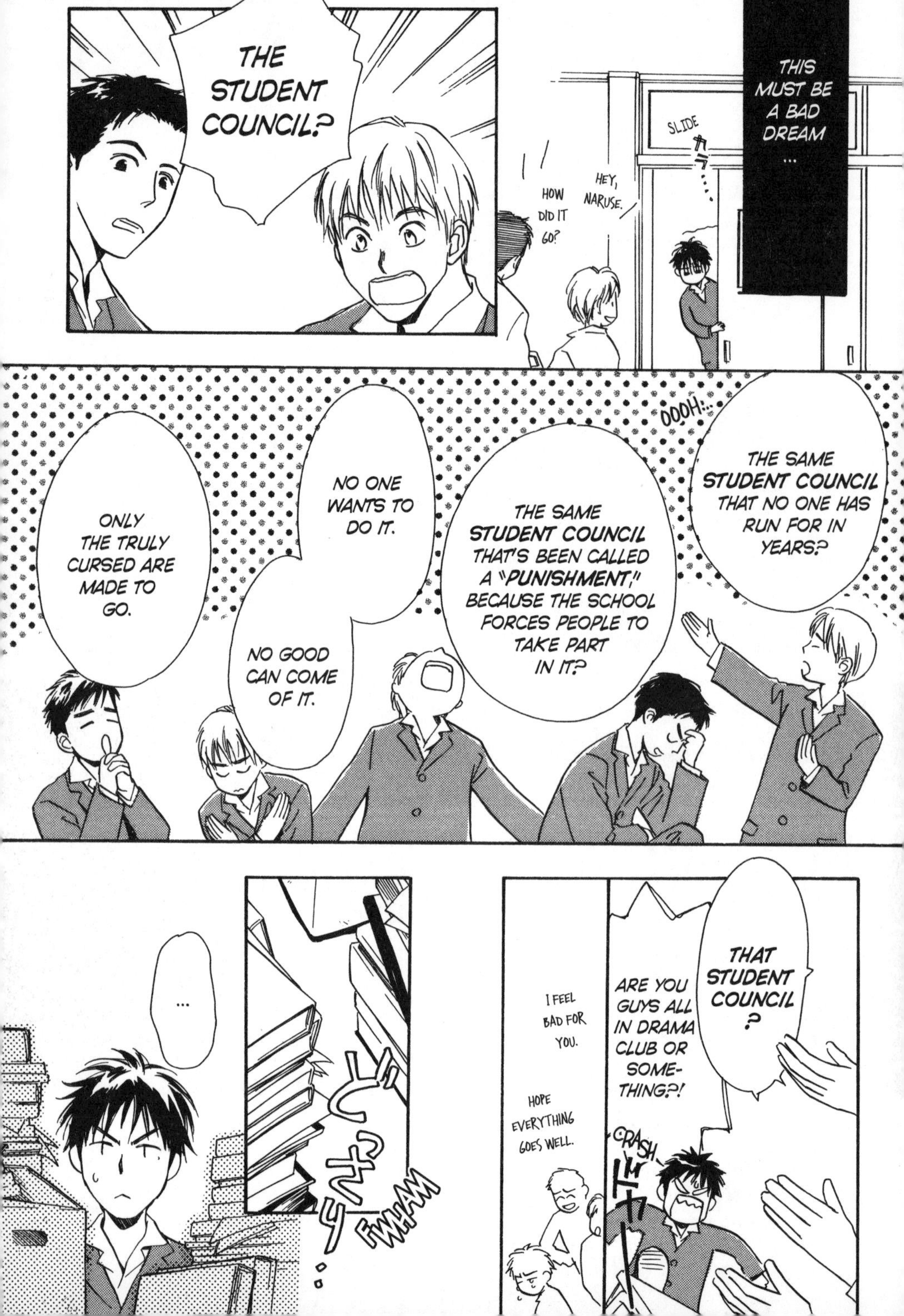
THIS MUST BE A BAD DREAM ...
SLIDE
HEY, NARUSE.
HOW DID IT GO?
THE STUDENT COUNCIL?
OOOH...
THE SAME STUDENT COUNCIL THAT NO ONE HAS RUN FOR IN YEARS?
THE SAME STUDENT COUNCIL THAT'S BEEN CALLED A "PUNISHMENT," BECAUSE THE SCHOOL FORCES PEOPLE TO TAKE PART IN IT?
NO ONE WANTS TO DO IT.
NO GOOD CAN COME OF IT.
ONLY THE TRULY CURSED ARE MADE TO GO.
THAT STUDENT COUNCIL?
ARE YOU GUYS ALL IN DRAMA CLUB OR SOME-THING?!
I FEEL BAD FOR YOU.
HOPE EVERYTHING GOES WELL.
CRASH
FWHAM
...

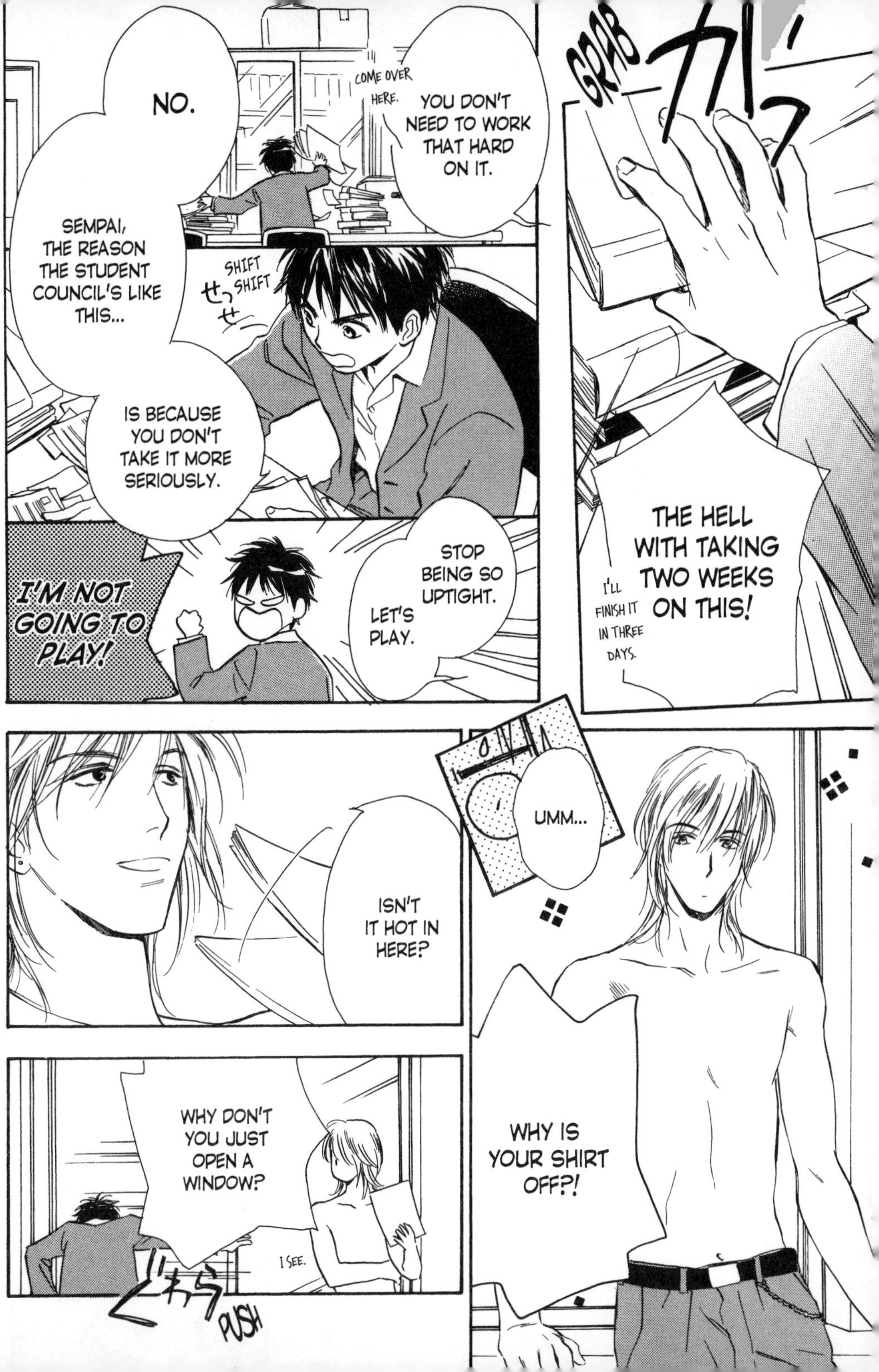
GRAB
THE HELL WITH TAKING TWO WEEKS ON THIS!
I'LL FINISH IT IN THREE DAYS.
YOU DON'T NEED TO WORK THAT HARD ON IT.
COME OVER HERE.
NO.
SEMPAI, THE REASON THE STUDENT COUNCIL'S LIKE THIS...
SHIFT SHIFT
IS BECAUSE YOU DON'T TAKE IT MORE SERIOUSLY.
STOP BEING SO UPTIGHT.
LET'S PLAY.
I'M NOT GOING TO PLAY!
UMM...
WHY IS YOUR SHIRT OFF?!
ISN'T IT HOT IN HERE?
WHY DON'T YOU JUST OPEN A WINDOW?
I SEE.
PUSH

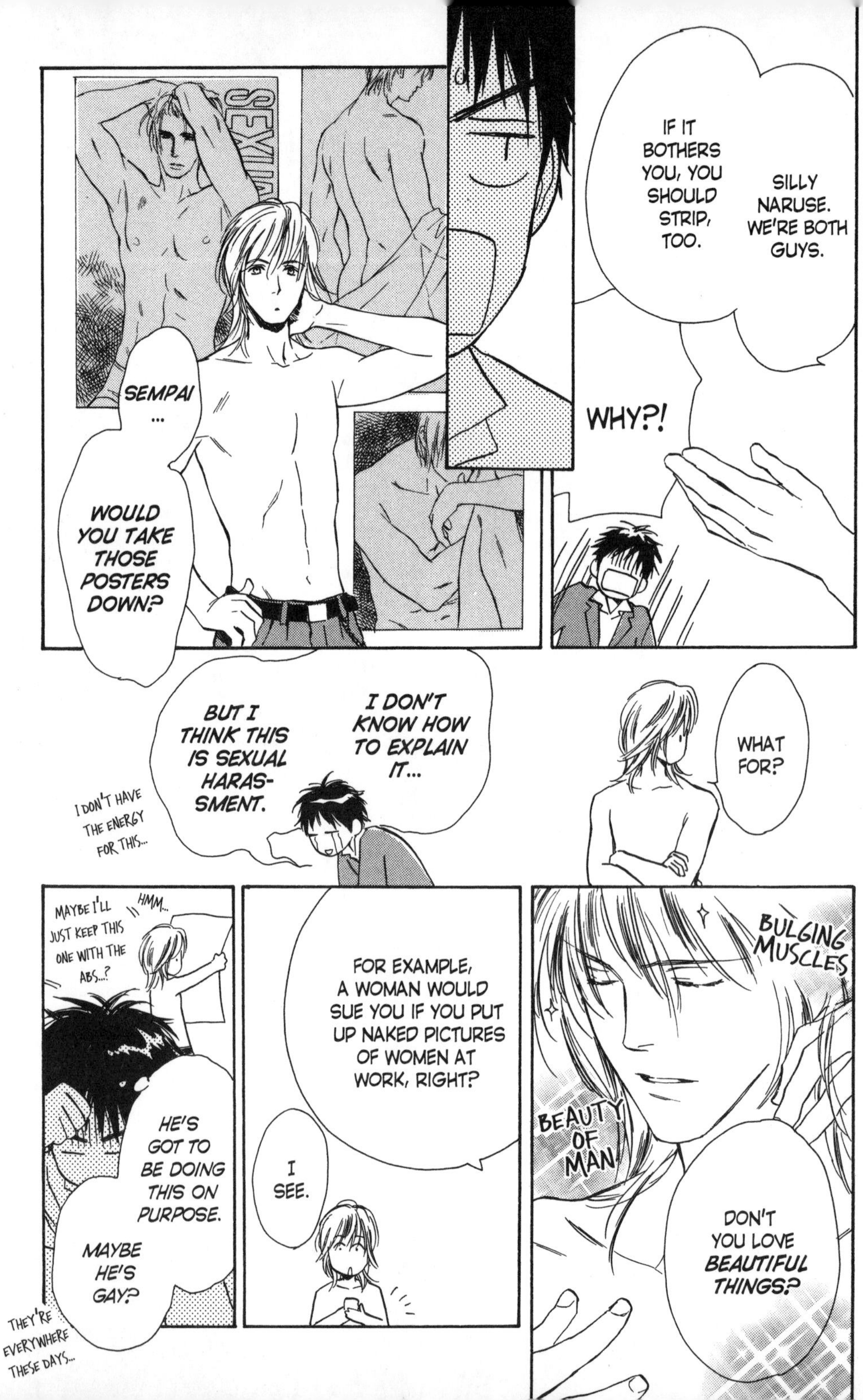
SILLY NARUSE. WE'RE BOTH GUYS.
IF IT BOTHERS YOU, YOU SHOULD STRIP, TOO.
WHY?!
SEXY
SEMPAI ...
WOULD YOU TAKE THOSE POSTERS DOWN?
WHAT FOR?
I DON'T KNOW HOW TO EXPLAIN IT...
BUT I THINK THIS IS SEXUAL HARAS-SMENT.
I DON'T HAVE THE ENERGY FOR THIS...
BULGING MUSCLES
BEAUTY OF MAN
DON'T YOU LOVE BEAUTIFUL THINGS?
FOR EXAMPLE, A WOMAN WOULD SUE YOU IF YOU PUT UP NAKED PICTURES OF WOMEN AT WORK, RIGHT?
I SEE.
HMM...
MAYBE I'LL JUST KEEP THIS ONE WITH THE ABS...?
HE'S GOT TO BE DOING THIS ON PURPOSE.
MAYBE HE'S GAY?
THEY'RE EVERYWHERE THESE DAYS...

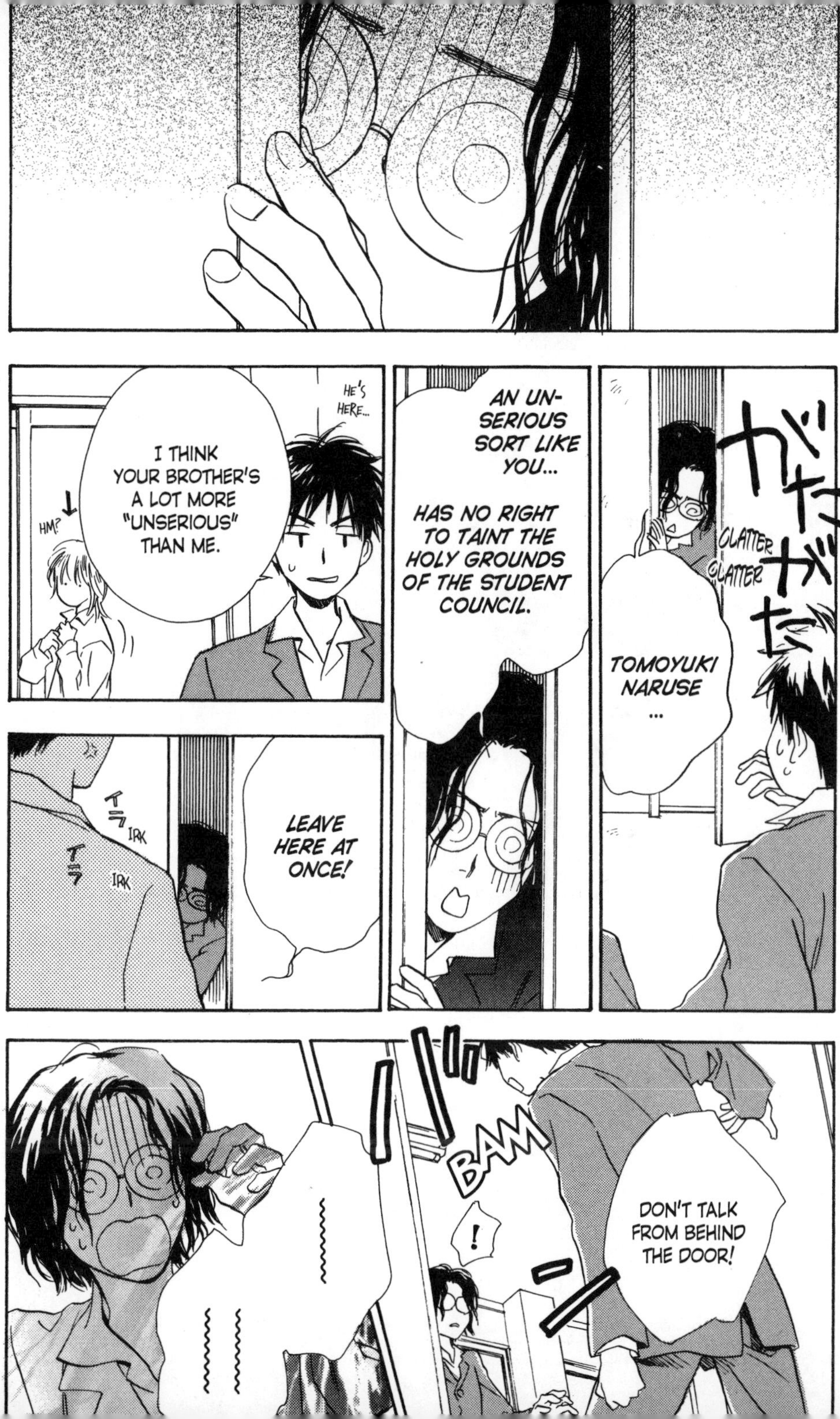

がたがた
CLATTER
CLATTER
TOMOYUKI NARUSE ...
AN UN-SERIOUS SORT LIKE YOU...
HAS NO RIGHT TO TAINT THE HOLY GROUNDS OF THE STUDENT COUNCIL.
HE'S HERE...
I THINK YOUR BROTHER'S A LOT MORE "UNSERIOUS" THAN ME.
HM?
LEAVE HERE AT ONCE!
イラ IRK
イラ IRK
BAM
DON'T TALK FROM BEHIND THE DOOR!
!

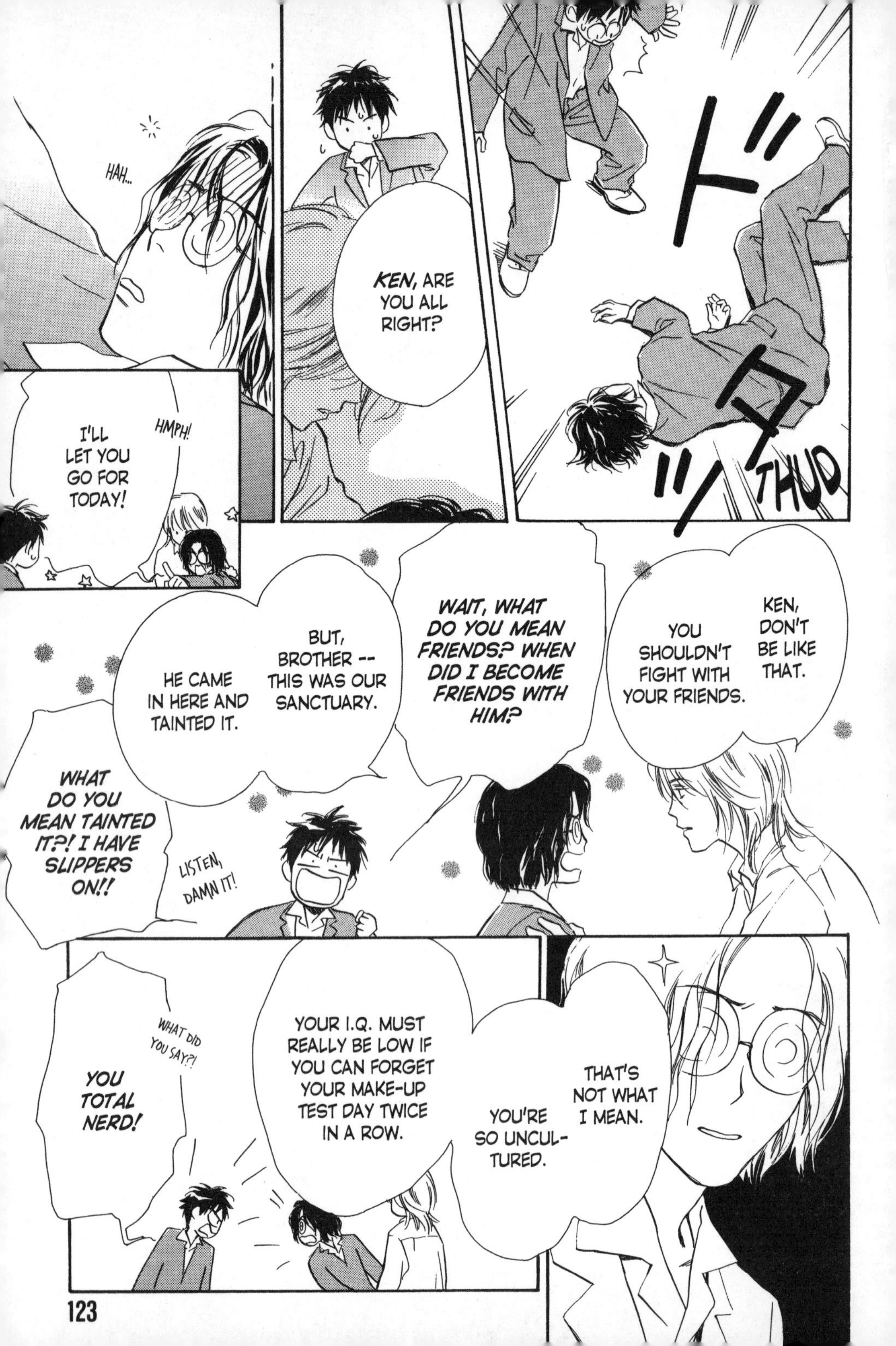
ドタッ
THUD
KEN, ARE YOU ALL RIGHT?
HAH...
I'LL LET YOU GO FOR TODAY!
HMPH!
KEN, DON'T BE LIKE THAT.
YOU SHOULDN'T FIGHT WITH YOUR FRIENDS.
WAIT, WHAT DO YOU MEAN FRIENDS? WHEN DID I BECOME FRIENDS WITH HIM?
BUT, BROTHER -- THIS WAS OUR SANCTUARY.
HE CAME IN HERE AND TAINTED IT.
LISTEN, DAMN IT!
WHAT DO YOU MEAN TAINTED IT?! I HAVE SLIPPERS ON!!
THAT'S NOT WHAT I MEAN.
YOU'RE SO UNCUL-TURED.
YOUR I.Q. MUST REALLY BE LOW IF YOU CAN FORGET YOUR MAKE-UP TEST DAY TWICE IN A ROW.
WHAT DID YOU SAY?!
YOU TOTAL NERD!

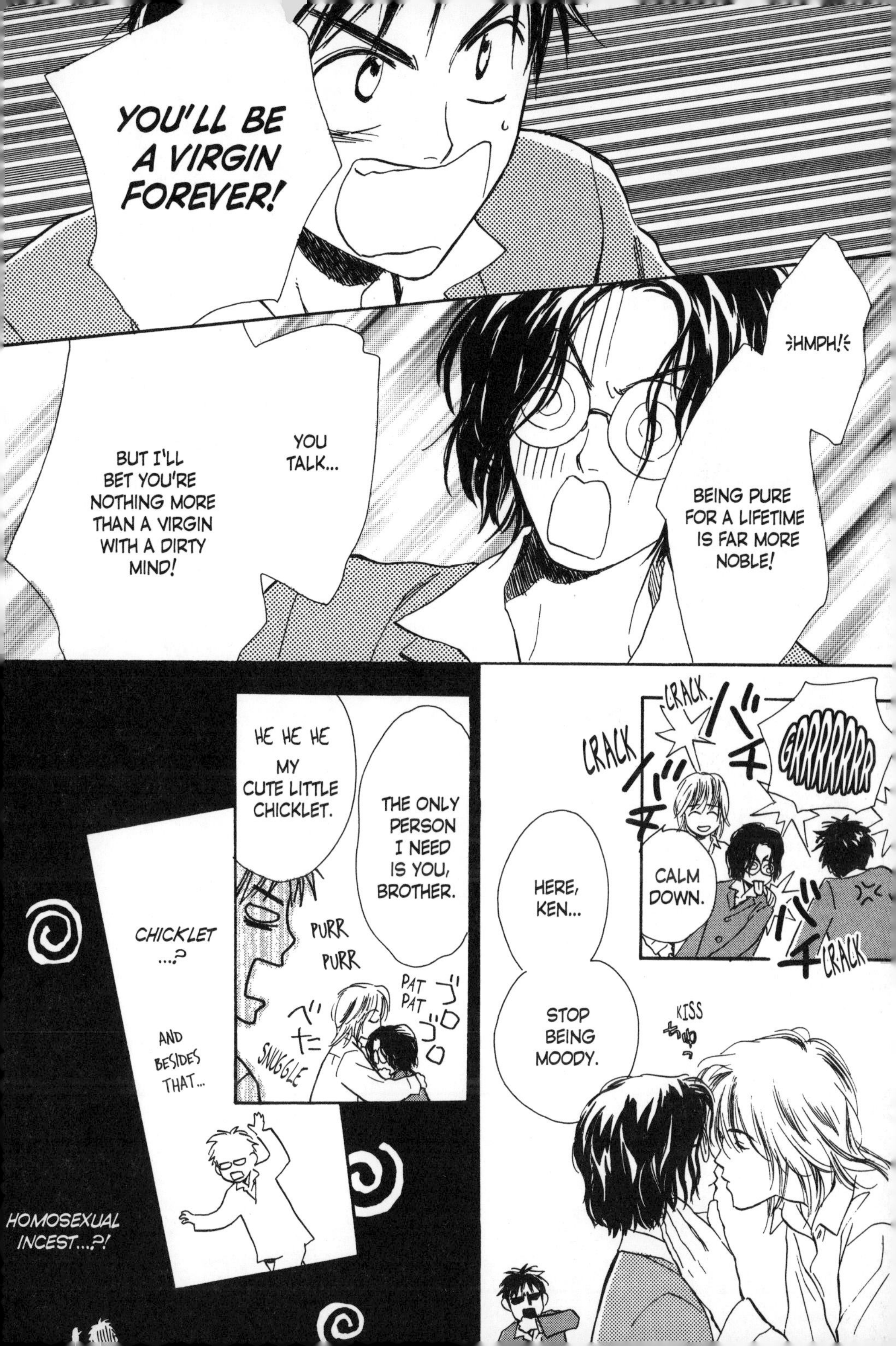

YOU'LL BE A VIRGIN FOREVER!
HMPH!
BEING PURE FOR A LIFETIME IS FAR MORE NOBLE!
YOU TALK...
BUT I'LL BET YOU'RE NOTHING MORE THAN A VIRGIN WITH A DIRTY MIND!
CRACK
GRRRRRRR
CRACK
CALM DOWN.
CRACK
HERE, KEN...
STOP BEING MOODY.
KISS
HE HE HE
MY CUTE LITTLE CHICKLET.
THE ONLY PERSON I NEED IS YOU, BROTHER.
PURR PURR
PAT PAT
SNUGGLE
CHICKLET ...?
AND BESIDES THAT...
HOMOSEXUAL INCEST...?!

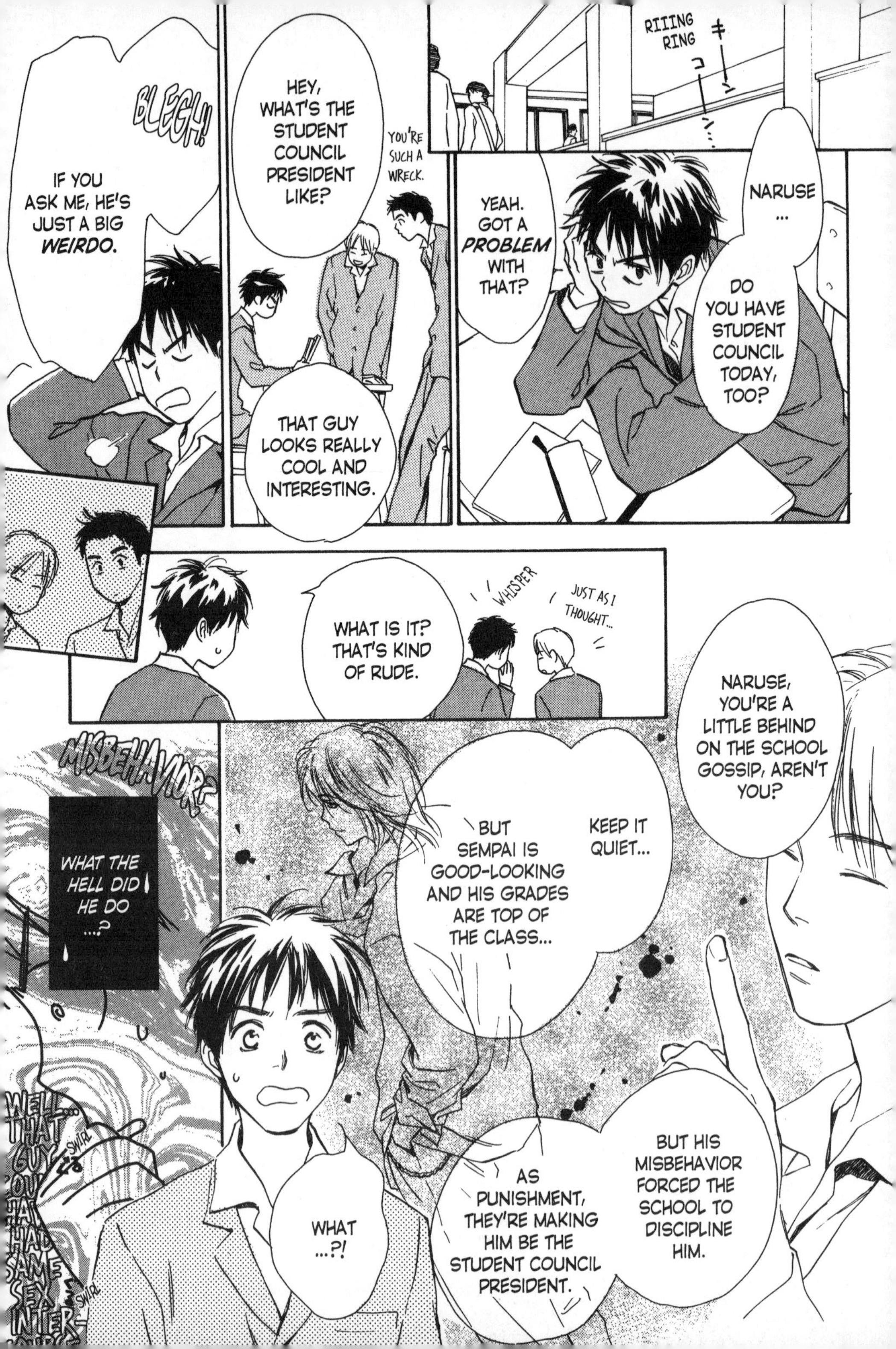
RIIING RING
キーンコーン…
NARUSE ...
DO YOU HAVE STUDENT COUNCIL TODAY, TOO?
YEAH. GOT A *PROBLEM* WITH THAT?
HEY, WHAT'S THE STUDENT COUNCIL PRESIDENT LIKE?
YOU'RE SUCH A WRECK.
THAT GUY LOOKS REALLY COOL AND INTERESTING.
BLEGH!
IF YOU ASK ME, HE'S JUST A BIG *WEIRDO*.
JUST AS I THOUGHT...
WHISPER
WHAT IS IT? THAT'S KIND OF RUDE.
NARUSE, YOU'RE A LITTLE BEHIND ON THE SCHOOL GOSSIP, AREN'T YOU?
KEEP IT QUIET...
BUT SEMPAI IS GOOD-LOOKING AND HIS GRADES ARE TOP OF THE CLASS...
BUT HIS MISBEHAVIOR FORCED THE SCHOOL TO DISCIPLINE HIM.
AS PUNISHMENT, THEY'RE MAKING HIM BE THE STUDENT COUNCIL PRESIDENT.
WHAT ...?!
MISBEHAVIOR?
WHAT THE HELL DID HE DO ...?
WELL... THAT GUY
SAME SEX INTER-
SWIRL
SWIRL

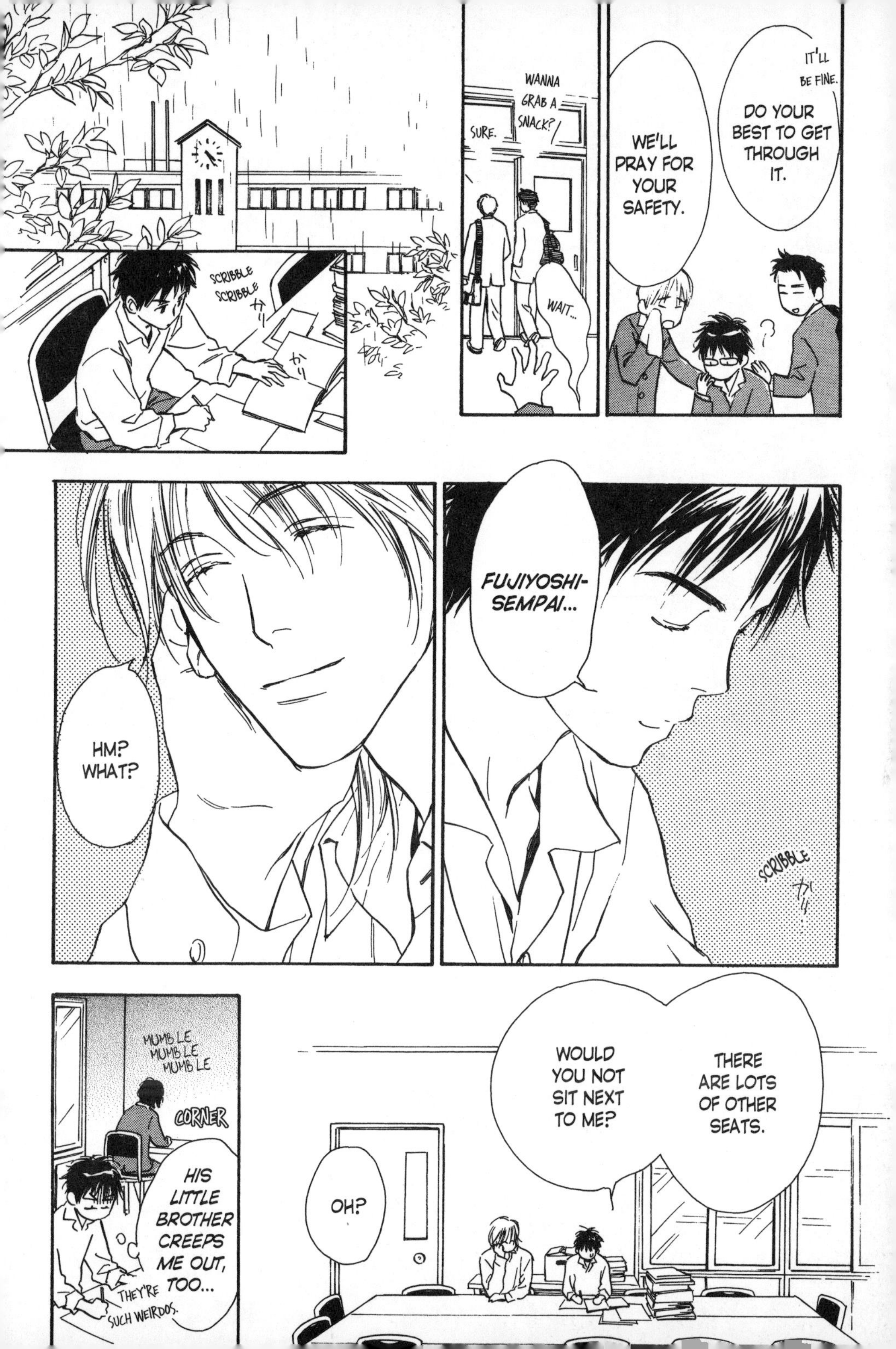
IT'LL BE FINE.
DO YOUR BEST TO GET THROUGH IT.
WE'LL PRAY FOR YOUR SAFETY.
WANNA GRAB A SNACK?
SURE.
WAIT...
SCRIBBLE SCRIBBLE
FUJIYOSHI-SEMPAI...
SCRIBBLE
HM? WHAT?
THERE ARE LOTS OF OTHER SEATS.
WOULD YOU NOT SIT NEXT TO ME?
OH?
MUMBLE MUMBLE MUMBLE
CORNER
HIS LITTLE BROTHER CREEPS ME OUT, TOO...
THEY'RE SUCH WEIRDOS.

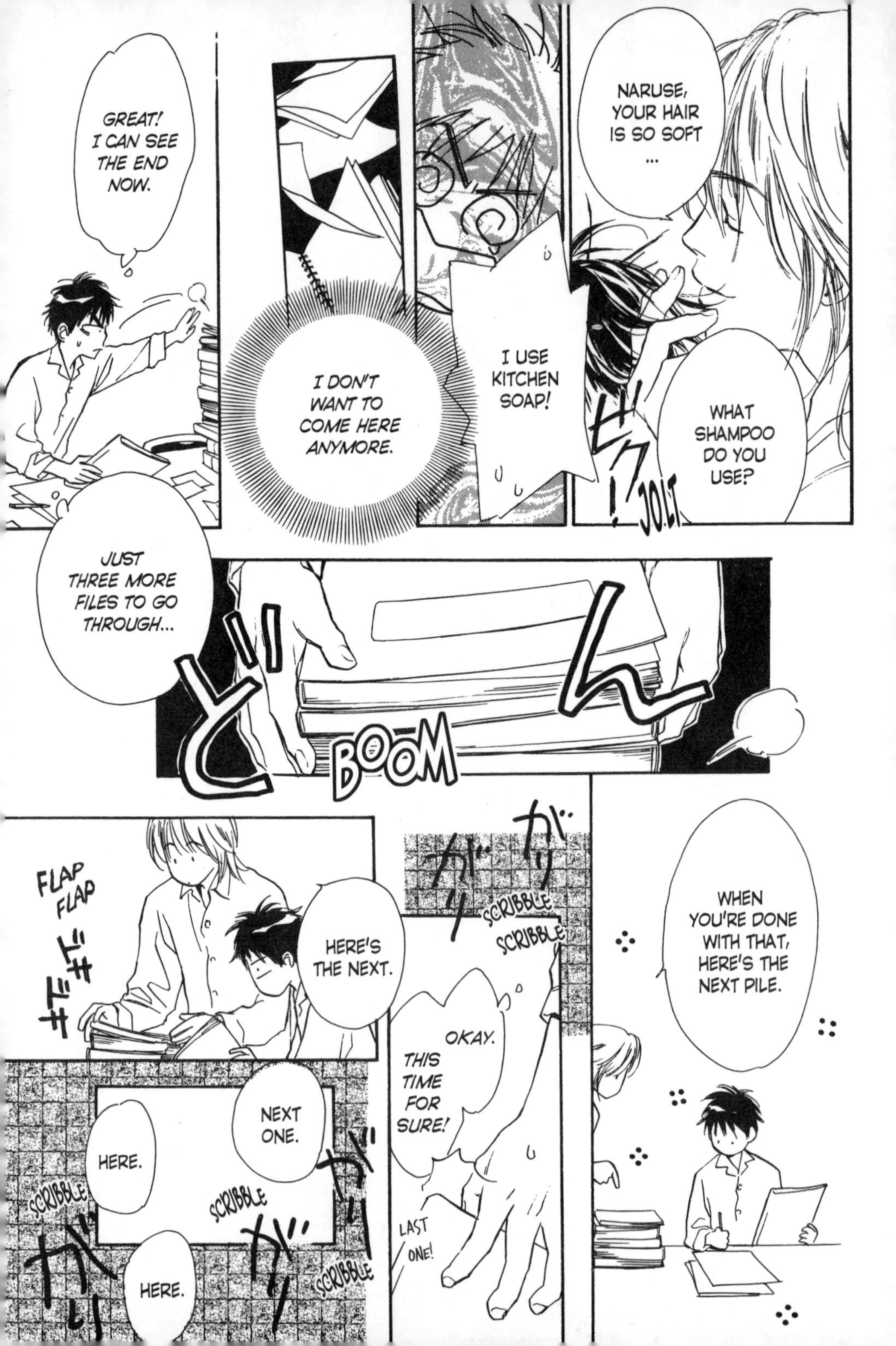
NARUSE, YOUR HAIR IS SO SOFT ...
WHAT SHAMPOO DO YOU USE?
JOLT
I USE KITCHEN SOAP!
I DON'T WANT TO COME HERE ANYMORE.
GREAT! I CAN SEE THE END NOW.
JUST THREE MORE FILES TO GO THROUGH...
BOOM
WHEN YOU'RE DONE WITH THAT, HERE'S THE NEXT PILE.
SCRIBBLE SCRIBBLE
OKAY. THIS TIME FOR SURE!
LAST ONE!
HERE'S THE NEXT.
FLAP FLAP
NEXT ONE.
HERE.
SCRIBBLE
SCRIBBLE
SCRIBBLE
HERE.

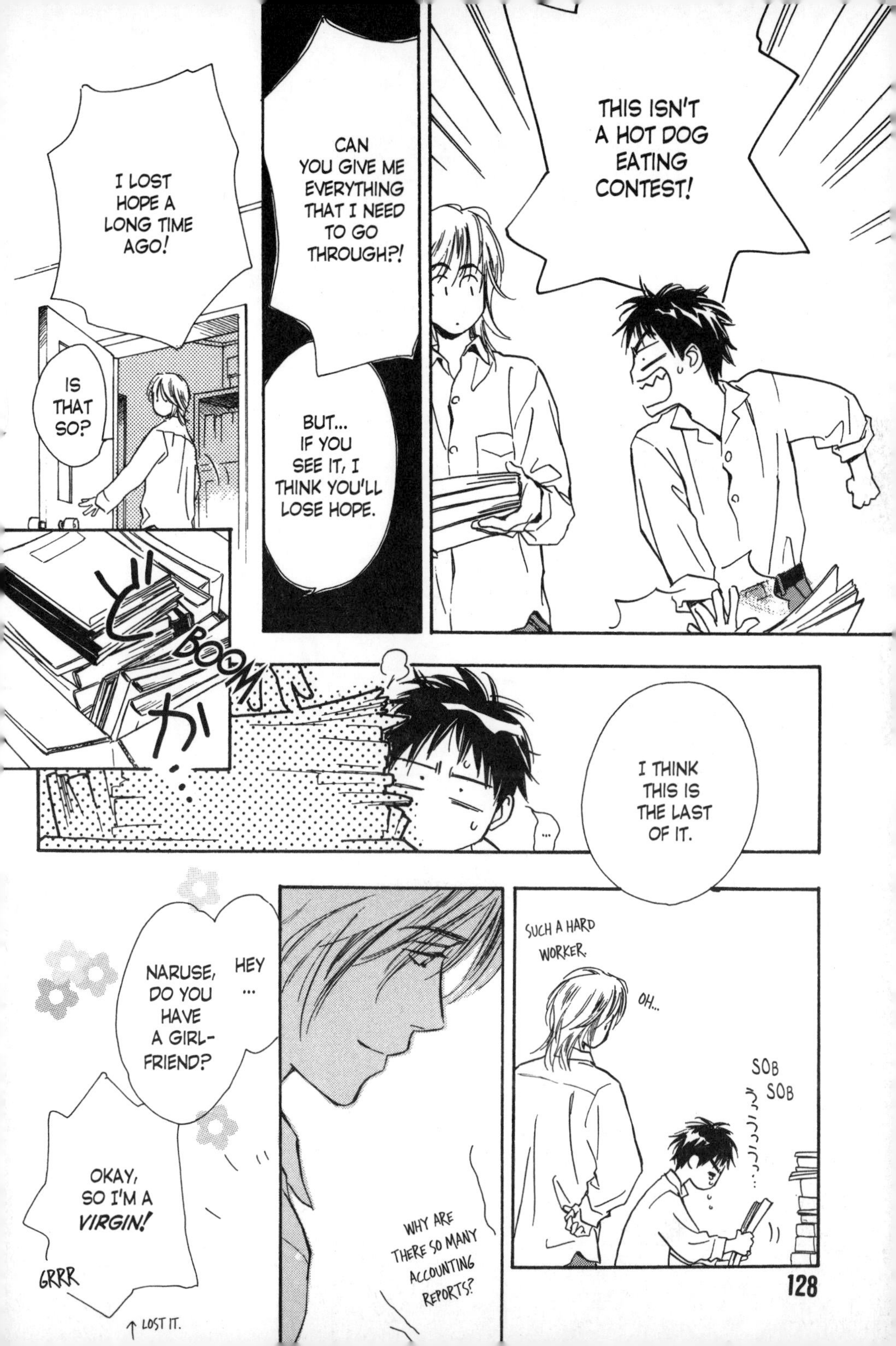
THIS ISN'T A HOT DOG EATING CONTEST!
CAN YOU GIVE ME EVERYTHING THAT I NEED TO GO THROUGH?!
BUT... IF YOU SEE IT, I THINK YOU'LL LOSE HOPE.
I LOST HOPE A LONG TIME AGO!
IS THAT SO?
BOOM
I THINK THIS IS THE LAST OF IT.
...
SUCH A HARD WORKER.
OH...
SOB SOB
WHY ARE THERE SO MANY ACCOUNTING REPORTS?
HEY ...
NARUSE, DO YOU HAVE A GIRL-FRIEND?
OKAY, SO I'M A VIRGIN!
GRRR
↑ LOST IT.

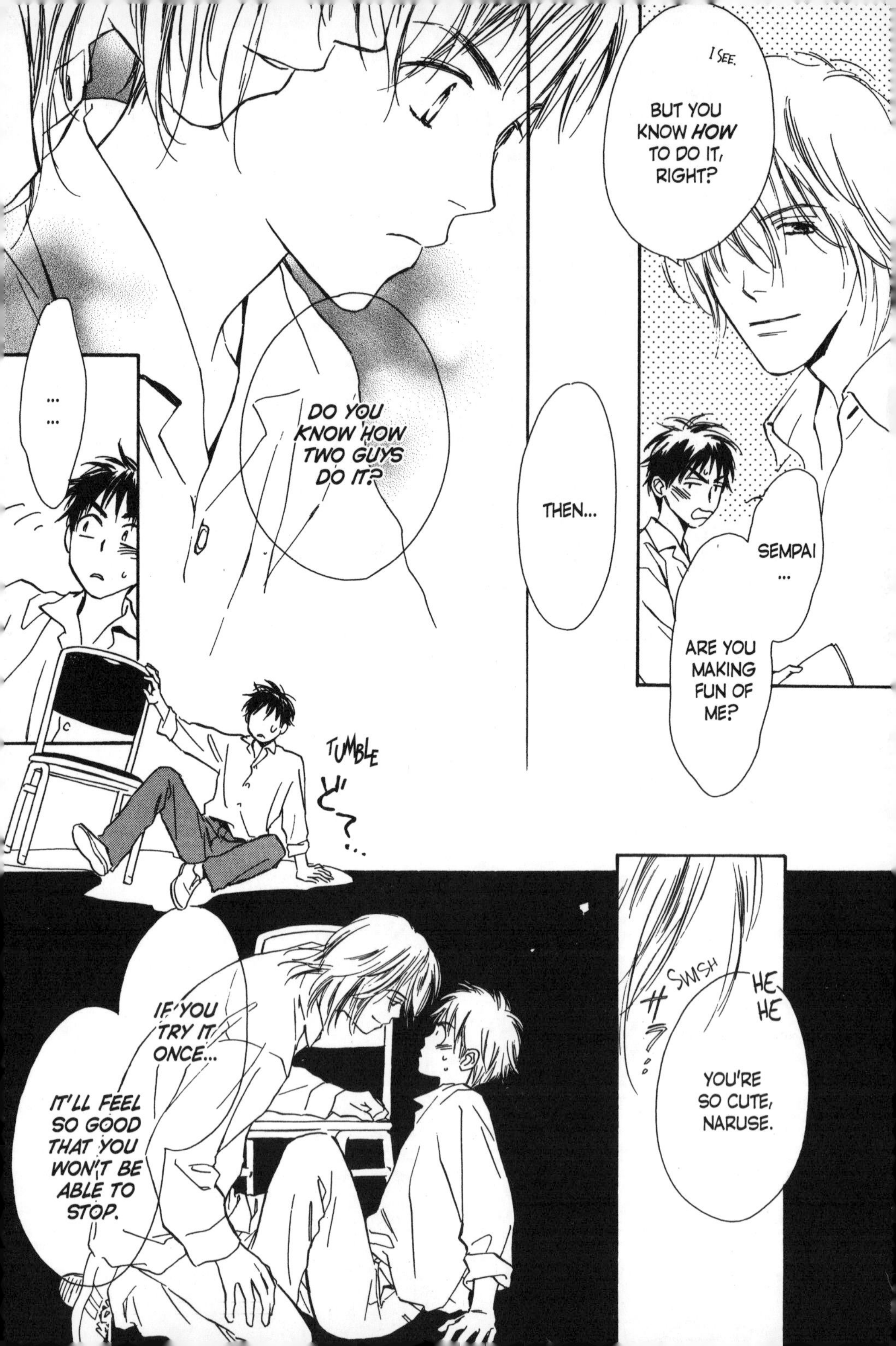
I SEE.
BUT YOU KNOW *HOW* TO DO IT, RIGHT?
DO YOU KNOW HOW TWO GUYS DO IT?
SEMPAI ...
ARE YOU MAKING FUN OF ME?
THEN...
... ...
TUMBLE
HE HE
SWISH
YOU'RE SO CUTE, NARUSE.
IF YOU TRY IT ONCE...
IT'LL FEEL SO GOOD THAT YOU WON'T BE ABLE TO STOP.

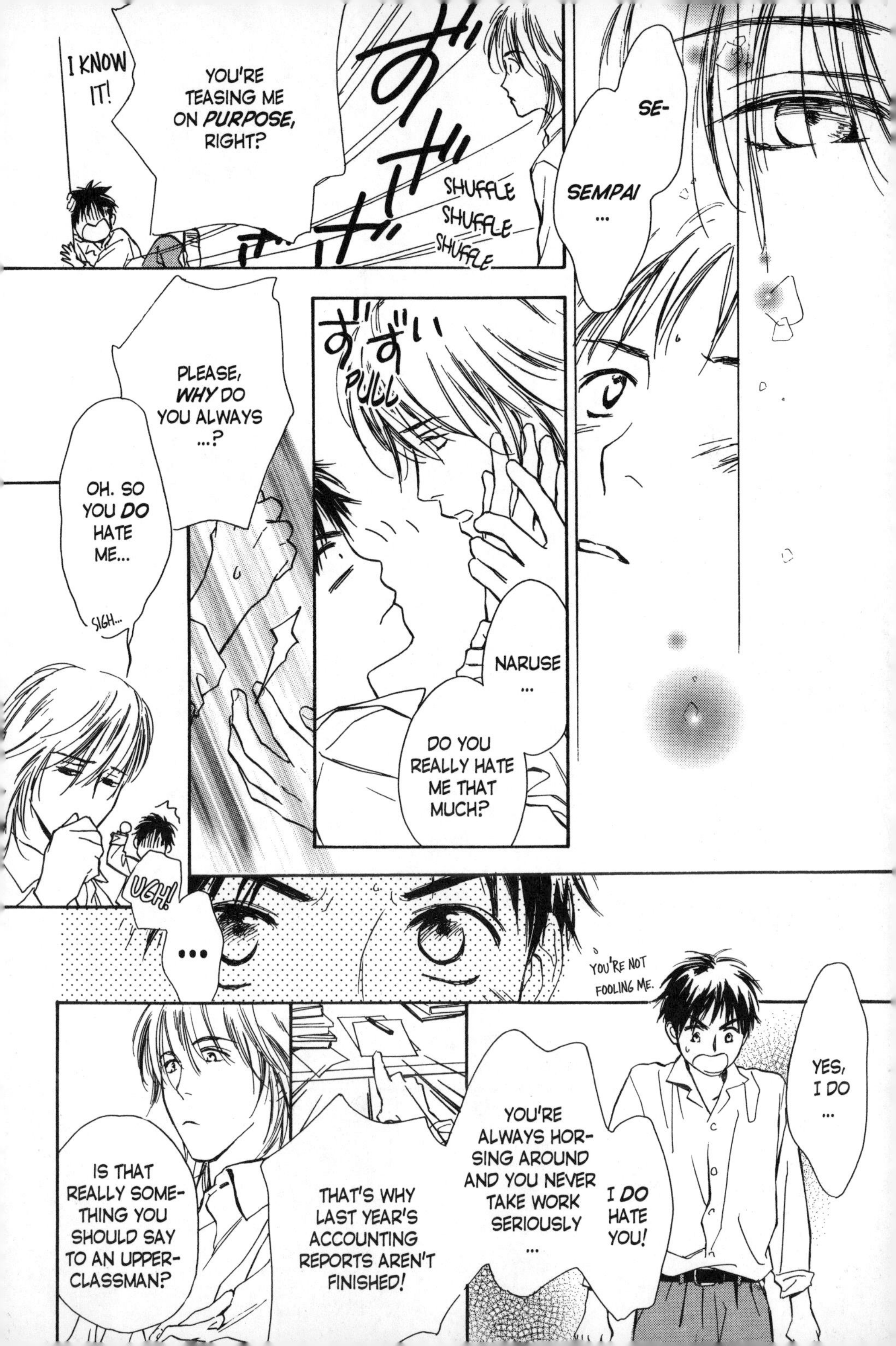
SE-
SEMPAI ...
YOU'RE TEASING ME ON PURPOSE, RIGHT?
I KNOW IT!
SHUFFLE SHUFFLE SHUFFLE
PULL
NARUSE ...
DO YOU REALLY HATE ME THAT MUCH?
PLEASE, WHY DO YOU ALWAYS ...?
OH. SO YOU DO HATE ME...
SIGH...
UGH!
...
YES, I DO ...
I DO HATE YOU!
YOU'RE NOT FOOLING ME.
YOU'RE ALWAYS HOR-SING AROUND AND YOU NEVER TAKE WORK SERIOUSLY ...
THAT'S WHY LAST YEAR'S ACCOUNTING REPORTS AREN'T FINISHED!
IS THAT REALLY SOME-THING YOU SHOULD SAY TO AN UPPER-CLASSMAN?

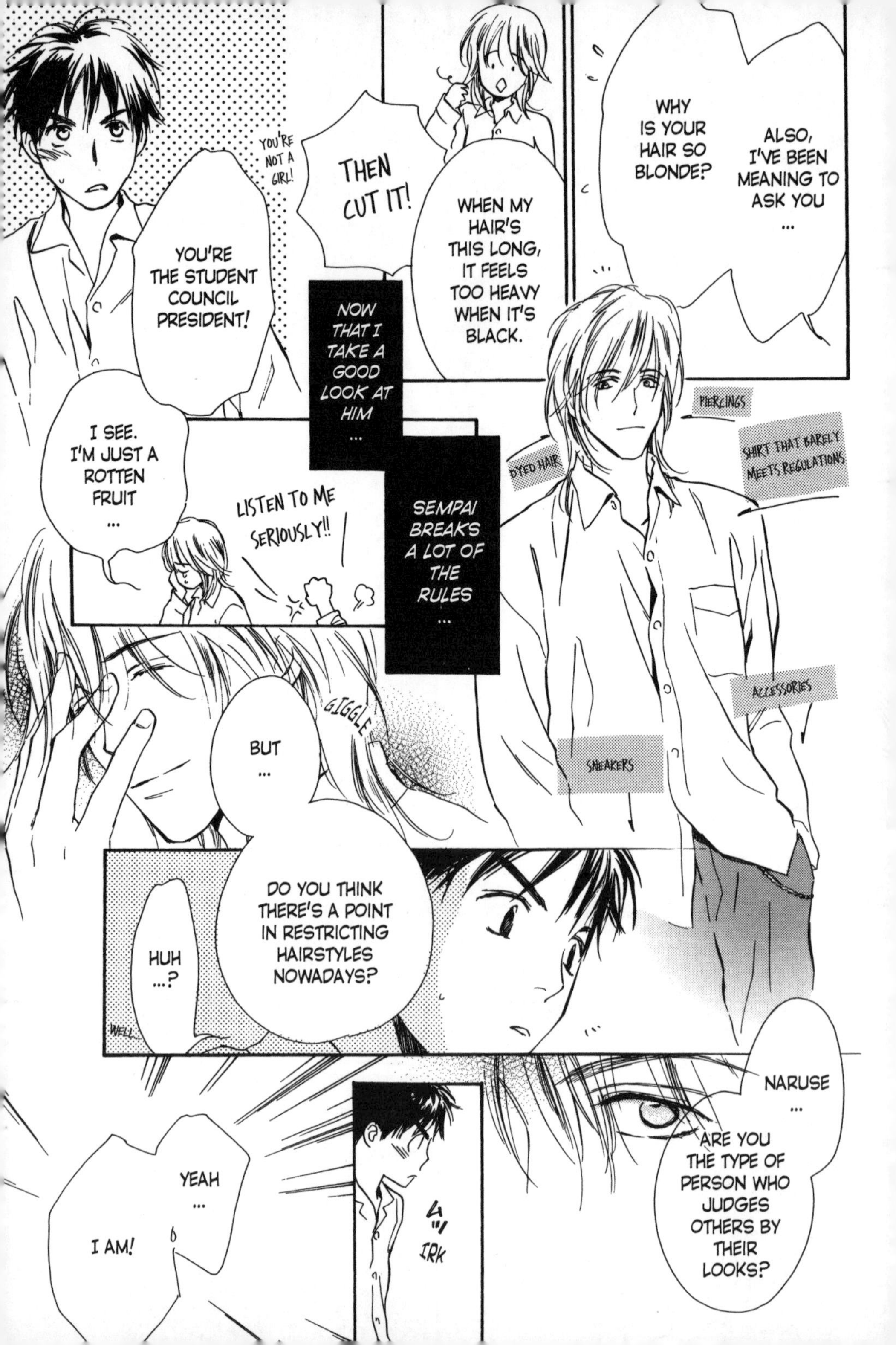
ALSO, I'VE BEEN MEANING TO ASK YOU ...
WHY IS YOUR HAIR SO BLONDE?
WHEN MY HAIR'S THIS LONG, IT FEELS TOO HEAVY WHEN IT'S BLACK.
THEN CUT IT!
YOU'RE NOT A GIRL!
YOU'RE THE STUDENT COUNCIL PRESIDENT!
NOW THAT I TAKE A GOOD LOOK AT HIM ...
SEMPAI BREAKS A LOT OF THE RULES ...
PIERCINGS
SHIRT THAT BARELY MEETS REGULATIONS
DYED HAIR
ACCESSORIES
SNEAKERS
LISTEN TO ME SERIOUSLY!!
I SEE. I'M JUST A ROTTEN FRUIT ...
GIGGLE
BUT ...
DO YOU THINK THERE'S A POINT IN RESTRICTING HAIRSTYLES NOWADAYS?
HUH ...?
WELL...
NARUSE ...
ARE YOU THE TYPE OF PERSON WHO JUDGES OTHERS BY THEIR LOOKS?
IRK
YEAH ...
I AM!

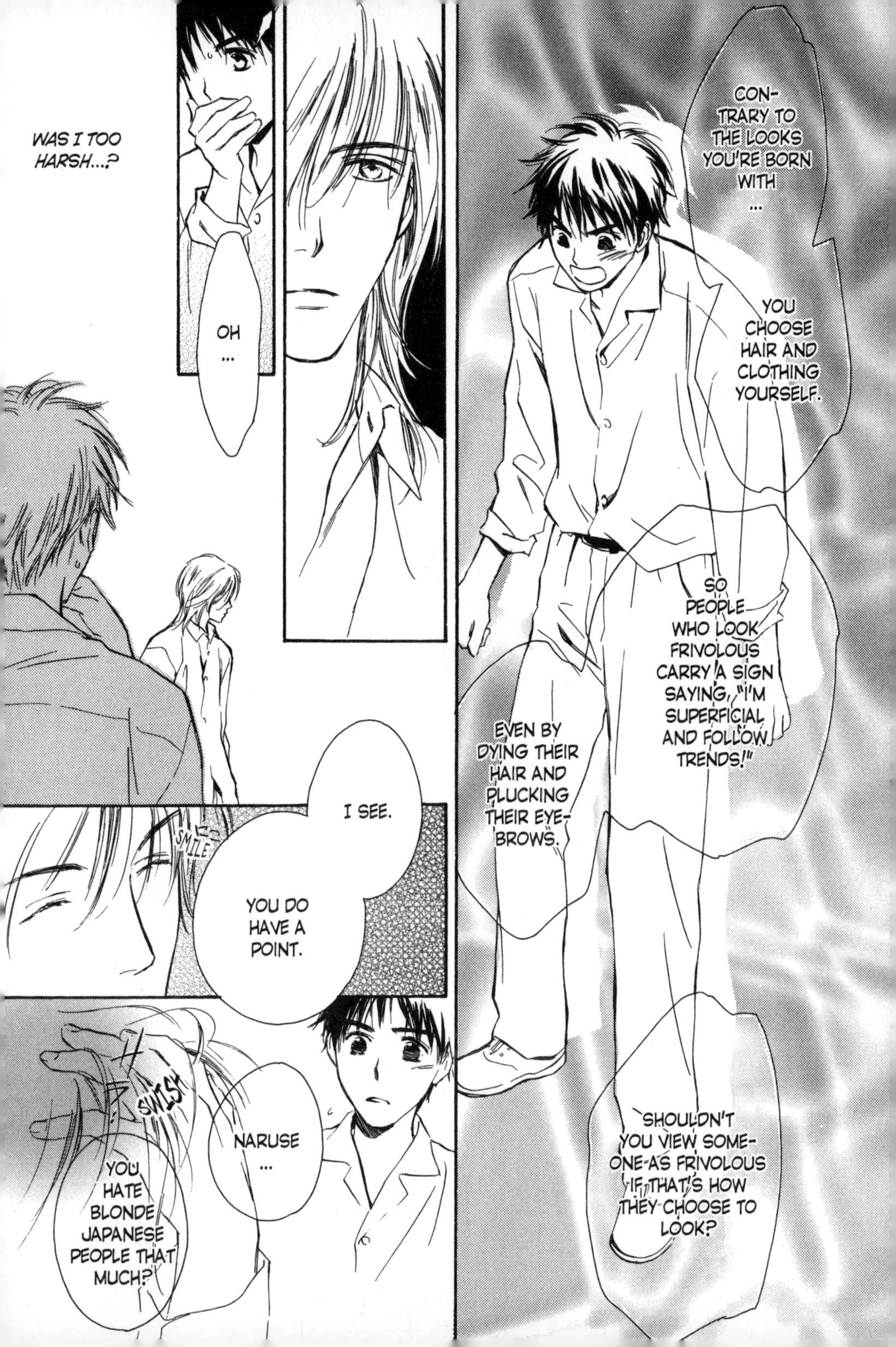
CON-TRARY TO THE LOOKS YOU'RE BORN WITH ...
YOU CHOOSE HAIR AND CLOTHING YOURSELF.
SO PEOPLE WHO LOOK FRIVOLOUS CARRY A SIGN SAYING, "I'M SUPERFICIAL AND FOLLOW TRENDS!"
EVEN BY DYING THEIR HAIR AND PLUCKING THEIR EYE-BROWS.
SHOULDN'T YOU VIEW SOME-ONE AS FRIVOLOUS IF THAT'S HOW THEY CHOOSE TO LOOK?
OH ...
WAS I TOO HARSH...?
SMILE
I SEE.
YOU DO HAVE A POINT.
NARUSE ...
SWISH
YOU HATE BLONDE JAPANESE PEOPLE THAT MUCH?

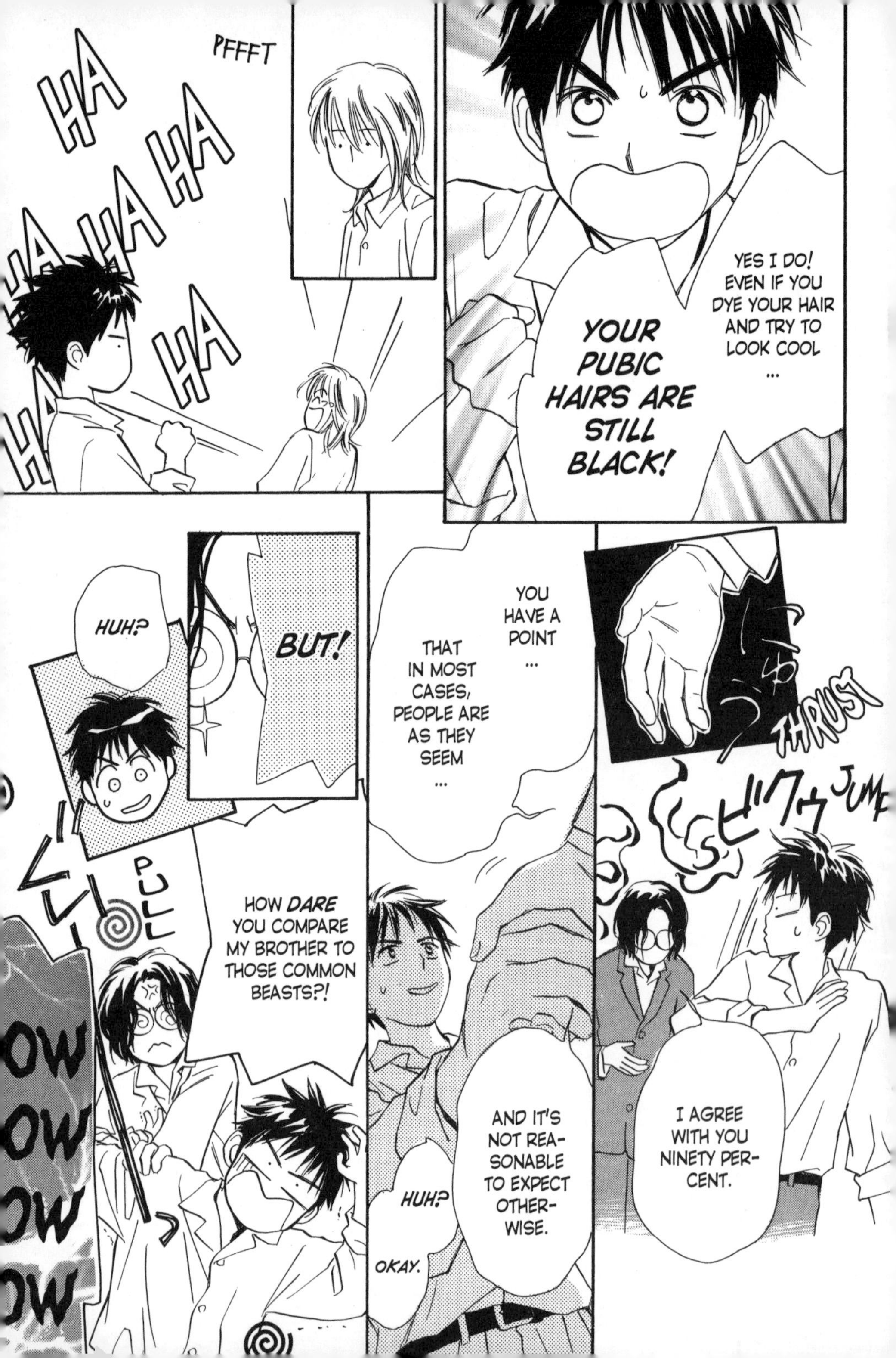

YES I DO! EVEN IF YOU DYE YOUR HAIR AND TRY TO LOOK COOL ...
YOUR PUBIC HAIRS ARE STILL BLACK!
PFFFT
HA HA HA HA HA HA HA HA
THRUST
ビクゥ
JUMP
I AGREE WITH YOU NINETY PER-CENT.
YOU HAVE A POINT ...
THAT IN MOST CASES, PEOPLE ARE AS THEY SEEM ...
AND IT'S NOT REA-SONABLE TO EXPECT OTHER-WISE.
HUH?
OKAY.
BUT!
HUH?
HOW DARE YOU COMPARE MY BROTHER TO THOSE COMMON BEASTS?!
PULL
OW OW OW OW

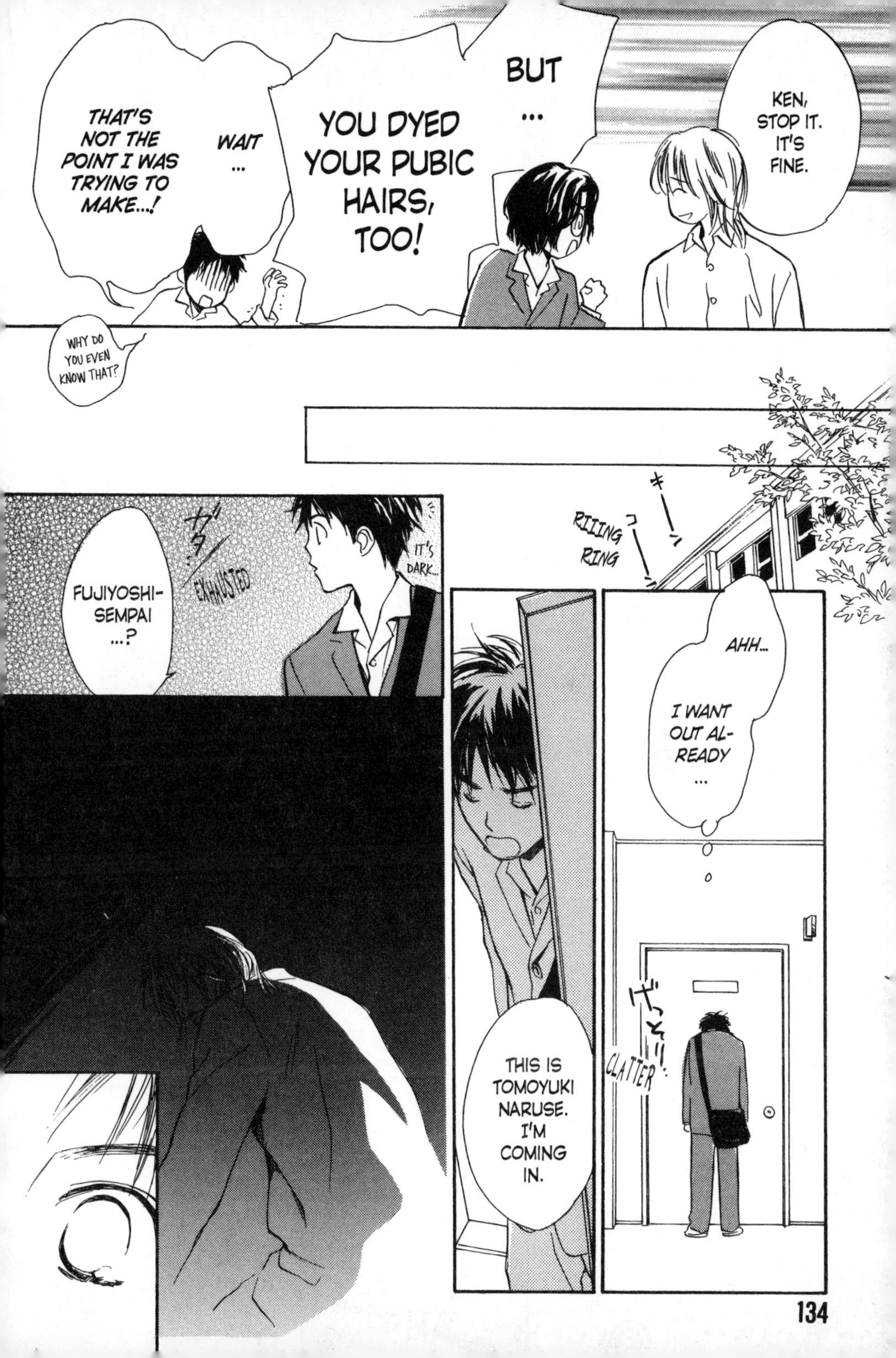
KEN, STOP IT. IT'S FINE.
BUT ...
YOU DYED YOUR PUBIC HAIRS, TOO!
WAIT ...
THAT'S NOT THE POINT I WAS TRYING TO MAKE...!
WHY DO YOU EVEN KNOW THAT?
RIIING RING
AHH... I WANT OUT AL-READY ...
CLATTER
THIS IS TOMOYUKI NARUSE. I'M COMING IN.
IT'S DARK...
EXHAUSTED
FUJIYOSHI-SEMPAI ...?

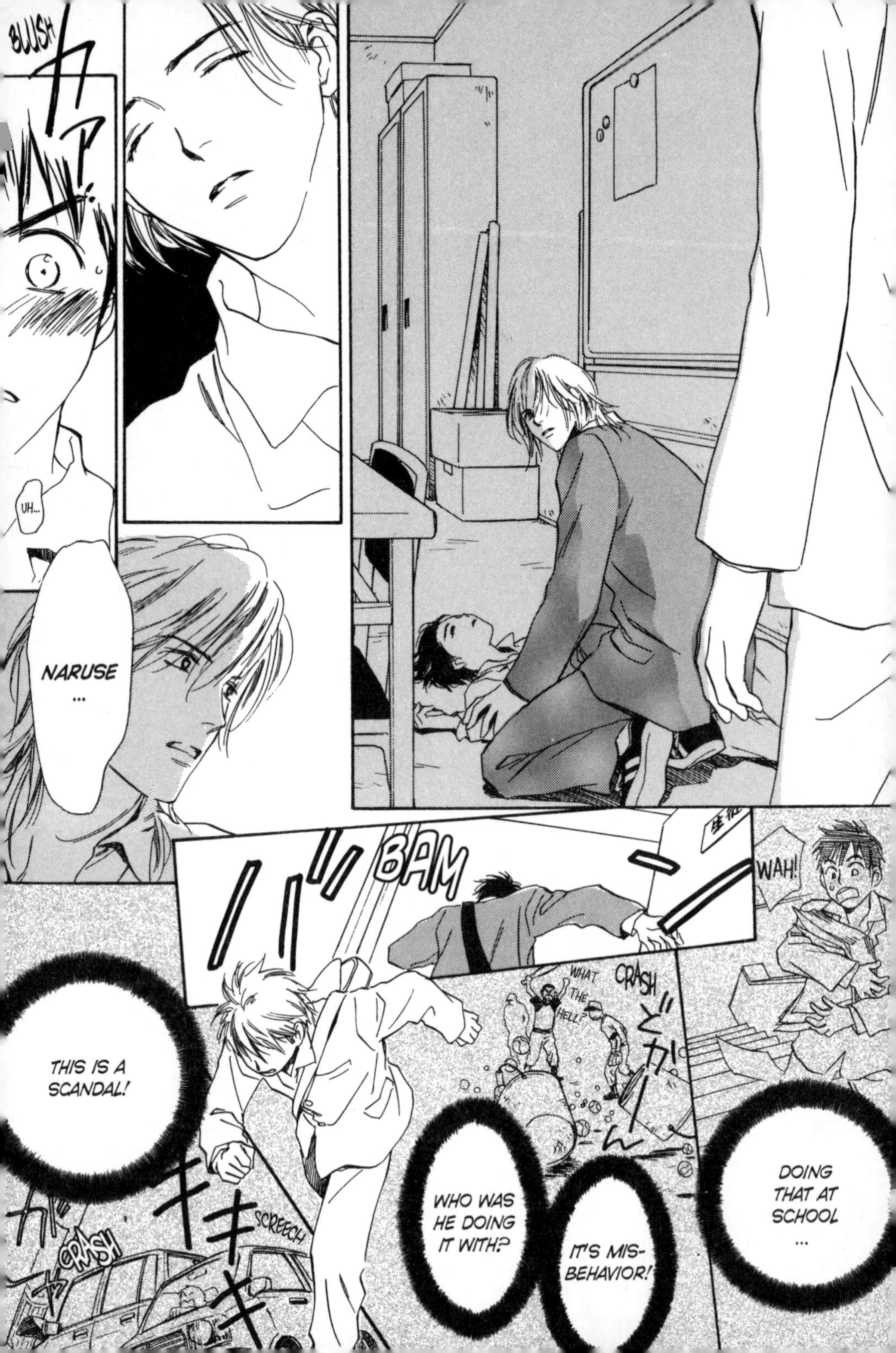
BLUSH
UH...
NARUSE ...
WAH!
DOING THAT AT SCHOOL ...
BAM
CRASH
WHAT THE HELL?
IT'S MIS-BEHAVIOR!
WHO WAS HE DOING IT WITH?
SCREECH
THIS IS A SCANDAL!
CRASH

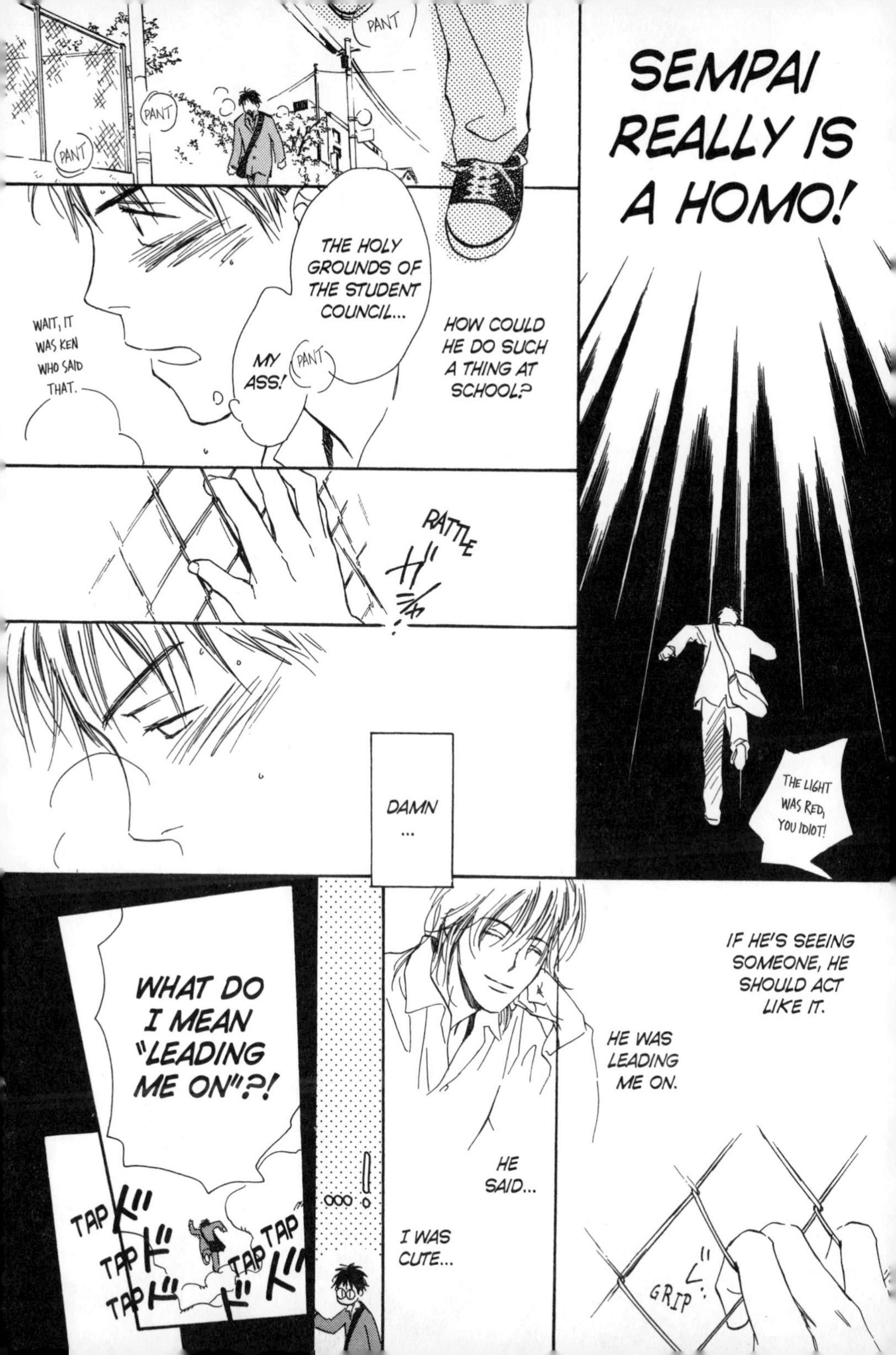
SEMPAI REALLY IS A HOMO!
THE LIGHT WAS RED, YOU IDIOT!
PANT
PANT
PANT
PANT
HOW COULD HE DO SUCH A THING AT SCHOOL?
THE HOLY GROUNDS OF THE STUDENT COUNCIL...
MY ASS!
PANT
WAIT, IT WAS KEN WHO SAID THAT.
RATTLE
DAMN ...
IF HE'S SEEING SOMEONE, HE SHOULD ACT LIKE IT.
HE WAS LEADING ME ON.
HE SAID...
I WAS CUTE...
GRIP
...!
WHAT DO I MEAN "LEADING ME ON"?!
TAP TAP
TAP TAP
TAP TAP

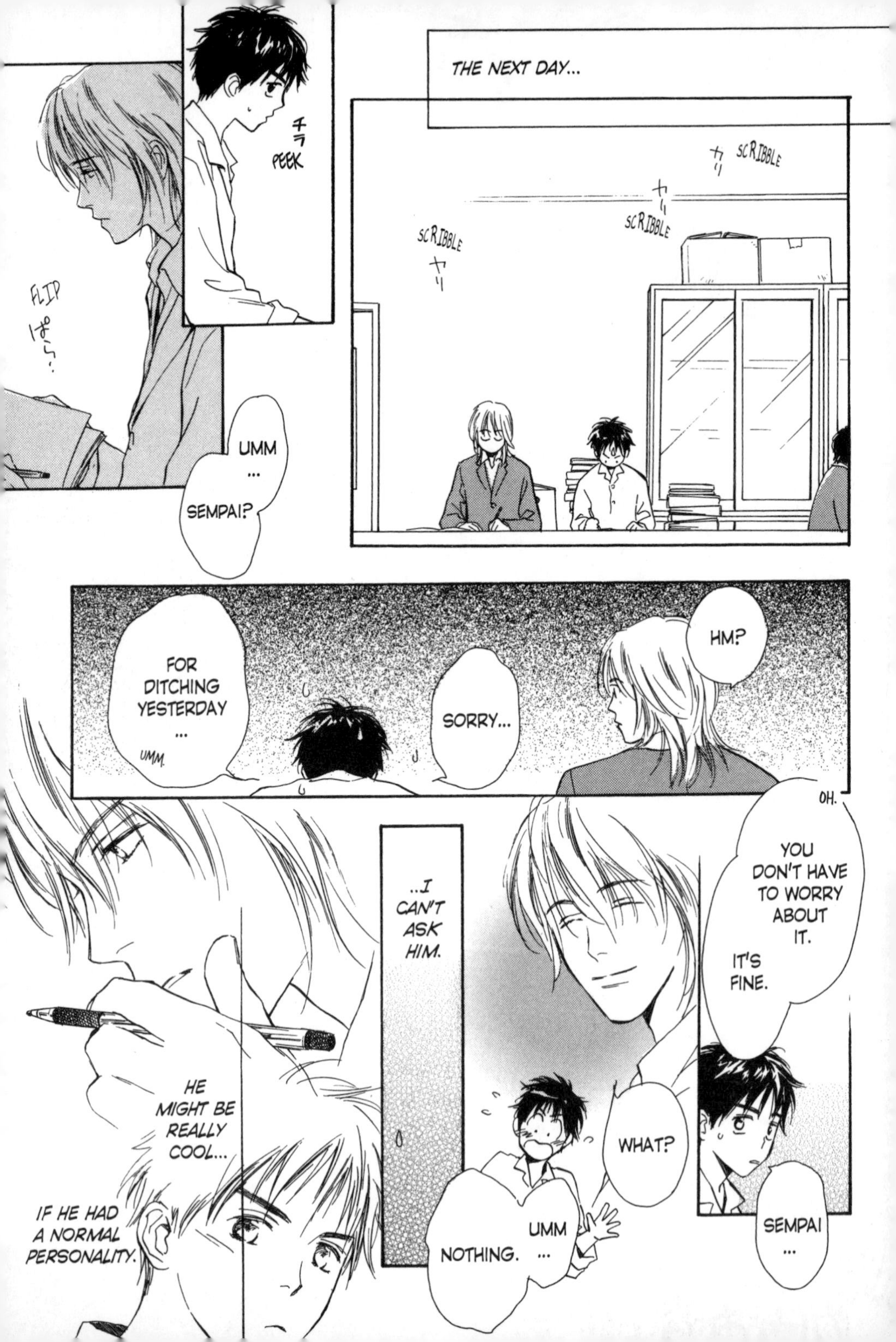
THE NEXT DAY...
ヤリ SCRIBBLE
ヤリ SCRIBBLE
SCRIBBLE ヤリ
チラ PEEK
FLIP ぱら..
UMM ... SEMPAI?
HM?
SORRY...
FOR DITCHING YESTERDAY ...
UMM.
OH.
YOU DON'T HAVE TO WORRY ABOUT IT.
IT'S FINE.
SEMPAI ...
WHAT?
UMM ...
NOTHING.
...I CAN'T ASK HIM.
HE MIGHT BE REALLY COOL...
IF HE HAD A NORMAL PERSONALITY.

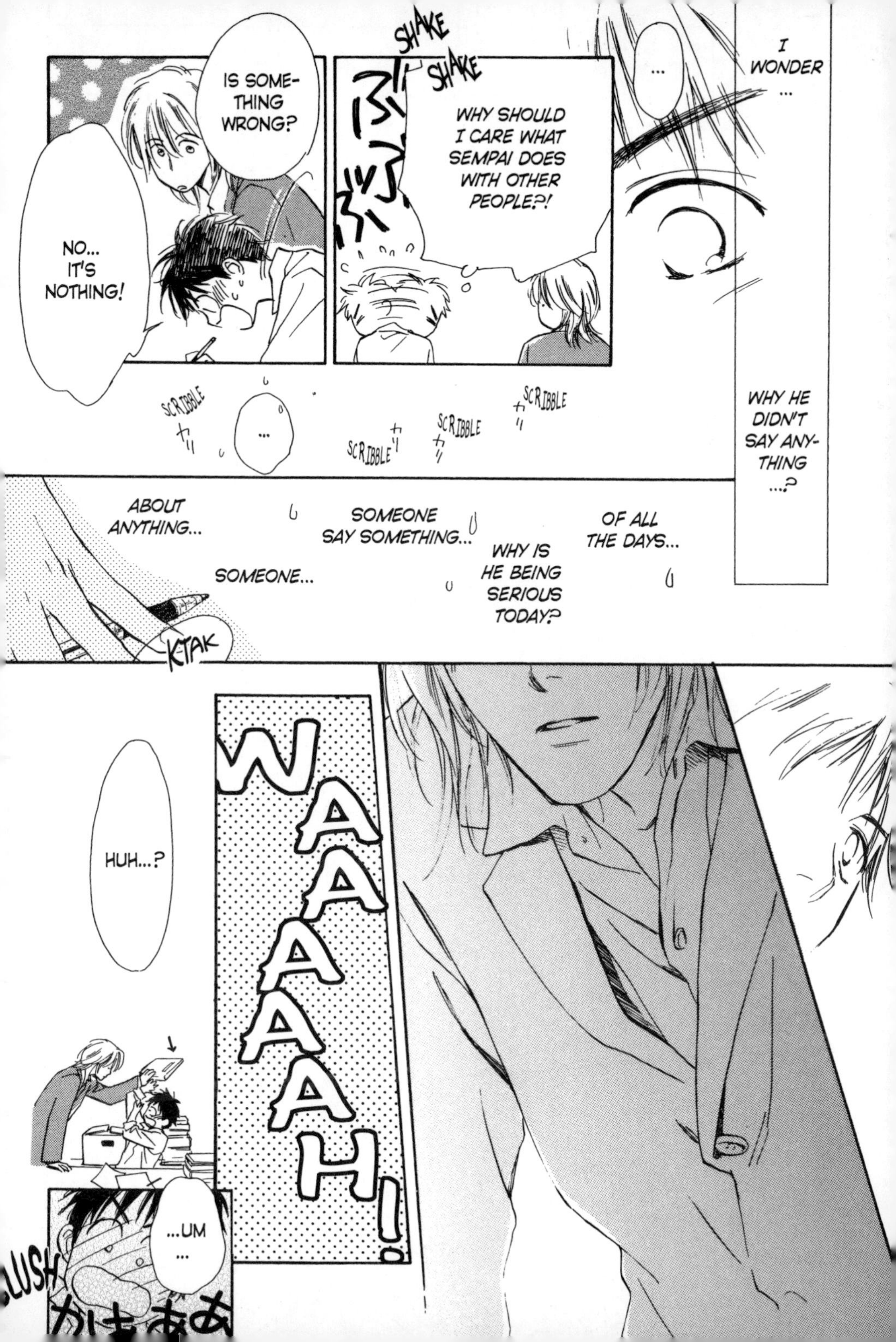
I WONDER ...
WHY HE DIDN'T SAY ANYTHING ...?
...
SHAKE
SHAKE
WHY SHOULD I CARE WHAT SEMPAI DOES WITH OTHER PEOPLE?!
IS SOMETHING WRONG?
NO... IT'S NOTHING!
SCRIBBLE
SCRIBBLE
SCRIBBLE
SCRIBBLE
...
OF ALL THE DAYS...
WHY IS HE BEING SERIOUS TODAY?
SOMEONE SAY SOMETHING...
SOMEONE...
ABOUT ANYTHING...
K-TAK
WAAAAAH!!
HUH...?
...UM ...
BLUSH

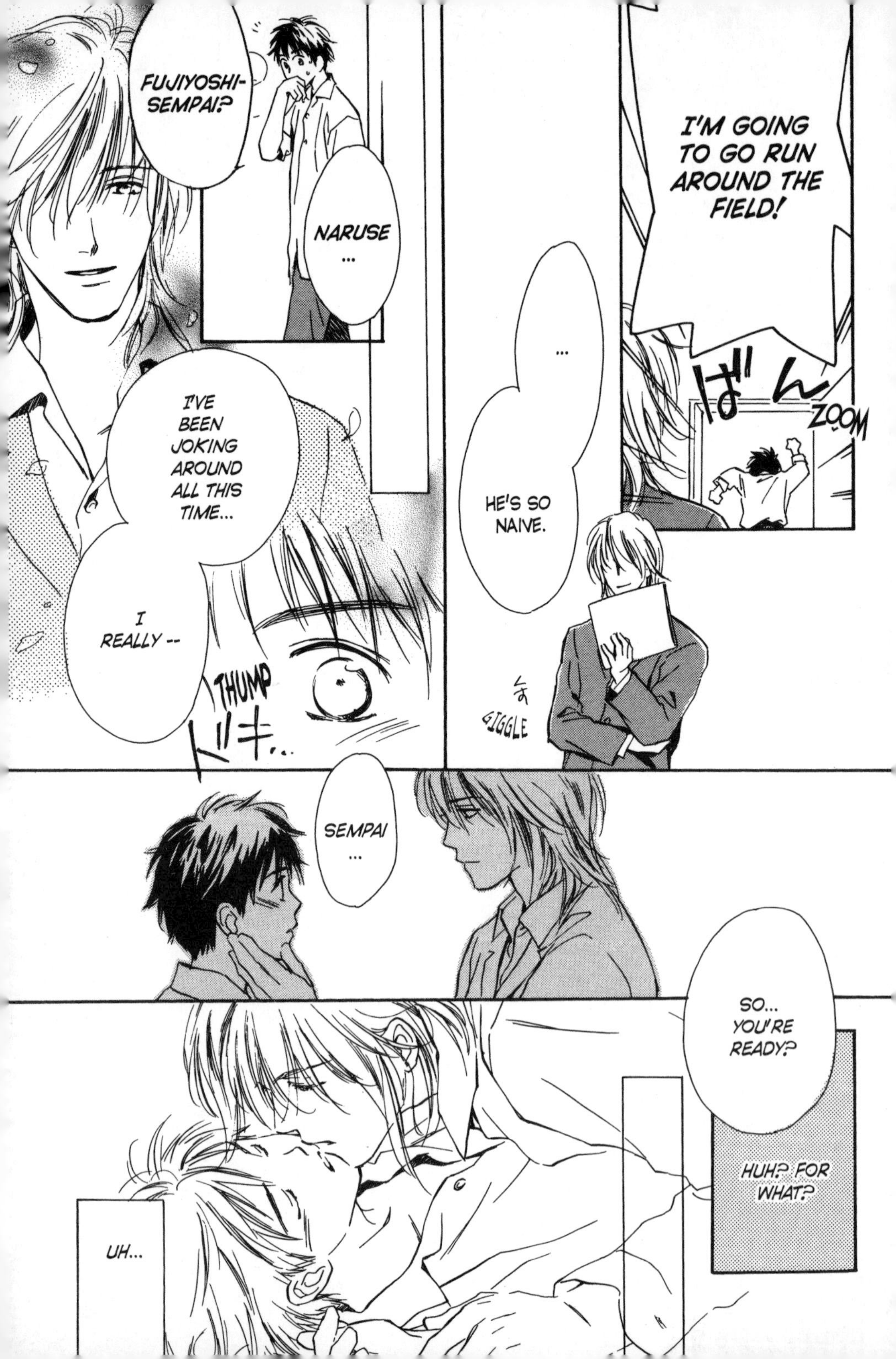

I'M GOING TO GO RUN AROUND THE FIELD!
ばん
ZOOM
...
HE'S SO NAIVE.
GIGGLE
FUJIYOSHI-SEMPAI?
NARUSE ...
I'VE BEEN JOKING AROUND ALL THIS TIME...
I REALLY --
THUMP
ドキ...
SEMPAI ...
SO... YOU'RE READY?
HUH? FOR WHAT?
UH...

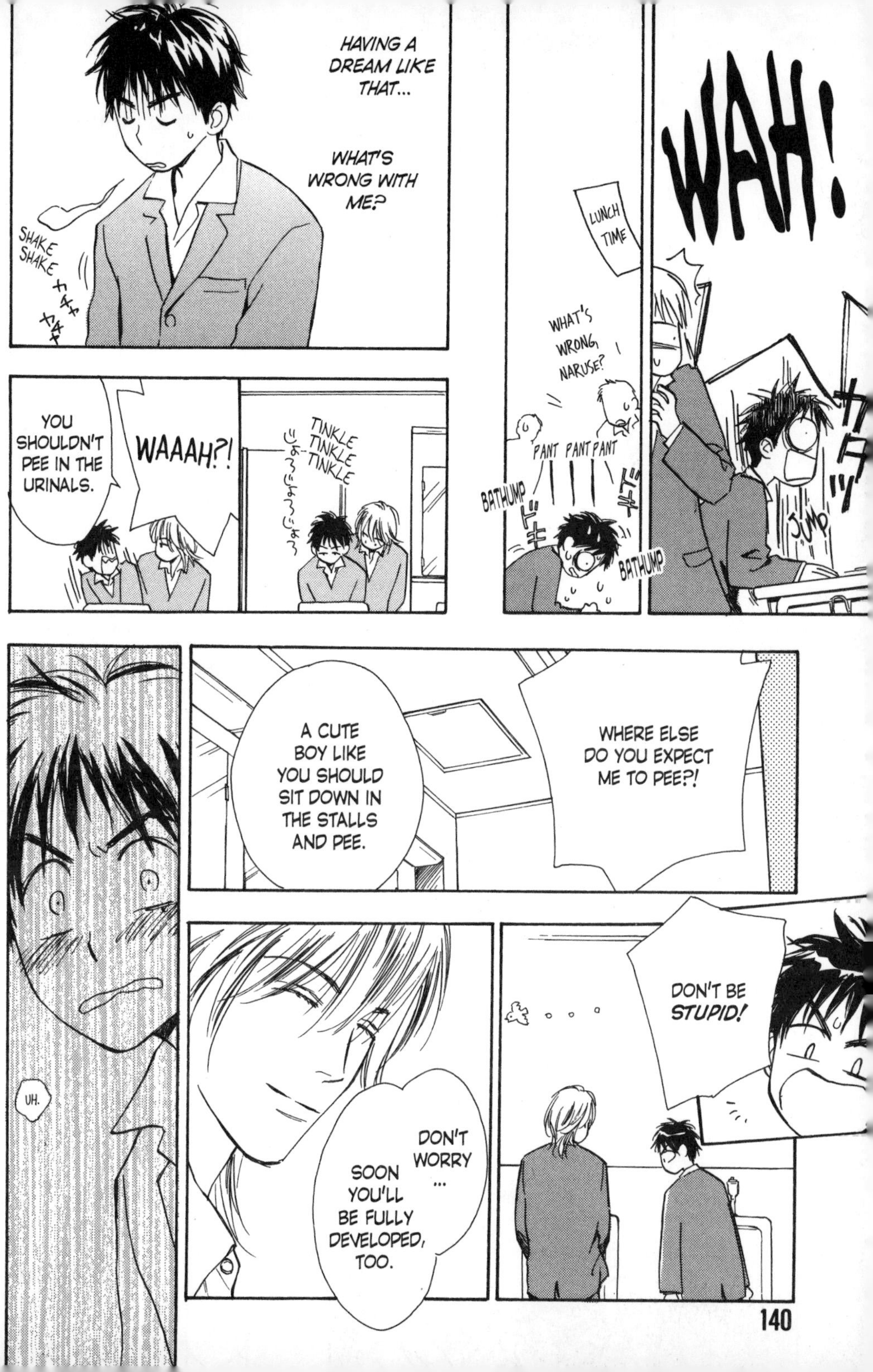
WAH!
JUMP
LUNCH TIME
WHAT'S WRONG, NARUSE?
PANT PANT PANT
BATHUMP
ドキ
ドキ
BATHUMP
HAVING A DREAM LIKE THAT...
WHAT'S WRONG WITH ME?
SHAKE SHAKE
TINKLE TINKLE TINKLE
WAAAH?!
YOU SHOULDN'T PEE IN THE URINALS.
WHERE ELSE DO YOU EXPECT ME TO PEE?!
A CUTE BOY LIKE YOU SHOULD SIT DOWN IN THE STALLS AND PEE.
DON'T BE STUPID!
DON'T WORRY...
SOON YOU'LL BE FULLY DEVELOPED, TOO.
UH.

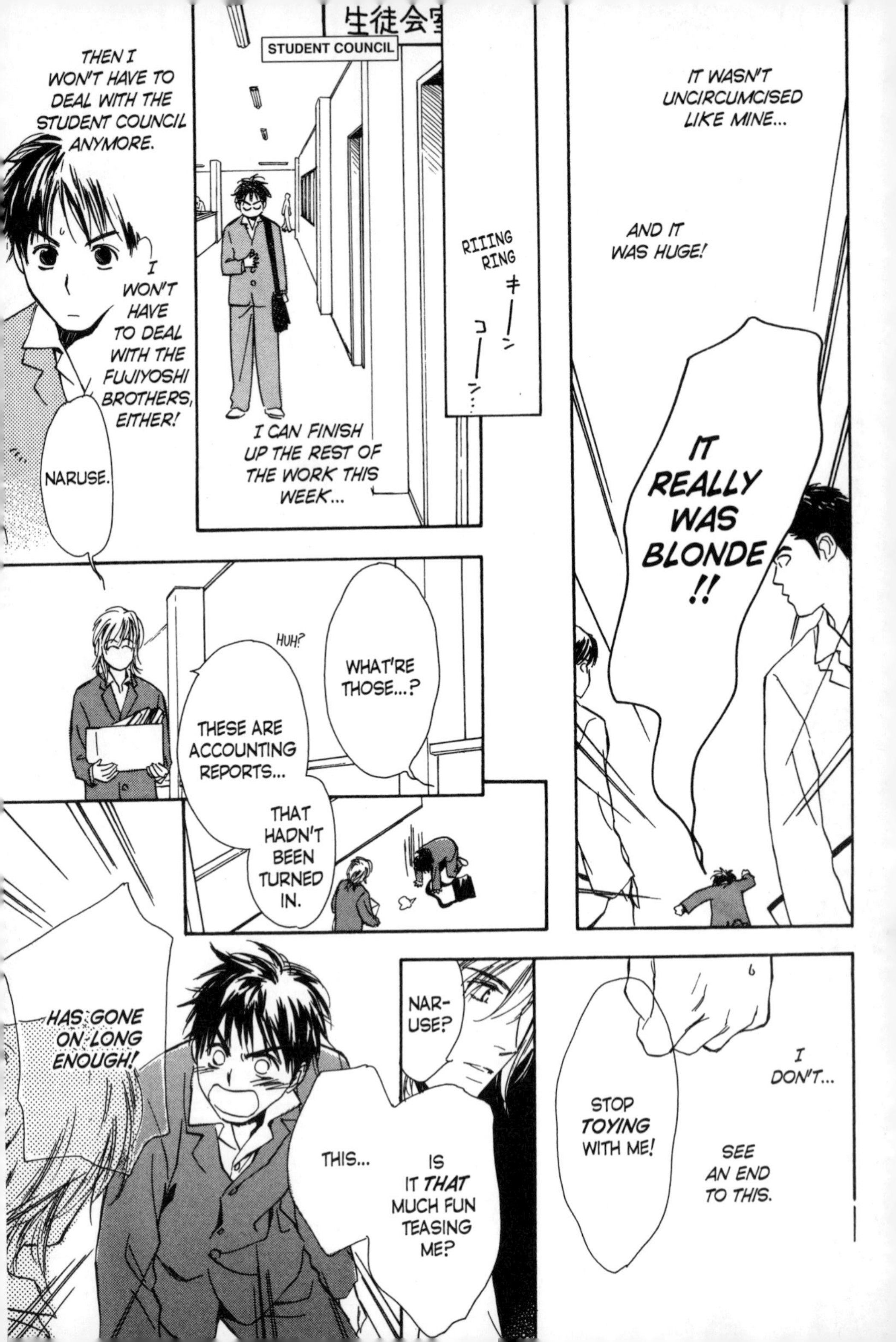
IT WASN'T UNCIRCUMCISED LIKE MINE...
AND IT WAS HUGE!
IT REALLY WAS BLONDE!!
RIIING RING
キーンコーン…
生徒会室
STUDENT COUNCIL
I CAN FINISH UP THE REST OF THE WORK THIS WEEK...
THEN I WON'T HAVE TO DEAL WITH THE STUDENT COUNCIL ANYMORE.
I WON'T HAVE TO DEAL WITH THE FUJIYOSHI BROTHERS, EITHER!
NARUSE.
WHAT'RE THOSE...?
HUH?
THESE ARE ACCOUNTING REPORTS...
THAT HADN'T BEEN TURNED IN.
I DON'T...
SEE AN END TO THIS.
STOP TOYING WITH ME!
NAR-USE?
IS IT THAT MUCH FUN TEASING ME?
THIS...
HAS GONE ON LONG ENOUGH!

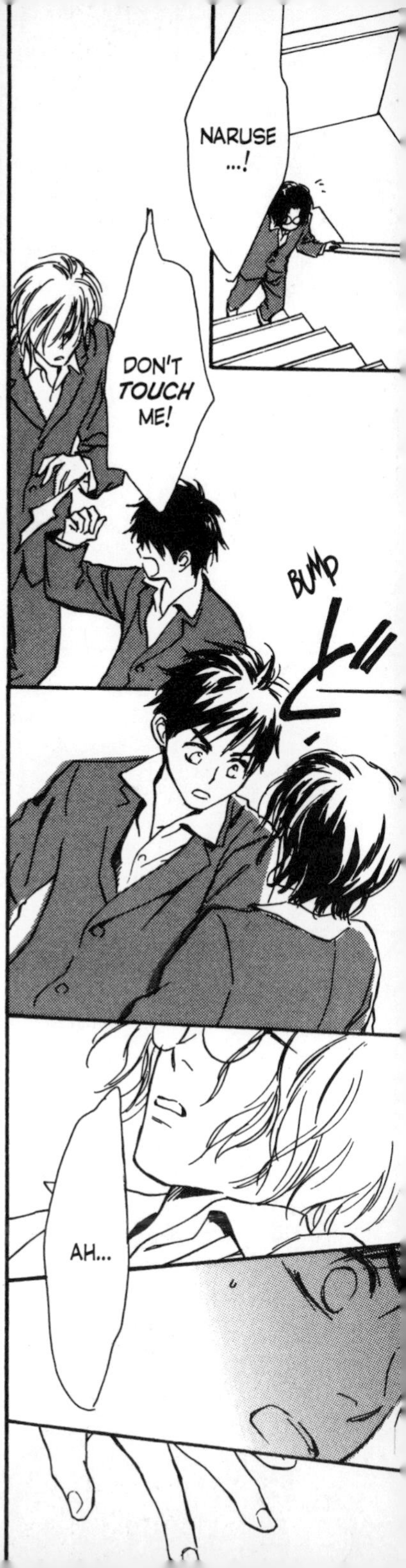
NARUSE ...!
DON'T *TOUCH* ME!
BUMP
AH...

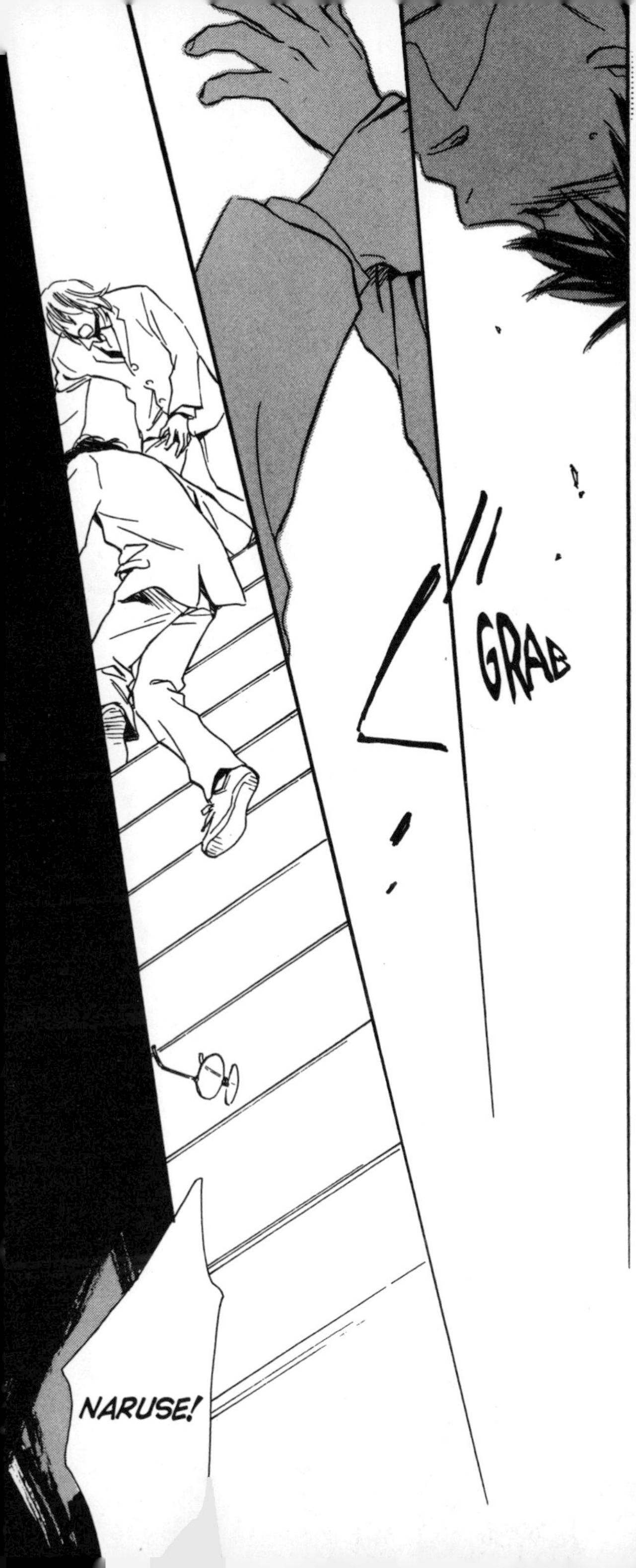
GRAB
NARUSE!

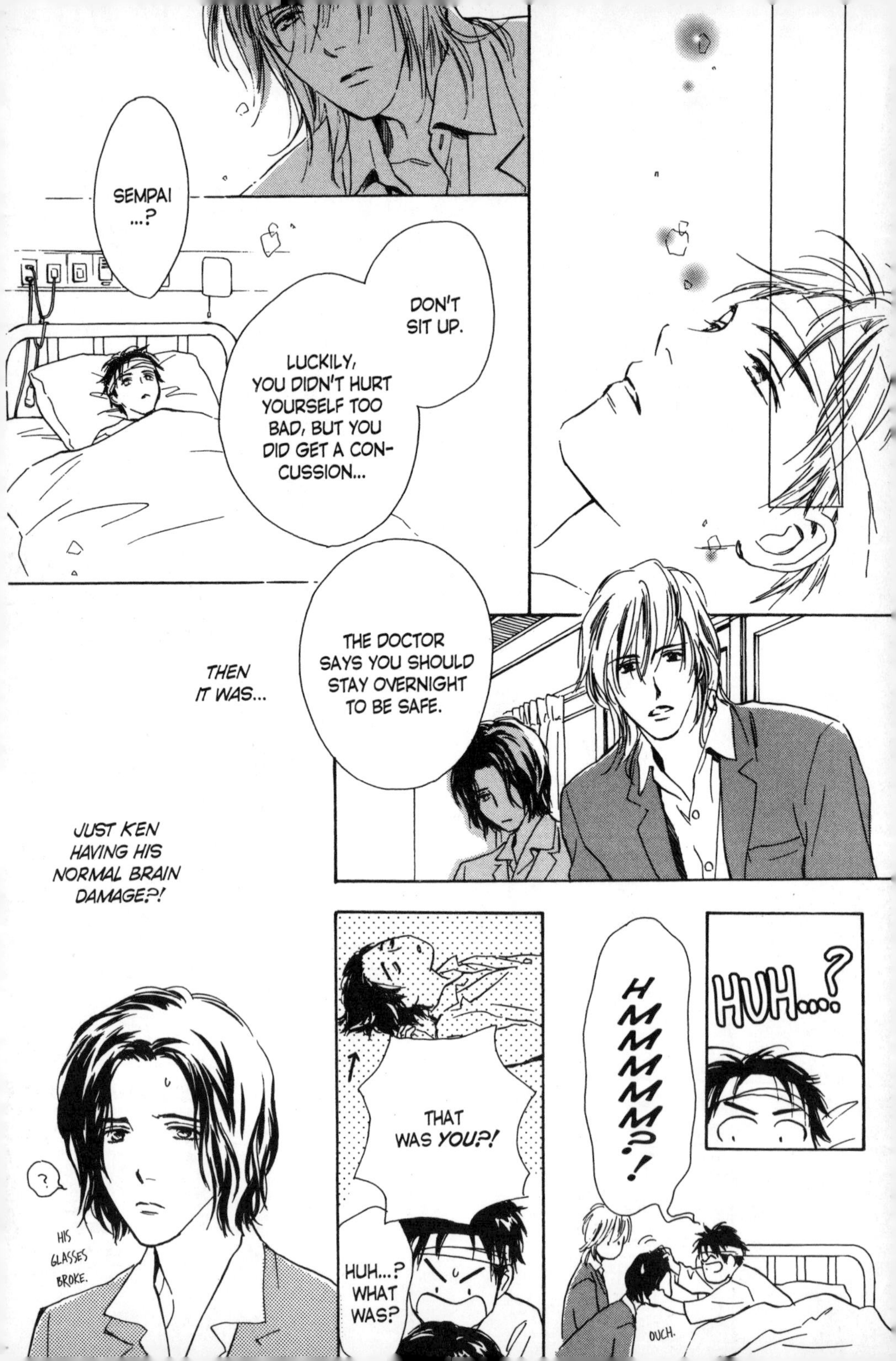
SEMPAI ...?
DON'T SIT UP. LUCKILY, YOU DIDN'T HURT YOURSELF TOO BAD, BUT YOU DID GET A CON-CUSSION...
THE DOCTOR SAYS YOU SHOULD STAY OVERNIGHT TO BE SAFE.
THEN IT WAS...
JUST KEN HAVING HIS NORMAL BRAIN DAMAGE?!
HUH...?
HMMMMMM?!
OUCH.
THAT WAS YOU?!
HUH...? WHAT WAS?
?
HIS GLASSES BROKE.

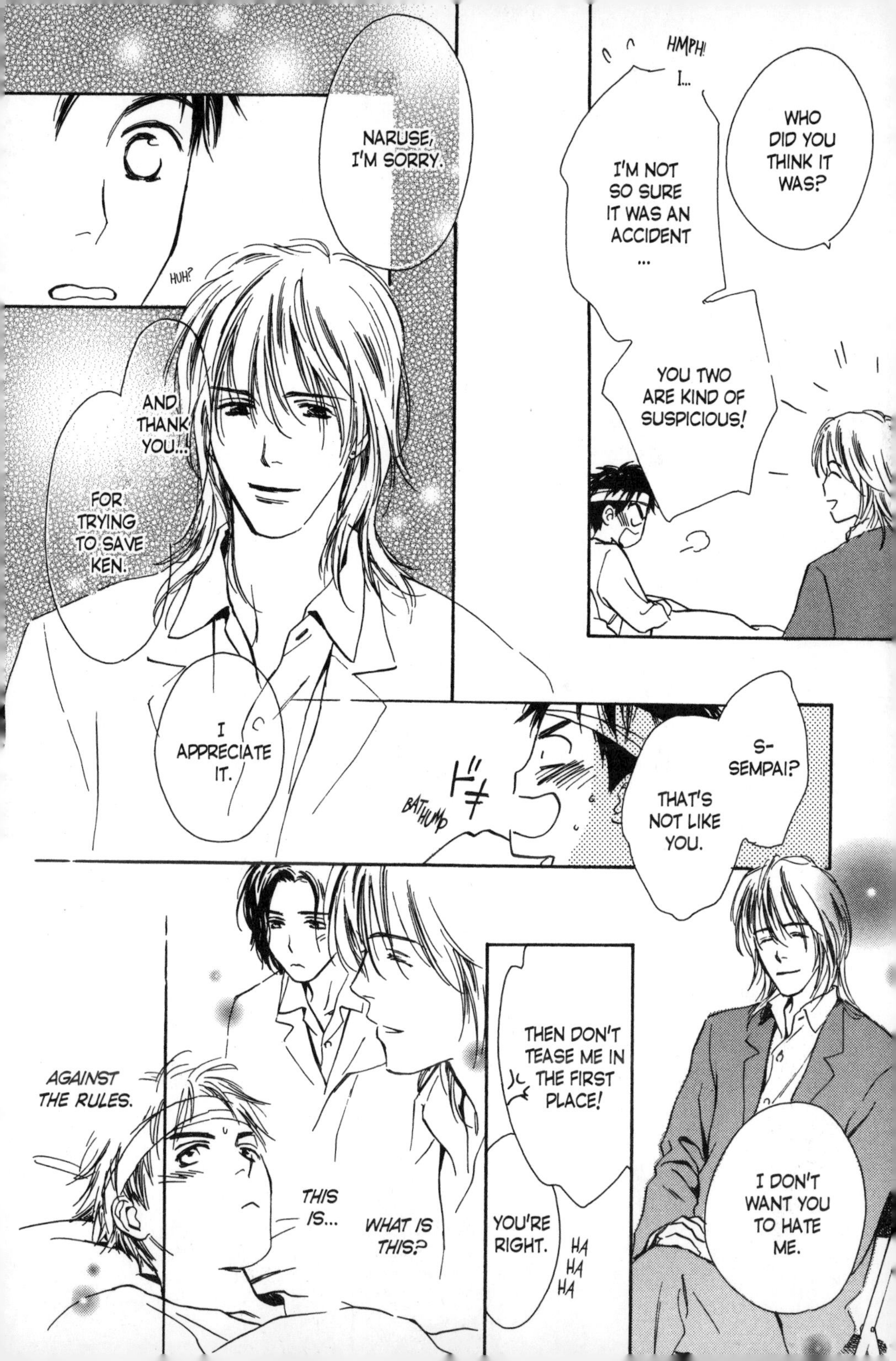
WHO DID YOU THINK IT WAS?
HMPH!
I...
I'M NOT SO SURE IT WAS AN ACCIDENT ...
YOU TWO ARE KIND OF SUSPICIOUS!
NARUSE, I'M SORRY.
HUH?
AND THANK YOU...
FOR TRYING TO SAVE KEN.
I APPRECIATE IT.
S-SEMPAI?
THAT'S NOT LIKE YOU.
BATHUMP
I DON'T WANT YOU TO HATE ME.
THEN DON'T TEASE ME IN THE FIRST PLACE!
YOU'RE RIGHT.
HA HA HA
WHAT IS THIS?
THIS IS...
AGAINST THE RULES.

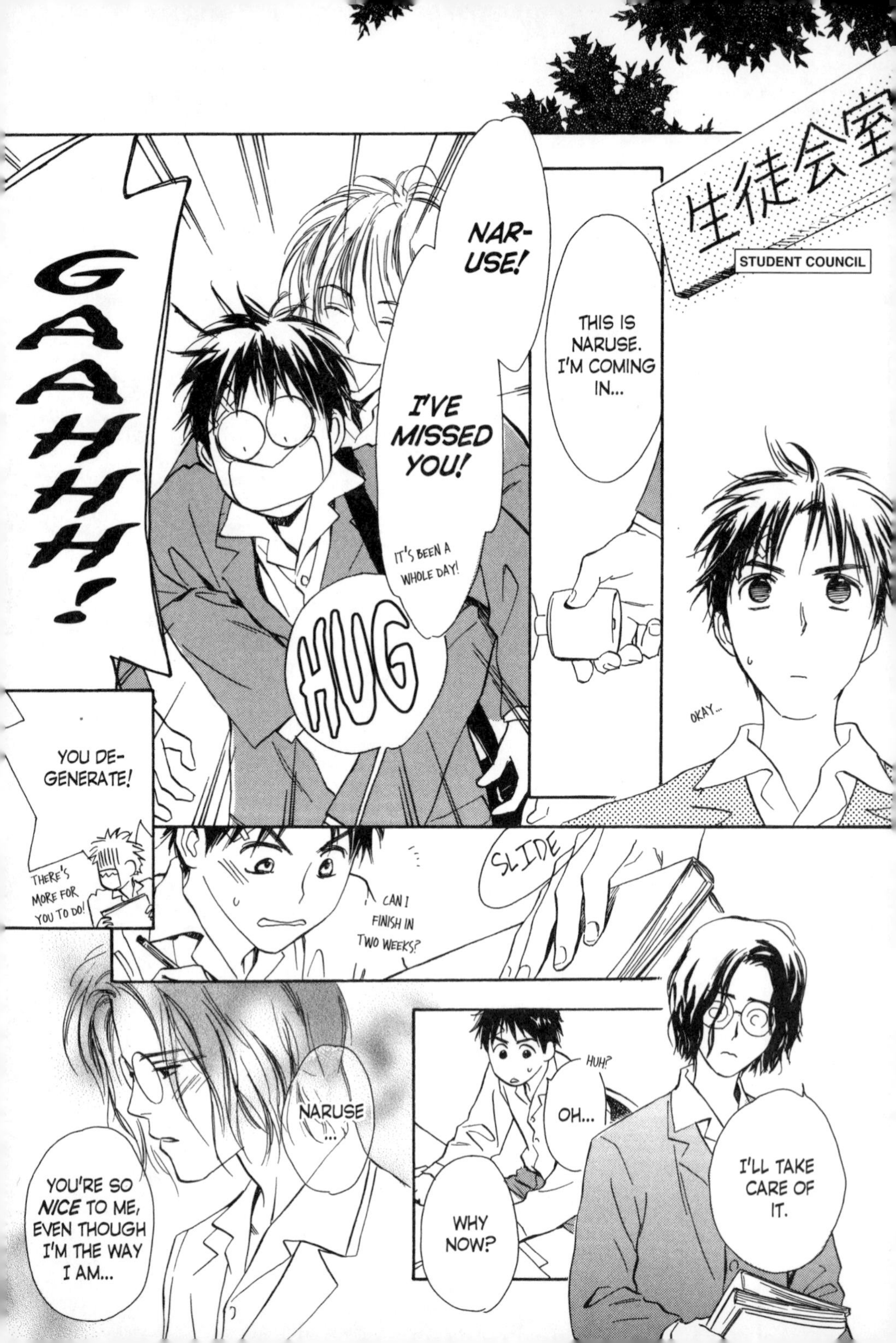

生徒会室
STUDENT COUNCIL
THIS IS NARUSE. I'M COMING IN...
OKAY...
NAR-USE!
I'VE MISSED YOU!
IT'S BEEN A WHOLE DAY!
HUG
GAAHHH!
SLIDE
CAN I FINISH IN TWO WEEKS?
YOU DE-GENERATE!
THERE'S MORE FOR YOU TO DO!
HUH?
OH...
I'LL TAKE CARE OF IT.
WHY NOW?
NARUSE...
YOU'RE SO NICE TO ME, EVEN THOUGH I'M THE WAY I AM...

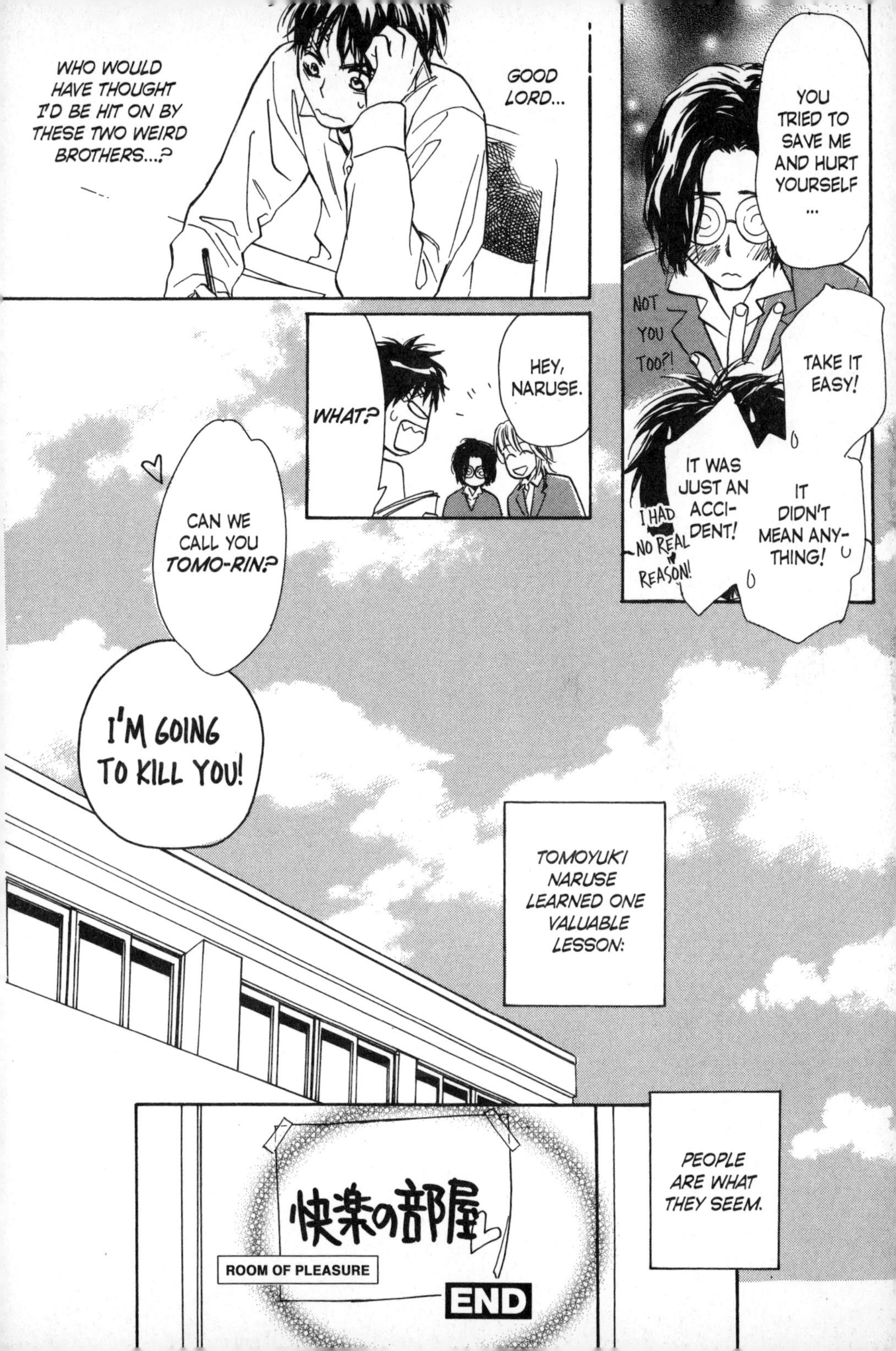
YOU TRIED TO SAVE ME AND HURT YOURSELF ...
NOT YOU TOO?!
TAKE IT EASY!
IT DIDN'T MEAN ANY-THING!
IT WAS JUST AN ACCI-DENT!
I HAD NO REAL REASON!
GOOD LORD...
WHO WOULD HAVE THOUGHT I'D BE HIT ON BY THESE TWO WEIRD BROTHERS...?
HEY, NARUSE.
WHAT?
CAN WE CALL YOU TOMO-RIN?
I'M GOING TO KILL YOU!
TOMOYUKI NARUSE LEARNED ONE VALUABLE LESSON:
PEOPLE ARE WHAT THEY SEEM.
快楽の部屋
ROOM OF PLEASURE
END

PEOPLE ARE WHAT THEY SEEM

THE "RELATIONSHIP BETWEEN THE INSIDE AND OUTSIDE OF PEOPLE" THAT NARUSE TALKS ABOUT IS SOMETHING MY HUSBAND SAYS, AND I USED IT WITHOUT TELLING HIM. MY HUSBAND READ THIS AND SAID... "WOW, IT'S LIKE TELEPATHY! YOU MADE AN EASY-TO-READ STORY ABOUT THE THINGS I WANTED TO SAY..." HE THINKS TOO HIGHLY OF ME. HE FORGOT THAT HE'D ALREADY TOLD ME ABOUT IT...

THIS WAS MY FIRST ATTEMPT AT WRITING A MANGA, AND HAVING SEEN THE END RESULT, I NOTICE THAT I PUT IN TOO MANY LITTLE DETAILS, AND I MADE HONAMI-SAN DO TOO MANY DETAILED DRAWINGS. I'M SO SORRY AND I'M FULL OF REGRET FOR MAKING HER DO THIS.

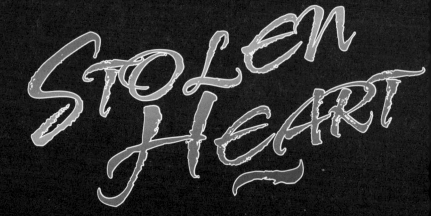

ISN'T IT RARE FOR HONAMI-SAN TO DRAW MODERN CAUCASIAN MALES? AREN'T THEY REALLY ATTRACTIVE, TOO?! I LOVE AMERICAN MOVIES, SO SETTING THE STORY IN THE UNITED STATES WAS LIKE MAKING MY OWN VERSION, AND WAS A LOT OF FUN.

THIS WAS MY FIRST TIME WRITING A MANGA AND IT MADE ME REALIZE A LOT OF THINGS. THE SUCCESS-OR-FAIL PORTION OF THE WORK IS CONTROLLED BY SOMEONE ELSE IN MANGA, WHERE IT'S CONTROLLED BY MYSELF IN NOVELS. ALSO, WHEN I WRITE NOVELS, IT'S A SOLITARY EXPERIENCE. IT WAS NEW FOR ME WORKING WITH OTHER PEOPLE AND CREATING A STORY, WHILE KEEPING THE DIVISION OF LABOR IN MIND. I KNOW THAT I WAS THE ONE SETTING THE SCENES AND WRITING THE SCRIPT, BUT BY THE TIME THE MANGA WAS FINISHED, THAT NOTION WAS COMPLETELY GONE, AND I WAS ABLE TO ENJOY IT PURELY AS A READER.

HONAMI-SAN, THANK YOU VERY MUCH. I LOVED EVERY CHARACTER, BUT I WAS ESPECIALLY THRILLED WITH COLLIN AND THE YOUNGER BROTHER, FUJIYOSHI. THEY WERE FAR BETTER THAN WHAT I IMAGINED THEY WOULD BE LIKE.

EDITOR TANAKA-SAN, THANK YOU SO MUCH FOR POINTING OUT SPECIFIC PROBLEMS AND ENCOURAGING ME ALL THE WAY THROUGH. THERE WERE SOME POINTS WHEN I THOUGHT TANAKA-SAN WAS THE SCRIPT WRITER.

TO ALL MY READERS, I HOPE YOU ENJOYED THIS TO YOUR HEART'S CONTENT.

TILL WE MEET NEXT TIME!

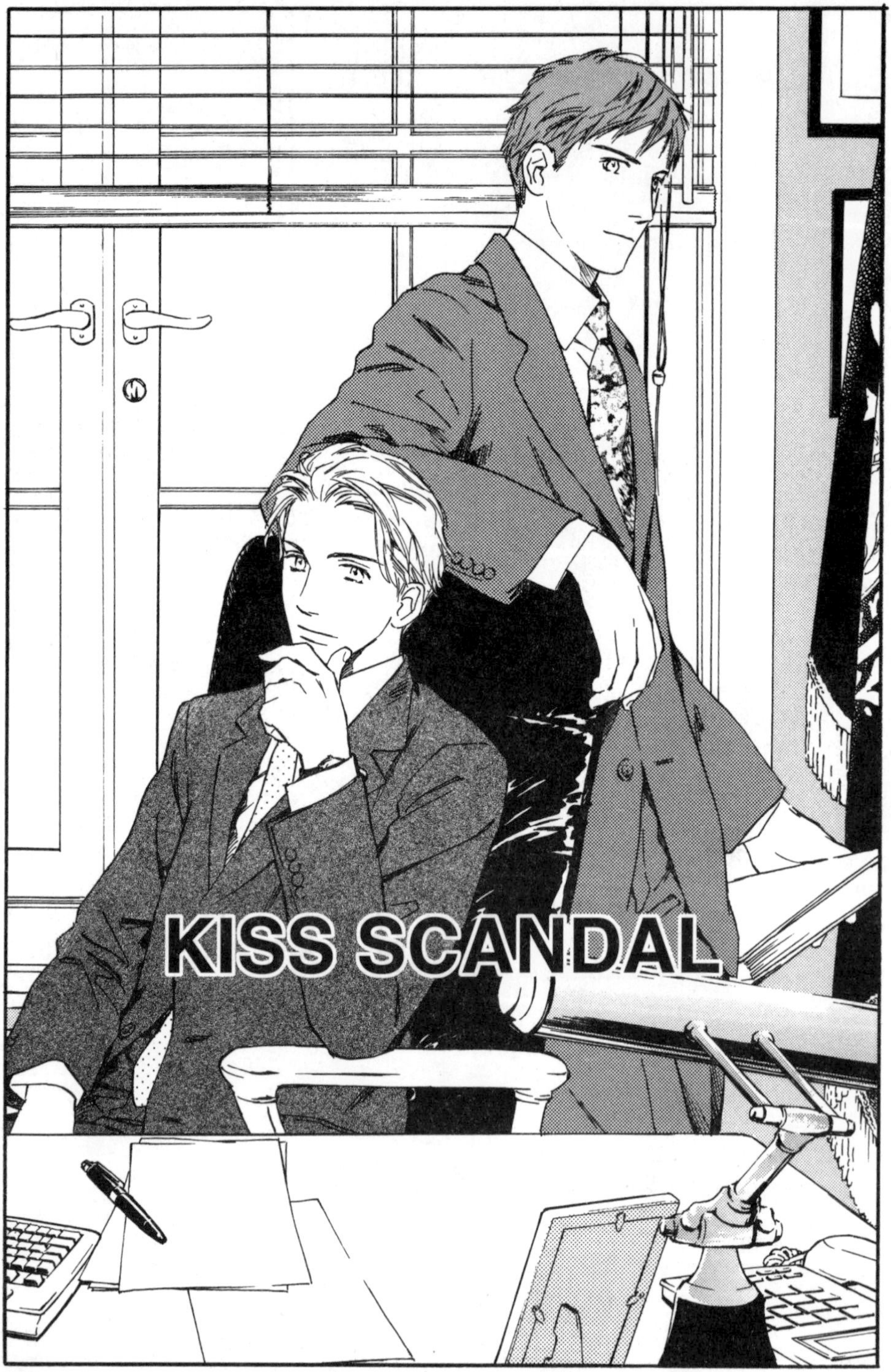
KISS SCANDAL

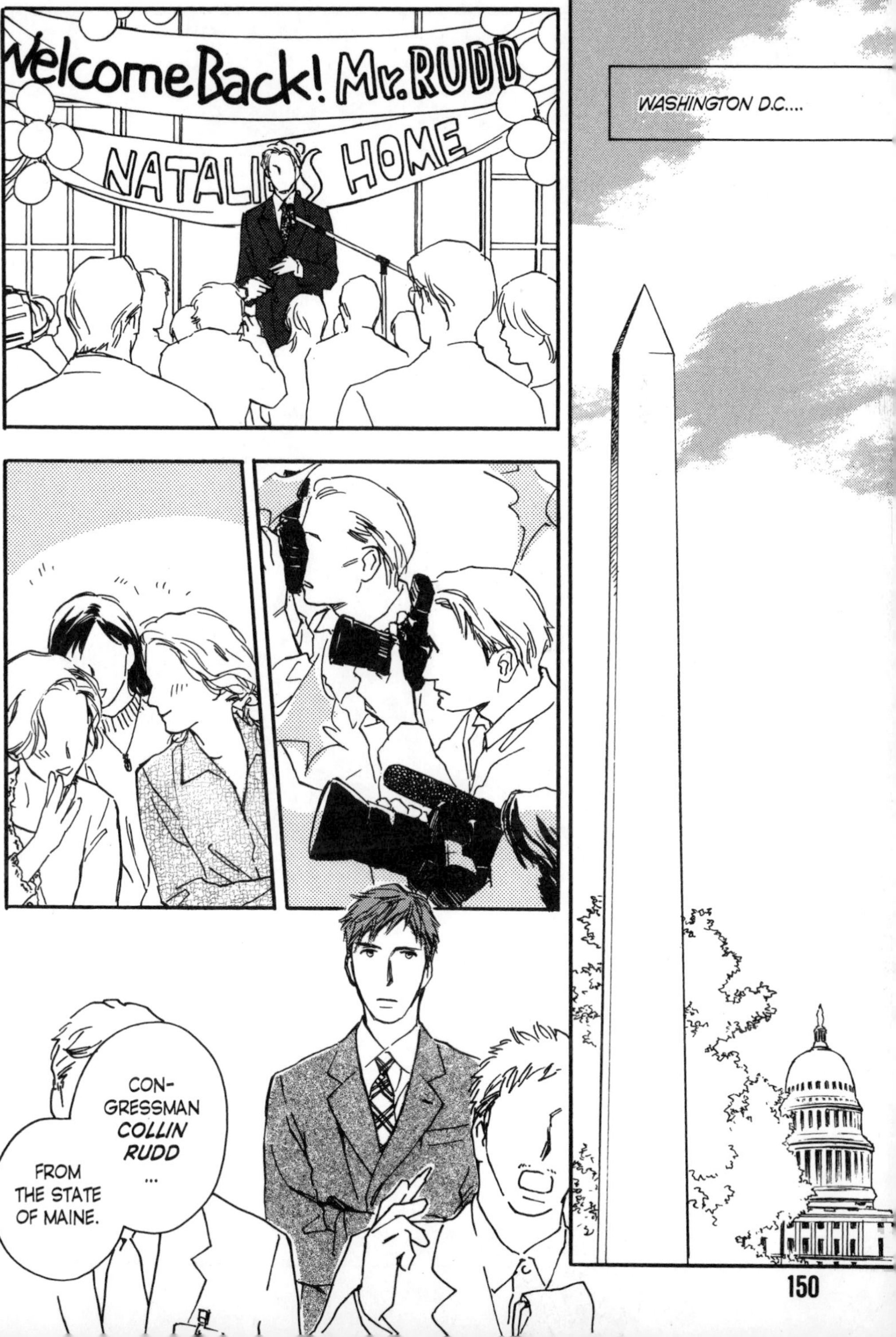
WASHINGTON D.C....
Welcome Back! Mr.RUDD
NATALI 'S HOME
CON-GRESSMAN COLLIN RUDD ...
FROM THE STATE OF MAINE.

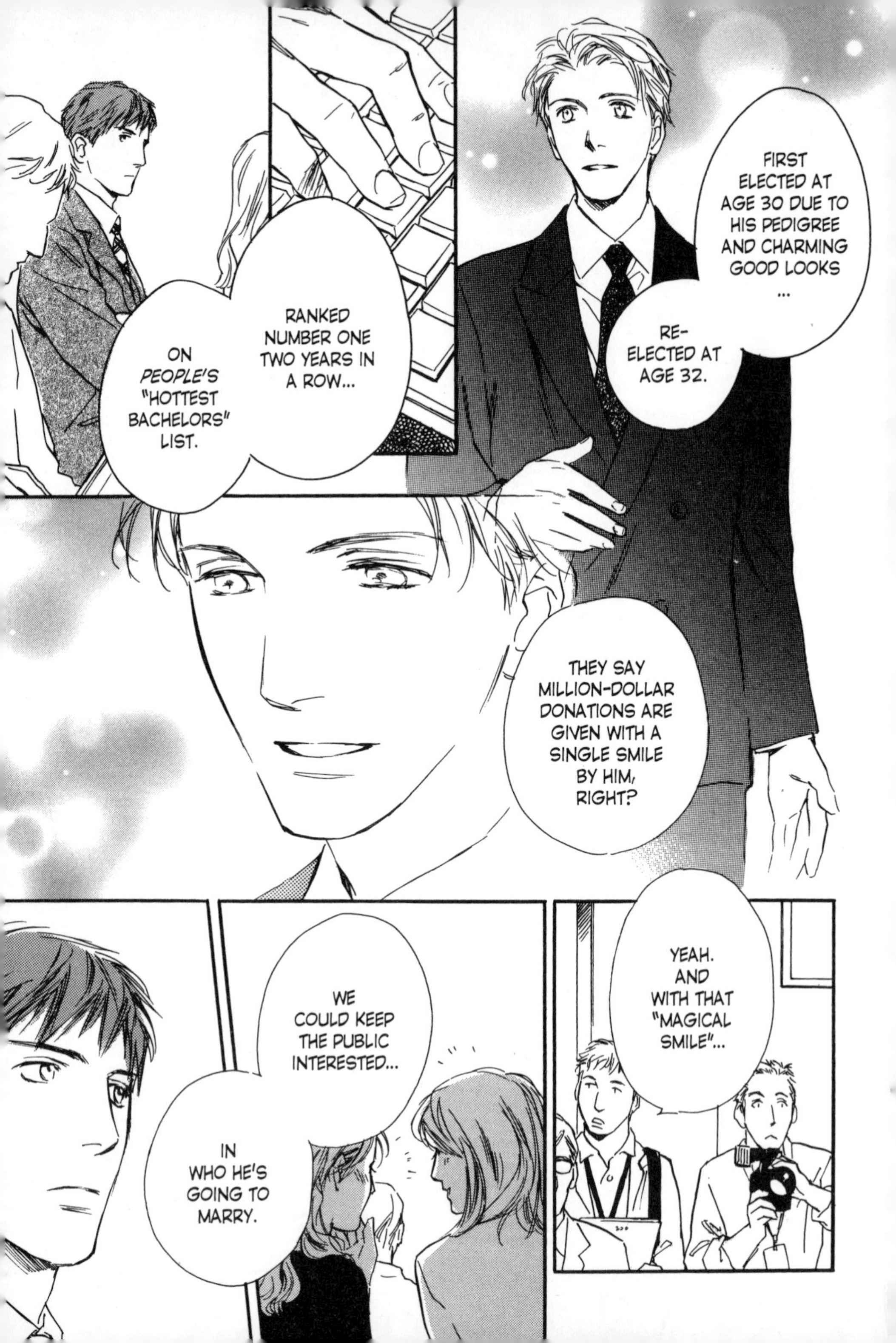
FIRST ELECTED AT AGE 30 DUE TO HIS PEDIGREE AND CHARMING GOOD LOOKS ...
RE-ELECTED AT AGE 32.
RANKED NUMBER ONE TWO YEARS IN A ROW...
ON *PEOPLE*'S "HOTTEST BACHELORS" LIST.
THEY SAY MILLION-DOLLAR DONATIONS ARE GIVEN WITH A SINGLE SMILE BY HIM, RIGHT?
YEAH. AND WITH THAT "MAGICAL SMILE"...
WE COULD KEEP THE PUBLIC INTERESTED...
IN WHO HE'S GOING TO MARRY.

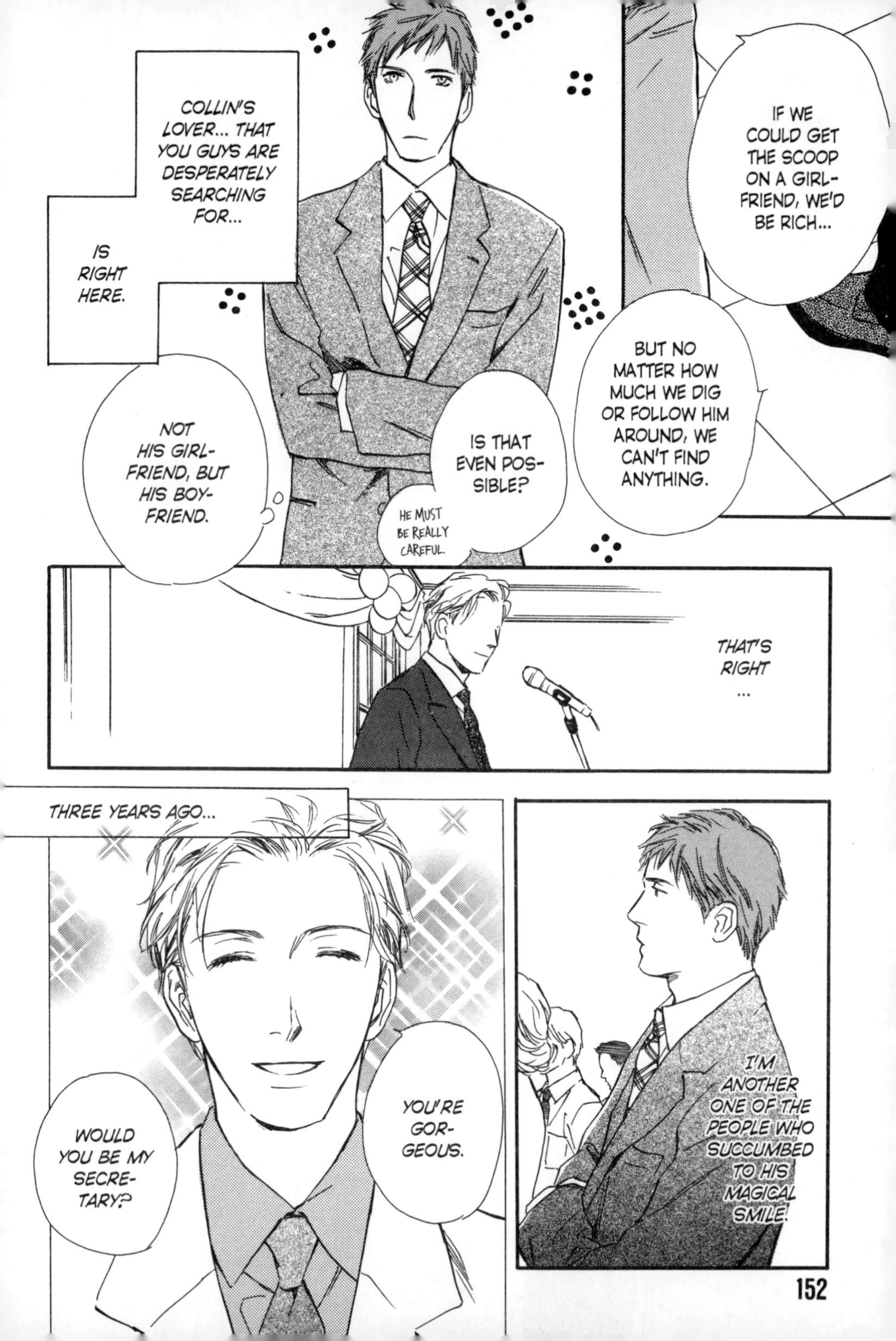
IF WE COULD GET THE SCOOP ON A GIRL-FRIEND, WE'D BE RICH...
BUT NO MATTER HOW MUCH WE DIG OR FOLLOW HIM AROUND, WE CAN'T FIND ANYTHING.
IS THAT EVEN POS-SIBLE?
HE MUST BE REALLY CAREFUL.
COLLIN'S LOVER... THAT YOU GUYS ARE DESPERATELY SEARCHING FOR...
IS RIGHT HERE.
NOT HIS GIRL-FRIEND, BUT HIS BOY-FRIEND.
THAT'S RIGHT ...
I'M ANOTHER ONE OF THE PEOPLE WHO SUCCUMBED TO HIS MAGICAL SMILE.
THREE YEARS AGO...
YOU'RE GOR-GEOUS.
WOULD YOU BE MY SECRE-TARY?

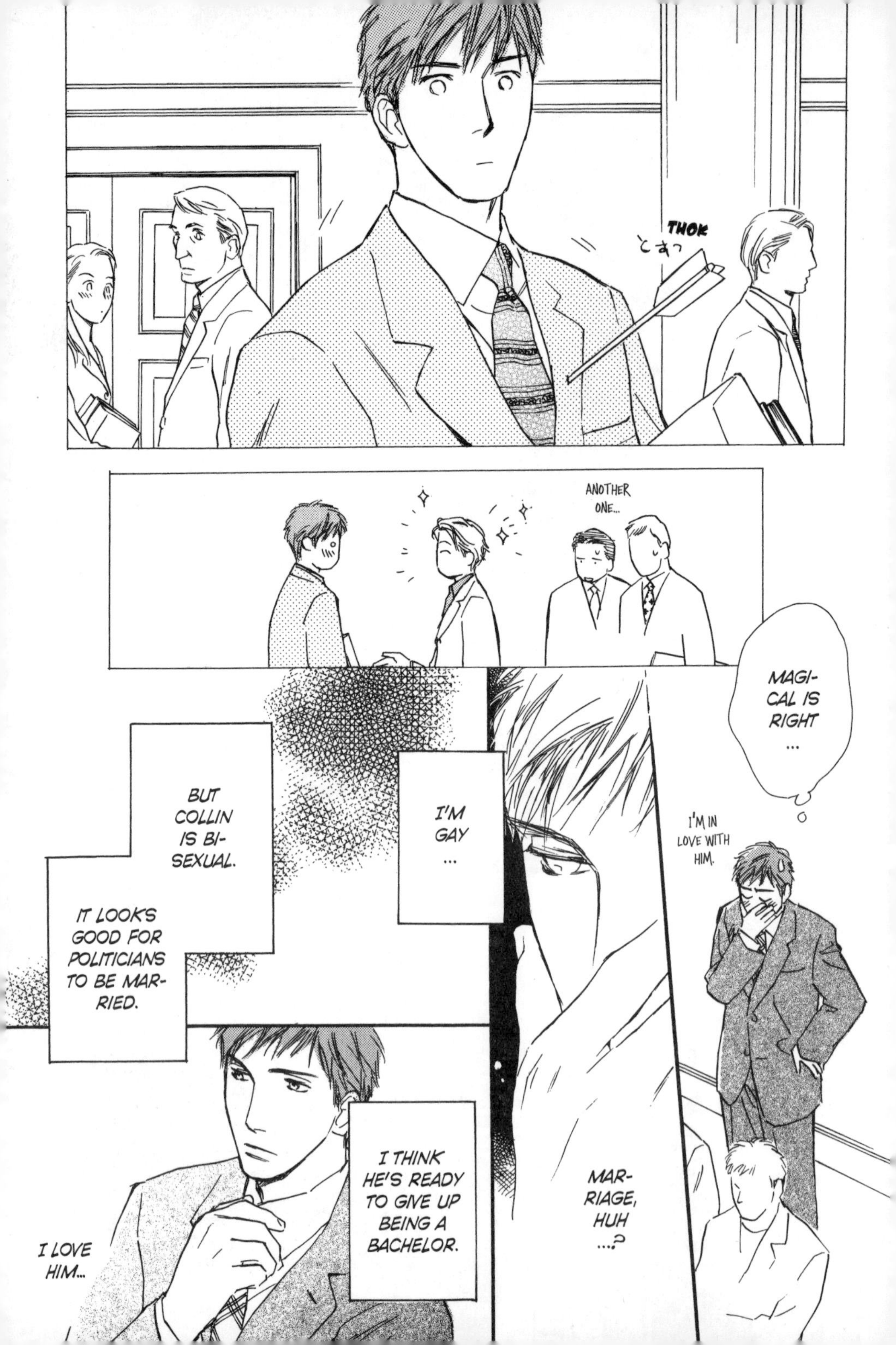
THOK
とすっ
ANOTHER ONE...
MAGICAL IS RIGHT...
I'M IN LOVE WITH HIM.
I'M GAY...
MARRIAGE, HUH...?
BUT COLLIN IS BISEXUAL.
IT LOOKS GOOD FOR POLITICIANS TO BE MARRIED.
I THINK HE'S READY TO GIVE UP BEING A BACHELOR.
I LOVE HIM...

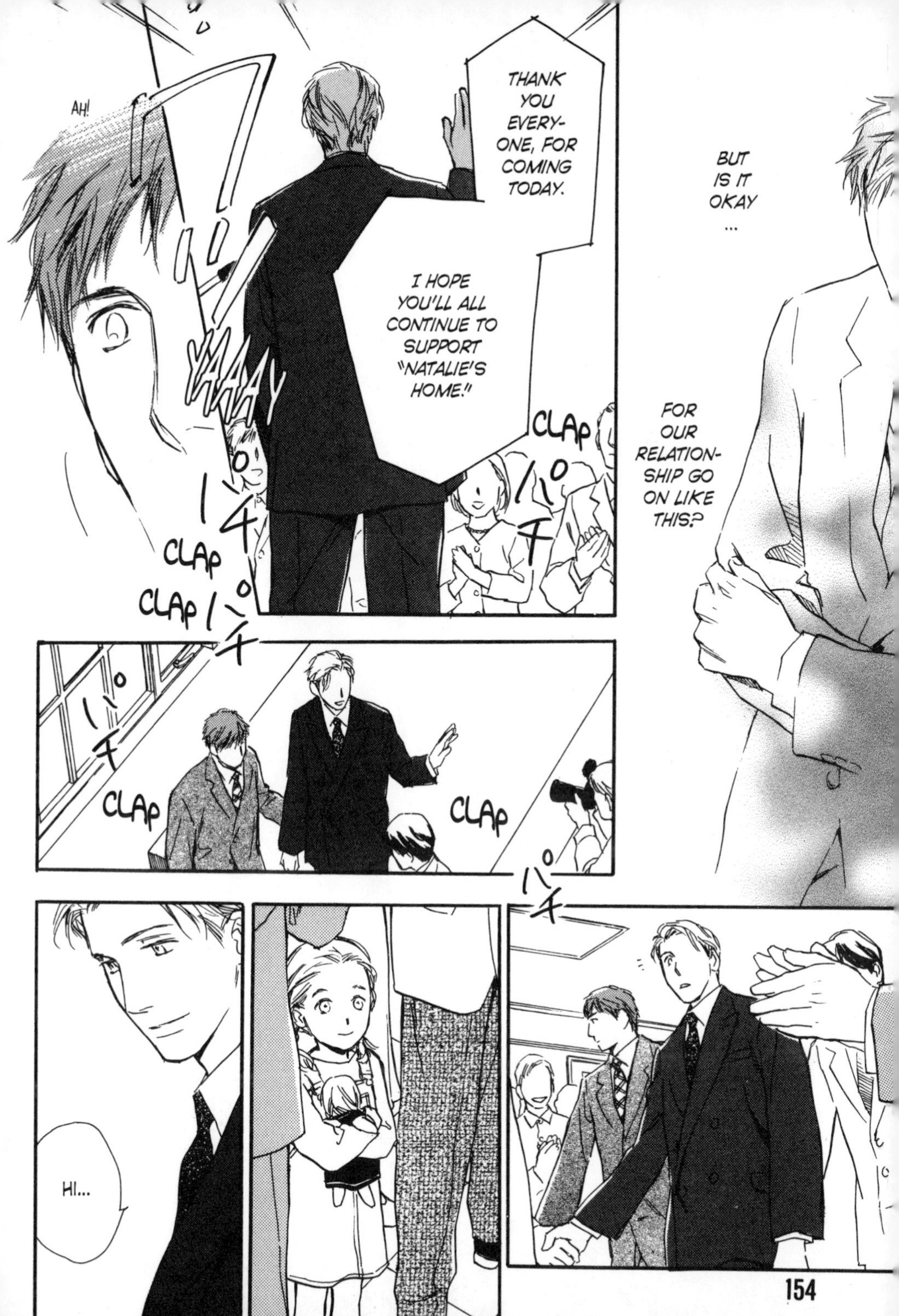
BUT IS IT OKAY ...
FOR OUR RELATIONSHIP GO ON LIKE THIS?
THANK YOU EVERYONE, FOR COMING TODAY.
I HOPE YOU'LL ALL CONTINUE TO SUPPORT "NATALIE'S HOME."
CLAP
パチ
CLAP
CLAP
パチ
パチ
YAAAY
AH!
CLAP
パチ
CLAP
パチ
HI...

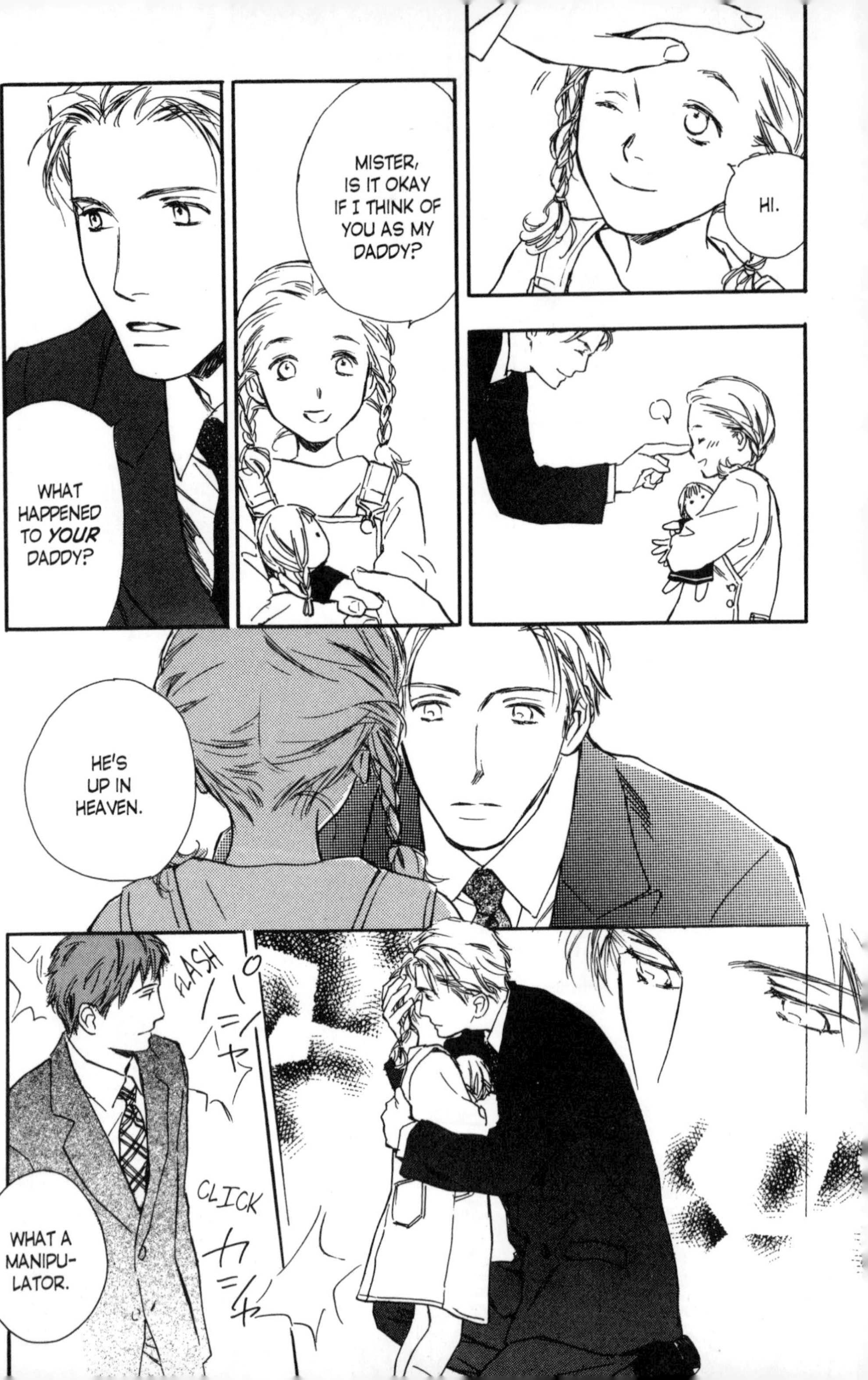
HI.
MISTER, IS IT OKAY IF I THINK OF YOU AS MY DADDY?
WHAT HAPPENED TO *YOUR* DADDY?
HE'S UP IN HEAVEN.
FLASH
CLICK
WHAT A MANIPU-LATOR.

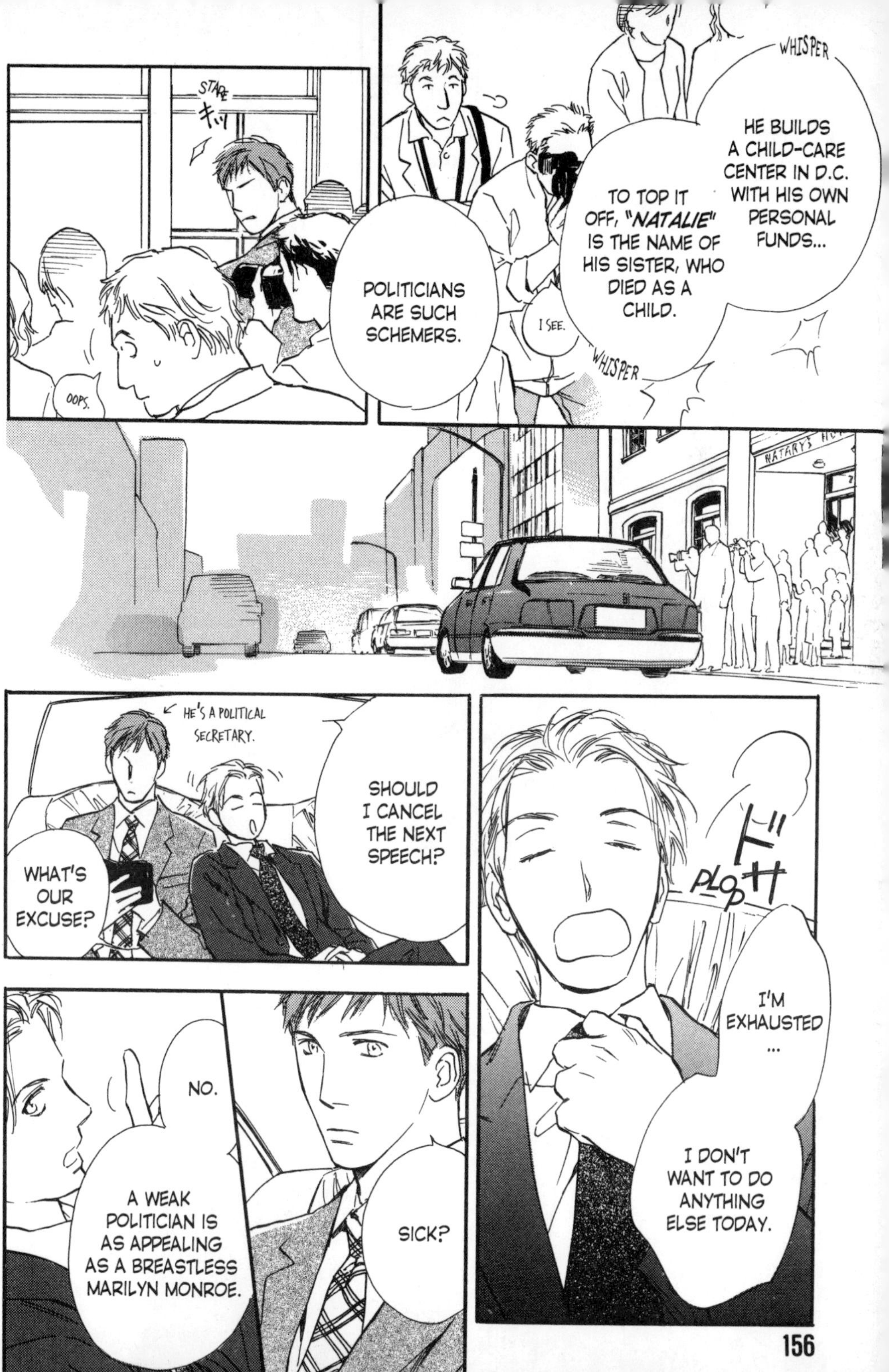
WHISPER
HE BUILDS A CHILD-CARE CENTER IN D.C. WITH HIS OWN PERSONAL FUNDS...
TO TOP IT OFF, "NATALIE" IS THE NAME OF HIS SISTER, WHO DIED AS A CHILD.
I SEE.
WHISPER
POLITICIANS ARE SUCH SCHEMERS.
STARE
キッ
OOPS.
PLOP
I'M EXHAUSTED ...
I DON'T WANT TO DO ANYTHING ELSE TODAY.
SHOULD I CANCEL THE NEXT SPEECH?
HE'S A POLITICAL SECRETARY.
WHAT'S OUR EXCUSE?
SICK?
NO.
A WEAK POLITICIAN IS AS APPEALING AS A BREASTLESS MARILYN MONROE.

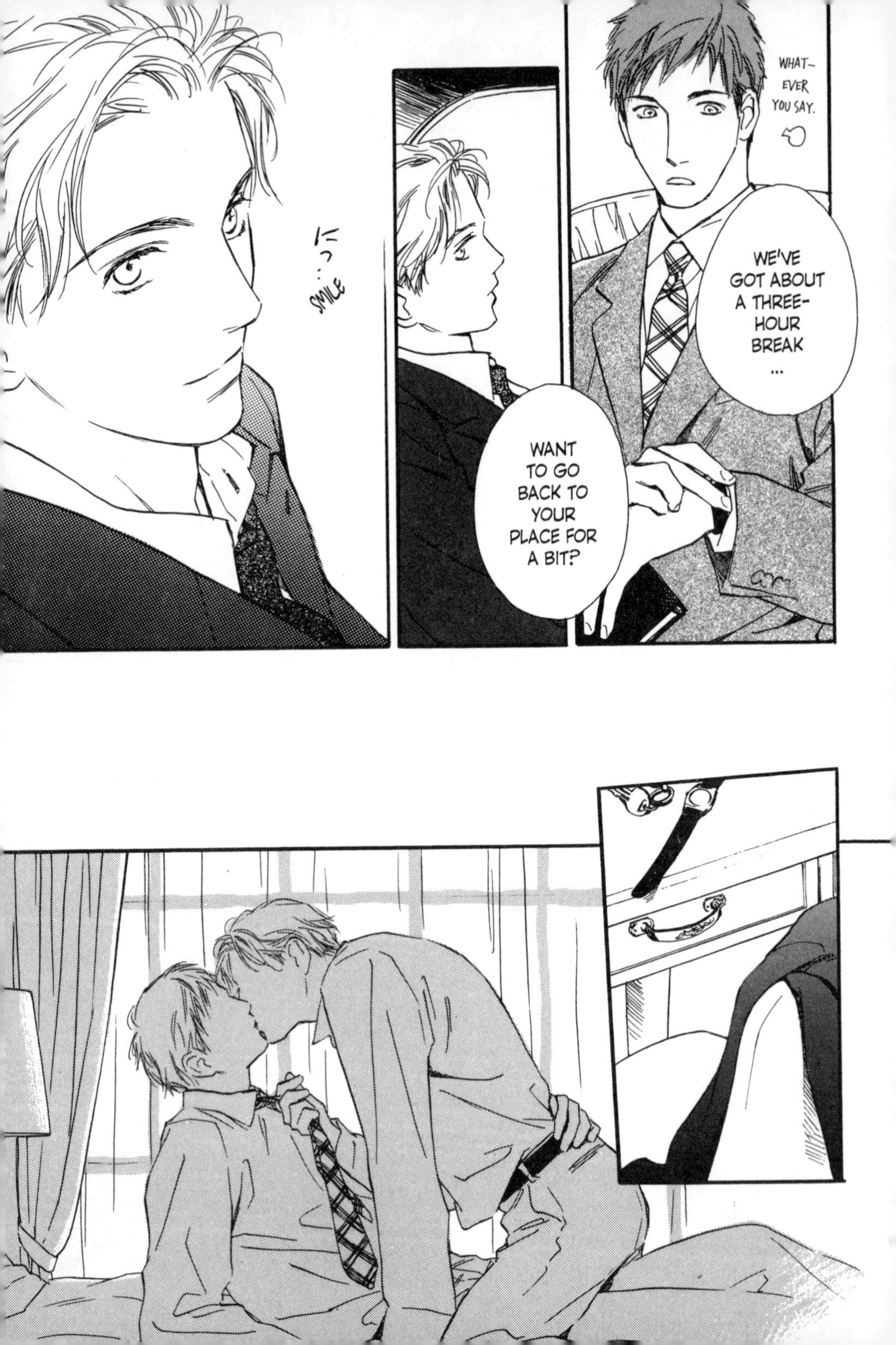
WHAT-EVER YOU SAY.
WE'VE GOT ABOUT A THREE-HOUR BREAK ...
WANT TO GO BACK TO YOUR PLACE FOR A BIT?
にっ
SMILE

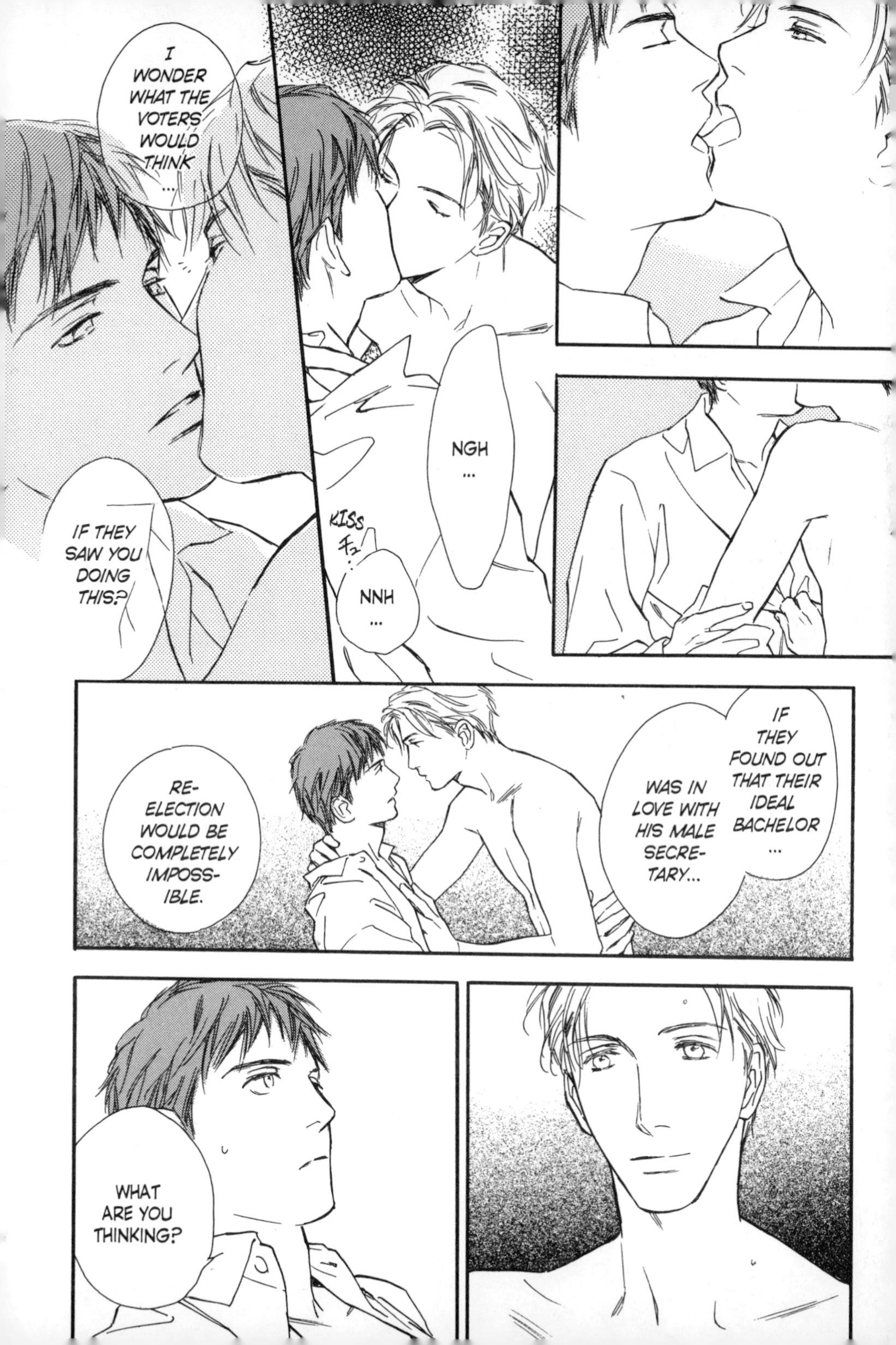
NGH ...
KISS チュ
NNH ...
I WONDER WHAT THE VOTERS WOULD THINK ...
IF THEY SAW YOU DOING THIS?
IF THEY FOUND OUT THAT THEIR IDEAL BACHELOR ...
WAS IN LOVE WITH HIS MALE SECRETARY...
RE-ELECTION WOULD BE COMPLETELY IMPOSSIBLE.
WHAT ARE YOU THINKING?

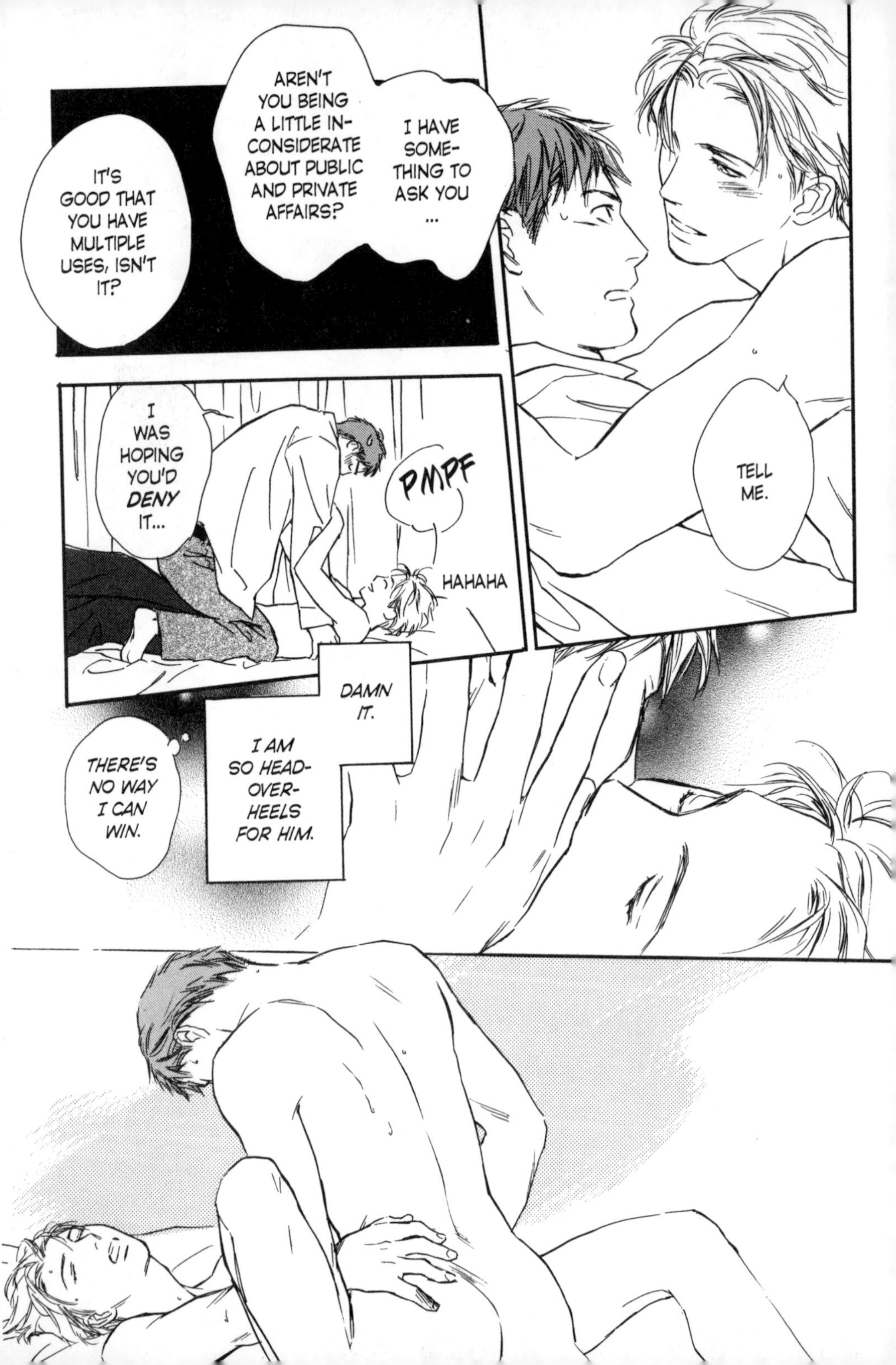
TELL ME.
I HAVE SOMETHING TO ASK YOU ...
AREN'T YOU BEING A LITTLE INCONSIDERATE ABOUT PUBLIC AND PRIVATE AFFAIRS?
IT'S GOOD THAT YOU HAVE MULTIPLE USES, ISN'T IT?
PMPF
HAHAHA
I WAS HOPING YOU'D *DENY* IT...
DAMN IT.
I AM SO HEAD-OVER-HEELS FOR HIM.
THERE'S NO WAY I CAN WIN.

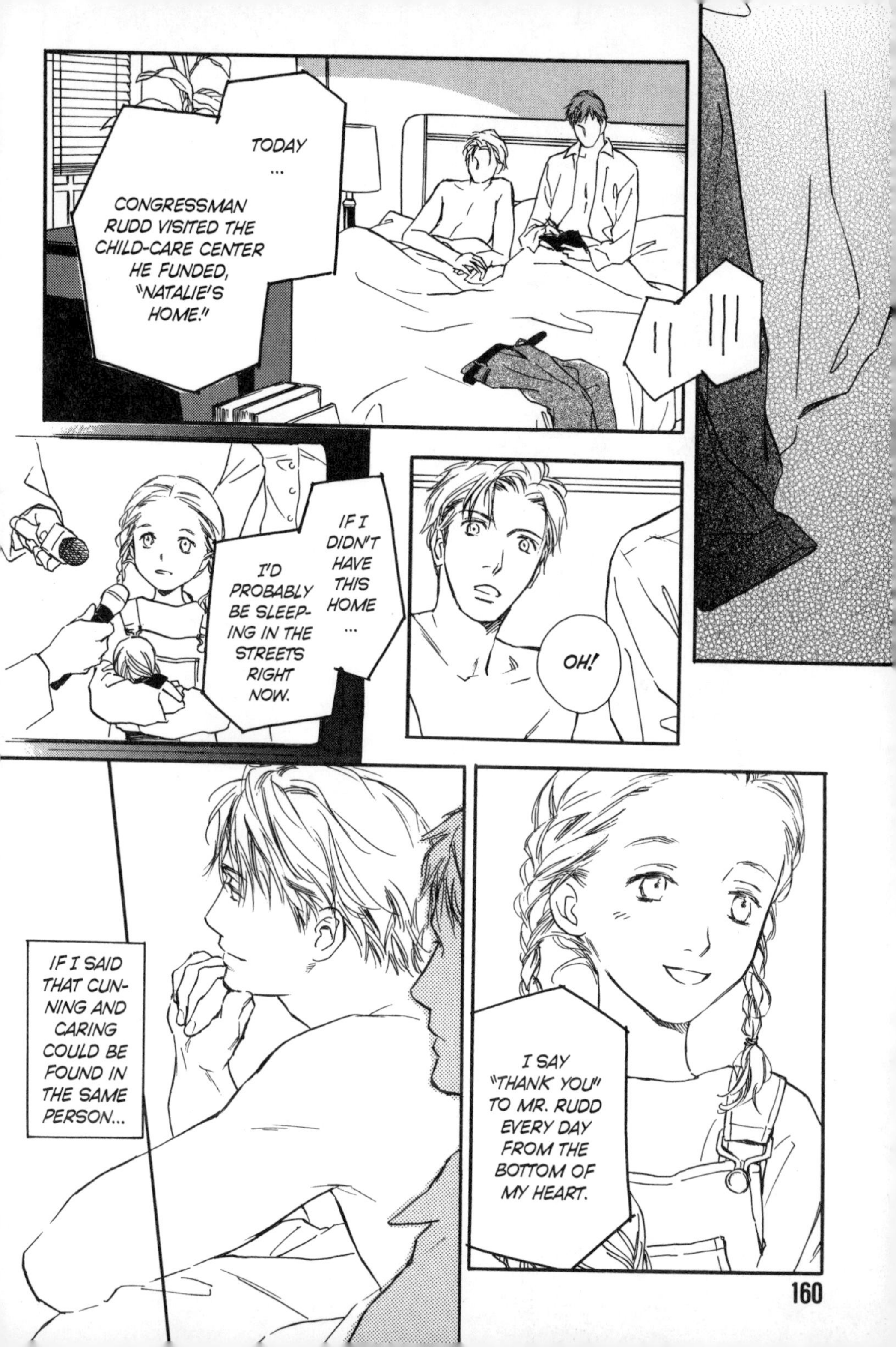
TODAY ...
CONGRESSMAN RUDD VISITED THE CHILD-CARE CENTER HE FUNDED, "NATALIE'S HOME."
OH!
IF I DIDN'T HAVE THIS HOME ...
I'D PROBABLY BE SLEEP-ING IN THE STREETS RIGHT NOW.
I SAY "THANK YOU" TO MR. RUDD EVERY DAY FROM THE BOTTOM OF MY HEART.
IF I SAID THAT CUN-NING AND CARING COULD BE FOUND IN THE SAME PERSON...

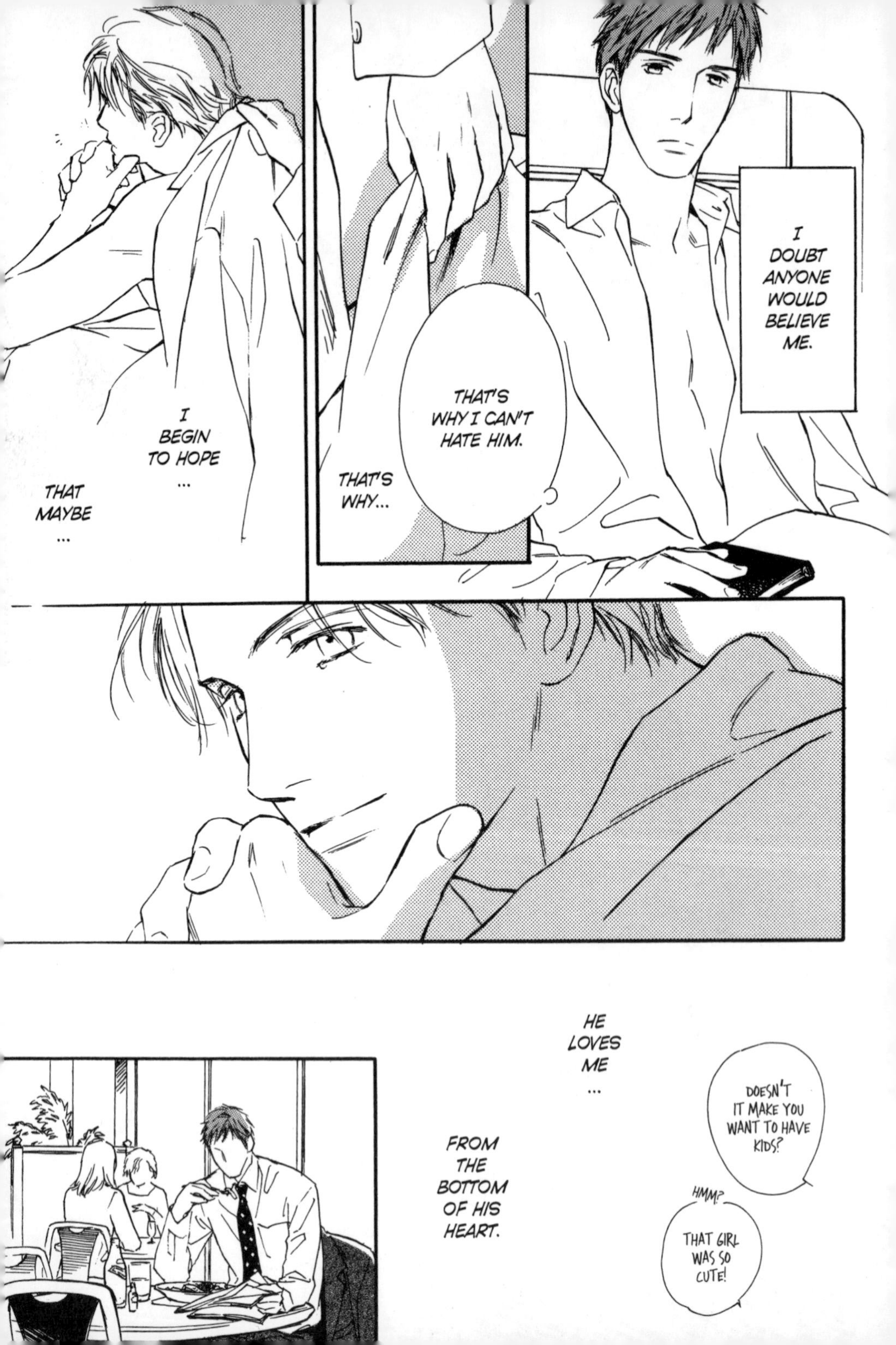
I DOUBT ANYONE WOULD BELIEVE ME.
THAT'S WHY I CAN'T HATE HIM.
THAT'S WHY...
I BEGIN TO HOPE...
THAT MAYBE...
HE LOVES ME...
FROM THE BOTTOM OF HIS HEART.
DOESN'T IT MAKE YOU WANT TO HAVE KIDS?
HMM?
THAT GIRL WAS SO CUTE!

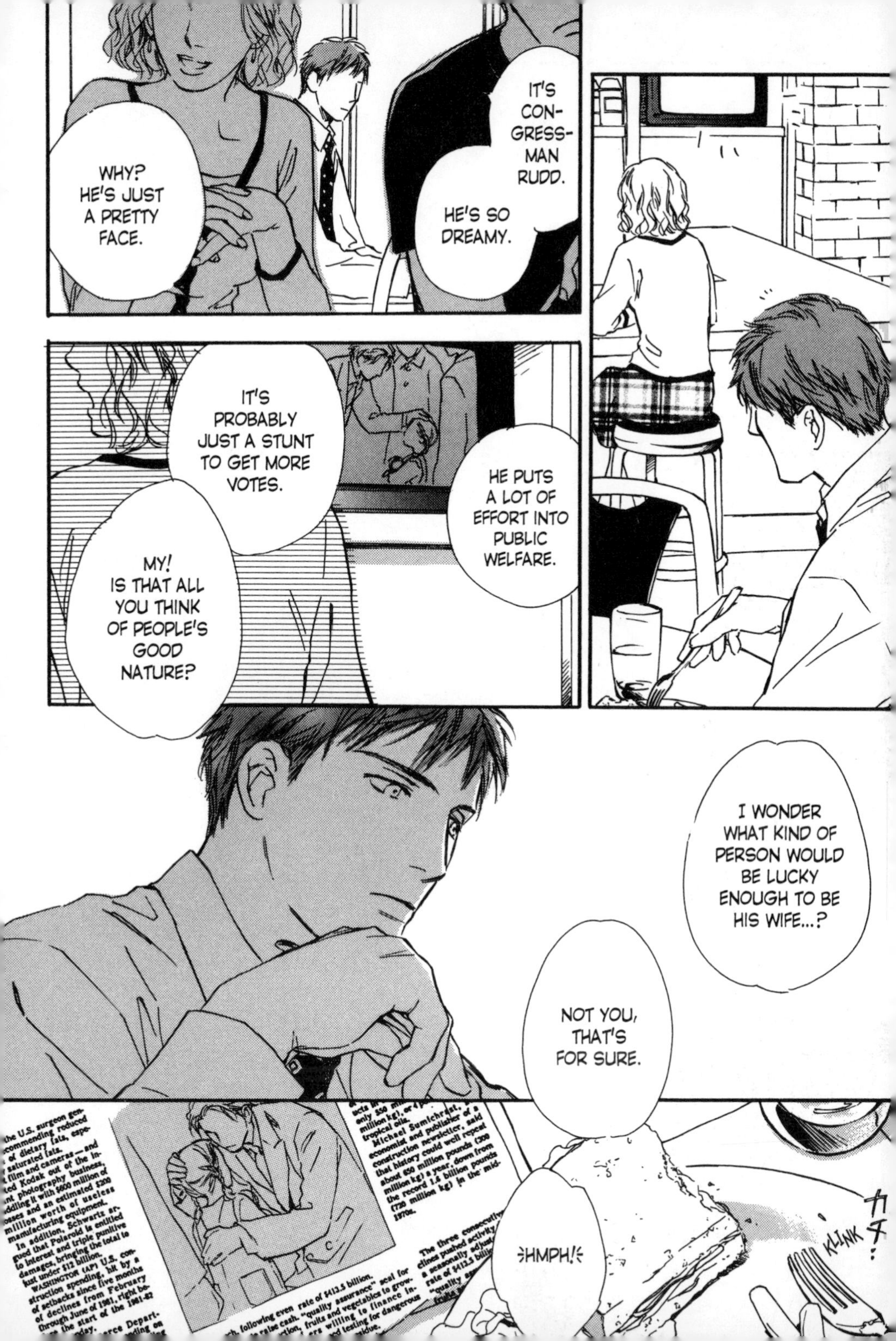
IT'S CONGRESSMAN RUDD.
HE'S SO DREAMY.
WHY? HE'S JUST A PRETTY FACE.
HE PUTS A LOT OF EFFORT INTO PUBLIC WELFARE.
IT'S PROBABLY JUST A STUNT TO GET MORE VOTES.
MY! IS THAT ALL YOU THINK OF PEOPLE'S GOOD NATURE?
I WONDER WHAT KIND OF PERSON WOULD BE LUCKY ENOUGH TO BE HIS WIFE...?
NOT YOU, THAT'S FOR SURE.
KLINK
HMPH!

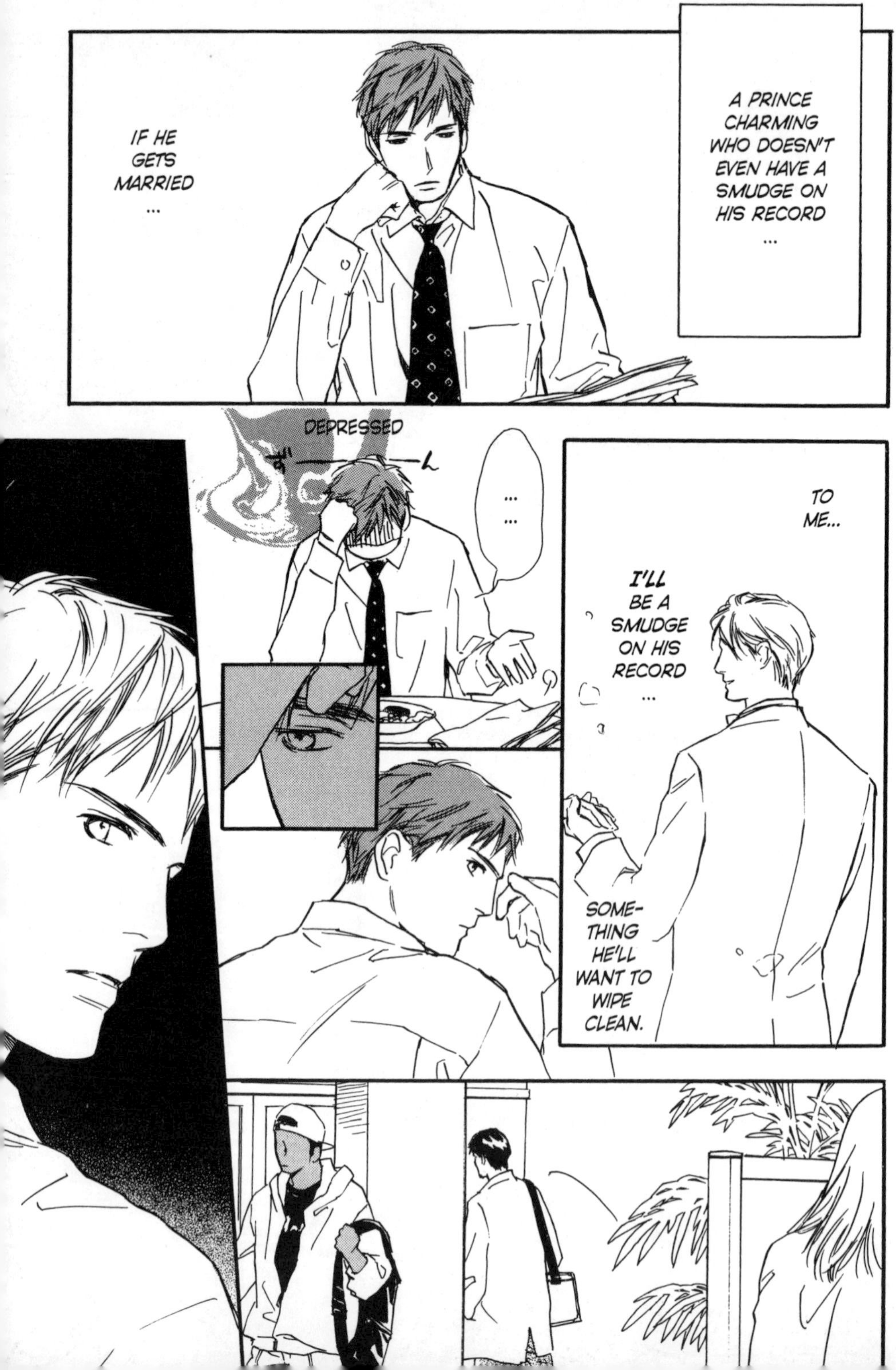
A PRINCE CHARMING WHO DOESN'T EVEN HAVE A SMUDGE ON HIS RECORD ...
IF HE GETS MARRIED ...
TO ME...
I'LL BE A SMUDGE ON HIS RECORD ...
SOME-THING HE'LL WANT TO WIPE CLEAN.
DEPRESSED
ず――ん
... ...

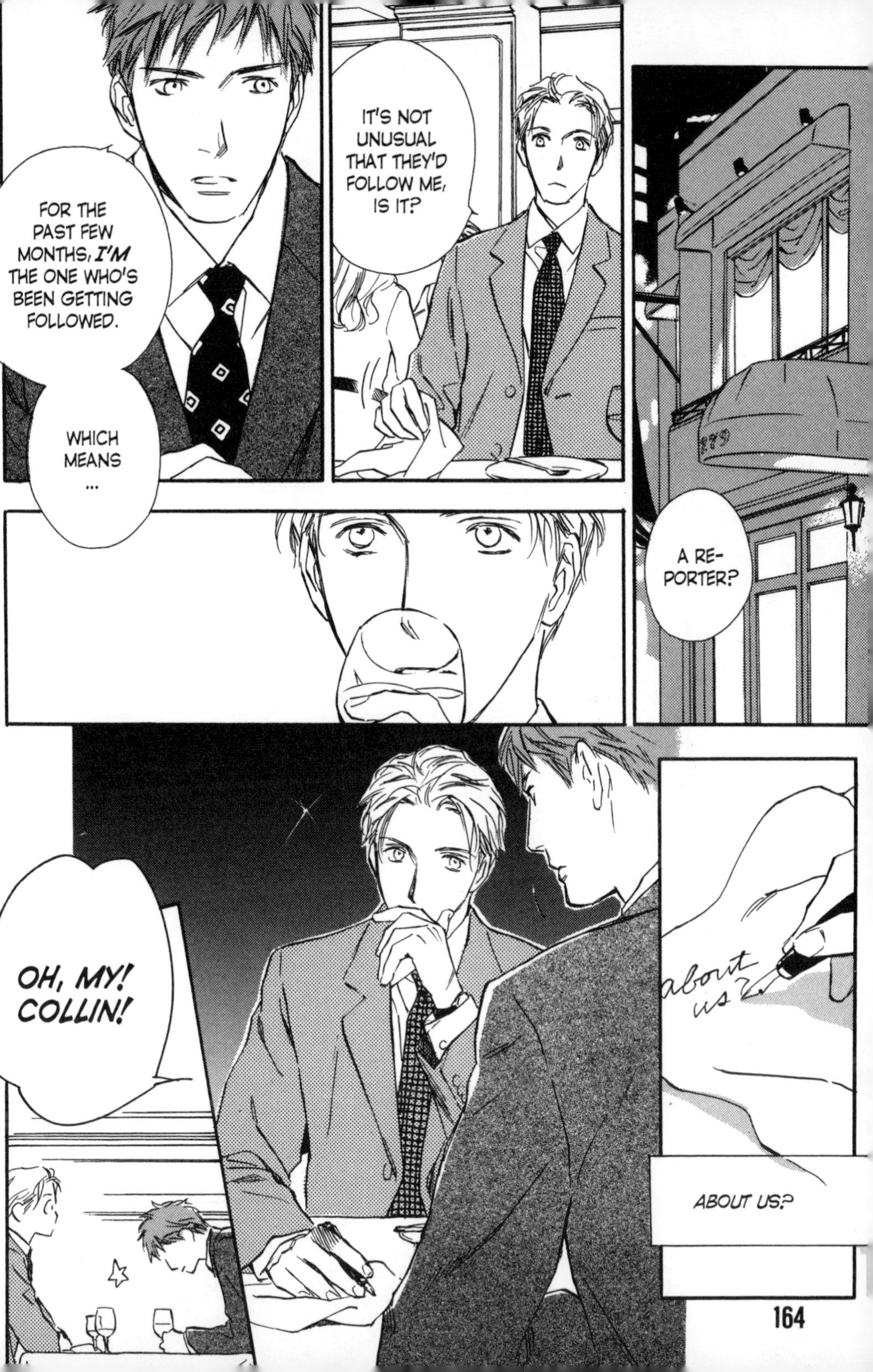
A RE-PORTER?
IT'S NOT UNUSUAL THAT THEY'D FOLLOW ME, IS IT?
FOR THE PAST FEW MONTHS, ***I'M*** THE ONE WHO'S BEEN GETTING FOLLOWED.
WHICH MEANS ...
about us?
ABOUT US?
OH, MY! COLLIN!

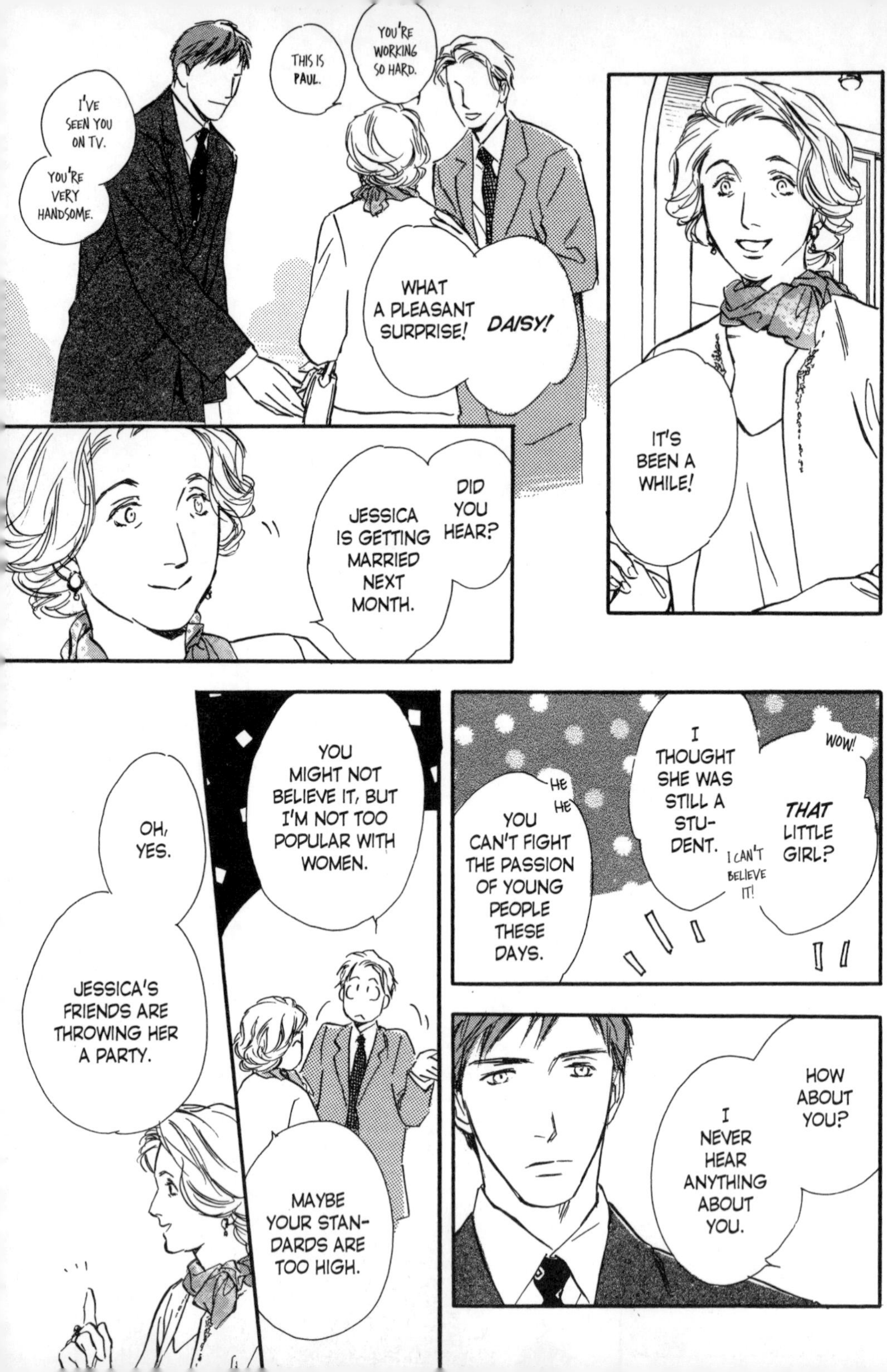
DAISY!
WHAT A PLEASANT SURPRISE!
YOU'RE WORKING SO HARD.
THIS IS PAUL.
I'VE SEEN YOU ON TV.
YOU'RE VERY HANDSOME.
IT'S BEEN A WHILE!
DID YOU HEAR?
JESSICA IS GETTING MARRIED NEXT MONTH.
WOW!
THAT LITTLE GIRL?
I CAN'T BELIEVE IT!
I THOUGHT SHE WAS STILL A STU-DENT.
HE HE
YOU CAN'T FIGHT THE PASSION OF YOUNG PEOPLE THESE DAYS.
HOW ABOUT YOU?
I NEVER HEAR ANYTHING ABOUT YOU.
YOU MIGHT NOT BELIEVE IT, BUT I'M NOT TOO POPULAR WITH WOMEN.
MAYBE YOUR STAN-DARDS ARE TOO HIGH.
OH, YES.
JESSICA'S FRIENDS ARE THROWING HER A PARTY.

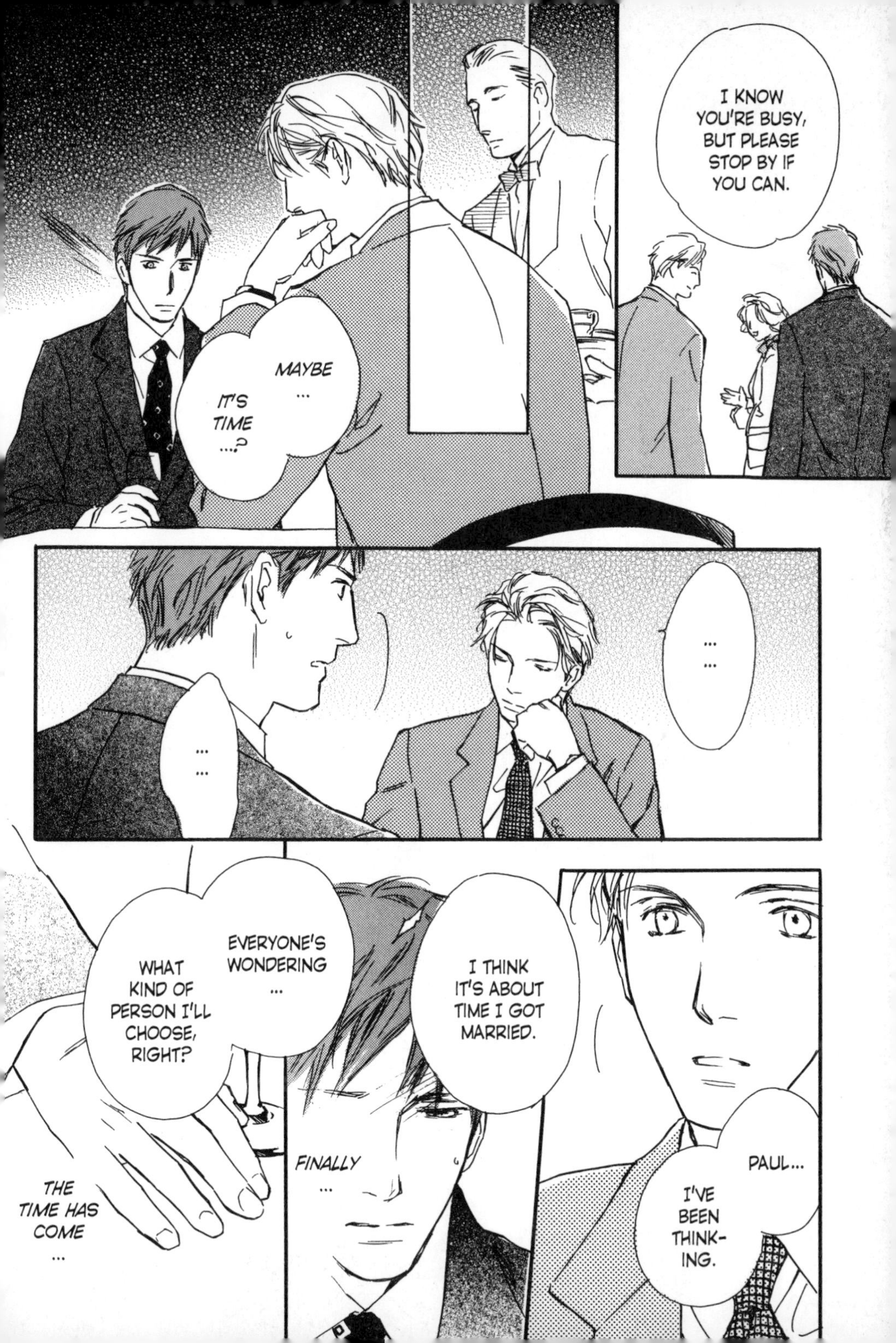
I KNOW YOU'RE BUSY, BUT PLEASE STOP BY IF YOU CAN.
MAYBE ... IT'S TIME ...?
... ...
... ...
PAUL... I'VE BEEN THINKING.
I THINK IT'S ABOUT TIME I GOT MARRIED.
FINALLY ...
EVERYONE'S WONDERING ... WHAT KIND OF PERSON I'LL CHOOSE, RIGHT?
THE TIME HAS COME ...

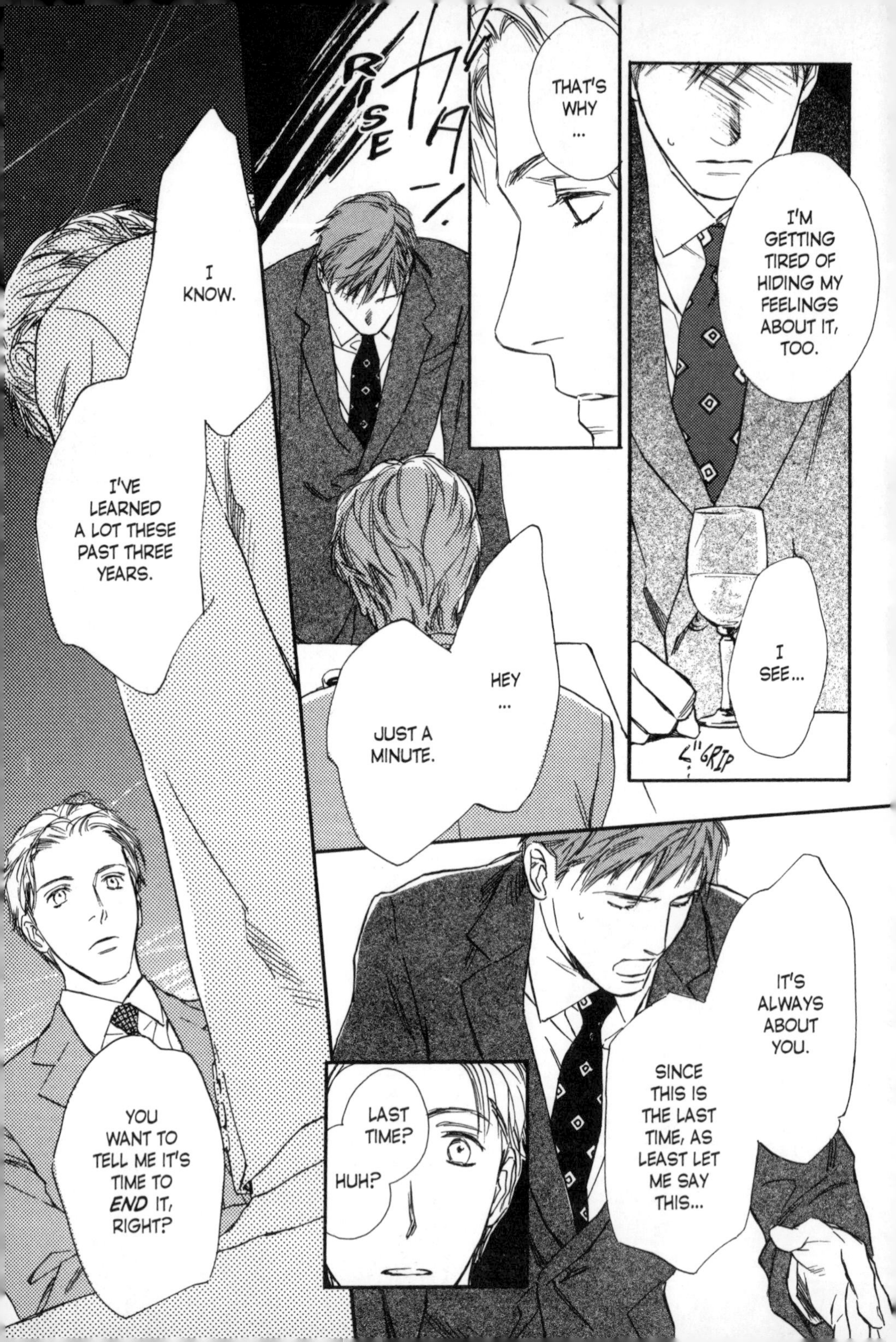
I'M GETTING TIRED OF HIDING MY FEELINGS ABOUT IT, TOO.
I SEE...
GRIP
THAT'S WHY ...
RISE
HEY ...
JUST A MINUTE.
I KNOW.
I'VE LEARNED A LOT THESE PAST THREE YEARS.
IT'S ALWAYS ABOUT YOU.
SINCE THIS IS THE LAST TIME, AS LEAST LET ME SAY THIS...
LAST TIME?
HUH?
YOU WANT TO TELL ME IT'S TIME TO *END* IT, RIGHT?

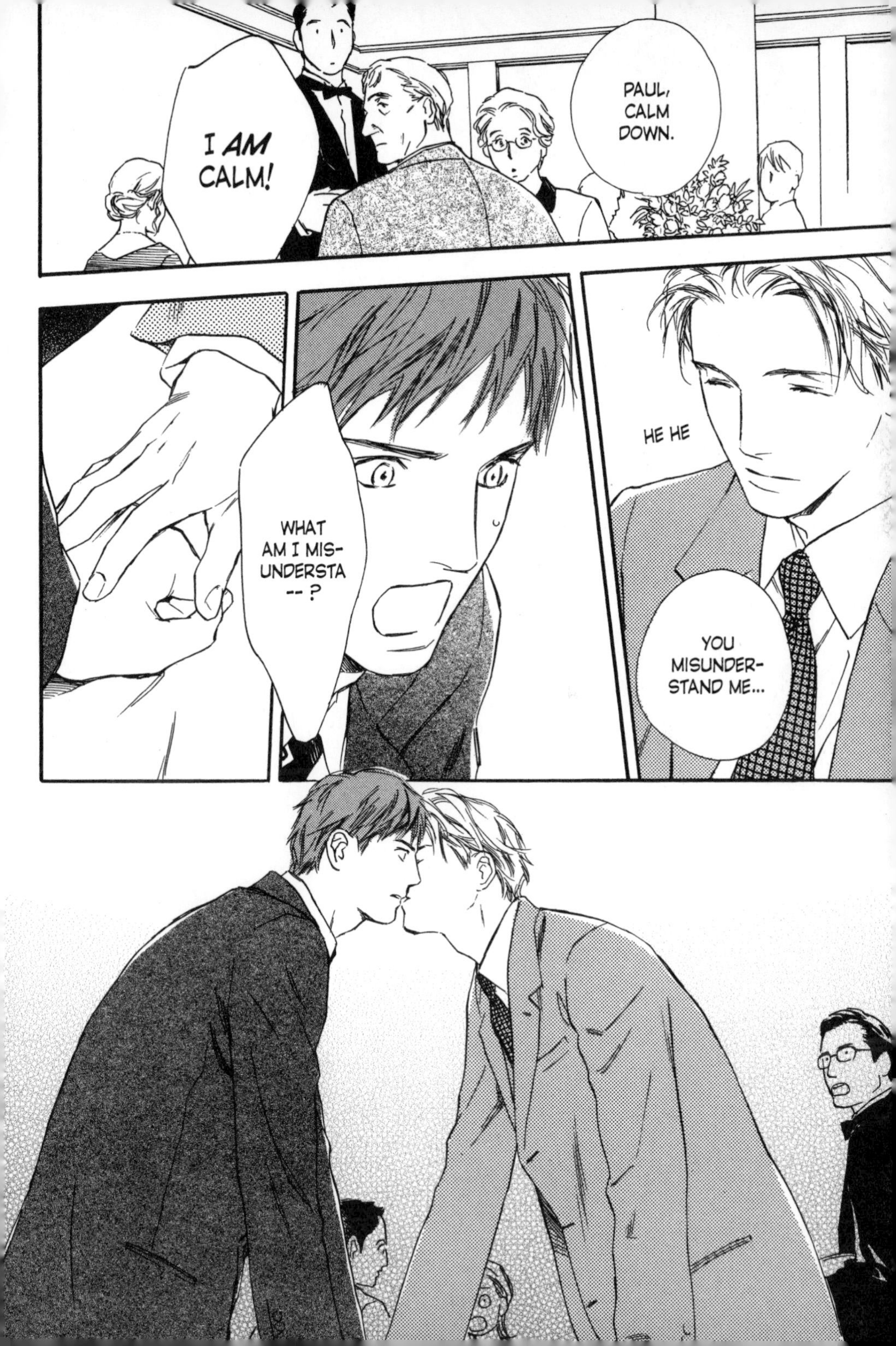
PAUL, CALM DOWN.
I AM CALM!
HE HE
YOU MISUNDER-STAND ME...
WHAT AM I MIS-UNDERSTA-- ?

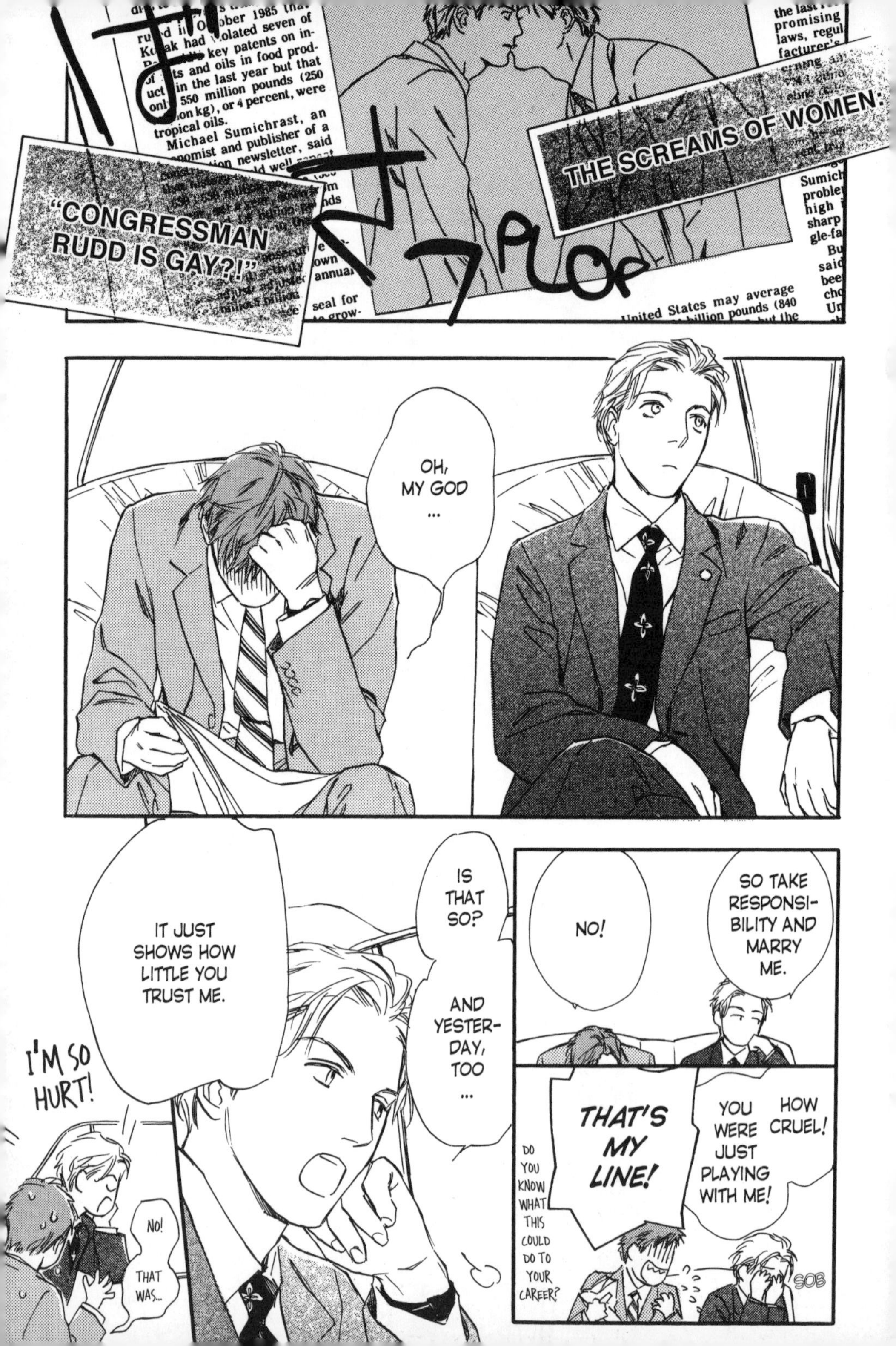
THE SCREAMS OF WOMEN:
"CONGRESSMAN RUDD IS GAY?!"
PLOP
OH, MY GOD ...
SO TAKE RESPONSIBILITY AND MARRY ME.
NO!
HOW CRUEL!
YOU WERE JUST PLAYING WITH ME!
THAT'S MY LINE!
DO YOU KNOW WHAT THIS COULD DO TO YOUR CAREER?
SOB
IS THAT SO?
AND YESTERDAY, TOO ...
IT JUST SHOWS HOW LITTLE YOU TRUST ME.
I'M SO HURT!
NO! THAT WAS...

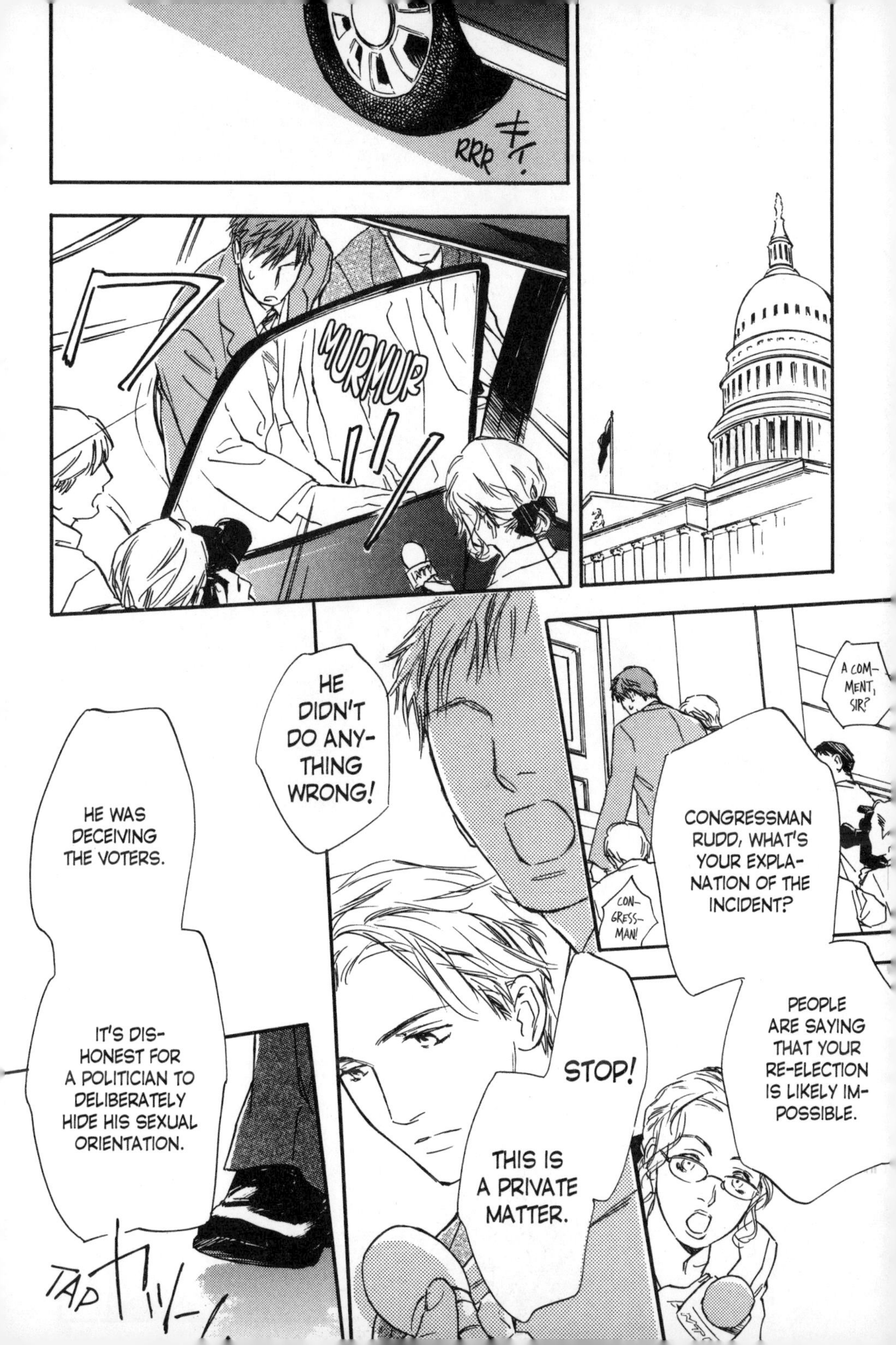
RRR
MURMUR
A COMMENT, SIR?
CONGRESSMAN RUDD, WHAT'S YOUR EXPLANATION OF THE INCIDENT?
CONGRESSMAN!
HE DIDN'T DO ANYTHING WRONG!
PEOPLE ARE SAYING THAT YOUR RE-ELECTION IS LIKELY IMPOSSIBLE.
STOP!
THIS IS A PRIVATE MATTER.
HE WAS DECEIVING THE VOTERS.
IT'S DISHONEST FOR A POLITICIAN TO DELIBERATELY HIDE HIS SEXUAL ORIENTATION.
TAP

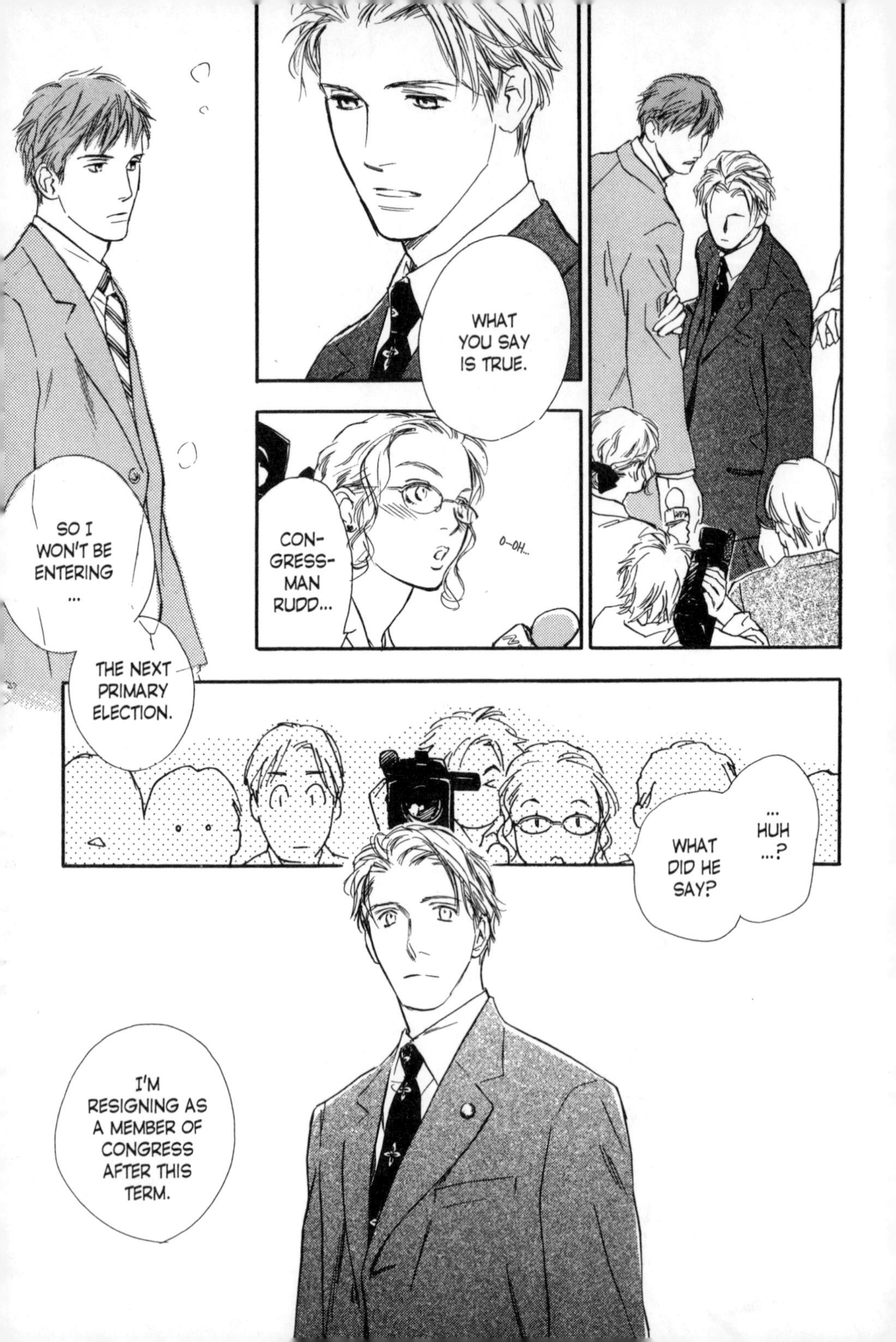
WHAT YOU SAY IS TRUE.
CON-GRESS-MAN RUDD...
O-OH...
SO I WON'T BE ENTERING ...
THE NEXT PRIMARY ELECTION.
... HUH ...?
WHAT DID HE SAY?
I'M RESIGNING AS A MEMBER OF CONGRESS AFTER THIS TERM.

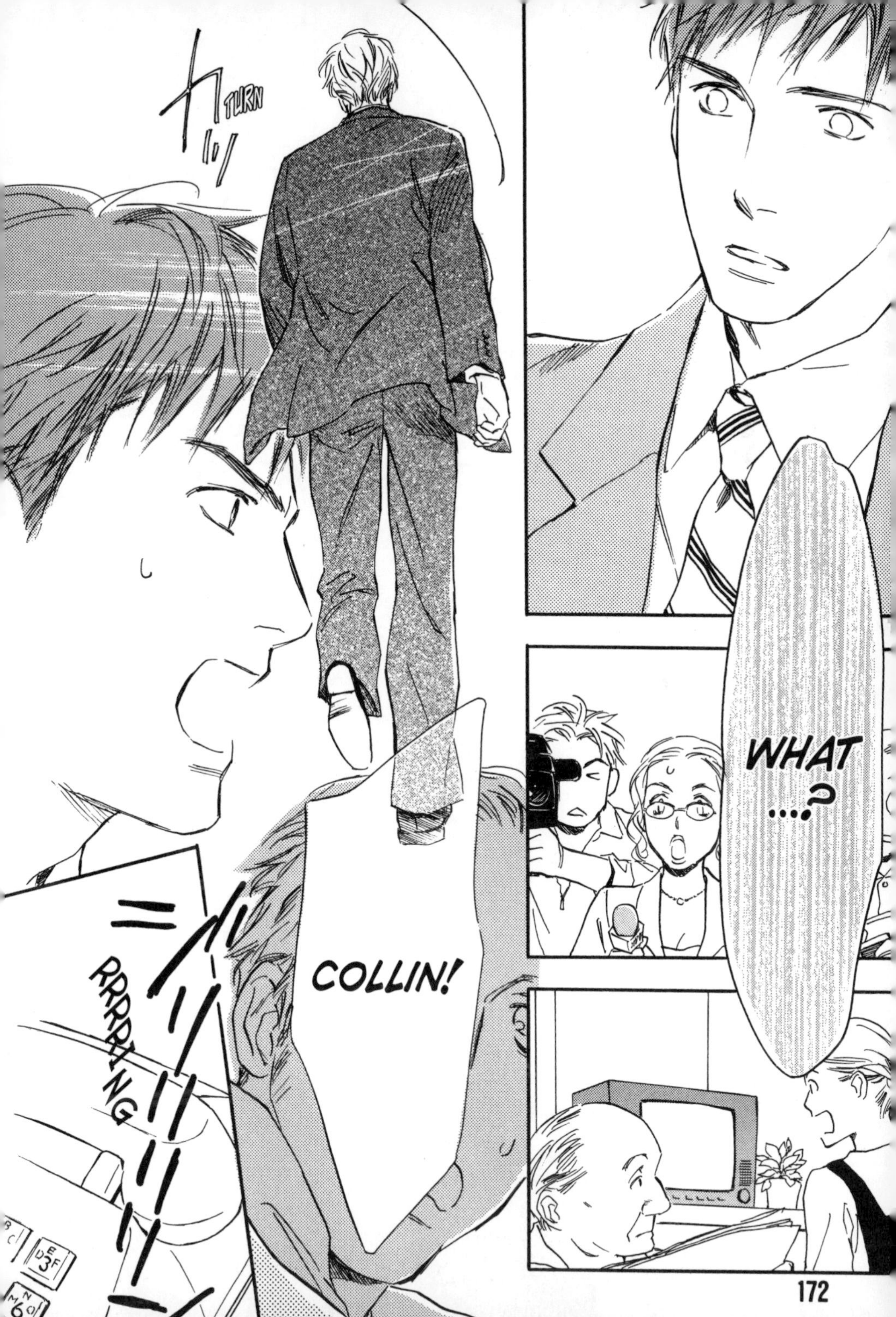
WHAT ...?
TURN
COLLIN!
RRRRING

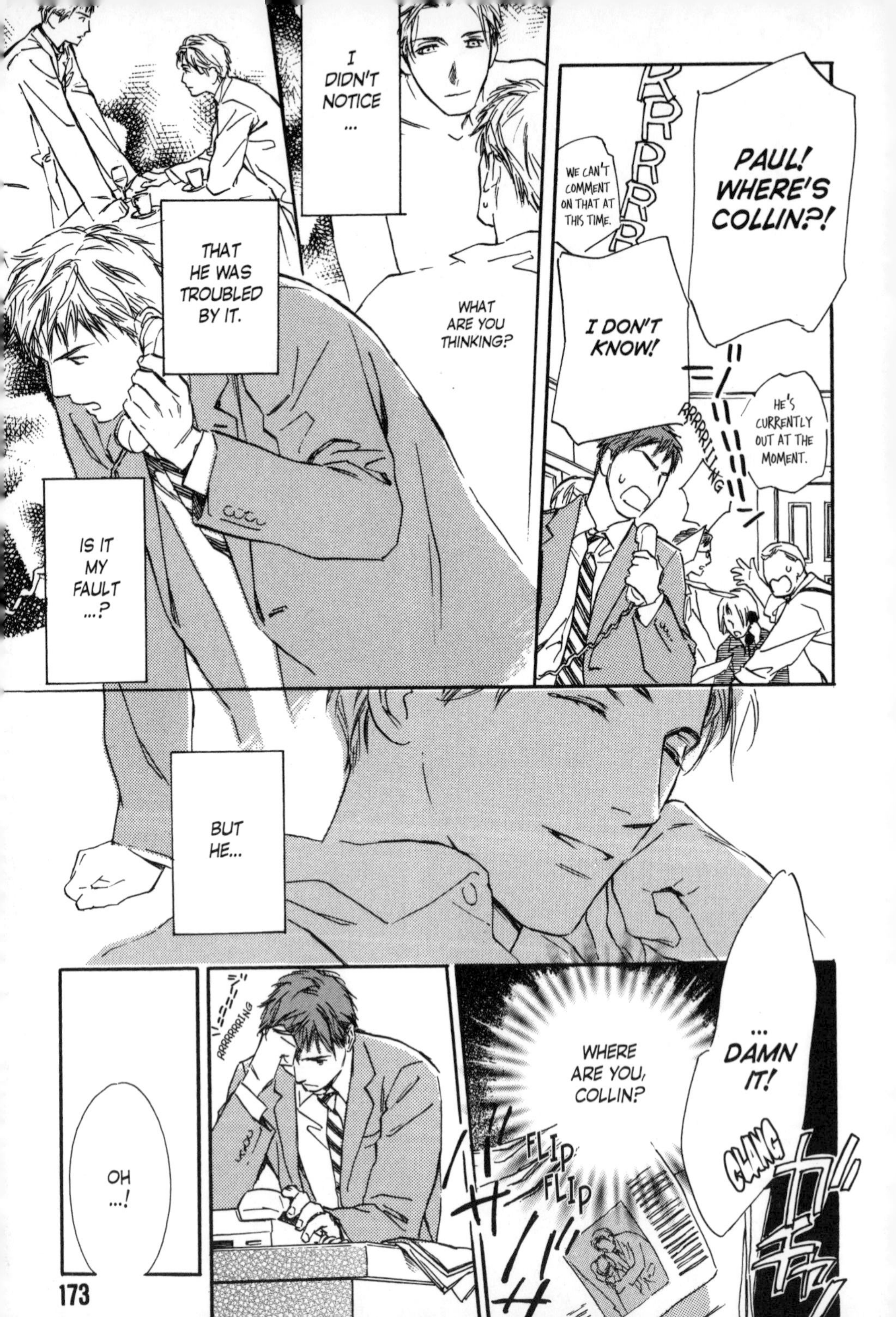

PAUL! WHERE'S COLLIN?!
RRRRRR
WE CAN'T COMMENT ON THAT AT THIS TIME.
I DON'T KNOW!
RRRRRIIING
HE'S CURRENTLY OUT AT THE MOMENT.
I DIDN'T NOTICE ...
WHAT ARE YOU THINKING?
THAT HE WAS TROUBLED BY IT.
IS IT MY FAULT ...?
BUT HE...
... DAMN IT!
CLANG
WHERE ARE YOU, COLLIN?
FLIP FLIP
RRRRRRRING
OH ...!

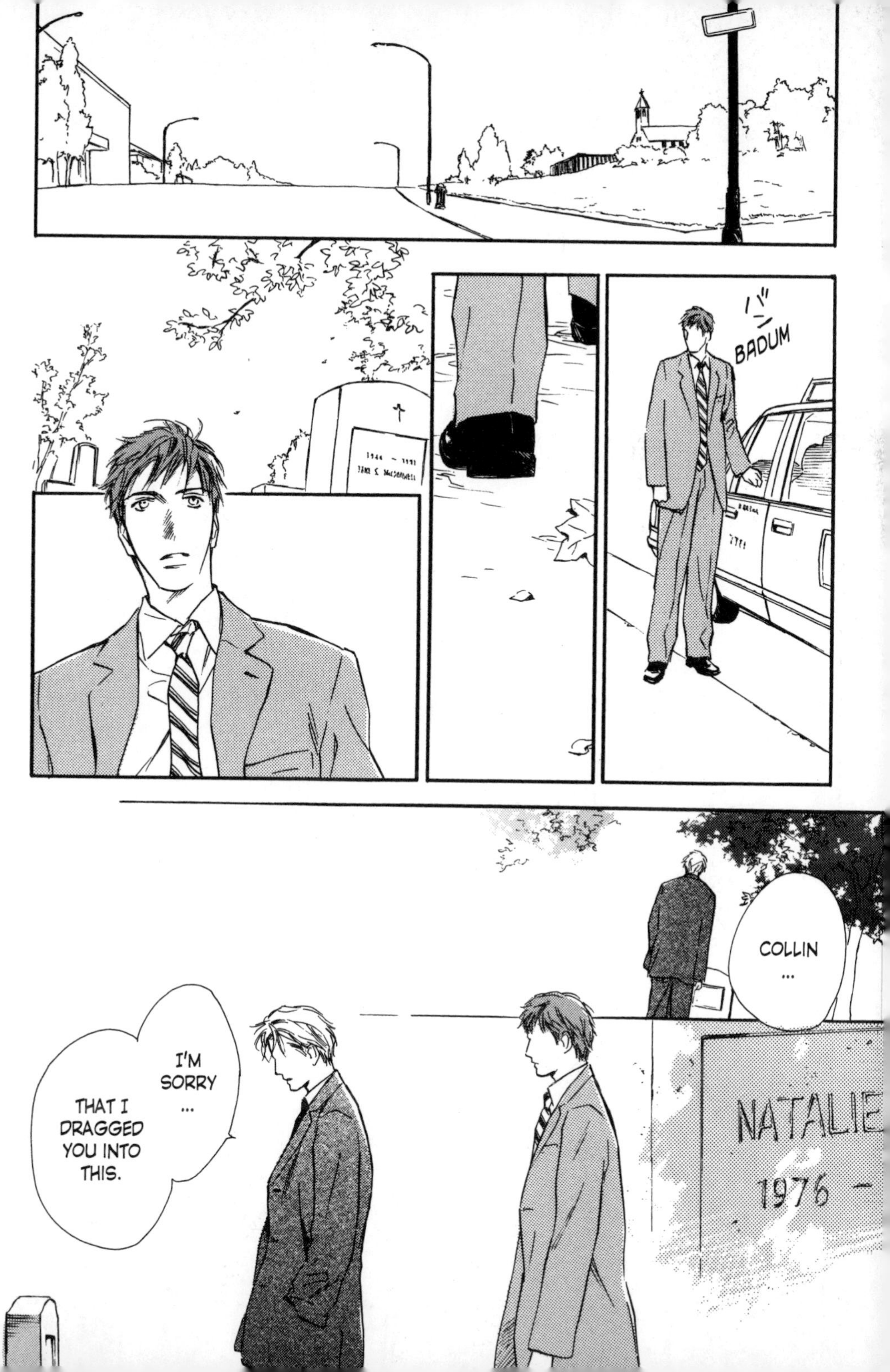
BADUM
COLLIN ...
NATALIE
1976 –
I'M SORRY ...
THAT I DRAGGED YOU INTO THIS.

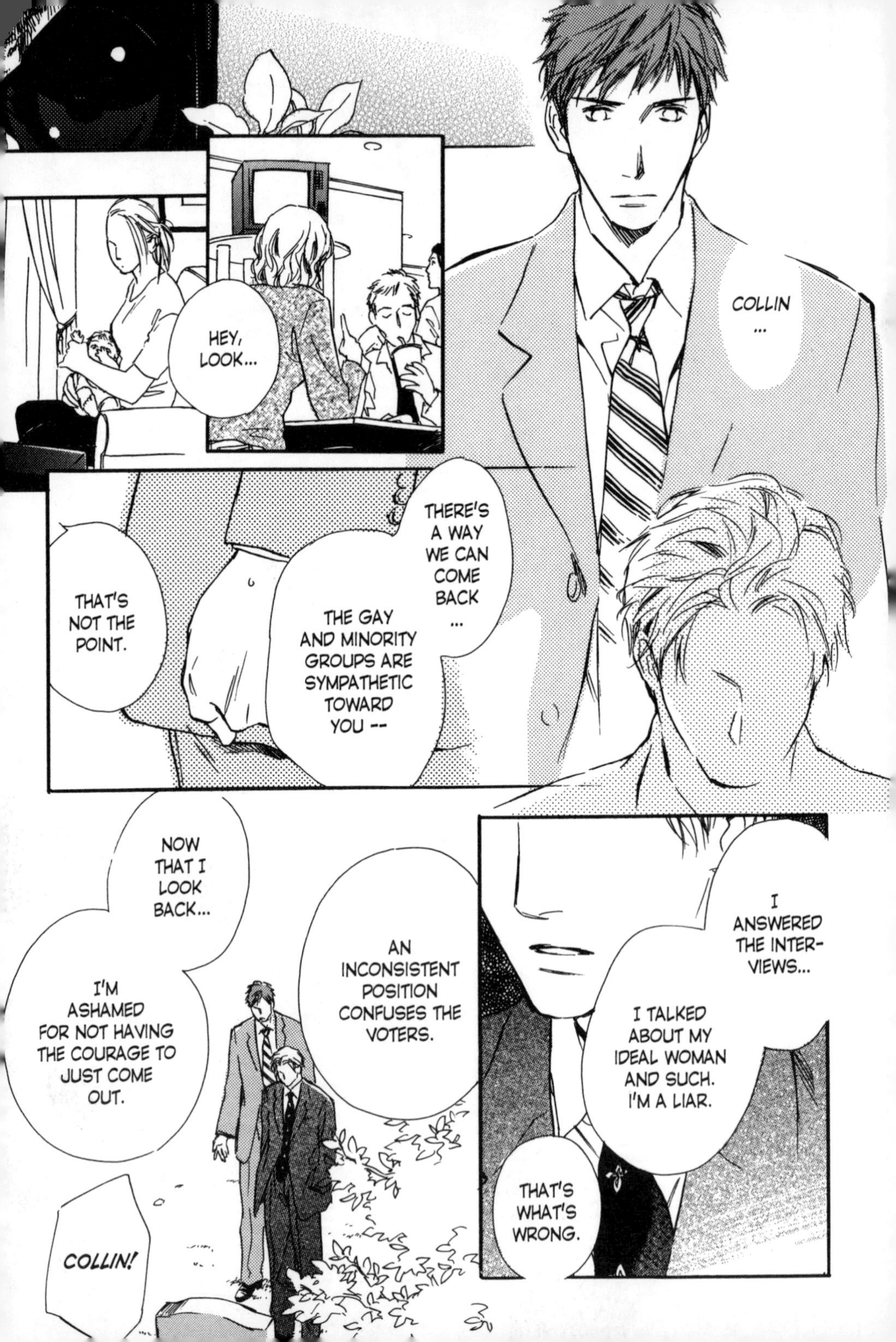
COLLIN ...
HEY, LOOK...
THERE'S A WAY WE CAN COME BACK ...
THE GAY AND MINORITY GROUPS ARE SYMPATHETIC TOWARD YOU --
THAT'S NOT THE POINT.
I ANSWERED THE INTER-VIEWS...
I TALKED ABOUT MY IDEAL WOMAN AND SUCH. I'M A LIAR.
THAT'S WHAT'S WRONG.
AN INCONSISTENT POSITION CONFUSES THE VOTERS.
NOW THAT I LOOK BACK...
I'M ASHAMED FOR NOT HAVING THE COURAGE TO JUST COME OUT.
COLLIN!

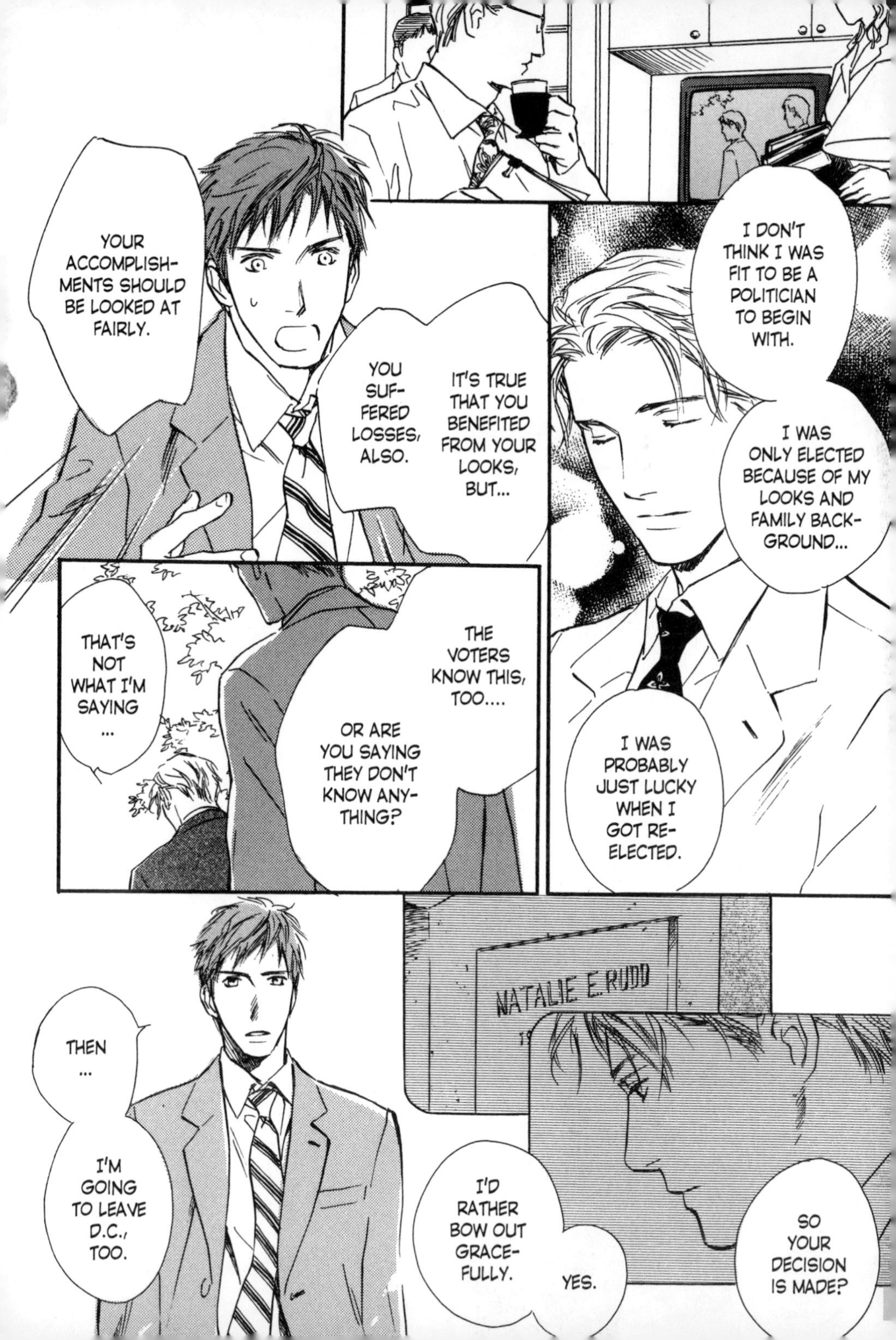
I DON'T THINK I WAS FIT TO BE A POLITICIAN TO BEGIN WITH.
I WAS ONLY ELECTED BECAUSE OF MY LOOKS AND FAMILY BACK-GROUND...
I WAS PROBABLY JUST LUCKY WHEN I GOT RE-ELECTED.
IT'S TRUE THAT YOU BENEFITED FROM YOUR LOOKS, BUT...
YOU SUF-FERED LOSSES, ALSO.
YOUR ACCOMPLISH-MENTS SHOULD BE LOOKED AT FAIRLY.
THE VOTERS KNOW THIS, TOO....
OR ARE YOU SAYING THEY DON'T KNOW ANY-THING?
THAT'S NOT WHAT I'M SAYING ...
NATALIE E. RUDD
SO YOUR DECISION IS MADE?
YES.
I'D RATHER BOW OUT GRACE-FULLY.
THEN ...
I'M GOING TO LEAVE D.C., TOO.

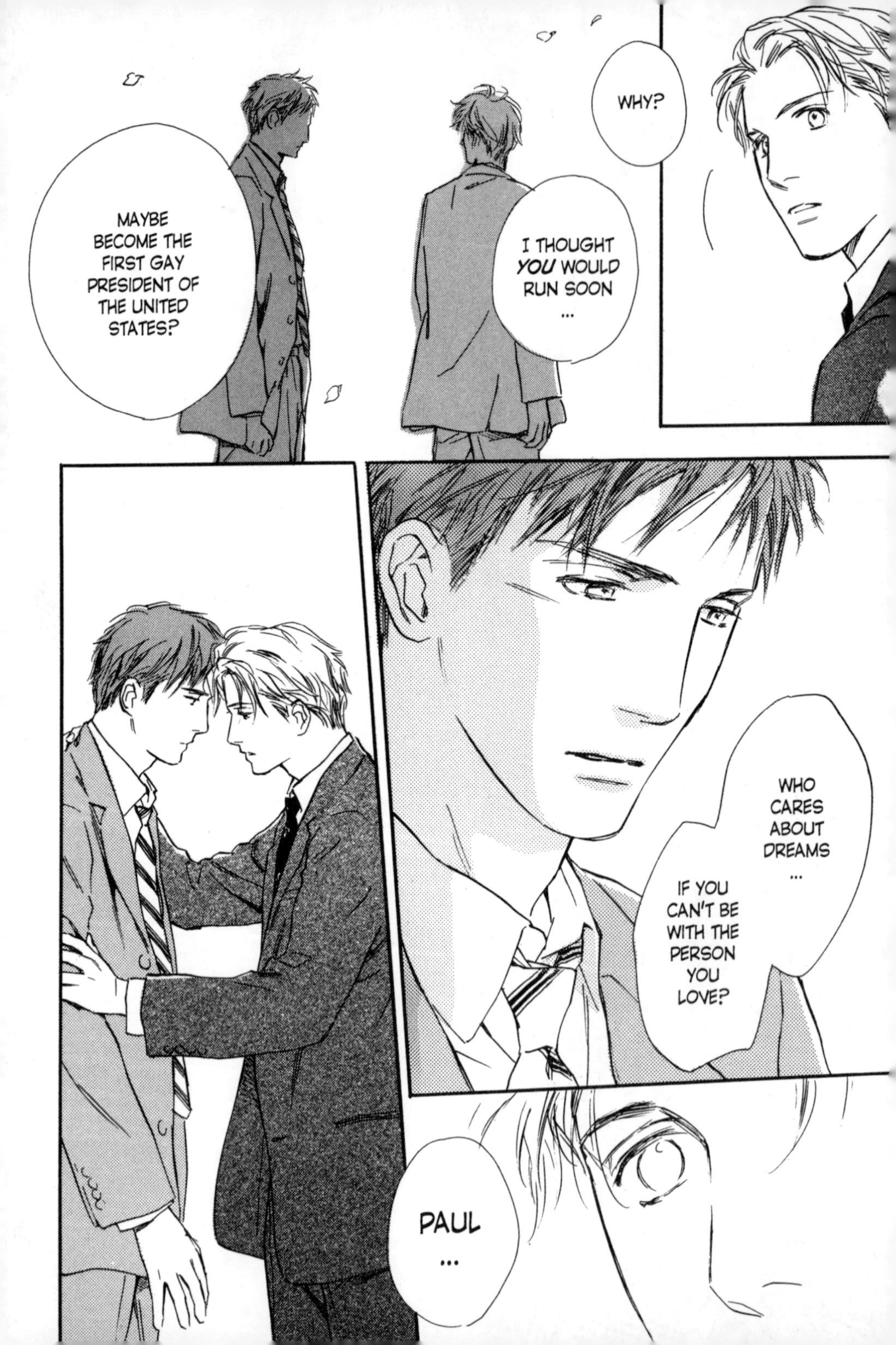
WHY?
I THOUGHT *YOU* WOULD RUN SOON ...
MAYBE BECOME THE FIRST GAY PRESIDENT OF THE UNITED STATES?
WHO CARES ABOUT DREAMS ...
IF YOU CAN'T BE WITH THE PERSON YOU LOVE?
PAUL ...

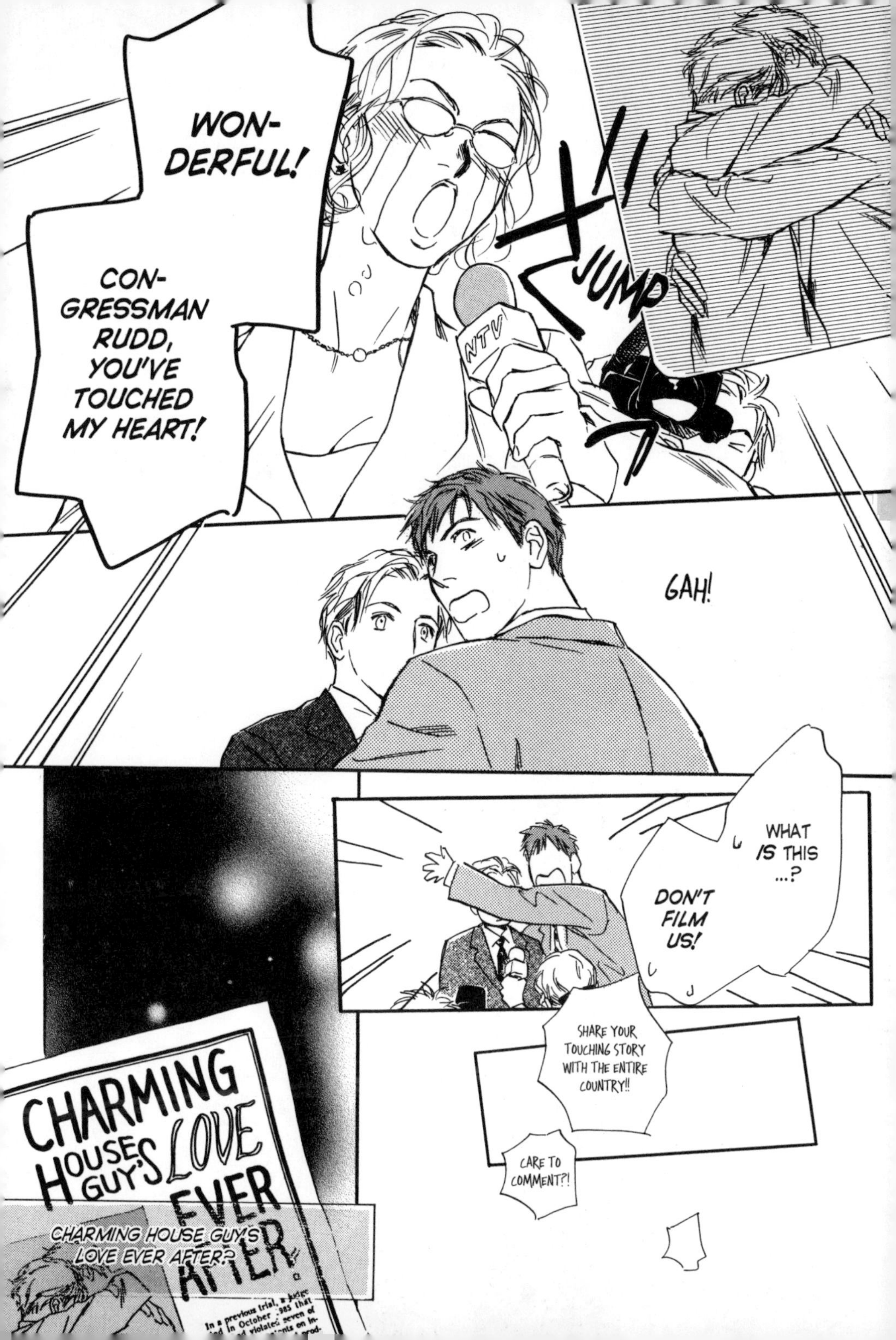
JUMP
WON-DERFUL!
CON-GRESSMAN RUDD, YOU'VE TOUCHED MY HEART!
GAH!
WHAT IS THIS ...?
DON'T FILM US!
SHARE YOUR TOUCHING STORY WITH THE ENTIRE COUNTRY!!
CARE TO COMMENT?!
CHARMING HOUSE GUY'S LOVE EVER AFTER
CHARMING HOUSE GUY'S LOVE EVER AFTER?

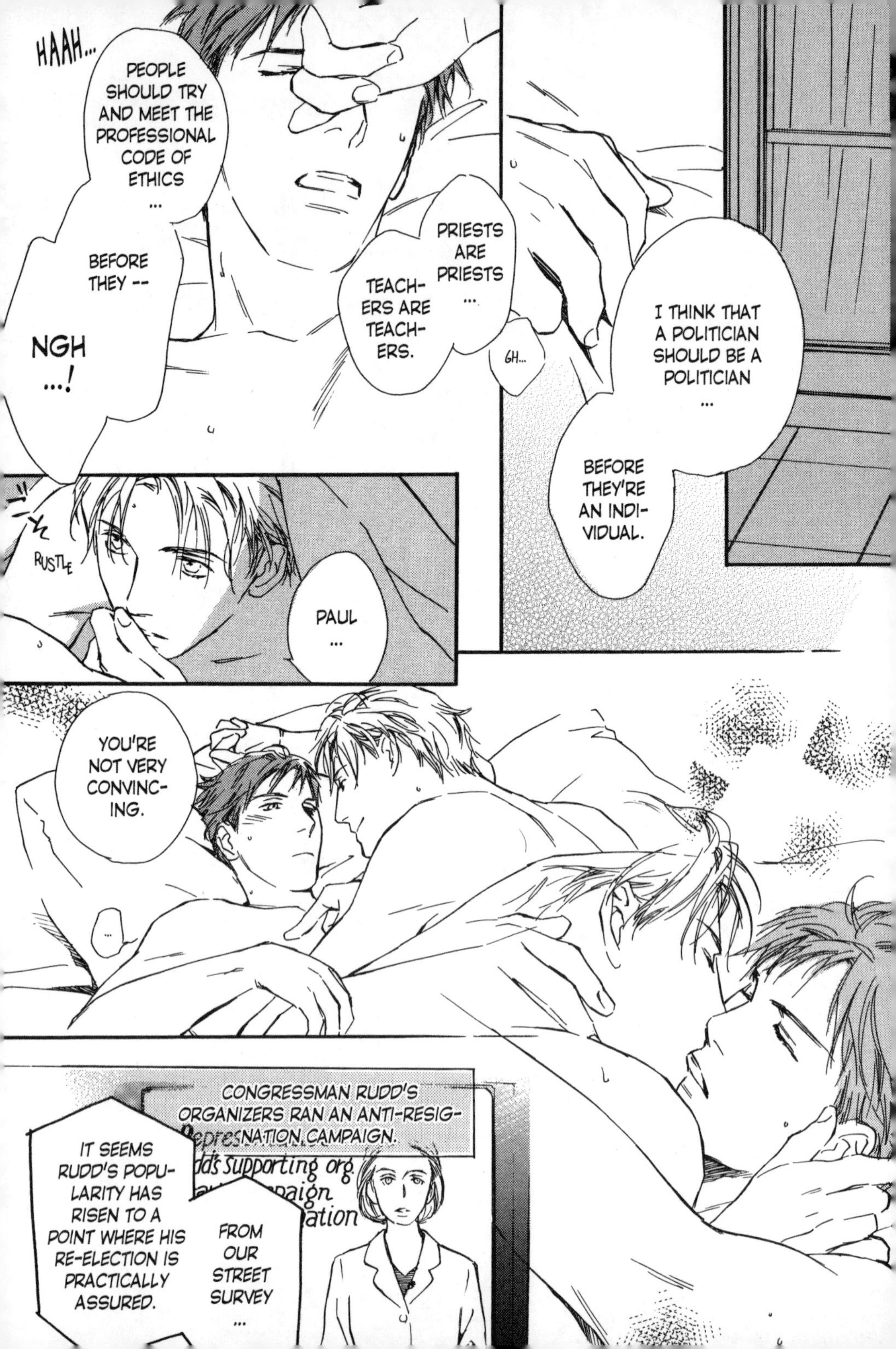
I THINK THAT A POLITICIAN SHOULD BE A POLITICIAN ...
BEFORE THEY'RE AN INDIVIDUAL.
PRIESTS ARE PRIESTS ...
TEACHERS ARE TEACHERS.
GH...
HAAH...
PEOPLE SHOULD TRY AND MEET THE PROFESSIONAL CODE OF ETHICS ...
BEFORE THEY --
NGH ...!
RUSTLE
PAUL ...
YOU'RE NOT VERY CONVINCING.
...
CONGRESSMAN RUDD'S ORGANIZERS RAN AN ANTI-RESIGNATION CAMPAIGN.
FROM OUR STREET SURVEY ...
IT SEEMS RUDD'S POPULARITY HAS RISEN TO A POINT WHERE HIS RE-ELECTION IS PRACTICALLY ASSURED.

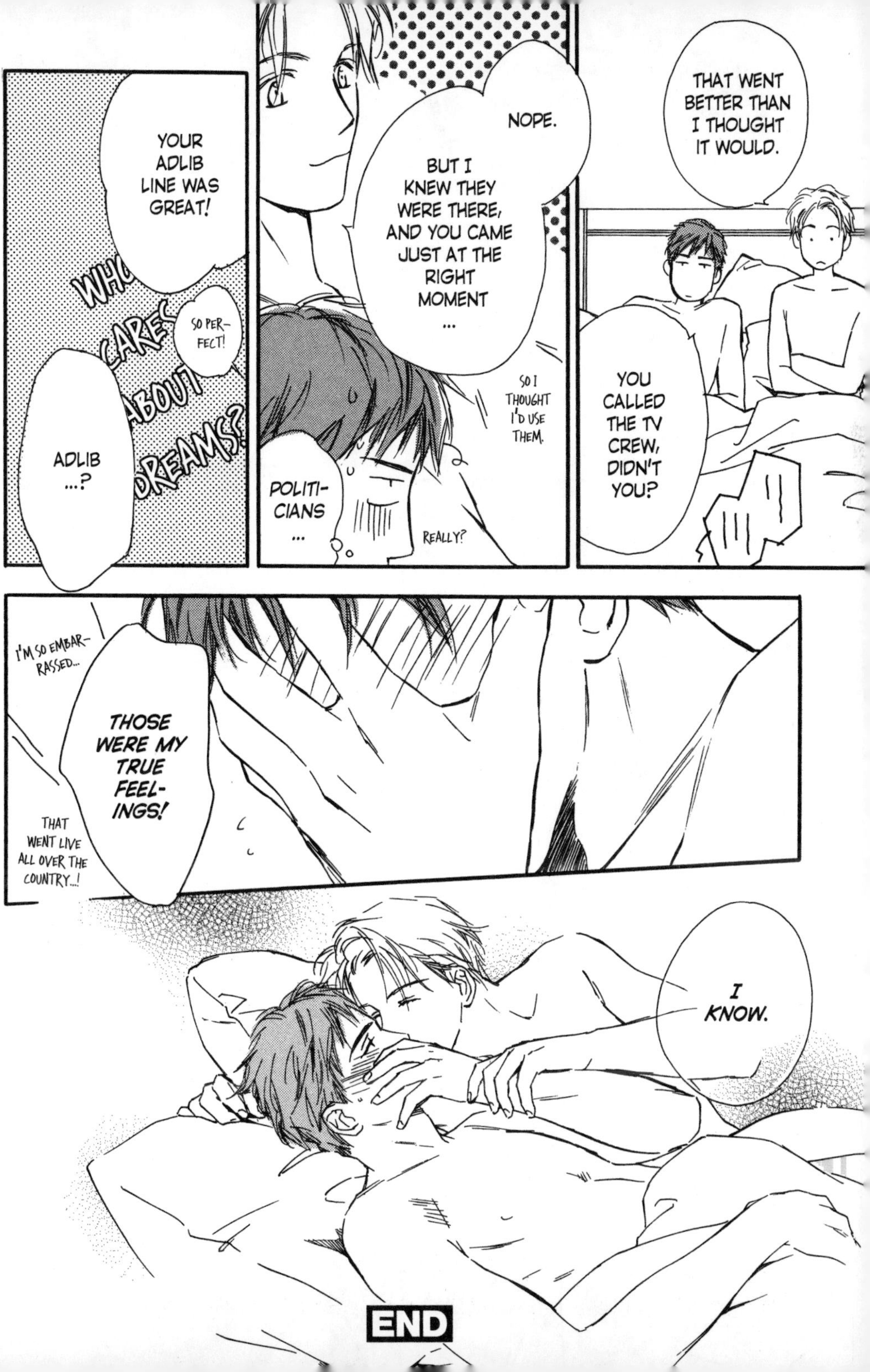
THAT WENT BETTER THAN I THOUGHT IT WOULD.
YOU CALLED THE TV CREW, DIDN'T YOU?
NOPE.
BUT I KNEW THEY WERE THERE, AND YOU CAME JUST AT THE RIGHT MOMENT ...
SO I THOUGHT I'D USE THEM.
POLITICIANS ...
REALLY?
YOUR ADLIB LINE WAS GREAT!
WHO CARES ABOUT DREAMS?
SO PERFECT!
ADLIB ...?
I'M SO EMBARRASSED...
THOSE WERE MY TRUE FEELINGS!
THAT WENT LIVE ALL OVER THE COUNTRY...!
I KNOW.
END

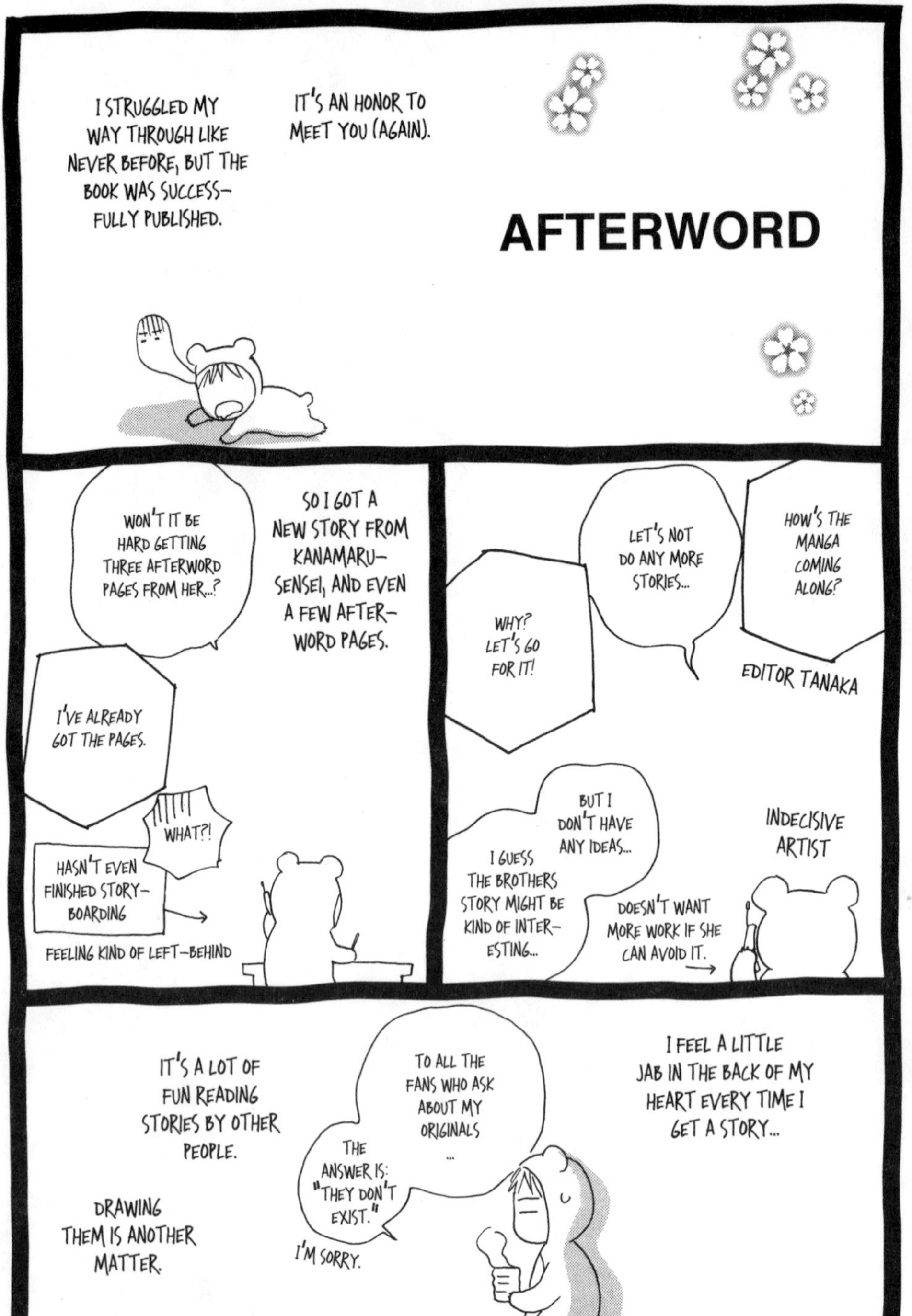
AFTERWORD
IT'S AN HONOR TO MEET YOU (AGAIN).
I STRUGGLED MY WAY THROUGH LIKE NEVER BEFORE, BUT THE BOOK WAS SUCCESS-FULLY PUBLISHED.
HOW'S THE MANGA COMING ALONG?
EDITOR TANAKA
LET'S NOT DO ANY MORE STORIES...
WHY? LET'S GO FOR IT!
INDECISIVE ARTIST
BUT I DON'T HAVE ANY IDEAS...
I GUESS THE BROTHERS STORY MIGHT BE KIND OF INTER-ESTING...
DOESN'T WANT MORE WORK IF SHE CAN AVOID IT.
SO I GOT A NEW STORY FROM KANAMARU-SENSEI, AND EVEN A FEW AFTER-WORD PAGES.
WON'T IT BE HARD GETTING THREE AFTERWORD PAGES FROM HER...?
I'VE ALREADY GOT THE PAGES.
WHAT?!
HASN'T EVEN FINISHED STORY-BOARDING
FEELING KIND OF LEFT-BEHIND
I FEEL A LITTLE JAB IN THE BACK OF MY HEART EVERY TIME I GET A STORY...
TO ALL THE FANS WHO ASK ABOUT MY ORIGINALS ...
THE ANSWER IS: "THEY DON'T EXIST."
I'M SORRY.
IT'S A LOT OF FUN READING STORIES BY OTHER PEOPLE.
DRAWING THEM IS ANOTHER MATTER.

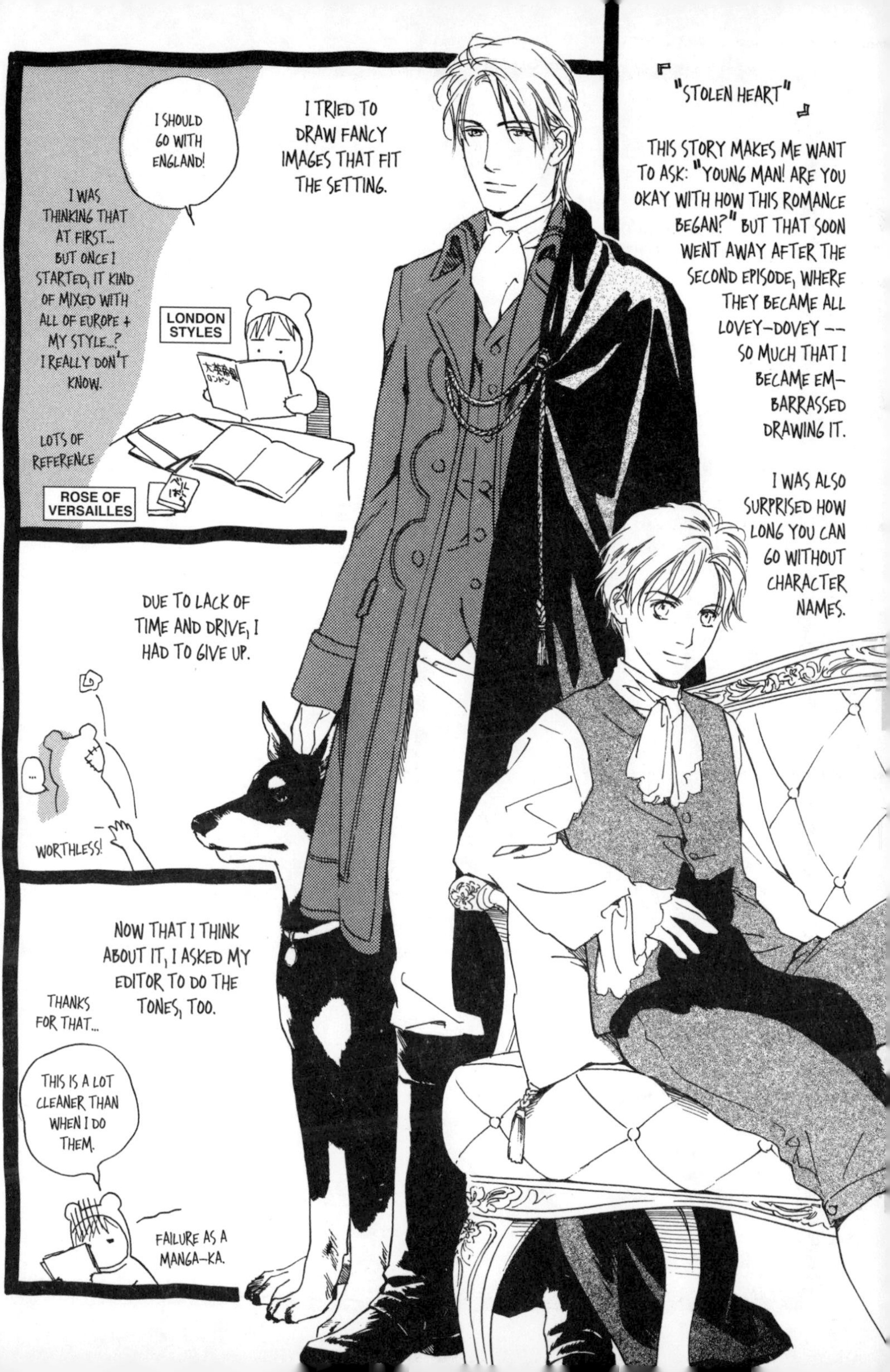

"STOLEN HEART"
THIS STORY MAKES ME WANT TO ASK: "YOUNG MAN! ARE YOU OKAY WITH HOW THIS ROMANCE BEGAN?" BUT THAT SOON WENT AWAY AFTER THE SECOND EPISODE, WHERE THEY BECAME ALL LOVEY-DOVEY -- SO MUCH THAT I BECAME EM-BARRASSED DRAWING IT.
I WAS ALSO SURPRISED HOW LONG YOU CAN GO WITHOUT CHARACTER NAMES.
I TRIED TO DRAW FANCY IMAGES THAT FIT THE SETTING.
I SHOULD GO WITH ENGLAND!
I WAS THINKING THAT AT FIRST... BUT ONCE I STARTED, IT KIND OF MIXED WITH ALL OF EUROPE + MY STYLE...? I REALLY DON'T KNOW.
LONDON STYLES
LOTS OF REFERENCE
ROSE OF VERSAILLES
DUE TO LACK OF TIME AND DRIVE, I HAD TO GIVE UP.
...
WORTHLESS!
NOW THAT I THINK ABOUT IT, I ASKED MY EDITOR TO DO THE TONES, TOO.
THANKS FOR THAT...
THIS IS A LOT CLEANER THAN WHEN I DO THEM.
FAILURE AS A MANGA-KA.

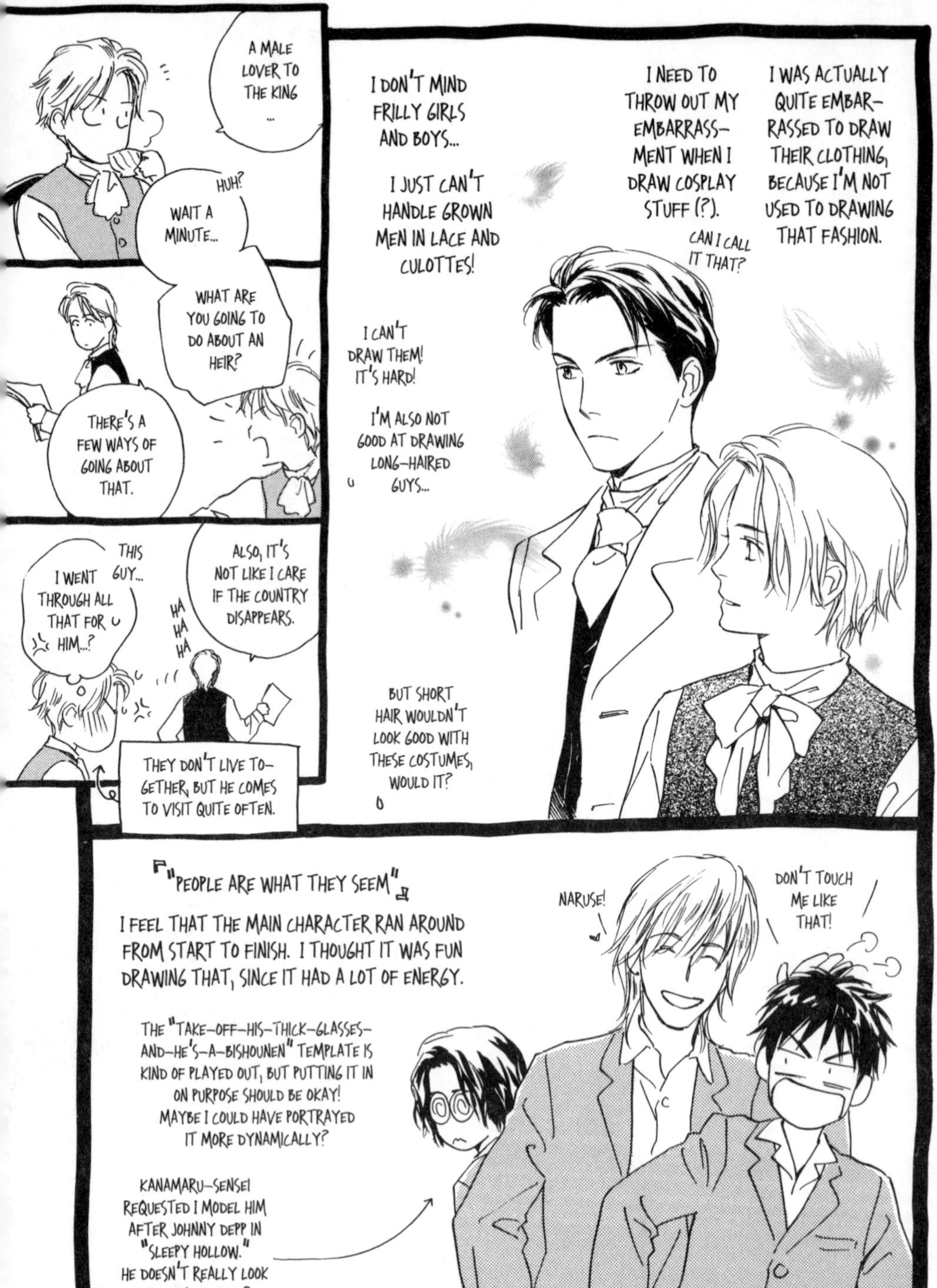
I WAS ACTUALLY QUITE EMBARRASSED TO DRAW THEIR CLOTHING, BECAUSE I'M NOT USED TO DRAWING THAT FASHION.
I NEED TO THROW OUT MY EMBARRASSMENT WHEN I DRAW COSPLAY STUFF (?).
CAN I CALL IT THAT?
I DON'T MIND FRILLY GIRLS AND BOYS...
I JUST CAN'T HANDLE GROWN MEN IN LACE AND CULOTTES!
I CAN'T DRAW THEM! IT'S HARD!
I'M ALSO NOT GOOD AT DRAWING LONG-HAIRED GUYS...
BUT SHORT HAIR WOULDN'T LOOK GOOD WITH THESE COSTUMES, WOULD IT?
A MALE LOVER TO THE KING ...
HUH?
WAIT A MINUTE...
WHAT ARE YOU GOING TO DO ABOUT AN HEIR?
THERE'S A FEW WAYS OF GOING ABOUT THAT.
ALSO, IT'S NOT LIKE I CARE IF THE COUNTRY DISAPPEARS.
HA HA HA
THIS GUY...
I WENT THROUGH ALL THAT FOR HIM...?
THEY DON'T LIVE TOGETHER, BUT HE COMES TO VISIT QUITE OFTEN.
DON'T TOUCH ME LIKE THAT!
NARUSE!
『"PEOPLE ARE WHAT THEY SEEM"』
I FEEL THAT THE MAIN CHARACTER RAN AROUND FROM START TO FINISH. I THOUGHT IT WAS FUN DRAWING THAT, SINCE IT HAD A LOT OF ENERGY.
THE "TAKE-OFF-HIS-THICK-GLASSES-AND-HE'S-A-BISHOUNEN" TEMPLATE IS KIND OF PLAYED OUT, BUT PUTTING IT IN ON PURPOSE SHOULD BE OKAY! MAYBE I COULD HAVE PORTRAYED IT MORE DYNAMICALLY?
KANAMARU-SENSEI REQUESTED I MODEL HIM AFTER JOHNNY DEPP IN "SLEEPY HOLLOW." HE DOESN'T REALLY LOOK LIKE HIM, DOES HE?
HE HE

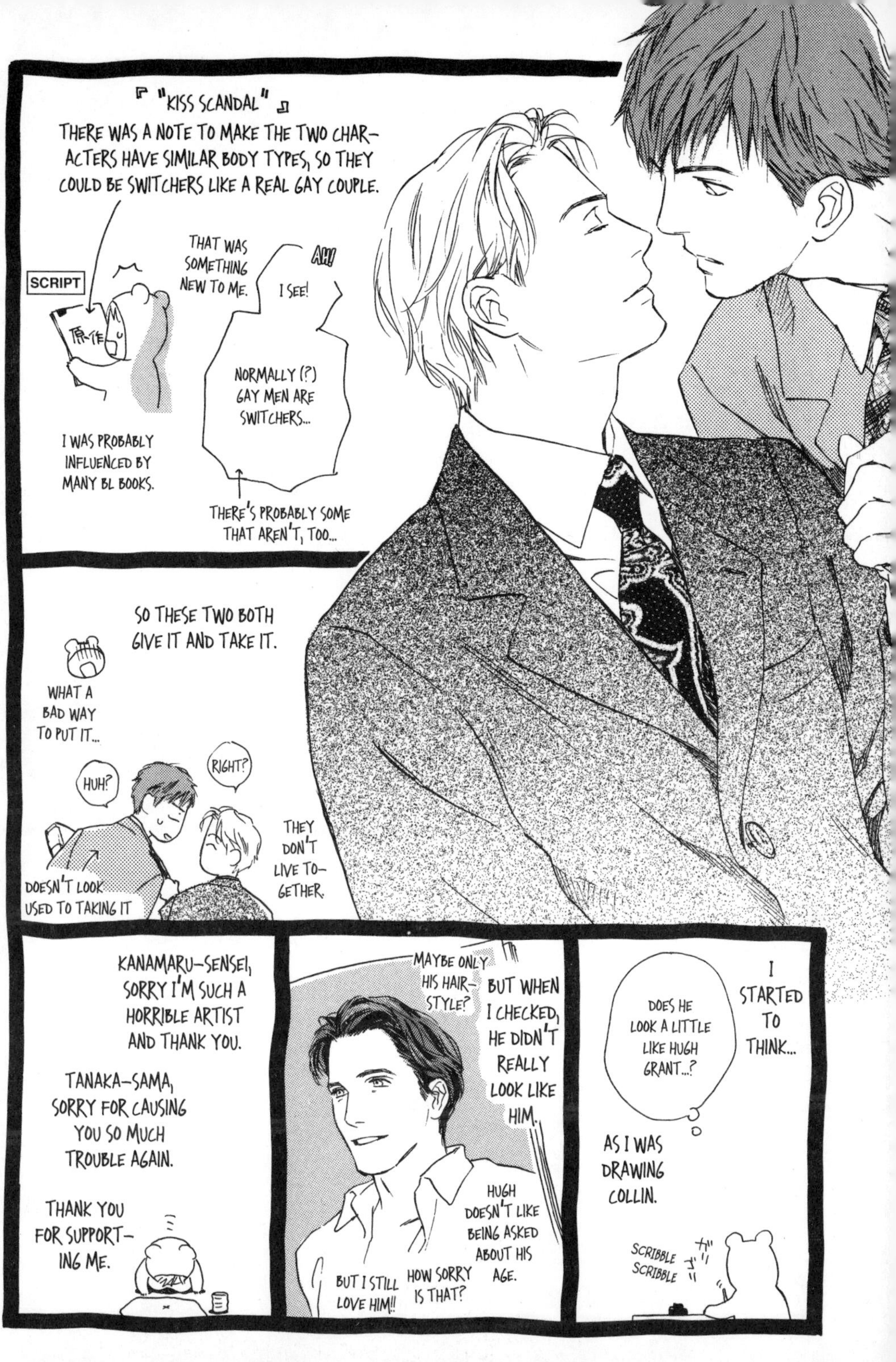
『"KISS SCANDAL"』
THERE WAS A NOTE TO MAKE THE TWO CHARACTERS HAVE SIMILAR BODY TYPES, SO THEY COULD BE SWITCHERS LIKE A REAL GAY COUPLE.
AH! I SEE!
THAT WAS SOMETHING NEW TO ME.
SCRIPT
NORMALLY (?) GAY MEN ARE SWITCHERS...
THERE'S PROBABLY SOME THAT AREN'T, TOO...
I WAS PROBABLY INFLUENCED BY MANY BL BOOKS.
SO THESE TWO BOTH GIVE IT AND TAKE IT.
WHAT A BAD WAY TO PUT IT...
THEY DON'T LIVE TOGETHER.
RIGHT?
HUH?
DOESN'T LOOK USED TO TAKING IT
I STARTED TO THINK...
DOES HE LOOK A LITTLE LIKE HUGH GRANT...?
AS I WAS DRAWING COLLIN.
SCRIBBLE SCRIBBLE
BUT WHEN I CHECKED, HE DIDN'T REALLY LOOK LIKE HIM.
MAYBE ONLY HIS HAIRSTYLE?
HUGH DOESN'T LIKE BEING ASKED ABOUT HIS AGE.
HOW SORRY IS THAT?
BUT I STILL LOVE HIM!!
KANAMARU-SENSEI, SORRY I'M SUCH A HORRIBLE ARTIST AND THANK YOU.
TANAKA-SAMA, SORRY FOR CAUSING YOU SO MUCH TROUBLE AGAIN.
THANK YOU FOR SUPPORTING ME.

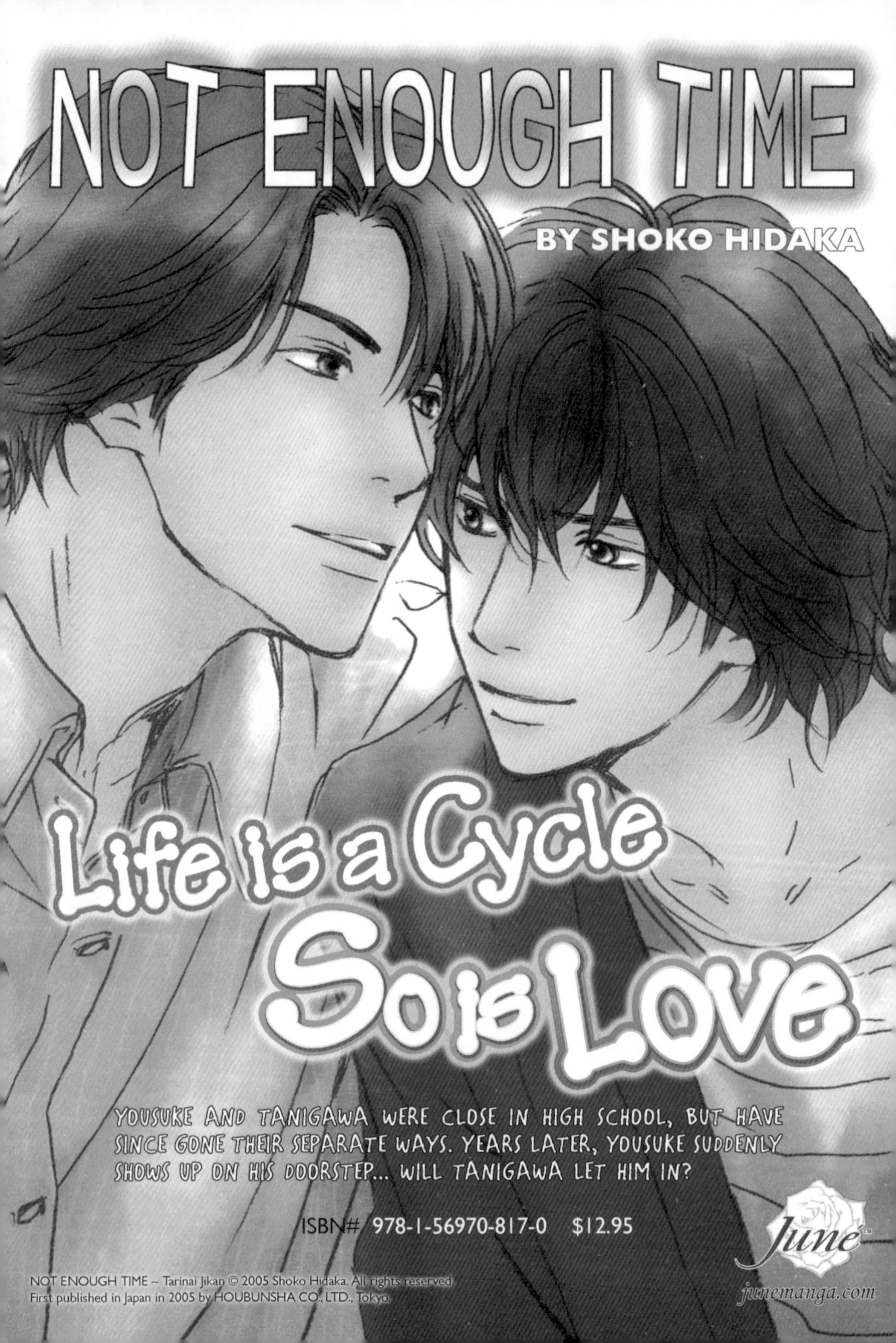
NOT ENOUGH TIME
BY SHOKO HIDAKA
Life is a Cycle
So is Love
YOUSUKE AND TANIGAWA WERE CLOSE IN HIGH SCHOOL, BUT HAVE SINCE GONE THEIR SEPARATE WAYS. YEARS LATER, YOUSUKE SUDDENLY SHOWS UP ON HIS DOORSTEP... WILL TANIGAWA LET HIM IN?
ISBN# 978-1-56970-817-0 $12.95
June™
junemanga.com
NOT ENOUGH TIME – Tarinai Jikan © 2005 Shoko Hidaka. All rights reserved.
First published in Japan in 2005 by HOUBUNSHA CO., LTD., Tokyo.

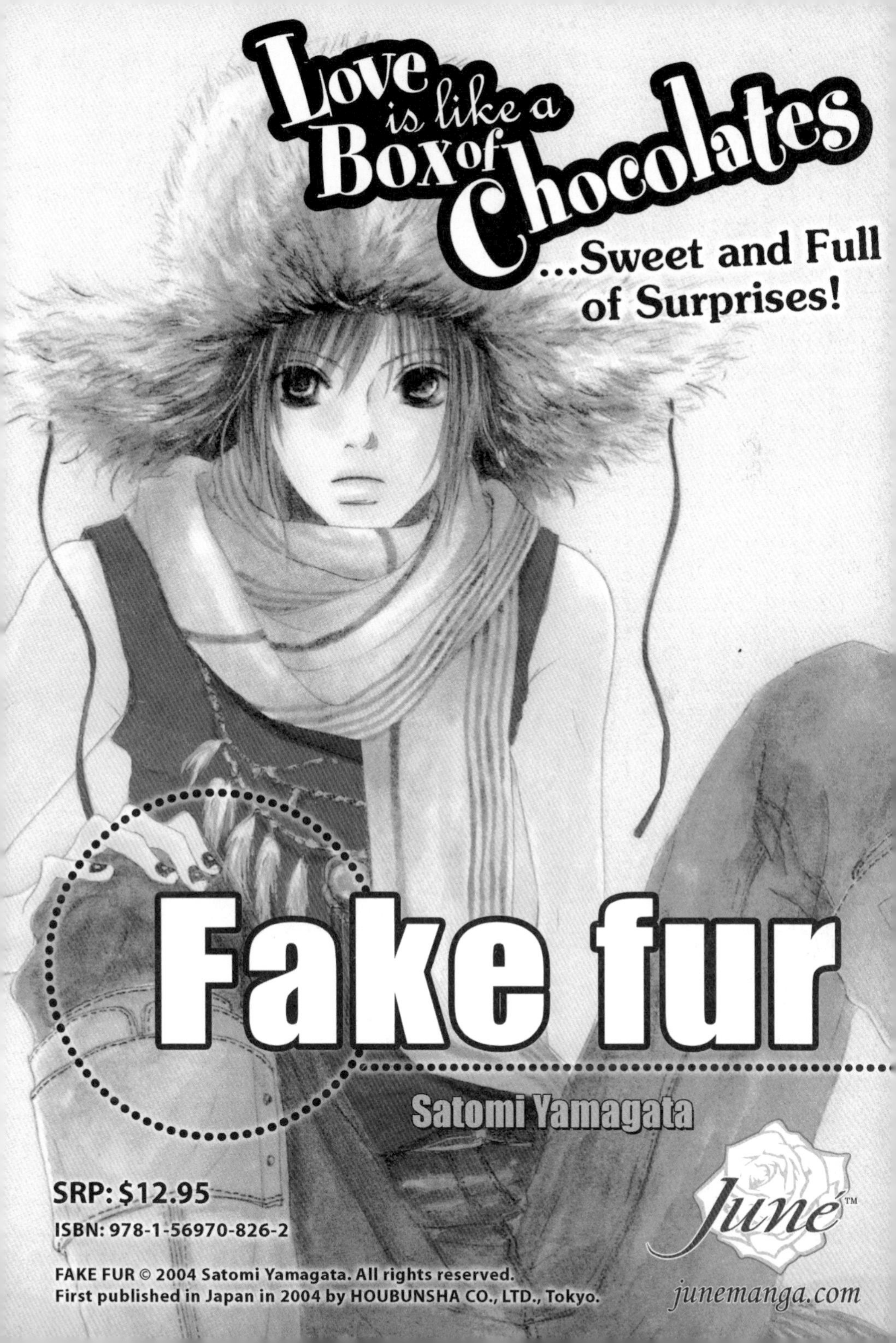

Love is like a Box of Chocolates

...Sweet and Full of Surprises!

Fake fur

Satomi Yamagata

SRP: $12.95

ISBN: 978-1-56970-826-2

June™

junemanga.com

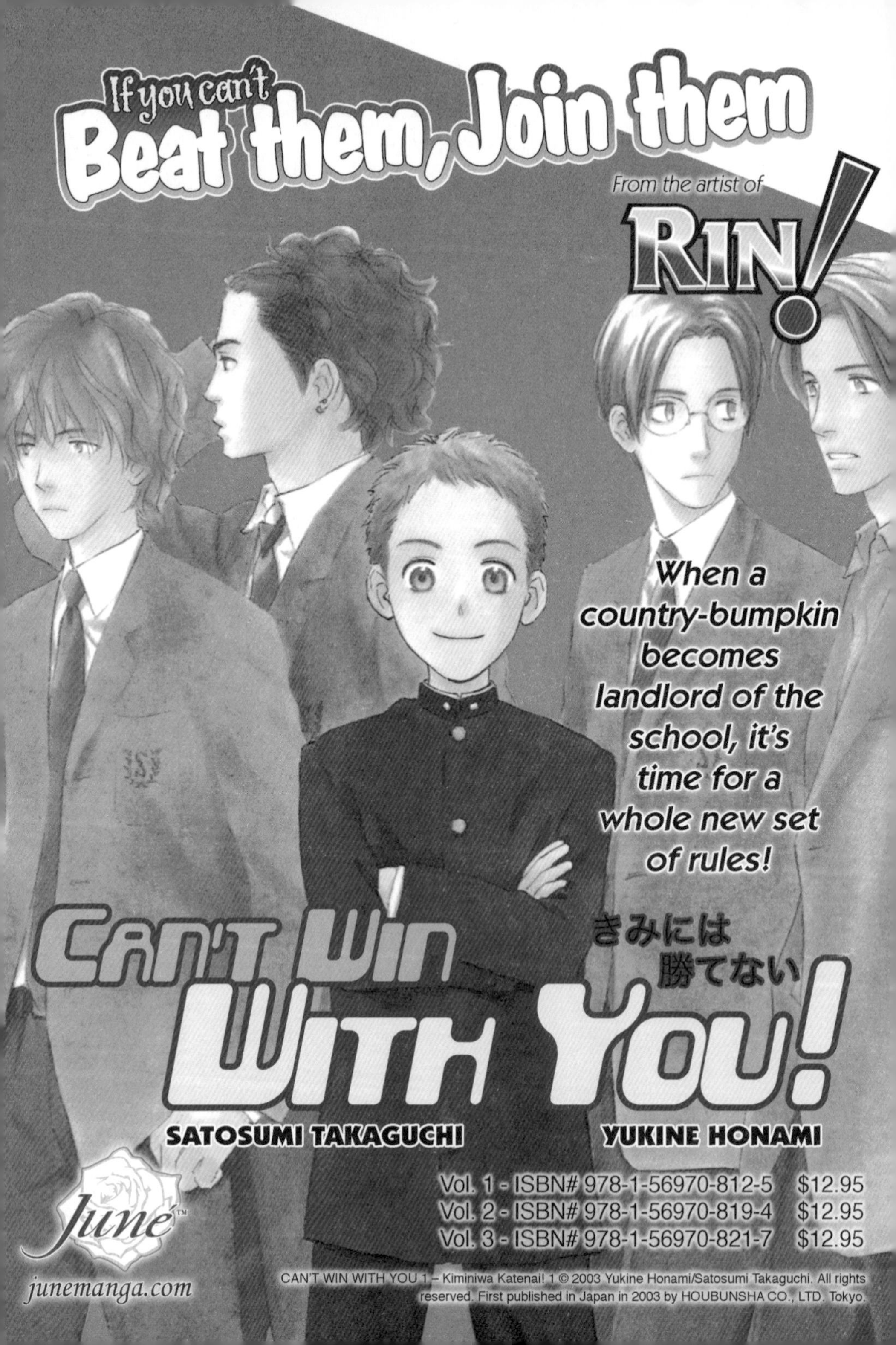
If you can't
Beat them, Join them
From the artist of
RIN!
When a country-bumpkin becomes landlord of the school, it's time for a whole new set of rules!
CAN'T WIN WITH YOU!
きみには
勝てない
SATOSUMI TAKAGUCHI
YUKINE HONAMI
Vol. 1 - ISBN# 978-1-56970-812-5 $12.95
Vol. 2 - ISBN# 978-1-56970-819-4 $12.95
Vol. 3 - ISBN# 978-1-56970-821-7 $12.95
June™
junemanga.com
CAN'T WIN WITH YOU 1 – Kiminiwa Katenai! 1 © 2003 Yukine Honami/Satosumi Takaguchi. All rights reserved. First published in Japan in 2003 by HOUBUNSHA CO., LTD. Tokyo.

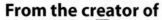

From the creator of
ANTIQUE BAKERY

A Duet Like No Other...

♪Solfege♪

Written & Illustrated by:
Fumi Yoshinaga

June™
junemanga.com

SRP: $12.95
ISBN: 978-1-56970-841-5

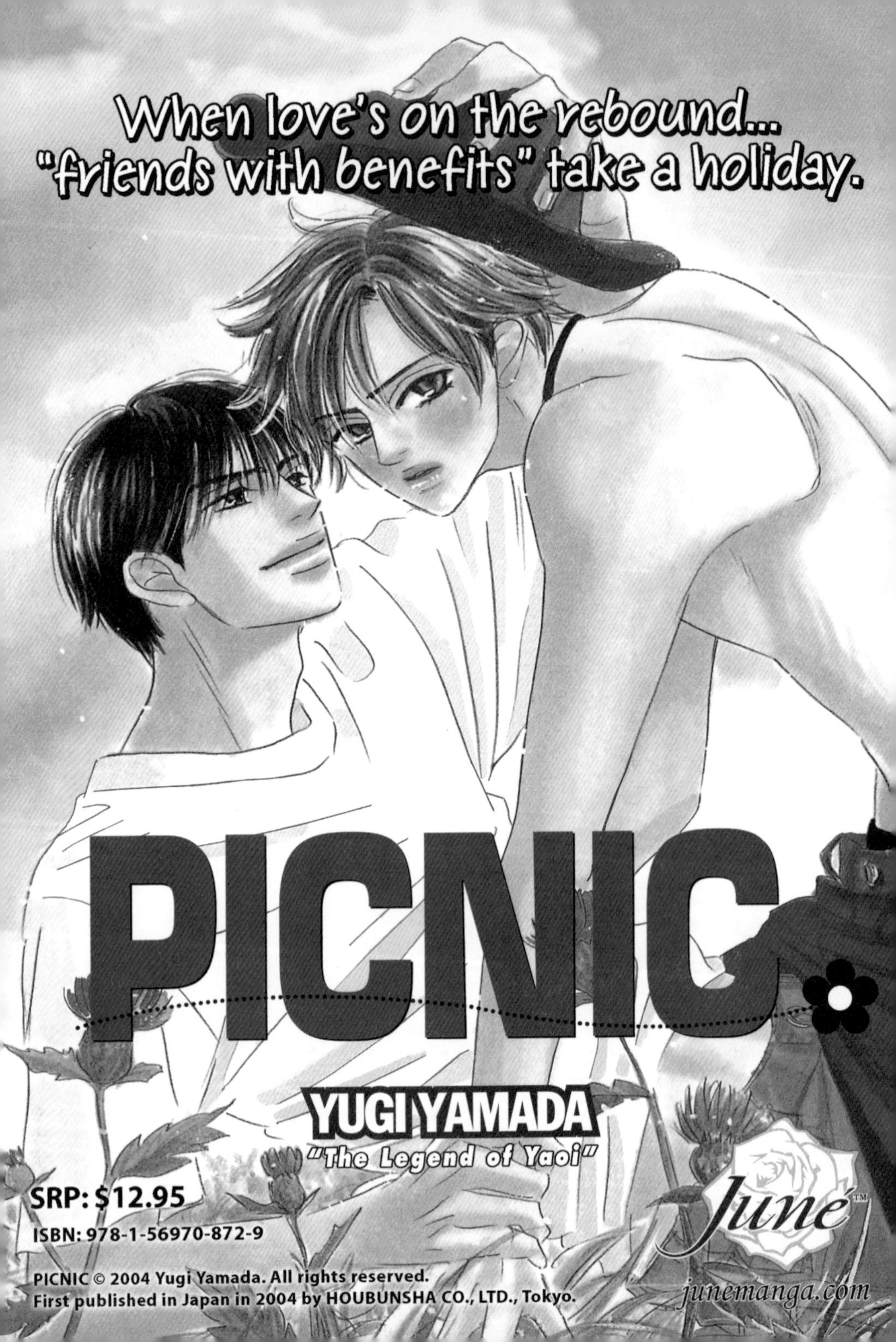
When love's on the rebound...
"friends with benefits" take a holiday.
PICNIC
YUGI YAMADA
"The Legend of Yaoi"
SRP: $12.95
ISBN: 978-1-56970-872-9
June™
PICNIC © 2004 Yugi Yamada. All rights reserved.
First published in Japan in 2004 by HOUBUNSHA CO., LTD., Tokyo.
junemanga.com

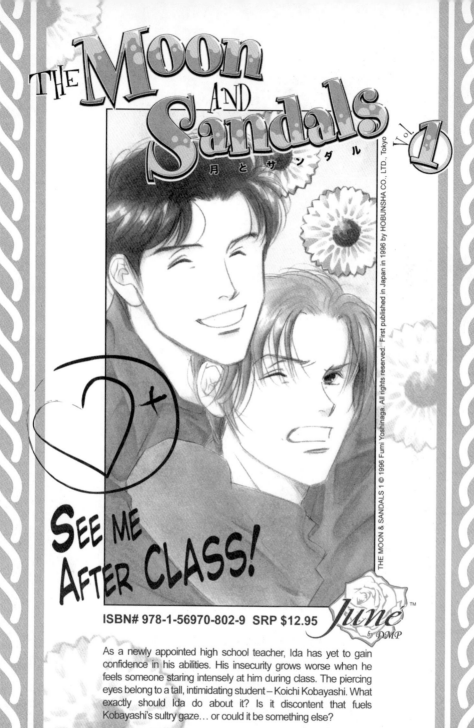

THE Moon AND Sandals Vol. 1
月 と サンダル

SEE ME AFTER CLASS!

ISBN# 978-1-56970-802-9 SRP $12.95

June
by DMP

As a newly appointed high school teacher, Ida has yet to gain confidence in his abilities. His insecurity grows worse when he feels someone staring intensely at him during class. The piercing eyes belong to a tall, intimidating student – Koichi Kobayashi. What exactly should Ida do about it? Is it discontent that fuels Kobayashi's sultry gaze… or could it be something else?

Written and Illustrated by:
Fumi Yoshinaga

junemanga.com

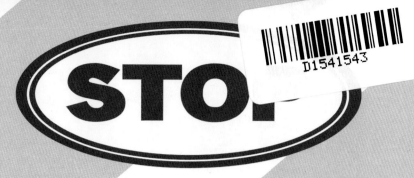

STOP

This is the back of the book! Start from the other side.

NATIVE MANGA
readers read manga from *right to left*.

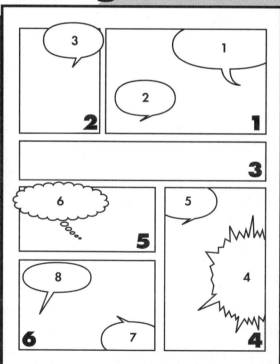

If you run into our **Native Manga** logo on any of our books... you'll know that this manga is published in it's true original native Japanese right to left reading format, as it was intended. Turn to the other side of the book and start reading from right to left, top to bottom.

Follow the diagram to see how its done. *Surf's Up!*

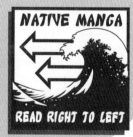

NATIVE MANGA

READ RIGHT TO LEFT